EST...

LATVIA

Seized by USSR 1940 with Hitler's consent. (U.S... not recognize USSR.)

LITHUANIA

...SR 1945 ...nsent.

Baltic Sea

DANZIG

GERMANY (E. PRUSSIA)

BYELORUSSIA

POLAND

Transferred by Soviets to Polish Administration 1945

P O L A N D

Seized by USSR 1939 with Hitler's consent and in 1945 per Yalta agreement.

UKRAINE

S O V I E T

ERMANY

S L O V A K I A

Seized by USSR 1945 with Beneš consent.

Seized by USSR 1940 with Hitler's consent.

HUNGARY

RUMANIA

Black Sea

JGOSLAVIA

BULGARIA

Col. Jan Bukar

KEY
Or to Further Soviet Aggression ?

CZECHO-SLOVAKIA
A CRITICAL HISTORY

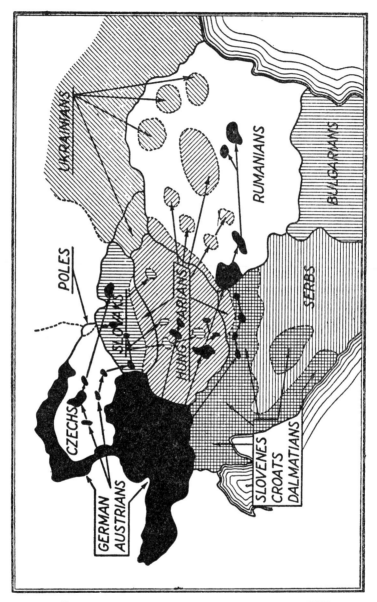

ILLUSTRATING THE INTERMINGLING OF PEOPLES IN THE
DANUBE BASIN

The Danube Basin is an ethnic mosaic which cannot be formed into states on
the basis of nationality. The population of the region is not homogeneous any-
where, although each of the more numerous peoples predominates in the heart
of its own territory. Groups of various nationalities are dotted about like islands
over the whole area. This is a simplified map. A detailed map shows over 150
ethnic islands, including a score of "islands within islands." (Reprinted by permission from F. O. Miksche, *Danubian Federation*.)

PLATE I

CZECHO-SLOVAKIA
A CRITICAL HISTORY

by

KURT GLASER

ASSOCIATE PROFESSOR OF GOVERNMENT

SOUTHWESTERN ILLINOIS CAMPUS

SOUTHERN ILLINOIS UNIVERSITY

THE CAXTON PRINTERS, LTD.
CALDWELL, IDAHO
1961

Printed, lithographed, and bound in the United States of America by
The CAXTON PRINTERS, Ltd.
Caldwell, Idaho
82452

to
AUSTIN J. APP

"Te autem . . . non solum
natura et moribus verum
etiam studio et doctrina esse
sapientem nec sicut vulgus
sed ut eruditi solent appel-
lare sapientem."
Cicero, *De Amicitia*, II, 7

PREFACE

IT IS probable that America's first two military ventures into European politics and the war policies of the Wilson and Roosevelt administrations will provide fuel for the disputes of historians and political scientists for some decades to come. About one fact, however, there can be little argument: the present political constellation, in Europe as in Asia, is to a large extent a consequence of the use—or as some view it, the misuse—of American power. It was the economic and military strength of the United States which swung the balance in World War I to the side of the Allies. Although President Wilson had initially opposed the dismemberment of the Austro-Hungarian Empire, he finally consented to it and affixed his signature to the Paris peace treaties, which helped France to a position of political hegemony which she lacked the economic or military potential to maintain.

Similarly, in World War II, it was American aid to Britain which enabled that state to hold out alone after Dunkirk. Lend-lease contributed significantly to the stopping of the German advance in Russia, and the military-political strategy of the Western Powers, largely dictated by the Roosevelt administration, led to the temporary total extinction of German power and to a Russian advance deep into Central Europe. Having eliminated the regional hegemony of the Japanese in East Asia, the United States has inherited many of the problems formerly faced by them, including that of holding the line against aggressive Communist governments.

Americans have inherited from earlier generations a

distaste for European "power politics," combined with
a profound ignorance of the historical, political, ethnic,
and economic roots of European quarrels. President
Wilson's knowledge of geography was so hazy that he
accepted Poland's demand for access to the sea without
realizing until some months later that this involved a
corridor through Germany—the corridor which provided
the *casus belli* for World War II.

Having become involved in two world wars with a
fragmentary understanding of the issues involved, we
concentrated on achieving "total victory," which George
Kennan correctly describes as a "dangerous delusion"
inimical to our own strategic interests. Our "war aims"
consisted largely of variations on the abstract; Woodrow
Wilson, ignoring the prizes of power and territory at
stake in World War I, strove to found an international
community based on law. Refusing, in the name of
idealism, to assert specific power interests on behalf of
the United States, he left the field open to those who
did assert them. The League of Nations became what
Wilson never intended it to be: an instrument for freez-
ing a *status quo* violently resented by the defeated states.

Franklin D. Roosevelt's call to arms in World War II
had a distinctly Wilsonian flavor. The Atlantic Charter
of August, 1941, was an echo of the Fourteen Points:
as Strausz-Hupé and Possony observe, it "was neither
a policy nor a program: for a program is the selection
of clearly defined, concrete, and attainable objectives, and
a policy is the selection of appropriate means to reach
these objectives."[1] Once more, refusal to formulate concrete political power objectives, this time coupled with
a refusal to permit the British to do so, opened wide
the gates to those who *had* goals of power and territory. Unconditional surrender created a vacuum, much
of which was filled by the man who knew exactly what
he wanted: Joseph Stalin. The United States then found
itself obliged to fill the rest of it.

Since World War II, the United States has become
for all practical purposes a European power. Across a

---

[1] Robert Strausz-Hupé and Stefan T. Possony, *International Relations*, New
York, 1950, p. 696.

thin line running from Lübeck to the Bohemian Forest and two buffer states, one weak and one unreliable, we face an enemy committed to our political destruction. Whether we like it or not, we are engaged in political warfare, success at which requires both a realistic program and a policy. Ignorance of European history and of the ramifications of European politics is a luxury which we can no longer afford. All too often, the Bolsheviks have won victories because they knew the facts, while responsible Americans did not. Since effective foreign policy in a constitutional state requires an informed public, we cannot leave the acquisition of knowledge to the "experts."

A country about which we need to know more is Czecho-Slovakia. Of its largest province, Bohemia, Bismarck once said: "He who rules Bohemia rules Europe." As a map of the continent shows, Czecho-Slovakia occupies a key position. Will the Russian Communists use this key for further aggression? Or will *we* use it to liberate the enslaved nations and to eliminate the Russian military threat to Western Europe and the United States?

Some years ago, the Kremlin moved the center of its espionage network for Western Europe from Moscow to Prague. As C. L. Sulzberger pointed out at the time in the *New York Times*,[2] much stealing of American military secrets in Europe is done by Czech rather than Russian agents. Important networks which undermine the security of United States forces in Germany are directed from Czech bases.

What follows is a short political history of Czecho-Slovakia from its origins to the present time, including its role in world affairs and as a subject of United States foreign policy. Since every state is largely a product of its history, this knowledge is essential for understanding the present situation and deciding what to do in the future.

Unfortunately, much of the "information" which has been circulated about Czecho-Slovakia is misinformation. Contrary to widespread belief, Communism did not come

---

[2] *New York Times*, January 21, 1954, "Reds Reshuffling European Spy Net."

to Czecho-Slovakia suddenly in 1948. Bolshevization of that country was prepared long in advance: the "February Revolution" was the culmination of a chain of events which began long before World War II. Only by understanding this process can we learn how to reverse it.

The author is deeply indebted to many friends throughout the world who contributed in various ways to making CZECHO-SLOVAKIA: A CRITICAL HISTORY possible. Particular thanks are due to Mr. V. L. Borin, St. Kilda (Australia); the late Dr. Karel Locher and Dr. Rudolf Storch, London; Professor Simeon Ghelfand, Brussels; Dr. Rudolf Hilf, Dr. Walter Becher, and Mr. Jiri Brada, Munich; Mr. Karel Stekr and Professor Bohdan Chudoba, New York; Dr. Joseph Kalvoda, Hartford; and Dr. Michal Zibrin, Chicago, for furnishing valuable and otherwise inaccessible source materials. Gratitude is also expressed to those who read and criticized—often energetically—the manuscript in its various stages, including Dr. Zbislav Peters, New York; Mr. Robert Heckert, Philadelphia; Mr. Philip A. Hrobak and Dr. Joseph Pauco, Middletown, Pennsylvania; the late Professor Francis Hrusovsky, Cleveland; Dr. Joseph Mikus, Washington; Deputy Wenzel Jaksch, Wiesbaden; and Dr. Walter Becher, Dr. Lothar Foltinek, Mr. Jiri Brada, and Mr. Kristof Greiner, of Munich.

The author also wishes to thank Mr. Heckert and Dr. Mikus, the Slovak Institute of Cleveland, and the Sudetendeutsche Landsmannschaft for the loan of photographs, and Lieutenant Colonel F. O. Miksche, of Paris, for permission to quote and reproduce a map from his pamphlet *Danubian Federation*. Appreciation is also expressed to Messrs. George Allen & Unwin, Ltd., of London, for permission to quote from the *Memoirs of Dr. Eduard Benes* (British edition).

KURT GLASER

Alton, Illinois
January, 1960

TABLE OF CONTENTS

LIST OF ILLUSTRATIONS

xv

CZECHO-SLOVAKIA
A CRITICAL HISTORY

I

CZECHO-SLOVAKIA AND ITS PEOPLES

THE "CZECHOSLOVAK LEGEND"

N OW THAT the Prague coup of February, 1948, is beginning to recede into history, it is difficult to imagine the shock with which news of that event was received by most Americans. True, the Communist leader, Klement Gottwald, had been premier since 1946. But non-Communist parties held a majority in the cabinet and in the parliament.

There had been a storm signal during the summer of 1947 when Stalin ordered Czecho-Slovakia to withdraw from the Marshall Plan, and the Prague cabinet complied—by unanimous vote. But few lost faith in the assurance of President Benes[1] that "any statement . . . that we are behind a curtain or occupied by the Russians is absolute nonsense. This country is absolutely democratic and we will remain so, come what may."[2] United States Ambassador Steinhardt declared: "There is definitely no iron curtain in Czecho-Slovakia."[3]

Yet overnight, without bloodshed, and to the infinite surprise of many Western statesmen, the supposedly democratic regime was replaced by a full-fledged Communist dictatorship.

Was the "February Revolution," as it is called, solely the result of a Communist plan which could not be thwarted? Or was it partially caused by mistaken United States and British policy, based on incorrect informa-

---

[1] In the text, Czech and Slovak names are given without the diacritical signs which affect the pronunciation. For exact orthography with English transliteration, see the Glossary beginning on page 255.

[2] *New York Times,* May 7, 1947.

[3] *Ibid.,* January 2, 1947.

tion? And if our policy was not realistic, what lessons can we learn for the future? More wrong information has been spread concerning Czecho-Slovakia than almost any other country. Misstatements of fact have not been limited to newspapers and speeches, but have crept into history books and encyclopedias. There is an entire "Czechoslovak legend," originated by Masaryk and Benes during World War I and then elaborated and propagated over thirty-five years by the government they founded, which appropriated millions of dollars for public relations. With secret funds the Czecho-Slovak Foreign Office bought reporters and professors, and sometimes entire newspapers.[4] During World War II, key positions in the Department of State and the Office of War Information were held by adherents of the "legend," which became the basis for United States policy on Central Europe. Since then, however, official faith in the "legend" has been punctuated by increasingly frequent expressions of skepticism, particularly in Congressional circles.

The fully developed "Czechoslovak legend" has numerous facets. It includes, among other things, the following propositions, none of which is true:

That there is a "Czechoslovak nation"—
That the Slovaks are not a nation, but only a branch of the Czech nation—
That the Slovak language is a dialect of Czech—
That a Czecho-Slovak state existed in the early Middle Ages—
That Czechs and Slovaks, since they began to struggle for freedom, have always wanted an independent Czecho-Slovakia—
That Thomas G. Masaryk and Eduard Benes were the greatest and most ethical statesmen of the twentieth century—
That the republic they established was a model democracy—

---

[4] V. L. Borin, "The Secret Funds of Benes' Intelligence Service," *Pravda* (anti-Communist), London, June, 1951, reprinted, *Slovak Newsletter*, Middletown, Pa., November, 1951. Using documents of the Czecho-Slovak Foreign Office, Borin shows how the Prague government bought control of the Vienna papers *Der Wiener Tag* and *Die Stunde*, and the Belgrade *Politika*. Its embassy in Paris paid the salary of Professor Fuscien Dominois, secretary of the Institute for Slavic Studies. On December 29, 1926, Consul-General Dr. Svetak, at Sydney, informed his superiors of amounts paid to Australian journalists for suppressing statements unfavorable to Masaryk and Benes. Czecho-Slovak Consul-General Moser, at Montreal, accounted on December 31, 1931, for money paid to several Canadian papers for articles praising Czecho-Slovakia. See also A. Bernauer, "Prague Bought European Public Opinion," *Sudetendeutsche Zeitung*, Munich, January 17, 1953; W. K. Turnwald, *Renascence or Decline of Central Europe*, Munich, 1954, p. 51.

That the Sudeten Germans were people sent by Adolf Hitler from the Reich to stir up trouble—

That the Slovak Republic established in 1939 was a Nazi puppet state—

That the "Czechoslovak" political exiles who came to the United States after February, 1948, were tried and true fighters against Communism, whereas anyone who fled *before* 1948 was probably a Nazi collaborator.

Rather than trying to refute these propositions one at a time, let us simply look at the facts as we find them.

THE CZECHO-SLOVAK REPUBLIC

Czecho-Slovakia was formed in October, 1918, as a result of the efforts of Thomas G. Masaryk and Eduard Benes, whose "Czechoslovak National Committee" in Paris had been recognized as a co-belligerent in World War I. Like the other "succession states," Austria and Hungary, it was carved entirely out of the old dual monarchy of Austria-Hungary.

Until 1938, Czecho-Slovakia contained 140,493 square miles, about as much as the states of New York, Pennsylvania, New Jersey, and Ohio together. Its western province, Bohemia, is a natural basin surrounded by forests, open to the east but with good rail connections to the west and access to the Elbe waterway in the north. The middle section, Moravia, including a small part of Silesia which remained with Austria after Prussia had annexed the rest of Silesia in 1763, was a central link in historic trade routes between northern and southern Europe. The two eastern sections, Slovakia and Ruthenia, belong to the Danube Valley and are separated from Polish and Ukrainian areas to the north by the Carpathian Mountains.

Forming a long east-west slice across Central Europe, Czecho-Slovakia was difficult to defend militarily. Lying athwart the direct routes between Berlin and Vienna and between Warsaw and Budapest, it was bound to be an object of interest for the major powers. For reasons which will become apparent as we proceed with our story, Czecho-Slovakia's internal weakness made it de-

pendent on great-power support.[5] The original protecting power was France, which took the initiative
in securing Allied agreement to dismembering Austria-
Hungary. But as French power weakened in the 1930's,
while Germany's attitude became increasingly unfriendly,
another protector had to be found. The only one available was Soviet Russia which, of course, had reasons of
its own for seeking expanded influence in Central Europe.

Having both heavy and light industry, coal, iron,
and timber, as well as a diversified agriculture, Czecho-
Slovakia was better off economically than its neighbors,
Austria and Hungary. But it also suffered from the
breaking up of the large market which the old Empire
had formed. As the retired premier, Dr. Karel Kramar,
said on December 25, 1932: "I cannot remember such
a sad Christmas as this. We are now feeling the full
weight of the loss to us of the Austro-Hungarian cus-
toms area. Anybody who thinks realistically and does
not forget that a state without sound economic founda-
tions cannot maintain its independence will realize that
these events must have serious consequences."[6]

CZECHS, SUDETEN GERMANS, AND SLOVAKS

Bohemia and Moravia-Silesia, the traditional lands of
the Bohemian Crown, were Austrian provinces with a
Czech majority and a German minority. The latter, constituting about one third of the population, had no desire to become part of a Czech state.

Slovakia, to the east, containing a solid core of Slovaks
with a sizeable fringe of Hungarians along the southern
border and a number of small German settlements, was,
before World War I, a part of Hungary. So was the
extreme eastern province of Ruthenia, also known as
Carpatho-Ukraine, which without any consultation of its
inhabitants was ceded to the Soviet Union in 1945.

The Czechs and the Slovaks are two distinct peoples.

---

[5] See F. O. Miksche, *Unconditional Surrender*, London, 1952, chap. 6, pp. 165-217, "The Balkanization of the Danube Countries," and Turnwald, *op. cit.*, pp. 53-55.

[6] For a detailed account of the economic decline in Czecho-Slovakia and the other states into which Austria-Hungary was divided after World War I, see Frederick Hertz, *The Economic Problem of the Danubian States*, London, 1947.

The ancestors of both were Slavic tribes which came to Europe during the great migrations of the fifth century, A.D. These tribes settled in different areas, where each people then lived its own distinctive history and developed its culture, traditions, and national aims. Although the two languages are enough alike so that Czechs and Slovaks can understand each other (as can Italians and Spaniards), each is a language in its own right.[7]

The Ruthenians or Carpatho-Ukrainians speak a Ukrainian dialect with a considerable admixture of words borrowed from other languages. Some Ruthenians consider themselves Ukrainians; others call themselves "Russians" (although they do not mean Muscovites or Great Russians), while still others feel that the Ruthenians are a people distinct in themselves. Some would prefer to remain with the Ukraine when that nation is liberated from Communism, while others wish to see Ruthenia federate with other peoples of the Danube Valley. How a majority of Ruthenians feel is an open question, since the exiles are seriously divided and the people at home have not recently been able to express freely their political will.

Eduard Benes advanced the idea of a "Czechoslovak people" during World War I to justify a state based on an artificial "majority."[8] Although the Slovaks, at the end of the war, were willing to form a common state with the Czechs, they insisted on doing so as Slovaks, retaining their identity as a nation. The Treaty of St. Germain, signed on September 10, 1919, guaranteed the autonomy of Ruthenia, but the Czecho-Slovak government did not fulfill the treaty until 1938.[9]

The republic conceived by Masaryk and Benes was governed as a unitary national state in which the "Czechoslovaks" were the ruling people or *Staatsvolk* and all others were treated as "minorities." The Slovaks soon

---

[7] See Joseph Skultety, *Sketches from Slovak History*, Middletown, Pa., 1930, chaps. I, V, and VI; Francis Hrusovsky, *This Is Slovakia*, Scranton, Pa., 1953, pp. 1-41; *Slovak Newsletter*, *passim*, articles headed "Out of the Slovak Past."

[8] Eduard Benes, *Détruisez l'Autriche-Hongrie!* ["Destroy Austria-Hungary!"] Paris, 1916, chap I.

[9] Julian Revay, "The March to Liberation of Carpatho-Ukraine," *Ukrainian Quarterly*, X, No. 3 (Summer, 1954), 226-34.

found themselves in the anomalous position of a "minority within the majority." Actually the republic was, like Austria-Hungary, a multi-national state.[10] According to the 1926 census it contained:

> 6.5 million Czechs
> 3.3 million Sudeten and Carpatho-Germans
> 2.5 million Slovaks
> 0.8 million Hungarians
> 0.4 million Ruthenians
> 0.1 million Poles
>
> ---
>
> 13.6 million people

If the new state had been named after its peoples in the order of their size, it would have been called "Czecho-Germano-Slovakia." In fact, the correct name, used in the Paris peace treaties, is Czecho-Slovakia with a hyphen.[11]

A GLANCE THROUGH HISTORY

In the early Middle Ages, the Slovaks were ruled by princes whose seat was the city of Nitra, where the first Christian church among western Slavs was built in A.D. 830. Prince Mojmir (830-850) and his successors Rostislav (850-870) and Svatopluk (870-894) extended their domain to include Czech lands as well as much of present-day Poland and Hungary. The Great Moravian Empire, as it is known in history, was based on the personal power of the rulers, and was not a "national state" in the modern sense.[12]

It was Rostislav who, in order to curb Frankish influence, requested the Byzantine Emperor Michael III to send a bishop to "enlighten and instruct his people

---

[10] See F. O. Miksche, *Danubian Federation*, Camberley, England, 1953, pp. 11-12, 16; Waller Wynne, Jr., *The Population of Czechoslovakia*, Washington, U.S. Bureau of the Census, 1953, pp. 15, 25-26.

[11] To avoid confusion, the term "Czech" is used in this book only in its correct sense, meaning the Czech people or a member thereof, never as an abbreviation for "Czecho-Slovak."

[12] Although some historians have attempted to appropriate Mojmir and his successors for the Czechs, there is no doubt that they were Slovaks. Skultety, *op. cit.*, pp. 1-40; Hrusovsky, *op. cit.*, pp. 9-13; B. S. Buc, "The Origins of Slovak Nationalism," *Slovakia*, Middletown, Pa., VIII, No. 1 (March, 1958) 46-59. See also Eugen Lemberg, *Die Ausweisung als Schicksal und Aufgabe* ["Expulsion as Fate and Challenge"], Gräfelfing/Munich, 1949, pp. 9-14, for a discussion of the non-national dynastic state of medieval and early modern times and the relatively recent emergence of nationality as a political factor.

in the true faith and in their own tongue."[13] The emperor sent two of his most learned doctors, Sts. Cyril and Methodius, who introduced a new alphabet and (with the permission of the Pope) a Slovanic liturgy. Svatopluk, however, favored the Frankish priests, so that when Byzantium split off from Rome in the wake of the Schism of Photius, Slovakia remained within the Western Church.

The Czech nobles of Bohemia, led by the Premyslides and the Slavniks, did not like being ruled by a Slovak prince. After Svatopluk's death, they revolted against his successor Mojmir II, and, in 895, pledged their allegiance to the Frankish emperor at Regensburg. The empire of those days, though called the "Holy Roman Empire of the German Nation," was no more a national state than had been Svatopluk's kingdom. The empire represented the heritage of Charlemagne, who had undertaken to weld European Christendom into a political unity corresponding to the unity of the Church.[14]

Soon after the fall of the Great Moravian Empire, the Slovaks had to turn their entire attention to defense against the pagan Magyars, who threatened to overrun the entire Danube Valley. The incursion of the Magyars prevented the re-establishment of any political connection between the Slovaks and the Czechs.

The Premyslides, particularly the ruthless Boleslav I (929-67),[15] achieved centralized rule in Bohemia, and participated actively in German imperial politics. Czech tribes fought with the Germans against the Magyars at Lechfeld in 955, and in 973 Prague acquired its own bishop, subordinate to the archbishop of Mainz. The immigration of German priests and monks, who supported the Premyslides against the feudal nobles, was encouraged by the rulers, and in the eleventh century King Bretislav I set an example for the Czech nobility by marrying a German princess.

During the centuries which followed, the Czech rulers

---

[13] Ludovit Zachar, *Borba za narodnu slobodu* ["Toward National Freedom"], Bratislava, 1931, cited by Buc, *op. cit.*, p. 53.

[14] Fritz Gause, *Deutsch-slawische Schicksalsgemeinschaft* ["Germans and Slavs as Partners in History"], Kitzingen, 1952, pp. 20-42 ; Turnwald, *op. cit.*, pp. 15-17.

[15] Boleslav attained the throne by murdering his brother, whose memory is preserved in the carol, "Good King Wenceslas."

encouraged Germans to settle in Bohemia and Moravia. The Czechs were mostly peasants, while the first German immigrants were city dwellers who founded towns where they introduced handicrafts, trade, and industry. The influx of Germans reached its peak in the thirteenth century, when the Czech nobles competed to obtain settlers to populate their domains. German production, particularly metal mining and glass blowing, raised the Czech standard of living. Under Charles IV, of the Luxembourg dynasty, Prague became the capital of the German Empire. The Charles University, founded at Prague in 1348, was a co-operative enterprise of Germans and Czechs.[16]

The Czech settlements were concentrated in the center of the Bohemian basin. German farmers moved in around the edges of this area, cleared the forests, and gradually settled the land as far as Saxony in the north and Franconia in the west. In this way, German settlers established what became the historical boundaries of Bohemia.[17]

The Czech nobility, whether or not of partial German descent, felt some antipathy toward the German townspeople, not because they were German but because the kings used them to strengthen central as against regional authority.[18] In general, however, relations between the Czechs and Germans of Bohemia were cordial until the appearance of Jan Hus, leader of a religious reform movement based on Bible teaching, simplicity, and communion in both parts (bread and wine) for laymen. In the university at Prague, where Hus was professor of theology, his "realist" teaching was opposed by the German professors who adhered to a school of philosophy called "nominalism." Hus also championed the peasants and poor country nobility, who were mainly

[16] Harriet Wanklyn, *Czechoslovakia*, London, 1954, pp. 146-51; Gause, *op. cit.*, pp. 54-71, 86-88; Turnwald, *op. cit.*, pp. 17-21; Rudolf Schreiber, "Die politische Entwicklung und Bedeutung der Sudetenländer" ["The Political Development and Importance of the Sudeten Lands"], in Helmut Preidel, ed., *Die Deutschen in Böhmen und Mähren* ["The Germans in Bohemia and Moravia"], Gräfelfing/Munich, 1950, pp. 34-59.

[17] Gause, *op. cit.*, p. 70; Schreiber, *op. cit.*, pp. 51-52; Göttingen Research Society, *Sudetenland*, p. 59.

[18] Wanklyn, *op. cit.*, p. 150. As Miss Wanklyn points out, this situation was repeated in other countries of medieval Europe. The writer takes rather strong exception to some of Miss Wanklyn's views, but agrees with her on this point.

Czechs, as against wealthy tradesmen and officials who were largely German. His movement became national and radical, anti-Catholic and anti-German, probably more so than Hus himself intended.

In 1409 the Czech party led by Hus prevailed on King Wenceslaus IV to sign the Kuttenberg Decree which gave the Czechs a majority voice in governing the university. Some four thousand German professors and students left Prague in protest. Many went to Leipzig, where the Elector of Saxony founded a rival university. Four years later the king decreed that Czechs should have half the seats in the Prague City Council, although the German citizens of the city were in a clear majority.

In 1415 the prelates of the Catholic church held a council at Constance, on what is now the German-Swiss border. Hus went there to defend his views. Although the emperor had promised him protection, he was burned at the stake for heresy.

Hus's followers then went on a rampage. A revolutionary army swept through Bohemia, murdering Catholics and burning their homes. The Hussite Wars, which lasted more than ten years, impoverished the country. A number of towns and over fifteen hundred villages were razed to the ground, and Czech as well as German farms were laid waste. The only winners were the Czech nobility, who took over for their private estates the lands of the Church, the peasants on which became serfs (slaves bound to the soil) in 1487.[19]

Slowly at first, Bohemia recovered from the Hussite disaster. Under King George Podiebrad (1457-71), who unintentionally paved the way for the accession of the Habsburgs by appointing King Wladislaw of Poland as his successor to the throne, relations between Czechs and Germans improved. After a Habsburg had become King of Bohemia in 1526, a new wave of German settlers arrived. It included artisans and tradesmen who moved to the Bohemian cities where the earlier German population had been liquidated by the Hussites.

Luther's Reformation produced new religious tension.

---

[19] For a brief survey of Hussite movement, see Turnwald, *op. cit.*, pp. 21-24; for economic and demographic effects see Preidel, ed., *op. cit.*, pp. 59-66, 127-29; for chronology see Gött. Res. Soc., *Sudetenland*, pp. 61-64.

In 1618 a group of Protestant nobles, including both Czechs and Germans, threw two of the Catholic emperor's officials out of a window. This act, known as the "Defenestration of Prague," set off the Thirty Years' War (1618-48) which soon engulfed the entire German Empire.

After the battle of the White Mountain, won by the Catholics in 1620, some thirty thousand Protestant families, Czech and German, were forced to leave Bohemia and settle in Germany, Poland and Slovakia. When the war ended in a stalemate in 1648, Bohemia was largely devastated, as was most of Germany,

The Thirty Years' War was a religious and dynastic struggle, not a national war in the modern sense. Although the battle of the White Mountain has gone down in legend as the end of Czech independence, its actual significance was that Bohemia and Moravia were henceforth ruled by a Catholic Habsburg rather than the German Calvinist Frederick of the Palatinate. While the Habsburgs undertook to liquidate Protestantism in their territories, Protestant monarchs elsewhere took equal advantage of the principle *cuius regio eius religio*.[20] Nor is there any evidence that the kings of the Palatinate would have been less autocratic than the Emperor Ferdinand II and his successors.[21]

Most continental European monarchies became autocratic and centralist during the seventeenth and eighteenth centuries, and the Habsburg Empire was no exception. Since the German language was used in government and business, and was rapidly replacing Latin

---

[20] The Peace of Westphalia (1648), which established a balance of power checking Austrian as well as French and Swedish ambitions, reduced the number of sovereign principalities in the German Empire from 900 to 355. Each ruler was accorded the right to prescribe the religion of his subjects.

[21] For developments from close of Hussite Wars (Prague compacts of 1433 to beginning of Thirty Years' War (1618), see Turnwald, *op. cit.*, pp. 23-24; Gause, *op. cit.*, pp. 115-16, 131-32; *Sudetenland*, pp. 66-76; Schreiber, *op. cit.*, pp. 66-70; and (also in *Die Deutschen in Böhmen und Mähren*) W. Weizsäcker, "Geschichte des Rechts in Böhmen und Mähren ["History of Law in Bohemia and Moravia"], pp. 140-41. For effects of Thirty Years' War on Bohemian lands and on German-Czech relations, see Turnwald, *op. cit.*, pp. 24-27; Gause, *op. cit.*, pp. 138-41, 151-52; Schreiber, *op. cit.*, pp. 70-76; Hugo Hantsch, *Die Nationalitätenfrage im alten Österreich* ["The Nationality Question in Old Austria"], Vienna, 1953, pp. 14-24. For general background, see Salomon Reinach, *Orpheus, A History of Religions*, New York, 1932, pp. 324-60; F. Palacky, *Geschichte von Böhmen* ["History of Bohemia"], Prague, 1936, *passim;* Ernest Denis, *La Bohème depuis la Montagne Blanche*, Paris, 1903, *passim;* Emil Krofta, *Geschichte der Tschechoslowakei* ["History of Czecho-Slovakia"], Prague, 1936. Caution is advised, however, in the use of encyclopedias.

as the language of literature and philosophy in most of Central Europe, the Czech language and culture were pushed into the background. At the University of Prague, where instruction had hitherto been in Latin, lectures in German were introduced in 1763. In 1784 German was made the official government language in all lands of the Habsburg monarchy. Yet the admittedly widespread process of "Germanization" was more automatic than deliberate. At no time did the Vienna government seek deliberately to suppress the Czech language. Under Queen Maria Theresia, Czech was introduced as a field of study in the military academy (1752) and at the University of Vienna (1775). The Theresian school law of 1774 provided for the use of Czech in the primary schools and German in the secondary schools. Toward the end of the eighteenth century, there was a revival of Czech national consciousness, viewed sympathetically by Goethe, Herder, and other Germans.[22]

The lesson to be learned from Bohemian history is that of national and religious tolerance. So long as Germans and Czechs, Catholics and Protestants, respected each others' rights, the country grew and prospered.[23] But when bigotry and hatred gained the upper hand, the results were mass murder and destruction, religious persecution, and slavery. This repeated itself in the twentieth century, when unbridled prejudice opened the door to totalitarian Bolshevism.

During all these centuries, Slovakia had her own troubles, which came from beyond her borders. In 955, Emperor Otto had defeated the Magyars at the battle of Lechfeld, forcing them to give up their life as marauding nomads and settle down in their present territory

[22] As Turnwald (loc. cit.) observes, governmental centralization in the Habsburg Empire was part of the general absolutist trend of the seventeenth and eighteenth centuries, and the attempt of certain historians (such as Palacky and Masaryk) to interpret it as a German attempt to "suppress" the Czechs is a distortion. See Gause's chapter on "Absolutism" (op. cit., pp. 154-86) ; J. Wiefels, Deutsche Verfassungsgeschichte ["German Constitutional History"], Stuttgart, 1949, pp. 62ff.; and Robert Ingrim, After Hitler Stalin?, Milwaukee, 1946, chap. VIII. On German attitudes to and participation in the Czech renaissance, see Eugen Lemberg, "Der deutsche Anteil im Erwachen des tschechischen Volkes" ["The German Role in the Awakening of the Czech People"], in Preidel, ed., Die Deutschen in Böhmen und Mähren, pp. 304-32.

[23] For graphic evidence of the fruits of Czech-German collaboration in Bohemia, see Turnwald, Sudeten German Picture Book, Munich, 1949.

in Hungary, which they proceeded to expand. About the year 1000, Slovakia was integrated into the Kingdom of St. Stephen, where her political tradition and geographical position enabled her to play a leading role in Hungarian politics. She was a bastion of Europe against barbarian invasions from the east, such as that of the Tartars in 1241. During the Turkish occupation of most of Hungary in the sixteenth and seventeenth centuries, Slovakia was the major area which remained unconquered and which bore the brunt of the effort needed to hold back and ultimately expel the invaders.

Hungary was a state of many nationalities, ruled since 1301 by kings of non-Magyar origin. The state language was Latin and the culture was the common product of the peoples of the Danube basin. Slovakia, therefore, retained and developed its language and national traditions. In 1526 Hungary, including Slovakia, came under the rule of the Habsburgs.

Difficulties in the relations between Magyars and Slovaks first became serious toward the end of the eighteenth century, when Maria Theresia and her son Joseph II (1780-90) introduced administrative and social reforms, including substitution of German for Latin as the official language. Fired with the nationalist ideas of the French Revolution, the Magyars reacted by moving toward a Hungarian state, to be achieved through "Magyarization" of the non-Hungarian peoples. The latter clung all the more tenaciously to their own languages and national traditions.[24]

---

[24] Skultety, *op. cit.*, pp. 46-128; Hrusovsky, *op. cit.*, pp. 12-44. For the history of ethnic German settlements in Slovakia, which were affected no less than the Slovaks themselves by "Magyarization," see Johann Liptak, ed., *800 Jahre Slowakei-Deutschtum* ["800 Years of German Settlements in Slovakia"], Stuttgart, undated (1948-1952).

II

THE FIRST CZECHO-SLOVAK REPUBLIC
1918-1938

DID THE CZECHS AND SLOVAKS WANT
CZECHO-SLOVAKIA?

UNTIL World War I, few Czechs or Slovaks thought of forming a national state separate from Austria-Hungary. The Czech national renaissance of the early nineteenth century, led by the historian Palacky and the journalist Havlicek, sought the development of Czech culture and fuller self-government within the empire. Although Palacky is primarily responsible for the myth that the Great Moravian Empire was a Czecho-Slovak national state, he was statesman enough not to wish to re-create it.

Justifying his refusal to lead a Czech delegation to the revolutionary Frankfurt Parliament of 1848, Palacky wrote of the Austrian Empire: "If it did not exist, we would have to invent it. The disintegration of the Austrian state into small republics would be an invitation to German and Russian imperialism." He exercised a moderating influence on the Slav Congress which met at Prague the same year. On January 23, 1849, Palacky proposed to the constitutional committee of the Austrian *Reichstag,* meeting at Kremsier, the reorganization of the empire as a federation of eight self-governing national groups. Had Emperor Francis Joseph accepted the liberal federal Kremsier Constitution, rather than dissolving the *Reichstag* in an arbitrary manner, Austria would have been on the way toward a peaceful solution of its national problems.[1]

---

[1] For a fuller treatment of Palacky's efforts toward a federal Austria, see Wenzel Jaksch, *Europas Weg nach Potsdam,* Stuttgart, 1958, esp. pp. 45ff. See also *Sudetenland,* pp. 70-72, and Gause, *op. cit.,* pp. 216-25, 248-54.

Havlicek, in arguing that Bohemia should not join the German Reich proposed by the Frankfurt Parliament in 1849,[2] wrote:

> Our federation is Austria. In the latter we will naturally retain a constant preponderance, while we would always have to be a small appendage in the German federation. . . . In association with the other Slavs of Austria we will be able, as a special "Bohemian Crown," to enjoy full autonomy and at the same time the advantages of a large state.[3]

Very few Czechs wanted to go further than the goal indicated by Palacky and Havlicek. Although promises made during the Revolution of 1848 were quickly forgotten, the Czechs realized substantial gains under the Imperial Decree of October 20, 1860, which guaranteed the rights of nationalities in the Austrian part of the empire. When Bismarck, during the Prussian-Austrian War of 1866, suggested freeing the Czechs from Habsburg rule, Palacky and his son-in-law, F. L. Rieger, swung Czech opinion against the proposal, since they foresaw that detachment from Austria would make the Czech lands too vulnerable to German domination.

The nineteenth century also witnessed a revival of Slovak national feeling, in which leading roles were played by the poets Jan Holly and Jan Kollar, and the political leader and writer, Ludovit Stur.[4] When the Hungarians revolted against the Habsburgs in 1848, an assembly of Slovaks drew up demands for political, social, and cultural equality. As Budapest responded by outlawing the action, the Slovaks took to arms. The Vienna government crushed the Hungarian revolt with Russian assistance, but did nothing about the Slovak

---

[2] Efforts to found an empire on liberal principles failed when King Frederick William IV of Prussia refused to become Kaiser "by the grace of bakers and butchers."

[3] Cited by Raupach, *Der tschechische Frühnationalismus* ["Early Czech Nationalism"], Essen, 1939, p. 92. As Schreiber (*op. cit.*, p. 82) and Weizsäcker (*op. cit.*, pp. 145-46) point out, however, Havlicek and the "Old Czech" party led by Palacky's son-in-law, Rieger, were not content with mere self-government for the Czechs. Basing their argument for a unitary Bohemia on the "Constitutional Law of the Bohemian Kingdom" (*böhmisches Staatsrecht*), they demanded a ruling status for the Czechs and a "minority" status with lesser political rights for the Germans of Bohemia. See also Jaksch, *op. cit.*, pp. 65-78.

[4] Hrusovsky, *op. cit.*, pp. 40-45; Eleonor Podkrivacky, "The Evolution of Slovak Literature—Anton Bernolak's Influence," *Slovakia*, September, 1953, pp. 18-25, with bibliography. On Ludovit Stur's Pan-Slavism and his opposition to Communism, see Joseph Kirschbaum, "Ludovit Stur and His Place in the Slavic World," *Slovakia*, March, 1958, pp. 1-24.

demands. Nor did Russia bring diplomatic pressure on behalf of the Slovaks, although she might well have done so. The 1860 decree on nationality rights did not apply to Hungary and therefore did not help the Slovaks. In 1867, Vienna granted full self-government to Hungary. But instead of extending this freedom to the non-Hungarian nationalities, the Budapest government began a systematic campaign of "Magyarization." Magyar was decreed as the only official language of Hungary and, finally, the Slovak language was forbidden in the schools of Slovakia. Even so, Slovak leaders continued thoughout the nineteenth century to seek national equality within the Hungarian state.[5]

In Austria (but not in Hungary), the principle of the 1860 decree was confirmed in the "Basic Law on the General Rights of Citizens" of December 21, 1867, which documented the equality of all nationalities. This law guaranteed each ethnic group the right to preserve its national character and its language, and recognized "the equality of all regionally customary languages (landesübliche Sprachen) in schools, administration, and public life."[6]

As successive governmental reforms widened the suffrage and expanded the powers of the provincial diets, certain national groups attempted to enhance their own status at the expense of others. In Galicia, the Polish-controlled diet embarked on a "Polonization" campaign, closing the Ukrainian schools. In Bohemia and Moravia-Silesia, where the diets now had Czech majorities, there was disagreement as to the meaning of "customary language." The Germans took it to mean that Czech would be used in Czech districts, German in German districts, and both languages in mixed areas. Czech nationalists, however, taking advantage of the fact that *Cechy* is the Czech word for the Bohemian Crown Lands, insisted

---

[5] Joseph A. Mikus, *La Slovaquie dans le Drame de l'Europe* ["Slovakia in the Drama of Europe"], Paris, 1955, pp. 13-25; Skultety, *op. cit.*, pp. 170-222; Hrusovsky, *op. cit.*, pp. 44-52; C. A. Macartney, *Problems of the Danube Basin*, Cambridge, England, 1942, *passim*.

[6] R. Laun, *"Die völkerrechtlichen und nationalitätenrechtlichen Grundlagen der Sudetenfrage"* ["International and Nationality Law and the Sudeten Question"], in *Mitteleuropäische Quellen und Dokumente* ["Central European Sources and Documents"], Munich, 1956, I, 39-53.

that the "Bohemian language" (i.e. Czech) be used in all parts of the provinces. During the latter part of the nineteenth century, Czech and German extremists engaged in a *Kulturkampf*, typified by the splitting of the Charles University into separate German and Czech schools in 1882, but there were many unsung moderate statesmen who worked earnestly to improve relations.[7] A practical solution was reached in Moravia with the "Equalization" (*mährischer Ausgleich*) of 1905, whereby each national group was assured proportionate representation in the diet and separate Czech and German administrations for schools and cultural institutions were established. Progress toward a similar arrangement in Bohemia was interrupted by World War I.[8]

In spite of ethnic friction, Czech political thought clung to the maxims of Palacky until nearly the end of World War I. It was felt that if Austria should fall, Bohemia would become the victim of German or Russian imperialism and would lose its home rule—which is precisely what happened later. Thomas G. Masaryk wrote in his book *The Czech Question,* published in 1908: "If Austria were defeated in a European conflagration and should break up, we would be integrated into Germany, alongside which we have lived for a thousand years."[9]

Dr. Eduard Benes, who later overshadowed Masaryk as a driving force in the movement for a Czecho-Slovak state, wrote in his 1908 doctoral thesis: "People have often spoken of a dismemberment of Austria. I do not believe in it at all." And Dr. Karel Kramar, later prime minister of Czecho-Slovakia, wrote in 1906:

[7] See Wenzel Jaksch, "Die Sudetenfrage im Mitteleuropäischen Kräftespiel" ["The Sudeten Question in the Central European Play of Forces"], *Mitteleuropäische Quellen und Dokumente,* I, 15-31.

[8] Concerning the constitutional and nationality policies of Austria-Hungary before World War I, and Czech-German relations in Bohemia, see Miksche, *Unconditional Surrender,* pp. 165-83 ; Hermann Raschhofer, *Die Sudetenfrage* ["The Sudeten Question"], Munich, 1953, pp. 26-37 ; Paul Molisch, *Vom Kampf der Tschechen um ihren Staat* ["The Czechs Battle for Their State"], Vienna, 1929, pp. 4-32 ; also Schreiber, *op. cit.,* pp. 84-87 ; Weizsäcker, *op. cit.,* pp. 145-48 ; Turnwald, *Renascence or Decline,* pp. 28-32. A more detailed treatment of Austrian nationality problems and policies is contained in Hugo Hantsch, *Die Nationalitätenfrage im alten Österreich* ["The Nationality Question in Old Austria"], Vienna, 1953. Classic Czech views are expressed in T. G. Masaryk's *The Making of a State,* London, 1929 ; in Benes' *Détruisez l'Autriche-Hongrie!,* and in S. Grant Duff, *Europe and the Czechs,* London, 1938.

[9] T. G. Masaryk, *Ceska Otazka* ["The Czech Question"], Prague, 1908. Quotation kindly furnished by Dr. Joseph A. Mikus.

Nobody will deny the clear and obvious fact that our people has comparatively the best conditions for cultural, political and economic development in Austria. There is no other way: the position of our people in the heart of Europe and the existing conditions of international policy compel us more than ever to see the best guarantees for the future of our people in a strong Austria.[10]

In addition to exercising majority control in Bohemia and Moravia-Silesia, the Czechs played an active role in Austrian imperial affairs. With 23 per cent of the population, the Czechs had, as of 1910, 21 per cent of the members of parliament, 25 per cent of the schoolteachers, 19 per cent of the army officers (including sixty-four generals), and 20 per cent of the civil servants in the Austrian government as a whole. A number of cabinets, including that in office at the beginning of World War I, had Czech ministers.[11] The Austrian railroad administration actually favored Czech employees to such an extent that the Czecho-Slovak railroads inherited a serious surplus of administrative staff.[12]

Liberal German-Austrian politicians were the first to admit that relations among the nationalities could be improved. The Moravian, Karl Renner (president of Austria, 1945-50), and the Bohemian, Josef Seliger, drafted a program for the reorganization of the empire as a federal state which was accepted by the Social Democrats of all national groups at their congress at Brno in 1899.[13] Similar proposals were advanced by Dr. Karl

---

[10] This and the preceding quotation from Benes cited from Frederick Hertz, *Nationality in History and Politics*, London, 1945, pp. 203ff.

[11] While Palacky had complained that the 1861 election law had favored German-Austrians over Czechs, this law was repealed in 1907. The Germans, meanwhile, had lost their majority in the *Reichsrat* ("Imperial Parliament") in 1879. Although in the central ministries in Vienna the Czechs accounted for only 653 (10.4 per cent) of the 6,293 civil servants, the situation was reversed in Bohemia where, with 63.2 per cent of the population (1910), the Czechs held 95 per cent of imperial and provincial civil service posts. See H. F. March, "Wahlpraktiken in der ersten Tschechoslowakei" ["Electoral Practices in the First Czecho-Slovak Republic"], *Sudetendeutsche Zeitung*, Munich, April 18 and 25, 1953 ; Miksche, *Danubian Federation*, pp. 10-12 ; Hantsch, *op. cit.*, pp. 25-35, 116-17 and sources there cited.

[12] Wanklyn, *Czechoslovakia*, p. 333.

[13] The Social Democratic program had five points, as follows:
1. Austria is to be reorganized as a democratic federation of nationalities.
2. The historic Crown Lands are to be replaced by self-governing areas limited by ethnic boundaries, the legislation and administration of which shall be the task of National Chambers, elected by universal, equal, and direct suffrage.
3. All self-governing areas of one and the same nation constitute a unified national federation, which administers national matters with full autonomy.
4. The rights of national minorities shall be guaranteed by a special law enacted by the Imperial Parliament.
5. We recognize no privileged nationality and therefore reject the demand for a

Lueger, mayor of Vienna; by the Transylvanian Rumanian Aurel Popovici; and by a group of adherents of Crown Prince Franz Ferdinand known as "The Workshop," to which the Slovak politician, Dr. Milan Hodza (later premier of Czecho-Slovakia), belonged. Franz Ferdinand's assassination on June 28, 1914, not only precipitated World War I but also eliminated the leader most capable of rebuilding Austria as a true federation. Even so, it may be offered as a sober judgment that the Austrian Empire would not have collapsed had not the Allies deliberately promoted its destruction.

When Thomas G. Masaryk decided in 1914 to agitate among the Allies for a Czecho-Slovak state, his only supporters at home were a small group of conspirators which he himself called the "Maffia."[14] The Austrian memorial presented at the 1919 Peace Conference lists many instances in which Czech members of the Imperial Parliament, political parties, and local government associations affirmed their loyalty to the Crown and their desire not for the dissolution of the Empire but for reorganization as a federation. When the Entente proclaimed the "liberation" of the Czechs and Slovaks in January, 1917, the Presidium of the Union of Czech Deputies (*Cesky Svaz*) declared that the Czechs did not want to be "liberated," an action later confirmed by the Czech deputies in parliament. As late as January 6, 1918, an assembly of 150 Czech deputies, including leaders of all parties, passed a resolution urging reorganization of Austria as a federation.

Although Masaryk and Benes enjoyed from the beginning a certain number of supporters at home, a widespread shift in public opinion did not set in until the summer of 1918. As Masaryk himself noted (*The Making of a State*, p. 284), even the National Council formed in Prague in October, 1918, was by no means unanimous on the issue of leaving Austria.[15]

---

state language. The Imperial Parliament shall determine the extent to which a language for negotiations is required.
    Cited by Jaksch, *op. cit.*, p. 22, appended to *Mitteleuropäische Quellen und Dokumente*, Vol. I, as Exhibit 1, pp. 101-2.
    [14] Thomas G. Masaryk, *The Making of a State*, London, 1927, pp. 46, 79, and *passim*. On Dr. Kramar's proposal for a Russian protected "Czech Czardom," see chap. III, *infra*.
    [15] For a brief account of Czecho-Slovak activity abroad during World War I

HOW THE CZECHO-SLOVAK REPUBLIC WAS ESTABLISHED

The birthplace of the Czecho-Slovak Republic was not at home, but abroad. With a small group of political exiles, Masaryk and Benes formed the "Czecho-Slovak National Council" in Paris. Then they convinced the Allies of the military advantages in recognizing this council as a Czecho-Slovak "government in exile." Benes wrote a book entitled *Destroy Austria-Hungary!* which had a considerable effect on French foreign policy.[16]

Lacking substantial support from home, Masaryk played eloquently on the Czech emigrants living in the United States and other Western countries, who organized demonstrations and passed resolutions which were palmed off on Allied statesmen as the will of the Czech people.[17] Czech military detachments, formed in Russia, France, and Italy, had great propaganda value, even though they did little fighting.[18] Masaryk's greatest achievement, of course, was convincing Woodrow Wilson that establishment of a Czecho-Slovak Republic would provide "the freest opportunity for autonomous development" for the peoples within its territory, as the President had demanded in his Fourteen Points.

When Austria was finally defeated, Masaryk was able to offer his countrymen, most of whom had taken part in the Austrian war effort, the chance to switch overnight from the status of a defeated nation to that of a victor. This was an attractive opportunity, and the Czechs are not to be blamed for accepting it.[19]

---

and at the Paris Peace Conference, see Turnwald, *Renascence or Decline*, pp. 32-47. A full account, covering both the policies of the Czecho-Slovak National Committee and the various governments and pertinent questions of international law, is found in Raschhofer, *Die Sudetenfrage*, pp. 47-144. Molisch, *Vom Kampf der Tschechen um ihren Staat*, also devotes a section (pp. 49-81) to this topic. For developments within Austria, see Raschhofer, *op. cit.*, pp. 34-46 (including the full text of the Austrian memorial to the Peace Conference), and Molisch, *op. cit.*, pp. 33-49 and 81-161. See also Miksche, *Danubian Federation*, pp. 13-19, and Gause, *Deutsch-slawische Schicksalsgemeinschaft*, pp. 253-77. For chronology, see *Sudetenland*, pp. 75-79.

[16] See chap. I, note 8.

[17] Molisch, *op. cit.*, pp. 49-55; Charles Pergler, *America in the Struggle for Czechoslovak Independence*, Philadelphia, 1926, *passim*. U.S. House of Representatives, 83d Congress, Select Committee on Communist Aggression, *Special Report No. 8: Czechoslovakia*, Washington, 1954, pp. 3-5.

[18] As the Czech military expert, Colonel Miksche, points out (*Unconditional Surrender*, p. 173), the main reason why Czech prisoners in Russia joined the Czech-Slovak Legion was to escape the oppressive and disease-ridden POW camps. Even then, large numbers refused to join. See *infra.* p. 50.

[19] *Ibid.*, pp. 174-76; Turnwald, *op. cit.*, pp. 36-37; Raschhofer, *op. cit.*, pp. 94-98.

Masaryk induced the Slovaks to join with the Czechs by offering them equality and self-government. To this end he endorsed the so-called Cleveland Agreement, signed by the Czech National Federation (of America) and the Slovak League of America in October, 1915. He also signed with the same organizations the more specific Pittsburgh Agreement of May 30, 1918, which provided: "Slovakia shall have its own administration, its diet (parliament), its own courts, and Slovak shall be the official language in the schools, state services, and public life." Masaryk assured Woodrow Wilson that relations between the Czechs and the Slovaks had been formulated to the satisfaction of both in the Pittsburgh Agreement.[20]

On October 18, 1918, the interim Czecho-Slovak "government" proclaimed the independence of the Czecho-Slovak Republic by a declaration issued in Washington. On the same day, President Wilson rejected Vienna's peace offer of October 7 on the ground that the United States recognized a state of war between Czecho-Slovakia and Austria-Hungary. After a delegation of Czech deputies have met with Dr. Benes in Geneva,[21] the Czecho-Slovak Republic was proclaimed in Prague on October 28, 1918, which is celebrated as Czech Independence Day.[22] Masaryk's followers at home, led by Dr. Kramar, took over from the Austrian authorities, who withdrew voluntarily to avoid bloodshed.

A revolutionary Slovak National Council met at Turciansky Sv. Martin on October 30, 1918, and adopted a declaration agreeing to join a Czecho-Slovak state on conditions of equality and self-government as exemplified by the Pittsburgh Agreement. The Declaration of Turciansky Sv. Martin did not, however, truly reflect the desires of the Slovak people, since Benes' representatives had foisted on the council the erroneous idea that the Allies would not permit separation of Slovakia from

---

[20] See Joseph Kirschbaum, "The Pittsburgh Pact: Its Significance in Slovak Politics," *Bulletin of the Slovak National Council Abroad*, Middletown, Pa., June, 1958, pp. 2, 4.

[21] The fact that Emperor Charles, however reluctantly, granted permission for the deputies to make the trip belies the existence of any "state of war."

[22] The Slovaks celebrate March 14, the anniversary of the founding of the Slovak Republic in 1939.

Hungary unless the Slovaks declared themselves a constituent part of the "Czechoslovak" nation. After the delegates had gone home, Dr. Milan Hodza, who many years later became Czecho-Slovak Prime Minister, took it upon himself to edit out a paragraph of the declaration providing for separate Slovak representation at the Peace Conference.[23] Czech-Slovak relations were soon clouded by the death of General Milan R. Stefanik, a Slovak scientist who had joined the "Czecho-Slovak National Council." The airplane taking him home was "accidentally" shot down near Bratislava on May 4, 1919. Many Slovaks refused to believe that it really was an accident. Nor were Slovaks gratified by the pronouncement of the Prague Council of State on April 14, 1919, that "Slovakia was annexed to the Czechoslovak state as a consequence of occupation of Slovakia by Czechoslovak armed forces." Monsignor Andrej Hlinka, who had led Slovak resistance to "Magyarization" and now led it against the new Czech imperialism, arrived in Paris in September, 1919, and presented a Slovak memorandum of protest to the Peace Conference. To add insult to injury, Benes induced the French police to deport Hlinka as a "Habsburg agent" and kept him six months in jail at Mirov, Moravia, while beguiling the Conference with claims that Czecho-Slovakia would be "like Switzerland."

Although Masaryk and Benes invoked the principle of self-determination to justify Czech independence and the separation of Slovakia from Hungary, they did not intend to permit the German population to reduce the territory of Bohemia and Moravia-Silesia by invoking the same principle. To forestall diplomatic interference with incorporation of the German as well as the Czech districts in the republic, the Czecho-Slovak National Council, in June, 1918, obtained French recognition of the historic boundaries of the Crown Lands as those of Czecho-Slovakia.[24]

---

[23] Ferdinand Durcansky, *The International Aspects of the Slovak Question*, New York, 1954, pp. 3-20; Hrusovsky, *op. cit.*, pp. 54-69; Mikus, *op. cit.*, pp. 28-41.

[24] Agreement of June 28, 1918, cited by H. Raschhofer, "Die Sudetenfrage als Völkerrechtliches Problem" ["The Sudeten Question as a Problem of International Law"], *Mitteleuropäische Quellen und Dokumente*, I, 55. Professor A. C. Coolidge, chief of the field mission attached to the American delegation to the Peace Conference, wrote in a memorandum of March 10, 1919:

On October 21, 1918, when it was clear that the Austrian war effort could no longer be continued, the German-speaking members of the Imperial Parliament, including the deputies from Bohemia and Moravia-Silesia, met in Vienna as a Provisional National Assembly. Accepting President Wilson's principle of self-determination, the assembly claimed for the German-Austrian state[25] "the entire territory settled by German Austrians," including the German parts of the Bohemian Crown Lands with the exception of linguistic exclaves, for which international minority protection was demanded. On the following day, the assembly resolved that Austria should seek to join the German Reich.

Upon receiving news that the Czecho-Slovak Republic had been proclaimed in Prague, the German deputies from northern and western Bohemia and from Moravia-Silesia constituted the Austrian provinces of German Bohemia and Sudetenland, which were officially recognized by the assembly on October 30, 1918. Dr. Rudolf Lodgman von Auen, noted for his efforts toward a liberal solution of the nationality problem, took office as *Landeshauptmann* of German Bohemia in Reichenberg, with the Social Democrat Josef Seliger as his deputy. On November 3, the German districts adjoining Lower and Upper Austria were merged into these provinces. Upon the abdication of Emperor Charles, the mayors and civil servants in all German areas took the oath of allegiance to the Republic of Austria.

The new government in Prague, however, declared that all parts of Bohemia and Moravia-Silesia were Czecho-Slovak territory, and began to mobilize forces to overthrow the Austrian regional authorities. The Vienna government called upon the Allies to hold a referendum, but London, Paris, and Rome rejected the proposal. Dep-

---

"The clearest case of a contradiction between nationality rights and those of history and geography is that involving the boundary desires of the Czechs, who—illogically but humanly—base their claims to the two halves of their territory on opposite principles. In Bohemia they demand their 'historic boundaries' without regard to the protests of the large number of Germans, who do not wish to be taken over in this way. In Slovakia, on the other hand, they insist on nationality rights and ignore the old and well marked 'historical boundaries' of Hungary."
U.S. Department of State, *Papers Relating to the Foreign Relations of the United States—The Peace Conference of Paris, 1919*, Washington, 1942-47, XII, 271ff.

[25] The term "Deutschösterreich" was used to distinguish German-speaking Austria from the multi-national Austrian Empire.

uty Landeshauptmann Seliger, sent to Prague to negotiate, was told that "We do not negotiate with rebels." Using the irrelevant pretext of difficulties with Hungary over Slovakia, Prague obtained Allied approval for a military occupation of the German districts, which was undertaken in December, 1918. The Austrian government considered resistance hopeless, and its regional and local authorities were replaced by a Czech military government. Dr. Lodgman was forced to flee to Austria, where he continued the struggle for self-determination. Looking back on this episode, some German participants say: "We should have fought. Even a losing battle would have attracted world attention and perhaps brought us justice. Lack of armed resistance strengthened Dr. Benes's contention that we *wanted* to join Czecho-Slovakia." At the time, however, things looked quite different. Austrian resistance to the Allied-approved occupation could have been interpreted as a violation of the armistice terms, and would have given substance to the fiction of a "state of war" between Austria and Czecho-Slovakia. Secondly, neither Vienna nor Berlin (which was wholly occupied fighting the Spartacists or German Bolsheviks) had forces to spare, and the Communist government in Munich disarmed Bohemian troops on their way home. Finally, Central Europe had not yet lost faith in the noble words of the Allies, and the Vienna government hoped that the Peace Conference would put matters to rights.

On March 4, 1919, the day on which Austria elected its new Constitutional Assembly, demonstrations for self-determination took place in many German cities in Bohemia and Moravia. While the demonstration in Teplitz, addressed by Josef Seliger, was permitted to proceed undisturbed, the Czech army crushed other demonstrations by force, wantonly killing 54 and injuring 107 unarmed demonstrators.[26]

---

[26] This massacre, which provided the Germans of Bohemia and Moravia with their first political martyrs, was described by the neutral *Neue Zürcher Zeitung* (Zurich, Switzerland) of March 7, 1919, as follows:
"The events in German Bohemia and the acts of Czech brutality against the German Bohemian demonstrators give rise to utter abhorrence. After the Czecho-Slovak military, the day before yesterday, had unleashed rifle salvoes and bayonet charges against the German people of Karlsbad, Reichenberg, Eger, Aussig, Sternberg, Brüx, Mies, and Neutitschein, who had assembled . . . for entirely peaceful demonstrations for the self-determination

Pinning its hopes on the Peace Conference, the Austrian government prepared a lengthy memorandum outlining its claim to all German areas within the Bohemian Crown Lands, but indicating its willingness to compromise if the southern border territories could be retained. On reaching St. Germain, however, the Austrian delegation found itself confined behind barbed wire, with no way to communicate with other delegations except through written notes. As published memoirs have since indicated, the Czecho-Slovak border question was already settled before the arrival of the Austrians in May, 1919. The "socially acceptable" Czecho-Slovak delegation, which had participated in the Conference from the beginning, had enjoyed ample opportunity to propagate its own version of history, demography, and international law. The best-known Czech document, Benes' Memoire III, underestimated the number of Germans in Bohemia by one million and "proved" the absence of contiguous German settlements by means of a falsified map.[27]

The Peace Conference actually gave Prague more than it had asked. Dr. Benes, who as Foreign Minister led the Czecho-Slovak delegation, offered to cede to the Reich a number of Bohemian salients outside the strategic border and containing only Germans. The "Big Four," however, refused to permit Germany to annex any territory whatever.[28] At the end of the Conference, in which neither Austrians nor Germans were allowed to par-

---

of the Germans of Bohemia, Czecho-Slovak soldiers proceeded yesterday to commit new atrocities against Germans in Kaaden and Karlsbad. In Kaaden, 17 persons were killed, 30 severely, and 80 lightly wounded. Two Germans were also killed in Karlsbad. . . . It is doubtless the intention of the Czech government to push its rule of violence and terror to the utmost, and not to shrink from invoking the worst brutalities. The effect of these indescribable deeds of violence can only be to produce an irreconcilable relation between the German Bohemians and the Czech government; the shooting has eradicated any possibility of understanding. . . . For German Bohemia now to yield to the Czech yoke is out of the question, and the Czech government is wrong if it thinks it can break the resistance of three and one-half million German Bohemians with terrorist methods. This act of the Czech government—like the refusal to assume an appropriate part of the old Austrian state debt—contradicts absolutely the will and intentions of Wilson and the Entente." For other accounts, see *Sudetendeutsche Zeitung*, February 28, 1953, and March 5 and 12, 1955; Turnwald, *Renascence or Decline*, pp. 38-40.

[27] For text of Memoire III (original French with German translation, see H. Raschhofer, *Die tschechoslowakischen Denkschriften für die Friedenskonferenz, 1919/1920* ["The Czecho-Slovak Memoranda for the Peace Conference, 1919/1920"], 2d ed., Berlin 1938, pp. 84ff.

[28] Karel Lisicky, "Das deutsch-tschechische Verhältnis gestern und morgen" ["German-Czech Relationships Today and Tomorrow"], *Mitteleuropäische Quellen und Dokumente*, pp. 82-83.

ticipate, Austria was handed a treaty ceding the whole of the Bohemian Crown Lands—as well as all other areas beyond its present borders—with an ultimatum demanding ratification by 1900 hours on September 9, 1919.[29] Unification of Germany and Austria was prohibited by the Treaty of Versailles.

These were the methods used to incorporate the Germans of Bohemia and Moravia-Silesia—henceforth known as Sudeten Germans—in the Czecho-Slovak Republic. Neither the Czech imperialists nor their Western supporters had paused to consider the prophetic warning of Josef Seliger:

. . . Rule by force and democracy are mutually exclusive. For the making of states is governed by the inexorable rule that the means employed in founding a state continue to operate throughout its life and determine its character. If the state is created by violence, then it can only be maintained by violence, and democracy is forever impossible within it. This would be the fate of the Czechoslovak state, as the Czech ruling classes desire it—it could never be a democratic state. The Czech bourgeoisie intends to use force to compel the Germans, Slovaks, Magyars, and Poles to join this state. It subjugates the German territories with military power, occupies the German cities and villages with its troops, and suspends freedom of assembly, association, and the press in these districts. In German Austria too, the Revolution eliminated all the laws of police dictatorship. . . . The Czech bourgeoisie abolishes civil liberties anew, and revives the Stürkh emergency laws from the days of the worst military despotism in Austria. It sends its political commissars throughout the land and establishes them as magistrates over the German people. It decrees a state of seige in Slovakia, where military tyranny is accompanied by high-handed bureaucracy in the old Austrian manner. Polish and Magyar territories are to be conquered with military might. These are the methods and means with which it wants to found its state. It will have to use the same methods to maintain this state, if it ever achieves it. To maintain its tyrannical state with the Czech nation as master race, the Czech bourgeoisie must retain the means and methods of monarchical tyranny. It must limit civil liberties, shackle the press, revive police tutelage, and rule the people through authoritarian bureaucrats. What would happen if it should relax its grip on the subjugated peoples? These peoples would immediately rise up to secure their rights. Once freed from the pressure of tyranny, the peoples would with-

---

[29] The Allied High Council "reserved all measures" to enforce its demands. The Austrians were given to understand that these measures would include a food blockade such as was later used to force German signature of the Treaty of Versailles.

out delay exercise their right of self-determination and found their own free and independent states. . . .[30]

THE CONSTITUTION OF 1920

On November 14, 1918, the Czecho-Slovak National Council transferred its governmental powers to the "Revolutionary National Assembly." This body consisted of the surviving Czech deputies elected to the Austrian parliament in 1911, plus Czechs and Slovaks *appointed* by the leadership of the various political parties, to a total number of 256 (later 270). Of the 270 members, 54 "represented" Slovakia (proportionately the Slovaks should have had 70) and of these, 12 were actually Czechs.[31] Three fourths of the genuine Slovaks were Protestants, whereas 80 per cent of the Slovaks are Catholics. The three and one-half million Germans, the Magyars, Ruthenians, and Poles had no representation whatever.

The Revolutionary Assembly, lacking any democratic legitimation, passed a number of drastic laws which bore heavily on the non-Czech minorities. These included the law on languages, the land reform of April 10, 1919, which expropriated the estates of "nobility and foreigners," the currency exchange law, and a capital levy. Western political norms require a specific mandate for radical legislation of this type; in Switzerland, which Benes held up to the Peace Conference as his model, such laws would inevitably have been the subject of a referendum.

When the time came to make a constitution for the Czecho-Slovak Republic, Masaryk and Benes did not care to risk an elected Constitutional Assembly, where

[30] From Seliger's leaflet, "Why We Fight for Self-Determination," cited by E. Paul, *Josef Seliger*, Munich, 1954, pp. 47ff. (Author's translation.) For a full account of the Sudeten Germans' efforts to remain in Austria, see Paul Molisch, *Die sudetendeutsche Freiheitsbewegung in den Jahren 1918-1919* ["The Sudeten German Freedom Movement in 1918-19"], Vienna, 1932. See also Turnwald, *op. cit.*, pp. 38-47 (with facsimile of falsified map) ; Schreiber, *op. cit.*, pp. 88-91 ; and (also in *Die Deutschen in Böhmen und Mähren*) Emil Franzel, "Die Politik der Sudetendeutschen in der Tschechoslowakei 1918-38" ["Sudeten German Politics in Czecho-Slovakia, 1918-38"], pp. 333-43. See further *Mitteleuropäische Quellen und Dokumente*, Vol. I, *passim*.

[31] March, *loc. cit.* Cf. Elizabeth Wiskemann, *Czechs and Germans*, London, 1938, p. 119. There were no Slovak deputies in the old Austrian parliament. Of the parties which participated in the assembly, all were Czech controlled, though some had a few Slovak members.

federalist or separatist elements might have jeopardized "Czechoslovak unity." So they assigned the task to the appointed and easily controlled Revolutionary Assembly. That body produced a constitution similar in most respects to the constitutional laws of the French Third Republic—a constitution reflecting Rousseau's theory of *volonté générale* or absolute majority rule, emphasizing the sovereignty of the state and minimizing the citizen's recourse against arbitrary authority.[32] The principal variation from the French model was the granting of unequal powers to the two houses of parliament: the cabinet was responsible only to the Chamber of Deputies, which could pass laws over the suspensive veto of the Senate. The president, furthermore, exercised substantially greater powers than his French colleague—both Masaryk and Benes gave personal consideration to major policy questions.

After enactment by the appointed assembly, the constitution was placed in effect without a popular referendum, which would have provided the Sudeten Germans and the Slovaks—by now thoroughly disillusioned—with the opportunity for a massive plebiscite against the Czecho-Slovak Republic. Thus, the Constitution of February 29, 1920, however much democratic language it may contain, lacks the essential element of a constitution—a *constituent power*. As Professor Durcansky correctly points out, the Slovak people acquired no moral obligation toward the Czecho-Slovak state, and certainly the same is true of the other non-Czech peoples of the republic.[33] The first act of the Sudeten German deputies elected in the spring of 1920 was to enter a formal protest against the Czecho-Slovak Republic in general and the "imposed constitution" in particular.[34]

---

[32] Those unfamiliar with political theory may be unaware that, although proceeding from different ideologies, French political thought and that of the Prussian *Obrigkeitsstaat* have much in common. Professor Marcel Prélot begins his standard work *Précis de Droit Constitutionnel* ["Summary of Constitutional Law"], Paris, 1948, with the statement: "The problem of differentiating between the governors and the governed is first in historical order and logical importance. Until this problem is solved, there is no state. . . ." We find almost exactly the same words in the authoritarian Hegel's *Philosophy of History*. (Quoted, W. Ebenstein, *Modern Political Thought*, New York, 1954, p. 303.)

[33] Durcansky, *op. cit.*, pp. 12-15; Raschhofer, *Die Sudetenfrage*, pp. 141-44; Mikus, *op. cit.*, pp. 39-43.

[34] The text of this document, issued by Dr. Lodgman on behalf of the "German Parliamentary Union," is reprinted in the *Sudetendeutsche Zeitung*, December 20, 1952.

CZECHO-SLOVAK NATIONALITY POLICY

Although Dr. Benes had presented to the Peace Conference a formal memorandum promising to make Czecho-Slovakia "a kind of Switzerland" with substantial equality among national elements, this resolve was quickly forgotten.[35] Slovaks and Sudeten Germans accuse the Czechs, themselves a minority in the republic, of attacking the substance of other national groups through a program of systematic "Czechification" during the years between World Wars I and II. They charge Prague with discrimination in economic and financial policy, in education, and in the civil service.

The Sudeten Germans complained particularly against the following governmental policies:

(1) *Land Reform*—Large estates were expropriated and divided into individual farms. Large numbers of farms in German districts were assigned to Czechs, so that many all-German neighborhoods assumed a mixed character.

(2) *Economic Policy*—Although ethnic discrimination was never officially admitted, the word was passed to German manufacturers that only those with a certain percentage of Czech employees would receive government contracts. This led to dismissal of a large number of German workers and an influx of Czechs into German towns. The Germans did not, of course, object generally to associating with Czechs: many Germans lived voluntarily in Czech cities such as Prague, Brno, and Olomouc, and there were many intermarriages. The objection was to

---

[35] Note of the Czecho-Slovak government to the Peace Conference, Paris, May 20, 1919—reprinted in *Mitteleuropäische Quellen und Dokumente*, I, 108-9, likewise in Raschhofer, *Die tschechoslowakischen Denkschriften für die Friedenskonferenz*, 1919/20. This note recognizes the Germans, but not the Slovaks, as a second nationality group, and does *not* promise *complete* national equality. Paragraph 8 of the note reads:
"The official language shall be Czech and the State shall be known abroad as the Czechoslovak State; but German shall be the second native language and shall always be used on an equal basis with Czech in the administration, before the courts, and in the central parliament. It is the intention of the Czechoslovak government to satisfy the wishes of the population in practice and in daily use, but to accord the Czechoslovak language and the Czechoslovak element a certain special position."
The interchangeability of *Czech* and *Czechoslovak* suggests that Benes considered the Czech language to be the Czechoslovak language. So far as the Sudeten Germans are concerned, Minister Lisicky (*op. cit.*, p. 86) contends that Benes intended to follow a liberal nationality policy, but was dissuaded by chauvinist politicians.

the misuse of Czech settlers to undermine the German claim to home rule.

(3) *Education*—A law was passed raising the number of children per class from 40 to 60, so that approximately 4,000 elementary classes were abolished. On the basis of the Minorities Treaty (originally intended to protect non-Czechs), smaller classes were permitted in *Czech* schools in *German* districts. While German schools were neglected, Czech schools were constructed in excess of current needs. To fill them, the authorities recruited German children by putting pressure on German civil servants and by offering free lunches and clothing (not available in German schools) to the children of unemployed.

(4) *Civil Service*—Under a law requiring all civil servants to speak Czech, some 33,000 Sudeten German officials—including many engaged in local duties in German districts—were dismissed in 1926. Many of the Czech officials who replaced them spoke no German.

While complaints of discrimination may in some cases have been exaggerated, there is no doubt as to the total effect of government policies: to increase the number of Czechs in the German districts from 150,000 in 1918 to somewhat more than 400,000 in 1938.[36]

The short-sighted policies of the Prague government did not, of course, destroy the bonds of historical association, common interest, and individual friendship which had linked Czech Bohemians and German Bohemians throughout seven centuries. After 1918, as before, there were Czechs and Germans who sought a reconciliation. Certain Sudeten German parties agreed to participate in the Czecho-Slovak cabinet, and in 1926 these "activist" parties gained a majority of the German vote. On the Czech side, President Masaryk attempted to correct the unfortunate impression left by an earlier reference to the Sudeten Germans as "colonists," by writing:

[36] See Turnwald, *Renascence or Decline*, pp. 49-53; Rudolph Schreiber, "Wirtschaftsgeschichte der Sudetenländer" ["Economic History of the Sudeten Districts"], and Franzel, *op. cit.*, in *Die Deutschen in Böhmen und Mähren*, pp. 287-89 and 343-61 respectively.

The Germans, as colonists, are not second-class citizens, for they were invited into our country by our kings, who guaranteed them all rights necessary to assure their full cultural and national expression. . . . I am a deliberate supporter of the nationality policy of the Premyslides, who protected the German national group. . . . The overcoming of the quarrel between ourselves and our Germans will be a great political accomplishment.[37]

It is unfortunate that Masaryk's "Premyslide" policy was never translated into concrete action.

Czech relations with the Slovaks ran into a storm during the first session of the elected Czecho-Slovak parliament. Slovak deputies demanded implementation of the Pittsburgh Agreement, but were told that it was "unconstitutional" and invalid because signed by American citizens. Later, Masaryk indicated that the agreement was not to be taken seriously, and that he had only concluded it "to appease a small Slovak fraction which was dreaming of God knows what sort of independence for Slovakia."[38]

Although the Slovaks were theoretically a constituent branch of the "Czechoslovak people," the impression spread that Slovakia was being treated as a Czech colony. Failure to develop Slovak industry was a source of dissatisfaction: it was felt that Prague could have saved the Krompacky iron foundry and the Svolen sheet-metal works from bankruptcy and dismantling. Although some help from Prague in reorganizing Slovak public services and schools was desirable to fill the vacuum left by the Hungarians, the Czech officials came not as temporary technical advisers but as permanent incumbents. Throughout the First Republic, the public services in Slovakia remained staffed largely by Czechs, while there were less than 200 Slovaks among the 8,000-odd civil servants of the central government. Half the schoolteachers in Slovakia were Czechs, whose anti-clericalism often irritated Slovak parents, yet the training of Slovak teachers was limited by a *numerus clausus* in the teachers' colleges.[39]

[37] T. G. Masaryk, *The World Revolution*, 1925, cited by Lisicky, *op. cit.*, p. 78. (Author's translation.)

[38] T. G. Masaryk, *The Making of a State*, London, 1929, p. 208 ; Miksche, *Danubian Federation*, pp. 19-20 ; Durcansky, *loc. cit.*

[39] Arved Grébert, "Was Czecho-Slovakia a Democracy?," *Slovakia*, September, 1953, pp. 1-12 ; Joseph Kirschbaum, "Why No More Czechoslovakia?" *ibid.*, De-

LIMITATIONS ON POLITICAL FREEDOM

Had the citizens of Czecho-Slovakia enjoyed the full freedom which the "Czechoslovak legend" attributes to them, abuses such as those cited in the previous section could have been corrected through democratic processes. Unrestricted political expression would doubtless have led to a federal reorganization providing true self-government for the Slovaks, Sudeten Germans, and Ruthenians, a reform which might well have saved Czecho-Slovakia from destruction.[40]

Actually, criticism of the institutions of the Czecho-Slovak Republic was considerably restricted by laws such as the "Law for the Protection of the Republic" of March 23, 1923; the "Law on Political Parties" of October 25, 1923; and later the more drastic law of April 30, 1936, "For the Protection of the State."[41] Such laws were supplemented by administrative censorship: in 1922 alone there were 1498 instances of censorship and confiscation of newspapers in Slovakia.[42]

The 1923 "Law for the Protection of the Republic" combined wholly reasonable provisions—such as penalties for physical attacks on state functionaries or usurpation of their functions (§ 10)—with others which could easily be employed to stifle criticism.[43] Prohibited utterances and acts included the following:

§ 11. Insulting the President of the Republic so as to offend his honor or expose him to public ridicule; making accusations which in the knowledge of the accuser seriously offend the honor of the

---

cember, 1951, pp. 16-27; Cernak-Kreutzmann, "Freiheitskampf der Slowaken" ["Slovakia's Fight for Freedom"], *Sudetendeutsche Zeitung*, March 21 and 28, 1953. Mikus, *op. cit.*, pp. 51-74, cites the printing of government and university notices in Bratislava in Czech, the concentration of industry in Czech areas, discriminatory rail tariffs, appointment of Czechs to 90 per cent of the higher positions in the Slovak railways, etc. Further details are given by Konstantin Culen, *Preco Slovaci nechcu ist s Cechmi?* ["Why Don't the Slovaks Want to Be With the Czechs?"] and *Tschechen und Slowaken im Staatsdienst der tschechoslowakischen Republik* ["Czechs and Slovaks in the Civil Service of the Czecho-slovak Republic"], both Bratislava, 1945. See also Wanklyn, *op. cit.*, pp. 210-12.

[40] See Turnwald, *op. cit.*, pp. 54-56; Wenzel Jaksch, *Sudeten Labour and the Sudeten Problem*, London, 1945, pp. 13-29.

[41] Czecho-Slovak laws were printed in official Czech and German texts, the latter appearing in the *Sammlung der Gesetze und Verordnungen* ["Collection of Laws and Decrees"].

[42] *Jednota*, Middletown, Pa., October 16, 1946.

[43] *Sammlung der Gesetze und Verordnungen*, 1923, No. 50, pp. 240ff. The citations which follow are summaries rather than literal translations of the pertinent paragraphs.

President. Proof of the truth of such accusations is not admissible as a defense.

§ 14. (1) Agitating, publicly or in the presence of several persons, against the state because of its origin, or against its independence, constitutional unitary structure, or democratic-republican form of government.

(3) Publicly inciting to hatred against individual groups of the population because of their nationality, language, race, religion, or lack of religion.

(5) Publicly reviling the Republic, a nation, or a national minority so as to lower the dignity of the Republic, or threaten the Republic's internal peace or its international relations.

§ 16. (1) Publicly approving a major or intermediate offense, honoring its author, or collecting money to pay a fine imposed on him.

(2) Publishing the picture of an offender, except for scholarly purposes or to facilitate his capture.

§ 17. Founding a secret organization for the purpose of undermining the independence, the constitutional unitary structure, or the democratic-republican government of the state, or joining such an organization.

§ 26. Failing to comply with a police order to remove a monument, statue, bust, picture, coat of arms, etc. of a character hostile to the state or glorifying members of former Austrian and German dynasties.

Legal provisions such as the foregoing could be, and were, invoked to suppress movements seeking fundamental changes in the structure of the republic, even when it was intended to bring about these changes by peaceful means. Advocacy of federalism constituted an attack on the "constitutional unitary structure" and could be prosecuted as subversion. Likewise, anyone who publicly declared that the Czecho-Slovak Republic had been created by force or fraud, that there were too many Czechs in Slovakia or in the Sudeten districts, or that the President had failed to keep a promise, was likely to find himself in jail. It is significant that certain acts treated as minor offenses (*Uebertretungen*) in the Czech lands were punished as intermediate offenses (*Vergehen*) in Slovakia.[44]

Slovak nationalists were particular targets of political repression. In January, 1928, Professor Vojtech Tuka published an article contending that Czecho-Slovakia

---

[44] *Ibid.*, § 40 (1).

would legally cease to exist on October 30 of that year.[45] He was immediately arrested, charged with conspiring with Austrian and German groups against the Czecho-Slovak state, and—despite a total absence of conclusive evidence—sentenced to fifteen years in prison.[46] Another of many similar episodes was the seizure of the Slovak People's party newspaper and the trial of its editor in 1933 after 100,000 Slovaks had demonstrated for autonomy in Nitra.[47]

If it is felt that some of the political maneuvers described violate the canons of fair play, it should be remembered that they were the acts of a particular group of Czech politicians. It would be most unfair to charge them to the Czech people as a whole, just as we do not hold the Russian or satellite peoples responsible for Communism. Our experience with Germany has taught us the bankruptcy of any doctrine of collective guilt.

Without taking a partisan position as between the Czechs, Slovaks, and Sudeten Germans, we can note a fact of importance for American policy: *the basic disunity of the Czecho-Slovak Republic.* As the map clearly illustrates, Masaryk and Benes tried to impose a national state based on a ruling people (the Czechs) in an area containing several nationalities. Less than half the citizens enjoyed the full benefit of the much-publicized democracy. The fact that some states treated their minorities worse was not enough to prevent widespread disillusionment among the non-Czech peoples, who were not inspired to the loyalty which every state needs for survival in time of stress.

[45] At the Turciansky Sv. Martin conference of October 30, 1918, Tuka had proposed that Slovakia join the republic for a ten-year trial period, to be followed by a referendum. This motion gained considerable support, but was never formally adopted. Tuka argued that the proviso had somehow become part of the Declaration of the Slovak Nation and that Prague, not having fulfilled the Pittsburgh Agreement, had voided its claim to Slovakia. The legal principle invoked by Tuka, that transfers of territory are voided by the violation of promises made at the time of acquisition would—whatever its moral appeal—produce chaos in international law.

[46] Many "Czechoslovak" authors dispose of Tuka by calling him a "pro-Magyar," a "Habsburg agent," or simply a "Nazi." The point which concerns believers in constitutional government is not whether Tuka was a democrat or an authoritarian, or whether his legal arguments would bear scrutiny, but the fact that the government railroaded him to prison on trumped-up evidence so as to silence an unpopular voice.

[47] Hrusovsky, *op. cit.,* pp. 71-73 ; Mikus, *op. cit.,* pp. 71-72.

THE MUNICH CRISIS OF 1938

"Czechoslovak" propaganda has always pictured Konrad Henlein as a "Sudeten German Nazi." The word "Nazi" is a psychological trigger, used to evoke suspicion and dislike, not only of Henlein, but of Sudeten Germans in general. Although Henlein visited Hitler twice in 1938 before Munich (the second time at Lord Runciman's request) and later took part in the public life of the Third Reich, to dismiss his Sudeten German party as a "Nazi movement" is a gross oversimplification.[48]

The Sudeten German districts contained important export industries, many of which (carpets, glass, porcelain, jewelry, furniture, musical instruments, etc.) catered to luxury markets. The depression of 1929-36 therefore struck these areas with particular force. Of the 3,318,000 Germans in Czecho-Slovakia (1930 census), 500,000 were unemployed breadwinners, whereas there were only 300,-000 unemployed among the 9,756,000 Czechs and Slovaks. Many government relief projects, however, tended to benefit Czech rather than German workers.

Since the "activist" parties had failed to obtain any significant concessions from Prague in the matters of relief or home rule, the Sudeten Germans turned increasingly to self-help. Voluntary organizations, such as the *Deutscher Kulturverband* and the *Bund der Deutschen*, built German schoolhouses, made emergency loans to save German farmers from foreclosure, and supplemented the meager government dole for the unemployed. These activities increased the solidarity of the Sudeten Germans, and a younger generation centering in the *Turnverband* (Gymnastic Association) became increasingly outspoken in the assertion of German demands.

In October, 1933, the gymnastics teacher Henlein founded the "Sudeten German Front" as an interparty group to support the Sudeten German claim to home rule. The front did not have a specific Nazi character, nor did it aim at the dismemberment of Czecho-Slovakia. Henlein himself said in a speech in 1934: "We do not

---

[48] Franzel, *op. cit.*, pp. 360-70; Turnwald, *op. cit.*, pp. 52-58. For a contrary view, see S. Grant Duff, *Europe and the Czechs*, London, 1938, pp. 118-32.

need to explain that there is a fundamental difference between ourselves and the National Socialists. We will never abandon the freedom of the individual."[49] The Sudeten German Front, which promised to press its political demands with vigor, grew rapidly. Its rise was helped both by the depression and by the political tactics of the Prague government. Shortly after Hitler's accession as German Chancellor, the Czecho-Slovak authorities had suppressed two Sudeten German parties. One was the German National party and the other was the German National Socialist Workers' party, similar in its ideology to Hitler's party in the Reich, the National Socialist German Workers' party. Some of the National Socialist leaders moved to Germany, where they obtained political jobs, but most of the members of both parties, having nowhere else to go, joined the Sudeten German Front.

The government assisted the more rabid German nationalist element in the Sudeten German Front in gaining influence by arresting without criminal charges and imprisoning for some time the principal moderate leaders of the organization. In 1935, Prague ordered Henlein to rename the Front the "Sudeten German Party." This was a serious tactical blunder, since the name suggested that there could be no other Sudeten German parties. In the May, 1935, election, the party won two thirds of the Sudeten vote. It thus polled the largest individual party vote in Czecho-Slovakia, although gerrymandering gave the Czech Agrarian party one more seat than the Sudeten German party in parliament.[50]

The aging President Masaryk resigned late in 1935, and, on December 18 of that year, Foreign Minister Dr. Eduard Benes was elected his successor. During the following months, Henlein made a number of offers to co-operate with the Czecho-Slovak government in settling nationality questions. But the new Foreign Minister, Kamil Krofta, reflecting the view taken by President Benes, declared that full equality for the Sudeten Ger-

[49] Quoted by Franzel, *op. cit.*, p. 365.

[50] *Sudetenland*, pp. 87-89; Turnwald, *op. cit.*, p. 54; Alfred Juettner, *Aus den Akten, München 1938* ["From the Files, Munich 1938"], Bonn, 1954, pamphlet, pp. 6-7.

mans was out of the question, a sentiment echoed somewhat less emphatically by Premier Hodza.[51] The Sudeten German "activist" parties also made efforts toward an understanding with the Czech cabinet parties, culminating in a "gentlemen's agreement" reached on February 18, 1937. While this agreement provided only for an easing of discrimination in the civil service, in the letting of public contracts, and in linguistic questions, it might have opened the way to a solution of other problems. The Czech parties, however, undermined the position of the "activists" by failing to introduce implementing legislation, while individual ministers ignored the agreement altogether. Finally, the impact of Hitler's occupation of Austria on March 11, 1938, coupled with the decision of the Czech Agrarian party to bypass the "activists" and seek agreement with Henlein, brought about the collapse of all "activist" parties other than the Social Democrats.[52]

Although the growing tension aggravated nationalist feeling and stimulated sympathy for the Third Reich, Nazi influence in the Sudeten German party did not become decisive until 1938 and, even then, the efforts of various Reich agencies to assert control were frequently contradictory. The party contained a Nazi element led by Karl H. Frank, but most leading offices were occupied by members of the *Kameradschaftsbund* which supported the doctrines of Professor Othmar Spann, a Catholic conservative branded a dangerous enemy by the Nazi party and the SS. After Munich, the Nazis dissolved the Sudeten German party and transferred its members to their own party.[53]

Failure of the Prague cabinet and the Sudeten German leaders to agree on terms for home rule culminated in the crisis of 1938. Early that year, France promised to aid Czecho-Slovakia if attacked, and Russia was already

---

[51] For an account of negotiations with the Sudeten Germans by Dr. Benes, see his *Memoirs—From Munich to New War and New Victory*, London, 1954, pp. 14-20. Benes feared that granting full rights to the Sudeten Germans would invite Nazi infiltration of Czecho-Slovakia. See also *Sudetenland*, pp. 89-91; Juettner, *op. cit.*, pp. 7-9.

[52] Jaksch, *Europas Weg nach Potsdam*, pp. 281ff.; Turnwald, *op. cit.*, pp. 55-56.

[53] Raschhofer, *Die Sudetenfrage*, pp. 162-63; Franzel, *op. cit.*, pp. 362-63; *Proceedings of the International Military Tribunal*, Nuremberg, 1947, Vol. X (English ed.), pp. 332-45 (Interrogation of von Ribbentrop and related documents).

pledged to assist if France did likewise. This circumstance encouraged President Benes to take an uncompromising attitude. But on March 24, 1938, after Hitler had annexed Austria, Prime Minister Chamberlain declared that Great Britain would *not* fight over Czecho-Slovakia.

The Sudeten German party, its ranks strengthened by the Christian Social party and the Farmers' Federation which had joined *en masse*, then formulated the so-called "Karlsbad Program," which it presented to Prague on April 24, 1938. The program demanded equality with the Czech people, legal organization of the Sudeten German ethnic group, home rule for German districts, and the end of discrimination against German-speaking citizens.[54]

Hitler, in the meantime, was becoming increasingly interested in the Sudeten territory. Alarmed at German military movements, Prague ordered partial mobilization on May 21, 1938. On the following day, the Sudeten Germans registered their support of Henlein by giving his party over 90 per cent of their votes in the municipal elections. President Benes, nevertheless, allowed negotiations with the Sudeten German leaders to drag on at a snail's pace. Every day's delay played into the hands of Hitler, who had been stirred to wrath by rejoicing of Western newspapers over the success of the mobilization, in which Sudeten German men, with few exceptions, had obeyed the call to the colors.[55]

With the tacit consent of France, the British government sent Lord Runciman to mediate the dispute. But even after his arrival (August 3, 1938), the Benes government still refused to grant adequate home rule and

---

[54] For text of Karlsbad Program, see Monica Curtis, ed., *Documents on International Affairs, 1938*, Royal Inst. of Int'l Affairs, London, Oxford University Press, 1943, II, 135-37. While certain features of the program might have required modification or interpretation, the program as a whole did no violence to the principles of constitutional-democratic federalism.

[55] For detailed accounts of Czech-German and diplomatic negotiations leading up to the Munich Conference of September, 1938, see Raschhofer, *op. cit.*, pp. 144-92 and Jaksch, *op. cit.*, pp. 300-325. A briefer account, but with additional details, is given by Juettner, *op. cit.* See also Sir Nevile Henderson, *Failure of a Mission*, New York, 1940; and R. G. D. Laffan, *Survey of International Affairs, 1938*, Vol. II, "The Crisis in Czechoslovakia," London, 1951. Benes says little on this phase in his *Memoirs*, since he planned to deal with Munich in another book. But see S. Grant Duff, *op. cit.*, pp. 133-86, and Bernadotte E. Schmitt, "The Road to Munich and Beyond," in Robert J. Kerner, ed., *Czechoslovakia*, Berkeley, 1945, pp. 409-40, for accounts by admirers of Benes.

equal treatment to German-speaking citizens. Negotiations between the Prague cabinet, Sudeten German leaders, and Lord Runciman remained in a hopeless deadlock throughout the month. Finally, in September, Premier Hodza produced his "Fourth Plan" which, in Runciman's opinion, was compatible with the Karlsbad Program. But Hitler had in the meanwhile seized the initiative. On September 12, 1938, at the Nazi Party Congress in Nuremberg, he demanded the Sudeten territories for Germany. Lord Runciman, whose main interest was to avoid war, recommended cession of these areas to the Reich. He reported to the British government on September 16:

> I have been left with the impression that Czechoslovak rule in the Sudeten areas for the last twenty years, though not actively oppressive and certainly not "terroristic," has been marked by tactlessness, lack of understanding, petty intolerance and discrimination, to a point where the resentment of the German population was inevitably moving in the direction of revolt. . . . Czech officials and Czech police, speaking little or no German, were appointed in large numbers in purely German regions. Czech agricultural colonists were encouraged to settle on land transferred under the land reform in the middle of German populations. For the children of these Czech invaders Czech schools were built on a large scale. There is a very general belief that Czech firms were favored as against German firms in the allocation of state contracts, and the state provided work and relief for Czechs more readily than for Germans. I believe these complaints to be in the main justified.[56]

Prague responded to Hitler's speech by outlawing the Sudeten German party and ordering the arrest of his leaders. Henlein and a few associates fled to the Reich, where they organized the "Sudeten German Free Corps." Once more, however, the vast majority of Sudeten German men took their places in the Czecho-Slovak army. For a few days it looked as though Hitler would give the order to attack Czecho-Slovakia which, because of the French commitment to Prague, might well have set off World War II a year early—or might very possibly have toppled the Nazi dictator from his perch. It was at this point that Prime Minister Chamberlain, whose

---

[56] A fuller citation is given in Turnwald, *op. cit.*, pp. 56-57.

devotion to peace was as sincere as it was unrealistic, made his famous flying visits to the Führer. The story of the Hitler-Chamberlain talks at Berchtesgaden and Bad Godesberg, of Prague's seemingly reluctant acceptance of the Anglo-French Plan of September 19 for cession of areas with a German majority—of Hitler's sudden additional demands, of German preparations to march and French and British mobilization—and of Mussolini's last-minute diplomatic intervention, is too long to be repeated here. There are, however, two important aspects which have escaped the attention of many writers. The first is that—after initially and publicly rejecting the Anglo-French Plan—the Prague government urgently requested a formal statement that France would *not* march if the Nazis invaded Czecho-Slovakia because of the Sudeten question. The request was repeated at least twice before the French and British envoys handed Benes the "ultimatum" which has become part of the "Czechoslovak legend" at 0200 hours in the morning.[57]

The second is that Czecho-Slovakia was by no means so helpless as apologists for Dr. Benes later indicated. It had a mobilized strength of forty-four divisions, as compared to the thirty-one German divisions then existing, of which a part were committed to the Western Front. The psychological shock which the "desertion" of Henlein and his staff produced among the Sudeten Germans, the utter collapse of anti-Czech agitation in the Sudetenland, and a last-minute resurgence of "activism" offered an ideal opportunity for the only formula which could have saved Czecho-Slovakia: self-government for the non-Czech nationalities coupled with an iron will to resist Nazi aggression. But since the Benes government had firmly made up its mind *not to fight,* the inevitable upshot was the Munich Conference of September 29, 1938, at which Hitler, Chamberlain, Mussolini, and Premier Daladier of

---

[57] French Minister Laroix had reported Hodza's statement that "The leading men of Czecho-Slovakia would require this cover in order to be able to accept the Franco-British proposal." Hodza never denied making this statement, although the telegram was published several times before his death. Georges Bonnet, *Vor der Katastrophe* ["Before the Catastrophe"], German edition, Cologne, 1951, pp. 87, 92; Jaksch, *op. cit.,* pp. 328, 492.
   Concerning President Roosevelt's curious role in the Munich affair, see Charles Callan Tansill and Frederic R. Sanborn in Harry Elmer Barnes, ed., *Perpetual War for Perpetual Peace,* Caldwell, Idaho, 1953, pp. 144-56 and 196-201.

France agreed on the details of the transfer of the Sudeten districts in three successive stages.[58]

It is, however, unfair to Neville Chamberlain to make his umbrella the symbol of political cowardice and sacrifice of principle to expediency.

In 1938, as today, Czech and Sudeten Germans would have profited from a federative agreement, guaranteeing each of the two Bohemian peoples self-government and equal rights. Furthermore, many Sudeten Germans were strongly anti-Nazi and did not want to join the Third Reich. But the decision reached at Munich was not necessarily immoral in itself. What was bad was the inconsistency of Western policy.

For almost two decades the Western Powers, bemused by Benes' propaganda about "model democracy," had looked on benevolently while Prague followed an ultranationalist policy which made agreement with the Sudeten Germans impossible. Then, when matters reached a crisis, Britain and France agreed that annexation of the Sudeten areas by Germany was the only reasonable solution which would avoid war. But because they shifted at the last moment, the entire transaction took on the color of immoral appeasement. Hitler was encouraged to think that he could get away with anything, and a *Putsch* which the German generals had planned to unseat him was foiled.

As German forces advanced into the Sudetenland in early October, 1938, Social Democrats and other anti-Nazi Sudeten Germans who had supported the Republic fled into the remainder of Czecho-Slovakia. The Czech police began shipping them back into the Reich. Eventually, after the British government, yielding to pressure, tardily produced an emigration scheme, some 3,000 anti-Nazi Sudetens were enabled to escape. But a larger

---

[58] The fact that Benes struck his colors in a far from hopeless situation is conclusively demonstrated by Jaksch, *op. cit.*, pp. 309-25.

It is sometimes contended that Czecho-Slovakia was not legally bound by the Munich protocol, to which she was not a signatory. The Prague government did, however, agree specifically to the cession in notes to Great Britain and France on September 21 and again in notes to the British on September 25 and 26. Nor can it be pleaded that the cession was invalid because made under duress: if this were true, then the treaties of Versailles and St. Germain would both be invalid. See Raschhofer, *op. cit.* pp. 180-92, 235-43.

number, sometimes estimated as high as 20,000, were turned over to the Gestapo.[59] In spite of the unsavory features of the Munich decision, the transfer of a German ethnic area to the Reich could be justified by the principle that—barring good reasons to the contrary—political boundaries should correspond to national areas. While there were and still are very good reasons for having some Germans *outside* the Reich as members of a multi-national Danube state, these reasons became theoretical after the dissolution of the Austrian Empire. It is therefore misleading to use the term "Munich" for agreements which are purely the result of appeasement and cannot be justified on their own merits, such as the division of Vietnam in 1954.

THE BREAKUP OF THE REPUBLIC— SLOVAK INDEPENDENCE

A Slovak provincial administration created by a law of 1927 did not satisfy the Slovak leaders, who continued to press for full autonomy. As a protest against Prague's centralism, the Slovak People's party, led by Monsignor Andrej Hlinka, withdrew from the government in 1929 and, as an opposition party, submitted proposals for Slovak home rule. As the largest Slovak party, Hlinka's organization polled consistently about one half the Slovak votes, but demands for autonomy were also heard from Slovak members of Czecho-Slovak parties, such as the Agrarians and the Social Democrats. The predominantly Catholic People's party agreed in 1932 with the small Slovak National party, headed by the Lutheran pastor Martin Razus, that both would press for full Slovak rights even though the disintegration of the Czecho-Slovak Republic might result. Hlinka's objective remained, however, autonomy within Czecho-

---

[59] Wenzel Jaksch and Walter Kolarz, *Der Weg der letzten freien Deutschen* ["The Trail of the Last Free Germans"], London, 1940. Although this pamphlet is understandably somewhat harsh in its judgment of the Sudeten German party, it contains an interesting and moving account of the fate of those Germans who supported the Czecho-Slovak Republic to the bitter end, only to find that the Prague government would (or could) do nothing for them.

Slovakia rather than the deliberate dismemberment of the Republic.[60] The Slovak People's party reluctantly supported Dr. Eduard Benes in the 1935 presidential election on the strength of a promise that Slovak demands for autonomy would be fulfilled. But although the Slovak Agrarian, Dr. Milan Hodza, became premier, nothing was done to provide Slovakia with a government of its own. Despairing of obtaining voluntary concessions from Prague, Hlinka conferred in 1936 with representatives of the Sudeten German and Carpatho-German parties, and an agreement for informal co-operation was reached.[61]

The events of 1938 had immediate repercussions in Slovakia. On June 5, 1938, a mass meeting of 120,000 at Bratislava demonstrated anew for Slovak political rights, after which the People's party introduced an autonomy bill in the Prague parliament. The excitement was intensified by the exhibition of the original Pittsburgh Agreement by visiting Americans of Slovak descent, and by the unsuccessful efforts of the Benes police to steal the document. After the death of Monsignor Hlinka on August 16, 1938, leadership of the Slovak People's party was assumed by his close associate, Monsignor Jozef Tiso, who was determined to seize the opportunity to secure self-government for his people.

Premier Hodza was forced to resign on September 22 by demonstrations in favor of armed resistance against the Germans, and President Benes took the reins of policy into his own hands. He appointed General Jan Syrovy to head an all-party coalition, to which the Slovak People's party was invited to send a minister. Since assignment of a major leader might have compromised the party's freedom of action, the choice fell on a young teacher, Matus Cernak, later to fill the diffi-

---

[60] Hrusovsky, *This Is Slovakia*, pp. 73-79; Cernak and Kreutzmann in *Sudetendeutsche Zeitung*, March 28, 1953; Joseph A. Mikus, "Martin Razus," *Bulletin of the Slovak National Council Abroad*, October, 1957, pp. 3-4.

[61] The Carpatho-German party, which had allied itself with the Sudeten German party in 1935, represented at that time somewhat less than half the 154,000 ethnic Germans in Slovakia. Henlein's emissaries in the discussions with Hlinka were Karl H. Frank of the Nazi wing of the SGP (later Reich Protector of Bohemia-Moravia) and Franz Karmasin, his deputy for the Carpatho-Germans. See German Federal Ministry for Expellees, Refugees, and War Victims, *Dokumentation der Vertreibung der Deutschen aus Ost-Mitteleuropa*, Vol. IV/1, "The Expulsion of the German Population from Czechoslovakia," Bonn, 1957, pp. 146ff., also Cernak/Kreutzmann, *loc. cit.*

cult post of Slovak minister in Berlin. Finding the cabinet in utter confusion, Cernak served President Benes a face-to-face ultimatum on October 3: either Slovak autonomy would be granted within twenty-four hours or he would resign and all the Slovak deputies would leave the parliament. Cernak resigned the following day, but before anything else could happen, Dr. Benes himself resigned on October 5, 1938, leaving Premier Syrovy as interim president until the parliament could elect a successor. The following day the leaders of the non-leftist Slovak parties met at Zilina and decided to take over the government of Slovakia, forming the Slovak National Unity party for that purpose. Prague accepted the Zilina Manifesto, and acting President Syrovy appointed Monsignor Tiso to head the Slovak cabinet. On November 19, 1938, the Czecho-Slovak parliament passed a constitutional law formalizing the autonomy of Slovakia, after which it elected Dr. Emil Hacha, a former president of the Supreme Administrative Court, as third president of the republic. Slovak elections were held on December 18, 1938, and the new Slovak parliament was formally convened on January 18, 1939.[62]

In the meantime Hungary made claim to the southern section of Slovakia, demanding those areas which the 1910 census (considered prejudiced by the Slovaks) showed to have a Magyar majority. The matter was arbitrated by the Italian and German foreign ministers who, in the First Vienna Award of November 2, 1938, assigned to Hungary a strip of territory including areas which the 1930 census had shown with a Slovak majority, including the important city of Kosice in eastern Slovakia.

There were difficulties in carrying out the new autonomy statute since the central ministries in Prague and their new counterparts in the Slovak capital of Bratislava claimed overlapping authority. Adolf Hitler, who had decided to liquidate the Czecho-Slovak Republic,

[62] Hrusovsky, op. cit., pp. 80-84; Mikus, La Slovaquie dans le Drame de l'Europe, pp. 89-109; "Milestones of Slovak History—October 6, 1938," Slovakia, September, 1953, pp. 13-17; "Dr. Edward Benes and Dr. Milan Hodza," Slovak Newsletter, May-June, 1958, pp. 1-4.

instructed his diplomats to aggravate the friction. While the Wilhelmstrasse encouraged the Tiso government to resist Prague, German officials in the latter city enticed the central authorities into continuing what Sir Nevile Henderson called their "unbelievably short-sighted and haughty . . . treatment of the Slovaks."[63]

Among the Slovak leaders, Monsignor Tiso, Deputy Premier Karol Sidor, and their supporters from the Agrarian party would have been content to have Slovakia remain an autonomous state within a federal Czecho-Slovakia, *had such a solution been possible.* Others, such as Professor Tuka (released from prison in October, 1938) and Minister Ferdinand Durcansky, favored complete independence. It is doubtful, however, whether Slovakia would have become an independent state in 1939 without pressure from Germany—particularly since Prague still had large contingents of Czech troops stationed in Slovakia, while the Slovak contingents of the Czecho-Slovak army were mostly in Bohemia.

While the Western Powers and Prague assumed that Hitler would respect the new boundaries drawn after Munich, Tiso and his ministers had better information. Through the Carpatho-German leader, Franz Karmasin, and other German contacts, they learned that the Führer planned to seize Bohemia and Moravia in the near future.[64] They also knew that Hungary planned to annex the remainder of Slovakia and that Hitler—who, like many Austrians, tended to believe that Slovaks liked Magyar rule—was not averse to this move.[65] Politics being the art of the possible, there was only one way in which Tiso and his friends could stave off the reconquest of Slovakia by Hungary. That was to convince the Nazi leadership that Slovak independence would be more to Germany's interest. To accomplish this end, the leaders of the Bratislava government, including Durcan-

---

[63] Henderson, *Failure of a Mission,* p. 232.

[64] Hitler stated on November 23, 1939: "It was clear to me from the first moment that I could not be satisfied with the Sudeten German territory. That was only a partial solution." *Proceedings of International Military Tribunal,* III, 112.

[65] *Ibid.,* X, 343-44. Cernak and Kreutzmann, in Part II of "Freiheitskampf der Slowaken" (*Sudetendeutsche Zeitung,* March 28, 1953), indicate that Foreign Office area experts urged Hitler to support Slovak independence rather than Hungarian annexation.

sky, Mach, Tuka, Karmasin (since October 10, 1938, State Secretary for German Affairs), and on one occasion Tiso himself, held extensive conferences with Reich officials.[66] These conferences alarmed President Hacha and the Prague ministers, who walked squarely into the trap which the Nazis had set for them.

Early in March, 1939, Hacha and his cabinet decided to liquidate the Slovak government, or at least its "separatist" wing. The Czech Minister in Berlin, Dr. Mastny, asked the Wilhelmstrasse how Germany would regard Czech military intervention in Slovakia, and was given to understand that the Reich viewed it as "a Czecho-Slovak internal matter." On the night of March 9, President Hacha dismissed Tiso and his cabinet, and declared a state of emergency in Slovakia. General Homolka, the local commander, arrested Ministers Cernak, Mach, and Tuka, while Durcansky escaped to Vienna, where he made a radio speech urging the Slovaks to revolt against the Czech oppressors. Reluctantly, Sidor assumed the premiership: his first act was to obtain the release of the arrested ministers.

Hitler, of course, had no intention of regarding Hacha's *coup de force* as a Czecho-Slovak internal matter. On March 12, 1939, a Nazi delegation headed by State Secretary Wilhelm Keppler of the Foreign Office and Reich Governor Arthur Seyss-Inquart of Austria arrived in Bratislava and urged Premier Sidor to proclaim the immediate independence of Slovakia. Sidor refused adamantly, stating that he lacked authority for such an act, but arrangements were made for Tiso and Durcansky to fly to Berlin and for a special session of the Slovak parliament to be held upon their return.

At a conference in the Chancellory, Hitler laid down the terms of the decision the Slovaks had to make. If Slovakia wished independence, he would support it and even guarantee it, but "if she hesitated or did not wish

---

[66] Jozef Lettrich, *History of Modern Slovakia*, New York, 1955, devotes almost an entire chapter (pp. 88-109) to these conferences, the significance of which he entirely distorts. Lettrich pictures the meetings as a "sell out" of Czecho-Slovakia and Slovakia as well. Actually, the Slovak negotiators were in the position of a dwarf treating with a temperamental ogre. Through skillful diplomacy, including an inevitable quantum of play-acting and "apple polishing," they obtained an arrangement for Slovakia which was the best possible in the objective situation, and the *only* arrangement which would enable the Slovaks to retain control of their internal affairs.

to dissolve the connection with Prague, he would leave the destiny of Slovakia to the mercy of events for which he was no longer responsible." At the psychological instant, Ribbentrop produced a telegram reporting Hungarian troop movements along the Slovak frontier. After Monsignor Tiso had reported to the Slovak parliament the following morning, a law was passed unanimously declaring the independence of Slovakia and transforming the regional parliament into that of the Slovak Republic. A new government was formed with Tiso as premier and Durcansky as Foreign Minister.[67]

President Hacha, meanwhile, had requested an audience with Hitler, who granted the interview after several days' delay during which the German Minister in Prague and his associates were instructed to be "not available."[68] By the time Hacha arrived in Berlin, the Slovak Republic was a *fait accompli*. During the night of March 14-15, Hitler, Goering, and Ribbentrop gave Hacha a "going over" which has become famous in diplomatic history. After Hitler had announced that German troops would invade at 0600 the following morning, Goering adding that Prague would be bombed if the Czechs resisted, the ailing Hacha—who actually collapsed during the interview—signed an agreement making the rump of Bohemia and Moravia a protectorate of the German Reich.[69]

During the autumn of 1938, Ruthenia also finally secured its autonomy within the Czecho-Slovak Republic. A constitutional law of November 22, 1938, provided for a three-member cabinet and for a regional parliament, elections for which were held on February 12, 1939. On January 1, the cabinet adopted a decree changing the name of the territory to Carpatho-Ukraine.

But the self-government of Ruthenia was to be short-lived. Hungary, which had received a portion of the region including its capital, Uzhorod, under the Vienna

[67] *Proceedings of International Military Tribunal*, Vol. X, pp. 255-56 and 342-45, and Vol. XXXI, Documents PS-2801 and PS-2802; Henderson, *op. cit.*, p. 233; Mikus, *op. cit.*, pp. 109-27; "The Causes of Czechoslovakia's Disintegration," *Slovak Newsletter*, February, 1951, pp. 1-3.

[68] *Proceedings of IMT*, Vol. XXXI, Document PS-2815.

[69] *Ibid.*, X, 257-59, 346-54; Raschhofer, *op. cit.*, pp. 199-233; Paul Schmidt, *Hitler's Interpreter*, New York, 1951, pp. 122-26.

Award of November 2, 1938, made open preparations
to conquor all Ruthenia. Hitler, however, found it expedient to make the Budapest government wait temporarily. When the Slovak parliament, on March 14, 1939,
declared the independence of the Slovak Republic, the
cabinet at Uzhorod adopted a resolution proclaiming an
independent state of Carpatho-Ukraine. The parliament
ratified this resolution the following day. But while
Nazi troops were marching into Prague, the Hungarian
army — this time with Hitler's approval — invaded Ruthenia which, in spite of vigorous resistance, was quickly
subdued. From March, 1939, until the entry of Soviet
troops in 1944, Ruthenia was administered as a part
of Hungary.[70]

---

[70] See *Ukrainian Quarterly*, Vol. X, No. 3, Summer 1954, particularly articles
by Augustin Stefan (pp. 219-26), Julian Revay (pp. 227-34), Vincent Shandor
(pp. 235-46), and Vasyl Markus (pp. 252-56).

III

INTO THE RUSSIAN ORBIT
1939-1945

THE BEGINNINGS OF CZECH RUSSOPHILISM

THE mortgaging of Czech and Slovak political freedom to Russia began well before the establishment of Czecho-Slovakia and before the Russian Revolution. Extreme Czech nationalism, following the tradition of the first Pan-Slav Congress held in Prague in 1848, has always been anti-German and pro-Russian. Masaryk, Benes, and their followers seemed to feel instinctively and to have reconciled themselves to the fact that creation and maintenance of a Czech national state in a multi-national area would ultimately depend on Russian hegemony in Central Europe.

Important politicians in the Masaryk-Benes camp conceived of Czecho-Slovakia as a Russian satellite within a chain of overexpanded Slav states to be created through dismemberment of Austria-Hungary and truncation of the German Reich. Plans to this effect were completed in 1912 by Hanus Kufner and in 1914 by chairman Klofac of the Czech National Socialist party (to which Benes belonged), who presented his ideas in person to Foreign Minister Sazonov in St. Petersburg and to Russian Ambassador Schebeko in Vienna. A project for an All-Slav Empire was sponsored by Dr. Karel Kramar, the most influential of Masaryk's supporters who remained in Bohemia during the war and was later first premier of the Czecho-Slovak Republic. On June 7, 1914, three weeks before the assassination of Archduke Franz Ferdinand at Sarajevo, Kramar presented his plan with a map and a "constitution" to Ambassador Schebeko, who promptly forwarded the papers to the Czarist Foreign Office. The

Kramar Plan contemplated a "Czech Czardom" (including Slovakia), Polish and Bulgarian "Czardoms," and a Kingdom of Greater Serbia (Yugoslavia) under the suzerainty of the Czar of Russia, who would become the supreme ruler of the All-Slav Empire. The Russian Empire, which would dominate All-Slavia as Prussia dominated the German Reich, would retain eastern Poland and would annex northern East Prussia including Königsberg, Galicia, Subcarpathian Ruthenia, and North Bukovina—gains achieved by Stalin during World War II—while Poland would be "compensated" in the west at German expense.[1] Both Kufner and Kramar advocated the partition of the Reich, since permanent Slav occupation of non-Slav territories requires the extinction of Germany as a political and military power.[2]

From the outbreak of World War I until shortly before the Russian Revolution, Masaryk based the policies of his exile movement on the hope and expectation that Russia would succeed in invading the Czech lands. On April 15, 1915, he wrote to the British Foreign Office: "Now Bohemia wishes and hopes that her Russian brethren will soon succeed in occupying the Bohemian and Slovak districts. . . . They must, however, on no account enter Bohemia except to stay." In 1916, Masaryk even indicated his willingness to see a Russian dynasty on the "Bohemian Throne."[3]

The Czecho-Slovak Legion in Russia, formed in 1917 with the consent of the Provisional Government, might have given decisive help to the anti-Bolshevik armies during the early stages of the civil war, but Masaryk

---

[1] Jaroslav Papousek, "Pred dvacety lety" ["Twenty Years Ago"], *Narodni osvobozeni* (organ of the Czecho-Slovak Legion), June 24, 1934, cited by Rudolf Staffen in *Sudetendeutsche Zeitung*, July 10, 1954.

[2] Kufner, whose plan was submitted to the Paris Peace Conference, proposed creating independent states of "Upper Rhine," "Weserland," "Lower Elbe," and "Upper Elbe-Oder" (including Berlin). Remaining territory west of the Rhine and along the North Sea would be transferred to Belgium and Holland. The new state of "Czechia" (of which Slovakia was of course a part) would annex Silesia, a triangle extending almost to Berlin, and Bavaria as far as Regensburg. This would leave a rump Germany with its four corners near Münster, Dresden, Passau, and Basel. Kramar's plan contemplated the creation of separate East and West German states with a boundary somewhat west of the present interzonal border. A map of the Kufner plan appears in the *Sudetendeutsche Zeitung* of September 11, 1954. That of the Kramar plan, included in Staffen's article in the same newspaper on July 10, 1954, shows a striking similarity to the post-World War II situation. It appears that the Bolsheviks studied with profit the archives of the old Czarist Foreign Office.

[3] For details, see Jaksch, *Europas Weg nach Potsdam*, pp. 120-33. Quotation after Miksche, *Danubian Federation*, p. 13.

ordered noninterference until after Commissar of War Leon Trotsky had demanded that the Legion be disarmed.[4] Even during the summer of 1918, when the Czecho-Slovak Legion spearheaded the anti-Bolshevist drive along the Volga, the legionnaires seemed less interested in fighting Communism than in their own safety and whatever booty they could obtain. As Masaryk himself admitted, many members of the Legion had joined merely to escape being returned to the Austro-Hungarian army,[5] and their conduct was such that Colonel Shvets, the commander of the Legion who committed suicide on October 5, 1918, wrote in his will:

> You refuse to obey all rules of order and discipline; you destroy the character of the Czech soldier. I cannot survive the shame into which our army has fallen through the wrongs of numerous, unrestrained, and fanatical demagogues, who in themselves and in us have killed the highest virtue, honor.[6]

All this, however, did not prevent Masaryk from inflating the exploits of the Czecho-Slovak Legion in Russia into a glorious Odyssey.[7]

In the political field, Masaryk's first reaction to the Bolshevik revolution was favorable: on April 4, 1918, he dispatched a memorandum to President Wilson urging *de facto* recognition of Lenin's revolutionary government. Shortly afterward, the Bolsheviks attacked the Czecho-Slovak Legion, causing Masaryk to change his attitude for the time being. During the summer of 1918

---

[4] Based on interviews with former members of the Czecho-Slovak Legion in Russia. But see Masaryk on "Why We Were Neutral in Russia," *The Making of a State*, pp. 130ff.
  Robert Ingrim, in Chapter 10 of his *After Hitler Stalin?* (Milwaukee, 1946), reports that the French government had urged Masaryk to have the Legion join the anti-Bolshevik forces, but that Masaryk preferred to accept the offer of Muravyev, the Red commander in the Ukraine, for a withdrawal without fighting. Although the Bolsheviks offered to send the Czecho-Slovak troops to Murmansk and Archangelsk, from which British ships could have carried them to the Western Front in time to participate in combat, the Czech command deliberately chose the long way home via Siberia and Vladivostok, later pretending that this was the *only* way—a contention believed by most historians. (See, for instance, Georg von Rauch, *A History of Soviet Russia*, New York, 1957, pp. 90ff.)

[5] Masaryk, *op. cit.*, p. 167.

[6] Quoted by Robert Ingrim, *Von Talleyrand zu Molotow*, Stuttgart, 1951, p. 113. (Author's translation.)

[7] The need to assist the Czecho-Slovak Legion was the excuse given by the Japanese for invading Siberia in 1918. President Wilson also sent American troops to Siberia, ostensibly to render additional assistance to the Legion, but more probably to keep an eye on the Japanese. See R. C. Snyder and E. S. Furniss, Jr., *American Foreign Policy*, New York, 1954, p. 39; also Chambers, Harris, and Bayley, *This Age of Conflict*, 2d ed., New York, 1950, pp. 261-63, 272, and 376.

he sent an explanatory memorandum to the Department of State, asserting *inter alia:*

The relation to the Bolsheviks I always imagined as a so to say working relation. . . . I was in contact with them (in Ukraine and in Moscow) : I know how to work with them, and I had a certain amount of influence over them. I never agreed with *the whole* of their program, and I utterly condemn their tactics. . . . Lenin is a Jesuit . . . an *honorable and moral* object cannot be achieved by dishonorable methods. Bolshevism is clearly amateurism in all respects. . . . The Bolsheviks keep their power only through the weakness and incompetency of their opponents. I, and with me our army, *did everything possible not to provoke the Bolsheviks:* we wanted to work in Russia without obstacles. Only when the Bolsheviks showed themselves openly faithless, when they combined with the Germans, were we forced to take the offensive. . . .[8]

Since military defeat, civil war, and famine had eliminated Russia for the time being as a factor in European politics, while Clemenceau was exploiting the dynamics of World War I to achieve French hegemony and German prostration,[9] Masaryk shifted his foreign policy, looking to France rather than Russia as the protecting power for Czecho-Slovakia. The Prague government became an active member of the Paris-sponsored "Little Entente" (Czecho-Slovakia, Rumania, and Yugoslovia), co-operating with France, Poland and its Entente partners in policies designed to curb German, Austrian, and Hungarian "revisionism." France, however, had in recent decades remained politically and economically stagnant alongside a growing Germany, and was helped to "victory" in World War I only through the intervention of the United States—which after Wilson's defeat on the League of Nations withdrew abruptly from European politics. Lacking the military and industrial power and the historical *"élan"* necessary to sustain the dominant

---

[8] Quoted by Charles Pergler, *America in the Struggle for Czechoslovak Independence,* Philadelphia, 1926, pp. 50-55. (Author's italics.) In the remainder of the memorandum, Masaryk explained that circumstances had changed since his recommendation for *de facto* recognition of the Lenin government. See also V. L. Borin in *Pravda* (London, anti-Communist), October, 1951.

[9] In his *American Diplomacy, 1900-1950* (Chicago 1951: Mentor reprint, pp. 64ff.), George F. Kennan contends that the real reason for American entry into World War I was not submarine warfare but the need to preserve the balance of power in Europe. This being the case, we might well have adopted a feature of earlier British balance-of-power policy: to support the defeated state at the peace table. A moderate peace, Kennan tells us, was precluded both by American "moralism" and by the all-out nature of modern war, in which the public, aroused like a "sleeping dinosaur," tends to demand the total annihilation of the enemy.

position granted it by the Treaty of Versailles, France fell into a decline and its system of alliances gradually disintegrated.

Dr. Benes, who had taken over the Foreign Office of the Czecho-Slovak Republic, noted that the Soviet government of Russia was in power to stay, and promptly took out a "reinsurance policy." In 1920, the first important center of Soviet foreign espionage was opened in Prague, cloaked as a "Ukrainian Legation." Its chief was the subsequent Russian secret police boss, Lavrenti P. Beria. Only Foreign Minister Benes knew about this agency at first. When other ministers learned the facts, Benes admonished them to keep silent about the whole matter.[10]

After Hitler had assumed power in Germany and had detached Poland from its alliance with France, Benes considered that it was now time for Czecho-Slovakia to cement its ties with the Soviet Union.[11] In May, 1935, he concluded an alliance with Moscow, which was followed by various measures of political and military cooperation.[12] Rumania and Yugoslavia did not approve, while relations with Poland and Hungary were clouded by minority problems. Czecho-Slovakia thus became increasingly isolated and was forced into growing dependence on the Soviet Union.

The Czech National Socialist party, of which Benes was intellectual mentor both as foreign minister and as president, became the center of a pro-Soviet school of thought. The most outspoken sovietophile was Dr. Hubert Ripka, who conducted a tour of newsmen to the U.S.S.R. in 1935 and was co-editor of a Czech-Soviet

[10] INFORM Special Report on Beria, Baltimore, 1953.

[11] Dr. Eduard Benes, *Memoirs*, pp. 5-25. On page 6, Benes writes: "I never agreed with the policy of the Western democracies, which for so many years isolated the Soviet Union and excluded it from cooperation in Europe and in the world. . . . It seemed to me that victory would go to the side to which the Soviet Union ultimately gave its support. . . ." And, on page 24: "I emphasized the main principles of our policy, the first and most important being that Czechoslovakia was convinced that without the participation of the Soviet Union in European and particularly Central European affairs, Germany would again be supreme in Europe and would endanger European peace."

[12] *Ibid.*, pp. 40-43. The pact, signed by Benes and Soviet Ambassador Alexandrovsky on May 16, 1935, provided that either power would aid the other in defense against unprovoked aggression. The protocol of signature, however, contained the reservation that the pact would operate *only if France should aid* the party attacked. France's failure to support Czecho-Slovakia in the 1938 crisis relieved the Soviet Union of obligation. See Max Beloff, *The Foreign Policy of Soviet Russia*, 1929-1941, New York, 1947-49.

friendship magazine named *Prague-Moscow*.[13] When Dr. Benes decided to resume political activity abroad, he placed Dr. Ripka in charge of the information program of the "Czechoslovak Liberation Movement," later known as the "Czechoslovak National Committee," which Benes and his friends established in Paris.

THE MYTH OF THE "TWO PUPPETS"

A favorite weapon of confusion employed by "Czechoslovak" historiography is the myth of the "two puppets," the Bohemia-Moravia Protectorate and the Slovak Republic. These two political entities do not, in fact, belong in the same category.

The term "puppet" is appropriate when applied to the protectorate of Bohemia and Moravia, the government of which had little more than administrative powers while the Reich Protector and the Gestapo exercised the real control. The Czechs did not want to be governed by the German Reich, and even the most determined opponents of Dr. Benes directed their efforts to replacing the protectorate with a free Czech government. Dr. Emil Hacha, who continued in office after March 15, 1939, as president of the protectorate, found himself in a position similar to that of Marshal Petain in France. Hacha, like Petain, made the best of a bad bargain, and like Petain he was punished for doing so.

It is true that the protectorate government contained its share of opportunists who climbed to power via the coattails of the Nazis and participated in illegal acts against their countrymen. Other officials, however, reasoned that Czech authorities, however limited their powers, would be less oppressive than direct administration by the Nazis. They remained in their posts, resisting the Gestapo terror as best they could, and not

---

[13] See *Bohemia* (Journal of Czech Democratic Federalists), Munich, April 15, 1954, special English annex, "Who is Mr. Hubert Ripka?" For a brief biography of Ripka, see the author's "Profile of an Exile Politician," *Overseas Research Special Bulletin*, November 28, 1954 (out of print), reprinted in *Slovakia*, September-December, 1954, pp. 85-92. The editor-in-chief of *Prague-Moscow* was Dr. Zdenek Nejedly, later Minister of Education, a veteran Communist. Dr. Ripka, whose activities in exile during World War II, in the postwar Prague government, and again in exile after 1948 form an important part of our story, died in a London hospital on January 7, 1958.

anticipating the blanket condemnation of protectorate functionaries which was to follow.[14]

The Slovak Republic was neither a puppet nor a protectorate. It was independent both in law and in fact, and was recognized as such by the majority of European states, including Great Britain, France, Sweden, Switzerland, and even the Soviet Union. It had a government capable of shaping and executing its own policies, not a mere administration like that of the protectorate. Most importantly, the Slovak Republic represented the Slovak people: independence was a logical culmination of Slovak aspirations. While, as we have noted, many Slovaks had been willing to continue in a federal relation with the Czechs, that arrangement was no longer possible in March, 1939. Faced with the choice they had to make, the Slovaks were practically unanimous for independence. Once a nation has tasted independence, it is seldom ready to relinquish it: many federalists and "Czechoslovaks" who at first accepted the republic *faute de mieux* became its warmest supporters. After several years had passed, few Slovaks wanted to return to a revived Czecho-Slovakia.[15]

1. WAS THE SLOVAK REPUBLIC TOTALITARIAN?

Detractors of the Slovak Republic often maintain that it was a fascist state dedicated to aping the Third Reich, and therefore could not represent the free aspirations of the Slovak people. Such charges are pressed most sharply in "Czechoslovak" writings such as Dr. Lettrich's *History of Modern Slovakia*, but are reflected in milder form in other publications.[16] The political orientation of

---

[14] See the discussion of the "Kosice Statute" of April 5, 1945, in the following chapter.

[15] Mikus, *La Slovaquie dans le Drame de l'Europe*, pp. 97-184; Durcansky, *The International Aspects of the Slovak Question, passim;* Edward L. Delaney, *False Freedom*, Los Angeles, 1954, pp. 62-82; Karol Sidor, "The Slovak Republic—Fruit of Hlinka's Struggle" and "What Led to the Proclamation of the Slovak Republic," *Slovakia*, December, 1951, pp. 13-15, and December, 1952, pp. 1-12, respectively; House of Representatives, 83d Congress, Select Committee on Communist Aggression, *Special Report No. 8: Czechoslovakia*, Washington, 1954, p. 12.

[16] The Select Committee on Communist Aggression, *loc. cit.*, states that the Slovak Republic was not "a perfect democracy in the traditional sense," but "in general it was an expression of the self-preservation instinct of the Slovak Nation." We read on pp. 148-49 of *Dokumentation der Vertreibung der Deutschen aus Ost-Mitteleuropa* ["Documents on the Expulsion of the Germans from East-Central

the Slovak Republic therefore requires careful examination.

It must, first of all, be remembered that Monsignor Tiso and his associates were forced to operate, not in a vacuum, but in a Central Europe torn by national tensions and saturated with Nazi power, at a time when the prestige of "classical" democracy was at its lowest ebb.[17] As political realists they faced the task, not of elaborating a platonic "ideal democracy," but of finding ways and means to assure the national existence of the Slovaks, with the maximum freedom which the objective environment would allow. They were not so naïve as to believe that Hitler harbored any true affection for the Slovak people—as Tiso pointed out, the Germans were not helping the Slovaks "because of our beautiful blue eyes," but because it was in their interest to do so.[18] Hitler would have liquidated the Slovak Republic without compunction had it ever seemed convenient. He would most likely have done so had the Tiso government permitted a political free-for-all such as typified the French Third Republic or the last years of the Weimar Republic in Germany.

Except for the German and Hungarian minority parties, the Slovak Republic had a one-party system, established at the Zilina Conference of October 6, 1938. At this meeting, representatives of all Slovak political parties and Slovak branches of Czech parties—except the Communists and the Social Democrats—agreed to form the Slovak National Unity party, in which the Hlinka

Europe"], Volume IV/1, "The Explusion of the German Population from Czecho-Slovakia," published by the Federal Ministry for Expellees, Refugees, and War Victims, Bonn, 1957:

"However determining the influence of the Third Reich in this event [the dismemberment of Czecho-Slovakia], it is nevertheless indisputable that the new state [the Slovak Republic] was at that time supported by the majority of the politically interested Slovaks. The certainty, on the one hand, that the small number of ethnic Germans in Slovakia did not endanger the existence of the state and, on the other hand, that Slovakia could counter the Hungarian demands for annexation only through close association with the German Reich determined the clearly pro-German policy of the Slovak government. The totalitarian system which the Hlinka Party had already introduced during the period of autonomy served as a further basis for German-Slovak agreement." (Author's translation.)

[17] Parliamentary democracy in France had broken down in 1935, after which government was conducted by decree. Every six months the Chamber of Deputies would meet briefly, overthrow the cabinet, and promptly grant emergency powers to its successor.

[18] Speech at Trnava, August, 1939, quoted by Charles Murin, "A Belated Report," *Slovakia*, June, 1957, p. 33.

Slovak People's party played the dominant role.[19] It has been contended that the merger was brought about through undue pressure, and there is no doubt that the Hlinka party promoted it with energy. The pressure that existed, however, came from outside Slovakia: the shock of Munich, the threat of war, and the Hungarian claim to Slovak territory. The Hlinka party lacked police power to force other parties into unwanted association, and Monsignor Tiso would never have employed such power had he possessed it. The creation of the Slovak National Unity party cannot, therefore, be compared with the forced merger of political parties in Sovzone Germany and Communist Czecho-Slovakia. It was the voluntary response of Slovak leaders to an international storm which threatened to engulf Slovakia and which could be withstood only by forsaking "politics as usual" in favor of disciplined national unity.[20]

When elections were held on December 18, 1938, for the Slovak Diet—which later became the parliament of the Slovak Republic—the National Unity party presented a consolidated list of candidates chosen among its constituent elements. Delayed publication of election procedures made it impossible for the Communists and Social Democrats to run competing slates. The use of this maneuver at the expense of the Communists requires no apology, but exclusion of the Social Democrats would appear to violate the principles of democracy which Tiso had repeatedly upheld.[21] In defense of the government's action, it may be argued that (a) there was, at the time, practically no organized Social Democratic party in Slovakia,[22] and (b) if there had been, its election propaganda might well have jeopardized Slovak negoti-

---

[19] Of the forty-five Slovak deputies in the Prague parliament, thirty-five signed the Zilina Manifesto; nineteen of the Hlinka party, eleven Agrarians, and five deputies of smaller parties. The five Communists and five Social Democrats did not sign.

[20] As Murin observes (loc. cit., p. 22), Westerners cannot reasonably criticize Central European politicians for accepting the consequences of Munich, for which the Western Powers share the responsibility.

[21] See Joseph Pauco, "Dr. Joseph Tiso: Christian Democrat," Slovakia, June, 1957, pp. 37-50.

[22] The Social Democrats were a Czech party with a small Slovak following. Their apparatus, concentrated in the Czech lands, had been badly shaken by the Munich debacle, and was in the throes of reorganization as the "Party of Labor." The Social Democratic party in Slovakia had suspended its activities on November 23, 1938.

ations with the Germans—negotiations which, as we have seen, were vital in the struggle against Hungarian annexation. Critics such as Dr. Lettrich[23] would have us condemn the Hlinka party for refusing to stake the existence of their nation on a point of constitutional principle, which may well have been academic in any case. The Slovak people, anyhow, endorsed their government's policies, since 97.5 per cent of the voters cast ballots for the unity list in an election which was substantially free from coercion.

The constitution of the Slovak Republic, adopted on July 21, 1939, was that of a typical parliamentary democracy. Legislative and fiscal powers were vested in a one-house assembly elected by universal suffrage, which also chose the president of the republic and approved the ratification of treaties. The president conducted the government with the aid of ministers responsible to the assembly and removable by vote of no confidence. The constitution provided for an independent judiciary and contained a full bill of rights and guarantees of due process of law.[24] Although the government, under constant pressure from the Nazis, was obliged to exercise a certain degree of censorship, there was no violation of basic human rights. Even the postwar Communist-dominated government was obliged to admit that "not a single political execution took place in the Slovak state."[25]

Article 79 of the Slovak Constitution grouped all citizens, regardless of social status, into six "estates"—agriculture, industry, commerce, banking, free professions, and public employees—which some writers have mistakenly identified with the corporations of Mussolini's fascist state. These estates were not, however, copied from Italian fascism: they were recommended by Pope Pius XI in his encyclical *Quadragesimo Anno,* and were self-governing bodies in which employers and workers

[23] Jozef Lettrich, *History of Modern Slovakia*, New York, 1955, pp. 119-21.

[24] John F. Gleiman, "The Spirit of the Constitution of the Slovak Republic," *Slovakia*, December 1952, pp. 20-23. The constitution also contained specific provisions guaranteeing the rights of non-Slovak minorities, and making "any activity aimed at de-nationalization" a punishable offense. For full citation of these provisions, see *Dokumentation der Vertreibung der Deutschen aus Ost-Mitteleuropa,* IV/1, 150.

[25] Pamphlet issued by Slovak Information Bureau in 1946, cited in "The Politics of Hlinka's Party in the Slovak Republic," *Slovakia*, May, 1951, p. 48.

in each branch of the economy could resolve their social conflicts in accord with Christian principle.[26] Another superficial resemblance to fascism lay in the para-military Hlinka Guard, the uniforms of which looked rather like those of Hitler's storm troopers. Here it might be commented that in borrowing some of the panoply of fascism, Tiso and his associates hoped to distract Nazi attention from the Christian orientation of the Slovak state. The Hlinka Guard conducted frequent drills, parades, and demonstrations, and helped the army and police in tasks of order and defense—it did not indulge in organized smashing of Jewish shops or liquidation of political dissenters.[27]

Although the Slovak National Unity party enjoyed a constitutional political monopoly,[28] it was not monolithic; unlike the Bolshevik and Nazi parties, the Hlinka party had not liquidated its political competitors, but had joined with them in a common undertaking. The party contained a political spectrum ranging from Nazi-like extremists to Christian socialists and even former Social Democrats. The various groups debated, maneuvered, and intrigued, and those who lost lived to intrigue another day: the government was, if anything, too lax in rooting out subversive intrigue directed at the overthrow of the republic.[29] Tiso and his moderate supporters resisted steadfastly the efforts of the extremists to gain control over the state, sometimes yielding reluctantly to Nazi pressure and sometimes regaining lost ground.

In the environment in which it was forced to exist, the Slovak Republic was necessarily somewhat authoritarian. It was *never totalitarian*: Tiso's government adhered firmly to Christian principles which forbid the

[26] Pauco, *op. cit.*, pp. 42-45 ; Gleiman, *op. cit.*, p. 22.

[27] Individual and local acts of violence were the exception and not the rule. In interwar Europe, totalitarian parties were not alone in having para-military detachments. The *Reichsbanner*, allied with the German Social Democratic party, fought frequent skirmishes with the Nazi SA until its dissolution in 1933. The Sudeten German Social Democrats also had a uniformed corps, which supported the Czecho-Slovak army during the 1938 crisis.

[28] The constitution also recognized the "registered" parties of national minorities insofar as they are "representative of the political will of the entire ethnic group" (Art. 59). As Gleiman observes (*op. cit.*, p. 23), provisions of this sort represented a concession to Nazi ideology.

[29] See account of the "Slovak Revolt" of 1944 in the concluding section of this chapter.

state to encroach upon the basic rights of individuals and families.[30] While overt opposition to the government was restricted, no one was forced to make a show of support, and no one was executed for refusing to do so. A comparison of the Slovak Republic with Hitler's Third Reich is, therefore, entirely misleading: the Slovak state was *at least* as liberal as Franco's Spain (as of 1958) or Salazar's Portugal, both of which the United States considers acceptable political partners.

2. THE JEWS IN THE SLOVAK REPUBLIC

Dr. Lettrich and other "Czechoslovak" writers blame the Tiso government for the fact that the Slovak Republic enacted anti-Semitic legislation and that over fifty-thousand Slovak Jews were liquidated in German Nazi concentration camps during the course of World War II.[31] This question, like that of the supposed "totalitarianism" of the Slovak Republic, needs to be considered in its proper perspective.

To begin with, anti-Semitism was rife in Slovakia— as in most of Central Europe—long before the Hlinka party assumed political power. While it is not our purpose to excuse racial antagonism in any form, its sociological explanation lies in the fact that the 137,000-odd Jews of Slovakia[32] belonged for the most part to the upper and middle classes, and thus occupied a disproportionate share of business and professional positions. Milan S. Durica writes that after the Vienna Arbitration of 1938, "when the Jews constituted only 3.35 per cent

---

[30] Although Tiso's concept of basic rights was founded in Catholic ideas of natural law, it was similar to that of the Protestant John Locke, who held the most fundamental rights to be those of life, personal liberty, and property. See John Locke, *Of Civil Government* (1690), London, 1924, "Everyman's Library," Book II, especially paragraphs 134-40 and 190.

[31] There is no record of any liquidation of Jews by the Slovak government. Dr. Lettrich's *History of Modern Slovakia* contains a series of "atrocity" photographs which, according to the *Slovak Newsletter* (December, 1957, p. 4), are the same as and presumably borrowed from those appearing in Louis Mandel's *The Tragedy of Slovak Jewry*, published under the Communist government in Bratislava in 1949. The mass murders depicted took place in Germany and German-occupied Poland, not in Slovakia.

[32] The 1930 census listed 73,000 persons of Jewish nationality and 137,000 of the Jewish religion in Slovakia, the discrepancy arising from the fact that many German-speaking Jews listed their nationality as German. Persons of Jewish race who did not profess the Jewish religion, and who registered as members of other nationalities (normally on the basis of language) were not included in either category. See Waller Wynne, Jr., *The Population of Czechoslovakia*, Washington, United States Bureau of the Census, 1953, pp. 25-27, 65.

of the population in Slovakia, they owned almost one half of the entire national wealth and occupied most of the economically and civically important public functions."[33] There was a general demand that "something be done about the Jewish problem," a demand voiced no less energetically by "Czechoslovaks" than by Slovak nationalists.[34] Even Thomas G. Masaryk, who had won his political spurs in a battle against anti-Semitism, delivered himself of the following:

Anti-Semitism in Slovakia is warranted. . . In your land the Jews are everywhere, without exception, against the cultural efforts of the people. They practise usury. People must be saved from the yoke of alcohol and Jewish capital. . . Priests must be national; the Church must be anti-Semitic so that the people might free itself economically from Jewish capital. . .[35]

Quite apart from Nazi influence, Monsignor Tiso faced a strong public demand for legislation to restrict the economic power of the Jews, and it is apparent that he favored such legislation himself. He insisted, however, that "the Jewish question in Slovakia shall be solved justly, socially, and humanly,"[36] threatening the prosecution of anyone who resorted to individual violence against Jews.[37] Dr. Tiso's firm stand put a damper on the activities of certain individuals in the Hlinka Guard who, without authority, had undertaken to emulate Hitler's storm troopers.[38] His Jewish program, embodied in a decree of April 30, 1939, and confirming laws passed

---

[33] Milan S. Durica, "Dr. Joseph Tiso and the Jewish Problem in Slovakia," *Slovakia*, September-December, 1957, pp. 1-22. Citation, p. 3. Mr. Durica adds in footnotes that Jews controlled 90 per cent of the textile industry, and that 72 per cent of the lawyers and 64 per cent of the physicians were Jews. The author cannot vouch for Mr. Durica's statistics, but their accuracy is less important than the fact that they represented what the public believed to be true.

[34] The most violent anti-Semitic blasts appeared in the *Narodnie Noviny*, edited by Dr. Martin Kvetko, now a high official of Radio Free Europe, and in the *New Yorksky Dennik*. On September 18, 1938, the *Narodnie Noviny* wrote: "Germany has shown us how we must deal with the foreign element. We must apply such methods even more than Germany." Typical quotations from the *Dennik*: "Send all the Jews to hell" (November 11, 1919) ; "The irrefutable fact is that something ought to be done about the Jews in Slovakia already now." (October 8, 1938) Cited by Constantine Culen, "Lettrich's History of Slovakia," *Slovakia*, December, 1955, pp. 21-38.

[35] Advice to "Hlasist" movement, cited by Culen, *op. cit.*, p. 33.

[36] *Slovak*, Bratislava, February 9, 1939, cited by Durica, *op. cit.*, p. 6.

[37] Speeches of October 8, 1938, and March 15, 1939, cited by Durica, *op. cit.*, pp. 3, 17.

[38] Acts of violence such as those described by Dr. Lettrich (*op. cit.*, p. 176), to the extent that they occurred, were not authorized by the government, the efforts of which to keep such incidents to a minimum were generally successful.

by the assembly on February 10 and April 25, 1940, permitted Jews to continue the management of their enterprises, provided that they sold 51 per cent of the capital shares to Slovak partners of their choice.[39] Jewish participation in the professions and public services was to be limited by gradual steps to four per cent, a little more than the proportion of Jews in the total population. The government also took steps to facilitate Jewish emigration to Palestine. Jews were identified by their religion, baptized Jews being considered Christians.

Although the Tiso government's Jewish laws were objectionable by American standards, they were much too mild for the radical anti-Semites in Slovakia. They were entirely unsatisfactory to the German Nazis, particularly since the government granted frequent "administrative exemptions." On July 28, 1940, Adolf Hitler summoned President Tiso and his ministers to Salzburg, where he "laid down the law," forcing the dismissal of Dr. Ferdinand Durcansky, Minister of the Interior and Foreign Affairs, who had assisted in the moderate solution of the "Jewish problem" and whose independent diplomacy was annoying to the Nazis.[40] The Führer then dictated his choice of replacements: as Foreign Minister the strongly pro-Nazi Premier Vojtech Tuka[41] and for the Interior post—which carried with it control over the police and over Jewish affairs—Alexander Mach, the leader of the extremist element in the Hlinka Guard.

Having lost control over a vital area of policy, Dr. Tiso returned from Salzburg determined to resign the presidency.[42] He was induced to remain in office, however, by the pleas of Slovak moderates and Jewish leaders,

---

[39] Durica, op. cit., p. 18. Jews are not considered a nationality in the United States, but were so regarded in Czecho-Slovakia and Slovakia. While forced sales necessarily caused losses to Jewish owners, there was no confiscation of their property at this time; Durica cites an estimate that Slovak Jews transferred abroad assets worth two billion Slovak crowns (about $100,000,000 in actual value). In some cases, the new Gentile owners were "straw men," so that the change of ownership was fictitious.

[40] Tiso endeavored to support Durcansky, whereupon Hitler flew into a rage and shouted: "ich will diesen Zigeuner nicht mehr sehen!" ["Get that gipsy out of my sight!"]

[41] When Monsignor Tiso became president in October, 1939, Tuka had succeeded him as premier. Since Tiso had retained personal control over the government, Tuka's authority prior to Salzburg had been somewhat less than his title would indicate.

[42] Joseph Pauco, Dr. Jozef Tiso o sebe ["Dr. Jozef Tiso on the Gallows"], Passaic, New Jersey, 1952, p. 35.

who knew that Tiso could curb the Nazi-inclined radicals, if not fully, at least better than anyone else. For the time being, the president was forced into a defensive position: on September 10, 1940, Prime Minister Tuka rammed an enabling law through the assembly, on the strength of which he decreed the so-called "Jewish Code," which copied the German Nuremberg Law.[43] President Tiso refused to sign the "Jewish Code," but he lacked authority to veto it. Again, he considered resigning, but finally decided to stay and take advantage of two loopholes in the code: provisions confirming "exceptions" already made under previous law and authorizing the president to make additional exceptions under the new law.[44]

Under German pressure, the Slovak cabinet agreed to a scheme for transferring the Jews of Slovakia to the area between the Vistula and Bug rivers in the *Gouvernement Générale* of German-occupied Poland. Here, the Jews of Europe were supposedly to be settled permanently in a "Jewish reservation" with some degree of local self-government. As a preliminary measure, the government began concentrating the Jews who did not enjoy presidential "exceptions" in labor camps.[45] A decree issued by Minister Mach on March 7, 1942, confined the remaining non-privileged Jews to their homes pending transfer, and the first shipment of Jewish workers to Poland began on March 10. This action was met with protests from the clergy, private citizens, and members of the cabinet who had begun to suspect the intentions of the Nazis. On March 14, the Vatican handed a note of protest to the Slovak Ambassador, Karol Sidor, who shortly thereafter returned to Bratislava with a demand that the deportations be stopped.[46] Only after the Reich officials Reinhold Heydrich and Adolf Eichmann had given personal assurance that the Jews would be humanely treated did the Slovak government begin to move the

---

[43] *Slovak Code*, Part 52, No. 198, September 10, 1941.

[44] *Ibid.*, Part X, paragraphs 255 and 256. See also Pauco, *op. cit.*, p. 323n.

[45] Lettrich, *op. cit.*, p. 182, lists five camps with a total population of 54,652. The weight of evidence does not support his statement that the inmates were generally mistreated or forced to work without pay.

[46] Karol Sidor, *Šesť rokov pri Vatikáne* ["Six Years at the Vatican"], Scranton, Pa., 1947, pp. 141-42.

families of the workers who had been transported the previous month.

Although Prime Minister Tuka wanted to remove the Jews from Slovakia, he never favored their liquidation. In April, 1942, he addressed a note to Berlin urging that the Slovak government be permitted to send an inspection team to observe the treatment of the Jews who had been resettled. The Wilhelmstrasse, however, gave an evasive reply, which intensified suspicions in Bratislava.[47]

Dr. Tiso sensed the opportunity for a counterattack. At his initiative, the Slovak Assembly met and passed the constitutional law of May 15, 1942, which, although ostensibly a mandate for the deportation of Jews from Slovakia, actually reduced the shipments to a mere trickle.[48] The new law confirmed all the "exceptions" previously granted by the president and the ministers, and created a new general exception for Jews baptized before March 14, 1939. Most importantly, it reduced greatly the authority of Interior Minister Mach, who was no longer able to deal with the Jews as he pleased.

Upon being informed by the Papal Nuncio in July, 1942, that Jews were being murdered in the Lublin area, Dr. Tiso declared that unless a Slovak inspection mission were admitted, there would be no further shipment of Jews from Slovakia. According to Durica:

. . . In August, Wisliceny went to Berlin with the matter. There Eichmann told him that Tiso was asking an impossible thing because those Jews were no longer alive. Thereupon he showed him a secret order, issued by the will of Hitler and signed by Himmler, according to which the entire Jewish race was to be gradually destroyed. Wisliceny returned to Bratislava again with an evasive reply. After this deportations from Slovakia were completely stopped.[49]

Under the law of May 15, 1942, most of the remaining Jews who did not enjoy "exceptions" were sent to

---

[47] Testimony of Dieter Wisliceny (SS-Hauptsturmführer detailed to work with Slovak Ministry of Interior on Jewish questions) at Nuremberg; *Proceedings of International Military Tribunal*, III, 276-78. Durica, *op. cit.*, p. 11.

[48] *Slovak Code*, No. 68, May 15, 1942. Lettrich (*op. cit.*, p. 183) misinterprets the significance of this law, making it appear that it led to a worsening of the treatment of the Jews.

[49] Durica, *op. cit.*, p. 12. See also G. Reitlinger, *The Final Solution*, London, 1953, p. 390.

labor camps—a measure which, as Durica suggests, was at least partially motivated by the desire to protect them from anti-Semitic extremists.[50] Conditions in these camps were characterized by the International Red Cross as follows:

> . . . At certain times Slovakia was regarded as a refuge of the Jews, especially Polish Jews; the Jews who remained in Slovakia were comparatively protected until the uprising against the German army at the end of August, 1944. It is true that the law of May 15, 1942, resulted in the arrest of several thousands of Jews, but in the camps, where living and housing conditions were adequate, the prisoners were allowed to work for pay under conditions which approximated the free economy; in Hungary, like in Slovakia, Israelites were spared as long as the local government had a certain freedom of action.[51]

When the Germans assumed control in Slovakia after the "Slovak Revolt" of 1944—a story to be dealt with later—Security Minister Stefan Hassik ordered the disbanding of the labor camps and the repeal of anti-Jewish regulations. The Germans deported a number of Jews on their own account and later forced the Slovak government to decree a reconcentration of Jews. The latter, however, simply ordered the Jews to report to a certain place and made no effort to arrest those who failed to do so.[52]

Lack of firm statistics makes it difficult to determine accurately how many of Slovakia's Jews perished at the hands of the Nazis and how many survived. Jewish organizations approached by the author could supply only fragmentary information. There is a wide spectrum of estimates. At the one extreme we have Gerald Reitlinger's reference to "the murder of three quarters of the Jews in Slovakia," which apparently forms the basis for Lettrich's statement to the same effect, but which is not supported by Reitlinger's own statistics. At the other end of the scale is the report of *The Evangelist*,

---

[50] Durica, *op. cit.*. pp. 12-13.

[51] *Revue Internationale de la Croix Rouge*, Vol. 29, No. 348, Geneva, December, 1947, translated in *Slovak Newsletter*, December, 1957, p. 3.

[52] Durica, *op. cit.*, p. 13. A delegate of the International Red Cross ascertained that only about 50 Jews answered the summons. "As the Slovak authorities had anticipated, the Jews hid themselves." The International Red Cross, the Slovak Red Cross, and the Catholic church were able to aid them. *Report of the International Committee of the Red Cross on its Activity During World War II*, Geneva, 1948, p. 675 (French edition).

diocesan organ of Albany, that "in Slovakia . . . during the reign of President Joseph Tiso, 85 per cent of the Jews were saved." The truth would seem to lie somewhere in the middle.[53]

Gregory Frumkin, the former editor of the *Statistical Yearbook of the League of Nations,* offers a "fairly reliable estimate" that 67,000 Slovak Jews were liquidated. If the 137,000 persons of Jewish religion registered in the 1930 census are accepted as the initial population, this means that 49 per cent of the Jews perished while 51 per cent were saved. Reitlinger, however, considers Frumkin's estimate too optimistic. The following table is based on Reitlinger's more detailed data:

ESTIMATED RESULTS OF ANTI-JEWISH PERSECUTIONS IN SLOVAKIA 1938-1945

	Total	Perished	Saved
Initial Jewish Population—Reitlinger has apparently allowed for emigration between 1933 and 1938	135,000		
Lost to Hungary, 1938—Outside jurisdiction of Slovak Republic	40,000		
Remaining in Slovak Republic, 1939	95,000		
Emigrated, 1939-1941	5,000		5,000
Deported in 1942 (mean between minimum and maximum figures cited by Reitlinger)	54,350	54,100	250
Deported by Germans in 1944—Not taken to Poland but to Germany where "a fair proportion survived"	9,000	5,000	4,000
Remaining in Slovak Republic, 1945	26,650		26,650
Summary, Slovak Republic		59,100	35,900
Regained from Hungary, 1945 — Reitlinger cites an estimated survival rate of 20% for Jews in Hungary		32,000	8,000
Summary, Slovakia		91,100	43,900

---

[53] Reitlinger, *op. cit.,* p. 394; Lettrich, *op. cit.,* p. 191; *The Evangelist* (date not given) is quoted in the *Slovak Newsletter* of December, 1957, pp. 3-4.

Estimated survival rates derived from Reitlinger's statistics are 37.6 per cent for the Jews of the Slovak Republic and 32.5 per cent for those of Slovakia as a whole.[54] Comparable estimates indicate that between 21.2 and 30 per cent of the Jews of the protectorate and 23 to 30 per cent of Polish Jews survived, while only 6.1 per cent of the 215,000 Jews still in Germany in 1939 escaped the gas chambers.

In passing judgment on the foregoing facts, it must be remembered that Monsignor Tiso was unable to control the situation between July, 1940, and May, 1942, while his ministers feared that overt resistance to Nazi racial concepts might provoke direct German intervention in Slovakia. Reitlinger, while critical of many acts of the Slovak government, speaks of its revolt against mass liquidation in 1942 as "the first outright failure of the 'Final Solution.'" It must be recognized, however, that while participation in the Nazi "resettlement scheme" may have been the price of continued Slovak independence, *any program of forced resettlement is morally wrong*. Even if the Jews had actually been resettled, as the Slovak government believed would be the case, they would still have had a valid claim to restitution for civil wrongs. It would also appear that Mach, Tuka, and others directly concerned with "resettlement" were obtuse in not suspecting the true intentions of the Nazis before it was too late. Tiso, Sidor, Durcansky, and the other moderates, however, never favored the deportation program, which they were powerless to prevent. They did what they could—unfortunately not enough—to save Slovak Jewry from extinction.

3. THE CONTINUITY DOCTRINE

Some weeks after his departure from Czecho-Slovakia,

---

[54] Gregory (Grzegorz) Frumkin, *Population Changes in Europe Since 1939*, New York, 1951, pp. 50-51 ; Reitlinger, *op. cit.*, pp. 385, 389, 392, and 493. The breakdown of the Jews deported in 1944 is the author's estimate ; although the concentration camps in Germany were terrible enough, few were outright death factories such as those in Poland. While an exact registration of Jews who emigrated from Slovakia to Palestine is not available, Dr. J. Kermisz, Director of the Archives of the Yad Washem (Remembrance Authority of the Disaster and Heroism) at Jerusalem, wrote the author that: "In our archives we keep a number of documents ascertaining that the Slovak authorities were until 1940 very much interested in the emigration of Jews. Especially those of the poorer strata of the population were encouraged and facilitated to leave the country."

Dr. Benes wrote to Dr. Emil Hacha, formally congratulating him on his election as the third president of the Czecho-Slovak Republic. And when Hitler marched into Prague on March 15, 1939, it was the *ex*-President of Czecho-Slovakia who protested to the Allied powers.[55] Soon afterward, however, Benes and his followers announced the thesis that Hitler's aggression and Hacha's acquiescence had wiped out the Munich Agreement and everything else which had occurred in the meantime. As Benes explains:

By Hitler's crime, by this fresh British and French failure to keep their pledged word and by Hacha's signature to the protectorate I felt freed of all earlier obligations which I had temporarily imposed myself and from all that I had been forced to take part in by violence and pressure since September 19th, 1938. All these ceased to operate! The so-called *First Republic again existed legally!* And its voice had to make itself heard at whatever price![56]

The continuity doctrine—that the Czecho-Slovak Republic continued legally to exist—was first broached in Dr. Benes' broadcast of March 19, 1939. It was repeated in a telegram which the "former President of the Czechoslovak Republic" dispatched on May 13 to Secretary-General Avenol of the League of Nations and the foreign ministers of Great Britain, France, and Russia. On May 28, as Dr. Benes relates, President Roosevelt "received me most cordially, greeted me as the President of the Republic, and added that for him there was no Munich so that I was still the President." Benes' followers and admirers were quick to follow F. D. R.'s example, and by the end of 1939 the "ex" had quietly been dropped from his title.[57] According to the full-blown doctrine of continuity, the First Czecho-Slovak Republic *never ceased to exist* and Benes *never stopped being its president.*[58]

[55] Benes, *op. cit.*, pp. 65-67 and 71-72. The Benes-Hacha correspondence appears on pp. 96-97.

[56] *Ibid.*, p. 64. (Italics in original.)

[57] *Ibid.*, pp. 65-66, 71-72, and 76. It is not clear from Dr. Benes' *Memoirs* exactly when the metamorphosis from "ex-President" to "President" took place.

[58] The continuity doctrine was most fully developed by Edward Taborsky in *The Czechoslovak Cause in International Law*, London, 1944. For a criticism and refutation of Taborsky's theses, see Raschhofer, *Die Sudetenfrage*, pp. 235-52. See also Benes, *Memoirs*, pp. 74-75, 86-94, 106-17, 123-27, and 197-237; Curt Beck, "The Government," in Busek-Spulber, p. 83; Durcansky, *op. cit.*, pp. 31-33; A. Grebert, "Czech Intrigues Against the Slovak State," *Slovakia*, December, 1951, pp. 56-59.

For Dr. Benes, the principle of a unified "Czechoslovak" national state was a basic precept of "law and . . . political morality, which must not be sacrificed at any price."[59] In his eyes and those of his followers, the Slovak Republic existed only as a treasonable conspiracy, notwithstanding its establishment by the freely elected deputies of the Slovak people and its recognition by England, France, and the Soviet Union (the United States recognized it as a *belligerent* in World War II). By the same token, all members of the protectorate government, whatever their actual attitude toward the Nazi tyranny, were *ipso facto* guilty of high treason—against a state which existed neither in law nor in fact. This astounding feat of legal jugglery provided the "constitutional" basis for the acts of judicial murder and mass terror to be recounted in later chapters.

THE "EXILE GOVERNMENT" AND ITS POLICIES

Although Dr. Benes had established an "underground connection" with friends in Prague during the fall of 1938, he waited until after Hitler's seizure of Bohemia and Moravia before organizing the "Czechoslovak Liberation Movement," which had its principal centers in London and Paris. When France fell to the German *Wehrmacht* in 1940, the Paris group, plus a small Czecho-Slovak air force and part of an infantry division (organized under French auspices), were evacuated to England. Shortly afterward, Great Britain recognized Benes' organization as a "Provisional Czechoslovak Government" and made available to it some $24,000,000 of impounded Czecho-Slovak funds. The following year, after the German attack on Russia, Britain, France, and the Soviet Union accorded full recognition to the "Czechoslovak Democratic Government."[60]

---

[59] Benes, *op. cit.*, p. 59. Benes' statist concept is incompatible with the instrumental view of the state expounded by Locke and implicit in American political theory.

[60] *Ibid.*, pp. 106-17, 123-27, 152ff., 175-80; for text of United States Ambassador Winant's note according recognition, see Margaret Carlyle, ed., *Documents on International Affairs, 1939-1946*, Vol. II, "Hitler's Europe," London, 1954 (hereinafter cited as *Doc. Int. Aff.*), p. 316.

The policy of the "exile government" throughout the war was that of close adherence to the Soviet Union. Writing in 1944 of the situation during the Soviet-Nazi pact, Dr. Ripka explains:

Since, in the new situation, it was impossible to collaborate officially with the Soviet Union, we . . . did nothing which might prejudice or prevent the renewal of cooperation at the earliest possible moment; I need only recall how strongly our attitude contrasted with that of many others during the Soviet-Finnish War. Moreover, even in that period, there was no interruption of the personal contacts and exchange of information between ourselves and important Soviet representatives in London, Paris, Washington and elsewhere.[61]

Dr. Benes relates in his *Memoirs* that he was never misled by the *seeming rapprochement* of Germany and the Soviet Union. He was always certain that the Soviet Union would be involved in the war against Germany sooner or later. From information culled from Soviet sources, he reached the conclusion that Russia itself would move against Germany after the Nazis had reached a state of exhaustion, combining their action with a revolution to be instigated by German Communists.[62]

Immediately after the German attack on Russia on June 22, 1941, Dr. Benes approached the Soviet ambassador in London, Ivan Maisky, the result being a preliminary agreement signed on July 18 of that year. This protocol provided that the U.S.S.R. and Czecho-Slovakia would exchange ministers and support each other in the war against Germany, and that Czecho-Slovak military units would be formed in the Soviet Union. The commander of these units would be appointed by the Czecho-Slovak "exile government" in agreement with the Soviet government, and they would operate under the direction of the Soviet High Command.[63]

[61] Hubert Ripka, *East and West*, London, 1944, p. 34.

[62] Benes, *op. cit.*, pp. 138-53. As George de Huszar points out ("The Soviet Union and Her Satellites," in Thorsten V. Kalijarvi and Associates, *Modern World Politics*, 3d ed., New York, 1954, pp. 479-80), World War II was in large part a result of Russian "chestnut strategy"—that of maneuvering the two blocs of capitalist powers into a war of exhaustion. This thesis finds confirmation in a conversation which Benes had with Soviet Ambassador Maisky on August 23, 1939, which left Benes with the impression "that the Soviet Union would try to remain neutral as long as possible so that when the war was nearing its end with both sides exhausted the Soviet Union could intervene decisively and bring about an automatic solution of European problems by means of social revolution." (*Memoirs*, pp. 138-39)

[63] For text of agreement, see *Doc. Int. Aff.*, p. 315.

A more formal treaty was negotiated early in 1943 with A. Y. Bogomolov, the Soviet ambassador to the "exile government," but not signed immediately. While it was pending, Benes journeyed to the United States to visit Roosevelt. The President appears to have received Benes cordially, to have confirmed the correctness of the London "government's" pro-Soviet orientation, and even to have charged Benes with explaining quietly to Stalin that United States protests against Russian annexation of the Baltic republics (Lithuania, Latvia, and Estonia) were not to be taken seriously. He did not, however, fulfill Benes' wish for a flat promise to support his group as the government of Czecho-Slovakia after the war. Upon Benes' return to England, the London "government" decided to proceed with the Soviet treaty, which was signed by Benes in Moscow on December 12, 1943.[64]

COMMUNIST INFILTRATION IN BRITAIN AND AMERICA

During the Hitler regime, a number of committees were set up to arrange escapes from Nazi-dominated territory. The Communists gained control of some of these committees and used them to give their own people preferred treatment, and also to place Soviet agents in strategic positions in the West. Anti-Communists were either betrayed to the Gestapo or, if they succeeded in escaping, denounced as "fascists" to the French and British governments. One of these agencies, the "Salda Committee" in Prague, was dominated by the Politburo of the Czech Communist party and managed by the German Communist, Rudolf Katz, and the Czech Communist, Hilda Matouskova. When the Nazis occupied Prague, Mrs. Matouskova became Dr. Ripka's secretary in Paris, while Katz went to London where he served throughout the war as secretary to Sir Neill Malcolm, British High

---

[64] Benes, *op. cit.*, pp. 180-96; for the conversation on the Baltic Republics, see p. 195. Benes' report of his talk with Roosevelt on May 12, 1943, is quoted in another connection under the heading "The National Front in Communist Strategy," in chap. IV, *infra*.

Further information indicating that Roosevelt did not give Benes the unconditional assurance of support he wanted was obtained from a former member of the Czecho-Slovak Council of State, who heard Benes report on his United States trip. It appears that his talks with Roosevelt were not quite as unruffled as the *Memoirs* would suggest.

Commissioner for Refugees. A British Communist, Miss
E. A. Allen, managed Czech affairs before the "tribunals"
that decided which refugees should be interned and which
freed, while her Canadian Communist associate, Beatrix
Wellington—who had worked with the Salda group in
Prague—held a strategic post in the Czech Refugee
Trust Fund operated by the British Home Office. The
director of the fund, Sir Henry Bunbury, had for his
secretary the German Communist, Ivone Kapp.[65]

The Czecho-Slovak "exile government" enjoyed excellent working relations with this Communist network,
the existence of which the British discovered much too
late. It was relatively easy to procure the arrest of anyone objectionable to the "government" or the Communist
party, which often amounted to the same thing. There
were "white lists" and "black lists": Benes was able
to have the British Home Office intern a number of
Czech conservatives simply because they opposed him
politically. The "government" had its own "secret police"—the Tastapo, headed by General Frantisek Moravec
—which collaborated at times with the Soviet NKVD.
Finally, the political indoctrination of Czech troops in
England was turned over to Communists and fellow
travelers.[66]

Dr. Ripka, who became Minister of Information, enjoyed close relations with the British Broadcasting Company, from whose studios he spoke frequently. One of
his typical speeches to the Czech people, broadcast on
November 7, 1942, contained the following passage:

". . . The Russian November Revolution not only increased the
strength of the Russian Soviet state; it also raised to greater
heights than ever before the standard of civilization, culture and
living of the wide masses of the Soviet peoples. . . .

"Bolshevism is a super-national ideal, an eternal ideal, a human
ideal, an ideal which has kindled the minds of the noblest of men
from the time of Plato and through the Christian era, through
the French Revolution and until today. . . . Just as the French

---

[65] V. L. Borin, "Bolshevik Conspiracy in Your Country," *Pravda* (London),
April, 1951, pp. 4-8, and "The Underground," *ibid.*, November, 1951, pp. 5-10.
The author was able to verify Mr. Borin's information through extensive cor-
respondence and interviews.

[66] *Ibid.*, plus information developed through investigation. It appears that
Vlado Clementis, the most important Communist in England at the time (later
purged), played a prominent role in the training of Czecho-Slovak troops.

Revolution strove to realize the ideal of freedom, so did the Russian Revolution try to realize the ideal of equality."[67]

A Slovak Communist named Vavro Hajdu was appointed to head the Czecho-Slovak section of the BBC, in which section a number of Communists were employed. One of the most prominent was Oto Biheler, later expelled from the United States for espionage under cover of diplomatic status.[68] The "government" also paid the salaries of persons on the staff of the London *Daily Worker*, such as Ludwig Freund (Frejka), whose association with Ripka was brought out in the Slansky purge trial of November, 1952.[69] Other well-known Communists whose close connections with the London "government" are a matter of record were Otto Katz alias André Simone (Ripka's assistant in Paris), Evzen Loebl, Ervin Pollak, Rudolf Margolius, and Vlado Clementis.[70]

A number of Communist agents were also infiltrated into the United States as "Czechoslovak democratic exiles." One of these was the Soviet Russian Bension Batt, whom the Kremlin had sent to Prague in 1925. There, under the Czech alias Stefan Budin, he was editor of the party paper *Rude Pravo* until October, 1938. He then came to the United States and, under the name Batt, edited the Czech-language *New Yorkske Listy*. The Slovak-language *New Yorksky Dennik*, under the same management as the *Listy*, employed the Hungarian Communist Dezider Benau as an editor from 1942 to 1946. Other Czech Communists active in America during the war were Karel Leitner of the *Listy* and Adolf Hoffmeister of the Office of War Information. All these persons returned to political life in Communist Czecho-

---

[67] Quoted in the appendix of Dr. Ripka's book, *East and West*.

[68] Biheler was Czecho-Slovak Military and Air Attaché in Washington from about September 1, 1948, to February, 1951. On his efforts to secure military information and samples in violation of United States law, see Press Release of Senator Herbert R. O'Conor, November 8, 1951.

[69] See Douglas Hyde, *I Believed, The Autobiography of a Former British Communist*, London, 1951, pp. 181-83. Of Freund, Hyde writes: "Freund achieved considerable standing with members of the Benes government and was able to put us [the Communist party] in touch with them at any time. He was able, also, of course, to keep us informed of most of what was going on in Czech government circles. Freund in cooperation with members of our Editorial Foreign Department would write articles to which non-Communist members of his government would willingly put their names."

[70] See references to Slansky trial under heading "More Orthodox Than the Kremlin" in chap. VI.

Slovakia, Hoffmeister becoming Information Minister and later ambassador in Paris.[71]

A REVOLUTION IS PREPARED

Like the first Czecho-Slovak Republic, the regime which followed World War II was organized abroad. During both wars, exile politicians obtained recognition by the victorious powers, creating a regime which could be imposed on the people at home. The principal sponsoring power this time was, of course, Soviet Russia rather than France.

While the ministers and diplomats were busy "cementing relations," the situation of the Czechs at home, as reported by the Czech author F. O. Miksche, was by no means as unbearable as many of us have been led to believe. Miksche tells us:

The situation of the Czechs in the so-called Protectorate during the war was not unfavorable. In the first place they were exempt from military service, and worked quite willingly for Hitler's war machine in the Bohemian industries, which were greatly developed by the Germans. Thousands of tanks, airplanes and guns were produced in the factories, many more than could possibly have been destroyed by the Legions which were organized by Benes in France, England and Russia. The Legion in the West, which consisted of about 5,000 men in the ground forces, never went into action, while the 12,000 men in Russia were engaged in only a few insignificant skirmishes. As Benes himself said, it was a "symbolical army," but propaganda made quite a respectable amount of political capital out of it, and the books and newspaper articles which were written about it during and after the liberation of Prague gave the impression that the war could scarcely have been won without its aid. However, it would be unjust not to mention here the well-deserved glory earned by some Czech airmen in the Battle of Britain.

Statistics show that Bohemia's war-time industrial and agricultural production was proportionately equal to that of Germany, and food shortages were no worse there than in the Reich. In contrast to Poland active resistance and sabotage scarcely existed in Bohemia until the last days of the war, although arrests were made by the Gestapo in Bohemia and Moravia as in the other countries occupied by Germany, and in Germany itself. The assassination of Heydrich was planned and organized abroad, and the

[71] V. L. Borin, *Against the Hangman*, London, 1951, p. 26; *Slovak Newsletter*, February, 1953, January and February, 1954.

Benes government in London cleverly exploited the severe reprisals that followed, and especially the shooting of the 168 male inhabitants of Lidice, to influence British and American public opinion in its favor. Care was taken, of course, to avoid mentioning the fact that the reprisals were not the responsibility of the Sudeten Germans but were carried out by German Nazis.[72]

Miksche's account is confirmed by Kenneth de Courcey, who wrote in 1944:

There is, in fact, almost no resistance movement at all in Ruthenia, Slovakia, Moravia and Bohemia. The Ruthenians are . . . anti-Russian. The masses in Slovakia are anti-Czech and anti-Russian. The attitude of the Czech population is curious. Quite a number are now actually serving in the German forces, viz., in the 5th and 8th Jaeger Divisions, the 18th Motorized Division, and the 81st, 122nd, 225th and 290th Infantry Divisions. Czech industry is most effectively supporting the German war effort and many workers seem very much to dislike the idea of risking the consequences of resistance. The Czech clergy is largely supporting President Hacha, partly because of its anti-Russian views and partly because it fears anti-clericalism from the radicals abroad. All these facts are everywhere well-known on the Continent, and it causes astonishment to many friends of the Allies that they should be so little known in Britain and America. *War-Time Rationing and Consumption*, published by the League of Nations, Geneva, 1942, states that the inhabitants of Bohemia had the same ration as Germany.[73]

Many Czechs were disposed to climb on the Nazi band wagon in 1941 and 1942 so as to share in the "inevitable victory" of the Third Reich. Chairman Kalal of the Veterans Association offered a military contribution to the campaign in Russia, while Bishop Picha of Hradec Kralove led the clergy in militant anti-Communism. As Jaksch comments, "Nowhere was the collaboration between the occupation power and the occupied closer than in the Protectorate, a fact reflecting the feelings of impotence of a small people."[74] As in World War I, the Czech people again contributed more to the German than to the Allied war effort. This circumstance gave the "exile government" its principal appeal: it represented "reinsurance" that the Czechs would be on the winning side in any case.

[72] Quoted by permission from F. O. Miksche, *Danubian Federation*, p. 25.

[73] Kenneth de Courcey, *Review of World Affairs*, London, April 28, 1944.

[74] Wenzel Jaksch, *Europas Weg nach Potsdam*, Stuttgart, 1958, p. 425.

Benes and his followers in London knew that their support at home was lukewarm in Bohemia and Moravia, and practically nonexistent in Slovakia. Their problem was how to climb back into office after the war. To achieve this, they hitched their wagon to the Soviet star. "We Czechoslovaks," wrote Dr. Ripka in 1944, "make no secret of our satisfaction that Soviet Russia is beginning to participate in European and world politics as a strong world power."[75] Ripka's confidential assistant, Dr. Ivo Duchacek, later chairman of the Foreign Affairs Committee in the postwar parliament, underlined the Benes government's dependence on the U.S.S.R. when he said: "Our alliance with the Soviet Union is the main pillar of our foreign policy. What other pillar unless one made out of paper could we have? Our alliance with the Soviet Union guarantees us the immediate help of the Soviet Armies in case of emergency."[76] Soviet support was particularly required to achieve two extreme Czech national aims to which Benes and Ripka had given top priority: the *expulsion of the Sudeten Germans* and the *re-establishment of Czech domination over Slovakia*. To accomplish the latter, the Slovak Republic and its leadership had to be liquidated.

In his *Memoirs*, which contain extensive discussions of political principles, Benes leaves no doubt that it was his purpose to bring about a revolution in Czecho-Slovakia although, as he said, "I want to do it by the path of evolution, without violence." He believed firmly that Western-type democracies could coexist peacefully with Soviet socialism. Existing differences, he contended, would be erased by assimilation—in the process of coexisting, the Western states would inevitably move toward socialism themselves.[77]

To fulfill the program he had in mind, Benes needed to outmaneuver conservative factions such as the Agrarian party and General Lev Prchala's Czech National Committee, which had quite different objectives. For this

[75] Ripka, *East and West*, p. 58.

[76] Slovak Liberation Committee, *Documents* (for full title see Bibliography), London, 1951, p. 15.

[77] Benes, *Memoirs*, pp. 281-86. Benes became an original apostle of coexistence *because* he considered it the best road toward world socialism.

purpose, and to assure themselves Soviet support, the London politicians co-ordinated their plans with the Communists. The intermediaries were the Communist Vlado Clementis in London and the left-wing Socialist Zdenek Fierlinger in Moscow. What this collaboration between London "liberals" and Moscow Communists boded for the future of Czecho-Slovakia is indicated by Dr. Benes' conversations with the Communist leader Klement Gottwald in Moscow in 1943. These talks, as reported by Benes in his *Memoirs,* included the following significant points:

[Gottwald] emphasized that [the Communists] held that this war could not end in the same way as the war of 1914-1918. We would have to fight, we would have to carry out a real revolution together with all our people against the Germans as well as against our war criminals at home. I replied that in general we did not greatly disagree with this conception of the end of the war. . . .

Gottwald then explained his idea of the procedure to be followed in preparing for this revolution. He stressed the necessity of forming national committees which would have to be used not only for the organization of revolutionary cells for the insurrection itself but also as the basis for the whole revolutionary civil administration. I did not oppose this conception. . . .

Deputy Gottwald next asked what the party structure in our country would be after the revolution. He took it for granted that there would be a great revolutionary shift to the Left, a clear Socialist majority and an overwhelming defeat of our former pre-war Right-wing bloc (Agrarians, National Democrats and Traders). Our Moscow Communists also appeared to regard co-operation of the three Socialist parties with the Sramek Party as acceptable. In December, 1943, our Communists did not commit themselves definitely on the future existence of the Agrarian Party. All of us without exception regarded the ruthless liquidation of all Fascism as a matter of course.[78]

In the same discussion, Benes and Gottwald projected the establishment of a *National Front,* under which all parties would participate in the government and no parliamentary opposition would be permitted. The National Front of "government parties" would jointly prepare a single post-revolution program and jointly undertake to

---

[78] *Ibid.,* pp. 270-71. The author is indebted to Messrs. George Allen and Unwin, Ltd., of London, for permission to quote from the *Memoirs.*

fulfill it. "I also agreed to the plan for the National Front on this occasion," Benes wrote.[79]

What Gottwald proposed and Benes accepted is more commonly known as a "United Front." As we shall see in the following chapter, it is the first phase in a well-conceived Communist strategy designed to lead by easy steps to a "people's democracy" under full Communist control.

Although Benes' account of the Moscow talks does not mention Ruthenia, it is evident from other passages that he was ready to yield the area to the Soviet Union as a condition for Russian support, without regard to the interests or desires of the Ruthenian people.[80]

The execution of Benes' and Gottwald's plans depended, of course, on having Prague and central Bohemia occupied by Russian rather than American forces. As Dr. Jozef Lettrich, a Slovak "liberal" who collaborated with the London "government" and its successor, the National Front, explained later: "We cannot stress enough the fact that without the help of the Soviet Army, we would not be able to meet here today."[81]

PLANNING THE EXPULSION OF THE SUDETEN GERMANS

The most fateful step prepared by the London "exile government" and executed by its successor, the 1945-48 National Front regime, was the expulsion of nearly three million Sudeten Germans from the districts where they had lived for centuries. This action eliminated the largest anti-Communist bloc in Czecho-Slovakia.

The chief promoter of the expulsion was Dr. Hubert Ripka, who was not only Minister of Information but also Deputy Foreign Minister of the London "government." To work out the details, Ripka maintained a secret section of the Foreign Office, run by a German, Wolfgang von Putlitz—a friend of the vanished British

---

[79] *Ibid.*, p. 272.

[80] *Ibid.*, pp. 139, 191.

[81] *Cas,* Bratislava, June 5, 1945. Dr. Lettrich remained in Slovakia throughout the war, emerging as a leader of the "Czechoslovak" opposition to the Tiso government.

diplomats Burgess and McLean, as well as of the turncoat West German security chief Dr. Otto John. Putlitz later became a political adviser to the Sovzone German Communist regime.[82] The "exile government" had planned from the beginning to reacquire for Czecho-Slovakia the territories which had been ceded to other states in 1938. If we are to believe Ripka, the plan to expel the Sudeten Germans was conceived in 1939 or earlier, but it was considered advisable to keep it under wraps temporarily.[83] Dr. Benes actually conducted extensive negotiations with Wenzel Jaksch, the leader of the anti-Nazi Sudeten German Social Democrats in London, finally breaking them off in 1943 with the excuse that Sudeten demands for political rights were incompatible with loyalty to the Czecho-Slovak state.[84] A clue to the intentions of the London "government" had, however, been provided as early as August 29, 1941, when Foreign Minister Masaryk announced Czecho-Slovak reservations to the Atlantic Charter amounting to a rejection of its fundamental principles on the self-determination of peoples.[85]

Between June and September, 1942, the Soviet Union, Great Britain, and the Free French agreed to revoke the Munich Agreement. Although Molotov stated flatly that the Soviet government "takes its stand on the pre-Munich Czecho-Slovak frontiers," Anthony Eden's note was more cautiously worded, indicating that: "At the final settlement of the Czechoslovak frontiers to be reached at the end of the war [His Majesty's Government] will not be influenced by any changes effected in and since 1938."[86] The anti-German feeling generated by the Lidice massacre indicated a strategic time to press the next demand: for permission to drive out the

---

[82] Information developed through investigation; but see the *Congressional Record*, April 25, 1955, Extension of Remarks of Hon. Usher L. Burdick.

[83] Ripka, *Czechoslovakia Enslaved*, London, 1950, p. 24.

[84] Jaksch gives a detailed account of these negotiations in his short book *Benesch war gewarnt!* ["Benes Was Warned"], Munich, 1949. Some of the correspondence between Jaksch and Benes may be found in the appendix of the latter's *Memoirs* (pp. 303-34).

[85] Benes, *Memoirs*, pp. 315-16.

[86] For text of Molotov's statement to Benes on June 9, 1942, and the notes exchanged on August 5 by Foreign Ministers Eden and Masaryk, see *Doc. Int. Aff.*, pp. 317-19. For General de Gaulle's letter of September, 1939, and Premier Sramek's reply, see Benes, *Memoirs*, pp. 232-33.

inhabitants of the border areas. A chronology of maneuvers to this end is given in the Göttingen Research Society's handbook *Sudetenland,* as follows:

December 5, 1942	Dr. Benes discusses his proposal for an expulsion of the Sudeten Germans in a lecture at the University of Manchester.
May 12, 1943	In a conversation with President Roosevelt, Dr. Benes asserts that he has already received Soviet approval of his proposal to expel the Sudeten Germans.
May 29, 1943	Dr. Ripka informs the Soviet Ambassador in London, Bogomolov, that the American Government agrees to an expulsion of the Sudeten Germans. Ripka expresses the expectation that the Soviet Government will now also agree. [Benes had reported on May 13 that F. D. R. had agreed that "after the war the number of Germans in Czechoslovakia must be reduced by the transfer of as many as possible."]
June 6, 1943	Ripka informs Benes, who is still in America, that Soviet agreement to the expulsion of the Sudeten Germans has now been received. [On June 7, Benes reported that F. D. R. had confirmed his approval of the "transfer."]
December 12, 1943	Benes concludes a treaty of friendship and alliance with the U.S.S.R. in Moscow. While in Moscow, Benes reaches agreement with the Czech Communists there on the complete expropriation and expulsion of the Sudeten Germans.[87]

Contemporary observers report that Gottwald was not very enthusiastic when he first heard of the plan to expel the Sudeten Germans. But Stalin saw immediately how the expulsion could further Soviet interests. The Kremlin stipulated only that the plan be advanced as a Czech rather than a Russian idea.[88]

---

[87] *Sudetenland,* p. 97; sentences in brackets have been added by the author and are based on Benes, *Memoirs,* pp. 210-27. See also Bohemicus, "Die Schuld Beneschs" ["The Guilt of Benes"], *Pressedienst der Heimatvertriebenen* ["Expellee Press Service"] Göttingen, October 23, 1952, article service pp. 1-2.

[88] Based on interviews with Czech politicians who were in touch with developments during the war. While this version cannot be positively verified, its correctness is suggested by Dr. Duchacek's statement that ". . . the Communist party in the years 1939, 1940 and 1941 showed little of that Slavic grasp of the problem which it so unmistakably and uncompromisingly shows today." (Speech of March

The expulsion of the Sudeten Germans promised to create chaos in the Reich, from which the Communists hoped to reap the profit. It also created an unstable international situation, making Czecho-Slovakia dependent on the permanent prostration of Germany as well as on overriding Russian power in Central Europe. Evidence that Dr. Benes knew that the expulsion meant the welding of Czech nationalism to Communism is supplied by Benes himself when he tells of his efforts to persuade Wenzel Jaksch to agree to the deportation of all Germans except a limited number of "anti-Fascists." At a tea party on January 7, 1942, Benes told Jaksch:

". . . in the social revolution which will certainly come it will be necessary to rid our country of all the German bourgeoisie, the pan-German intelligentsia and those workers who have gone over to fascism. That would be a final solution and, so far as we are concerned, the only possible solution which we would be able to implement, namely the coupling of our social revolution with the national one."

I added to Jaksch and his friends: "We must have the courage to speak about this openly. And especially you Social Democrats must have the courage to do so. This plan even contains an element of marxism and marxist dialectics in the revolutionary process which must inevitably accompany the changes in the social structure of the Nation as an outcome of this great and world-wide catastrophe. After the first World War . . . I foretold that the German nationalist bourgeoisie in our country would sometime in the future attempt a counter revolution and that there would be no peace between us until this bourgeoisie was forced to undergo a similar revolution to that the Czechs had to undergo in former centuries. Now, after the second World War, this revolution is inevitable. And the whole nationalities problem in our country will be radically solved at the same time."[89]

Speaking openly with the Sudeten Germans was, however, something which the Benes "government" did not do. Addressing a "Conference of German Anti-Fascists from the CSR" in London in October, 1943, Dr. Ripka declared that ". . . no German from Czechoslovakia has anything to fear, unless he has committed a crime against

8, 1946, in Provisional National Assembly, quoted in Slovak Liberation Committee, *Documents,* p. 27) After the Communists had determined that the expulsion would aid the "socialist revolution," they became its most enthusiastic promoters. An article in *Rude Pravo,* No. 53 of 1951, claims credit for the expulsion for Stalin.

[89] Benes, *Memoirs,* pp. 218-19. The dependence on Russia resulting from Dr. Benes' nationality policies is discussed in more detail in chap. VIII, *infra.*

the Republic." While supporters of "violent nazified Pan-Germanism" would be severely punished, he continued, such justice was "in the interest of sincere German democrats." He then went on to refer (quoting the Communist deputy Gustav Beuer) to a future "peaceful living together of the peoples on the basis of equal rights." In a lecture published together with the foregoing statement, Dr. Ripka commented: "And concerning indispensable measures as well as concerning policy as a whole with regard to the 'Sudeten' Germans, the decision will indeed not be made now nor here abroad, but only in the Republic after it has been restored in terms of the concrete situation. . . ." But as Benes later disclosed, "complete separation" of the Sudeten Germans from the Czecho-Slovak Republic had already become the firm objective of his regime.[90]

Efforts to obtain British approval for the expulsion of the Sudeten Germans were distinctly less successful. A commitment made by Minister Nichols in June, 1942, turned out, on closer examination, to relate only to Nazi activists.[91] Sometime between then and May, 1944, the British War Cabinet appears to have given consent to a population transfer, but the evidence indicates that its approval was likewise limited to political offenders.[92] In August, 1944, news leaked out that the War Cabinet was then considering a plan for mass deportations, from Germany east of the Oder-Neisse line as well as from Czecho-Slovakia. Although the V-bomb campaign did not exactly promote pro-German feelings, there were sufficient protests so that the cabinet deferred further action. That November, Dr. Benes' ministers submitted to the European Advisory Commission a somewhat weakened resettlement plan calling for the retention of some 800,000 Germans in Czecho-Slovakia.[93] Since the com-

[90] Hubert Ripka, *Die Tschechoslowakei in der Weltallianz* ["Czechoslovakia in the World Alliance"], London, November 2, 1943, pp. 13, 29, 30 ; Benes, *Memoirs,* pp. 220ff. See also Jaksch, *Benes war gewarnt,* pp. 7-20, and *Europas Weg nach Potsdam,* pp. 400-401.

[91] Benes, *op. cit.,* p. 206 ; Jaksch, *Benes war gewarnt,* p. 16.

[92] Until the pertinent archives become available, we have only the statement of Dr. Benes, who in May, 1944, told Compton Mackenzie: "I have discussed this transfer in detail with Mr. Churchill and Mr. Eden. The British War Cabinet has accepted this transfer, and they have already officially notified me that they are in favor of it. . . ." Compton Mackenzie, *Dr. Benes,* London, 1946, p. 293.

[93] Jaksch, *Europas Weg nach Potsdam,* pp. 404-6, 413 ; *Dokumentation der*

mission took no action, Benes sent the plan to Foreign Minister Eden, who rejected it flatly on January 15, 1945, adding that the Sudeten problem could not be settled in isolation, but only as part of the general postwar settlement with Germany.[94] Benes' uncertainty was so great that he promptly ordered his general staff to prepare an alternate plan, according to which 1,700,000 Germans would be expelled and 800,000 would remain in Czecho-Slovakia, while territory containing 600,000 Germans would be left to Germany.[95] Compromises of this sort could, of course, be avoided through the restoration of Czecho-Slovakia under Soviet auspices. This is why Benes and his followers—whatever they said *afterwards* —had good reason to prefer Russian rather than Western occupation of Prague.

THE "SLOVAK REVOLT" OF 1944

There remained the problem of liquidating the prosperous anti-Communist Slovak Republic. Plans for this purpose were initiated by Slovak Communists together with a small group of non-Communist "liberals" who were in touch with London. On December 25, 1943, they signed the so-called "Christmas Agreement" to "take over, at an expedient time, all political, legislative, military, and governmental executive power in Slovakia and use it according to the will of the people until such time as their freely elected representatives shall themselves

---

Vertreibung, IV/1, 45-47. The latter cites extensively the contribution of Karel Lisicky (a member of the Czecho-Slovak Foreign Office in London) to the discussion following a lecture by former Minister Jaroslav Stransky, *Odsun Nemcu z CSR z hlediska narodniho a mezinarodniho* ["The Expulsion of the Germans from Czecho-Slovakia from the National and International Standpoint"], *Doklady a rozpravy*, Volume 10, London, 1953. As described by Lisicky, the plan submitted to the EAC was based on a "Ten-Point Plan" formulated by Benes in 1944 and originally published by Jaromir Smutny in *Doklady a rozpravy*, London, 1956, XXVI, 64-68. A German translation of this plan appears in *Dokumentation der Vertreibung*, IV/1, 181-83.

The European Advisory Commission, consisting of the United States and Soviet ambassadors in London and a senior member of the British Foreign Office, was established by the Moscow Foreign Ministers' Conference of November, 1943, to prepare terms for the German surrender and to consider the political problems of postwar Europe.

[94] Instructions from Eden to Philip B. Nichols, British Minister to Czecho-Slovakia, January 15, 1945, mentioned by Jaksch, *op. cit.*, pp. 415, 503. *Dokumentation der Vertreibung*, Vol. IV/1, p. 48, is apparently in error in giving the date of this communication as January, 1944.

[95] Lisicky, *loc. cit.*

be able to take it over." A supplementary document contained the following provisions:

(1) It is our desire that the Slovaks and the Czechs, as the two most closely related Slav nations, shall unite their destinies in a Czechoslovak Republic which will be their common Government organized on the principle of equality.

(2) We desire close collaboration with all Slav states and peoples, particularly with the Soviet Union, in which we see a protecting shield for the free life and welfare of all small nations in general, and of the Slav nations in particular.

(3) The future Czechoslovak Republic shall conduct its foreign policy in the spirit of these principles and should therefore lean on the Soviet Union.

The underground Slovak National Council, founded by the Christmas Agreement, gained considerable support among the Protestant minority.[96] Except for the nationalist followers of the late Martin Razus,[97] Slovak Protestants tended to share the anti-clericalism of Masaryk and Benes and to look to the Czechs for support against what they considered the cultural and political Catholicism of the Hlinka party. Disaffection against the Tiso government also spread among the officers of the Slovak army and police, most of whom had originally received a "Czechoslovak" political indoctrination and many of whom resented the newly-attained prestige of the Hlinka Guard. General Golian, the chief of staff, co-ordinated military preparations for a revolt, moving combat divisions and materials into Protestant districts of central Slovakia.

Entirely separate from the military conspiracy, partisan detachments were formed in the remote mountain regions of central and eastern Slovakia. Although these groups established liaison with the Slovak National Committee, they were controlled by Soviet partisan headquarters in Kiev and led by Russian, Slovak, and Czech Communist agents dropped by parachute. They were joined by Slovak and Czech Communists, escaped prisoners of war and forced laborers, and by Slovak "liberals"

[96] According to the 1930 census, 556,000 (16.7%) of the inhabitants of Slovakia belonged to the Evangelical church and 11,000 (0.3%) to the Czechoslovak church. See Wynne, *The Population of Czechoslovakia*, Table 19, p. 65.

[97] See J. A. Mikus, "Martin Razus (1883-1937)," *Bulletin of the Slovak National Council Abroad*, October, 1957, pp. 3-4.

motivated by opportunism or misplaced idealism.[98] On February 7, 1944, Professor Vladimir Jershov of Russian origin, Second Lieutenant Gregorij Soloshenko of the Red Army, and the Slovak partisan leader Viliam Zingor agreed that ". . . all future partisan activities in Slovakia would follow instructions from Moscow." Operating under these instructions and supplied by air from the Ukraine, the partisans grew rapidly in number and strength and by midsummer of 1944 controlled sizeable areas in eastern and central Slovakia.[99]

The "Slovak Revolt" was launched by the partisans and not by the Slovak National Committee. Between August 25 and 28, 1944, Communist-led forces seized a number of towns in central Slovakia, including Turciansky Sv. Martin, Ruzomberok, Banska Bystrica, and Zvolen. On August 26, they waylaid a train containing a German military mission returning from Rumania, shooting the thirty German officers without ceremony. They also conducted massacres in Carpatho-German and mixed villages such as Deutsch Proben, Kremnitz, and Prievizda, where the Germans had lived for centuries and were on the best terms with the Slovaks. The entire male population of Glaserhau, one hundred strong, was forced to dig its own mass grave and was then mowed down with machine guns. Some four thousand Germans of Krickerhau escaped a similar fate by hiding in the coal mines.[100] The Slovak National Committee, seeing its hand forced by events, proclaimed the revolt officially on August 29 over the Banska Bystrica radio, constituting itself a "provisional government" and ordering general mobilization.

[98] See *Dokumentation der Vertreibung*, Vol. IV/1, pp. 158-59, and Vol. IV/2, Report No. 129; Jozef Lettrich, *History of Modern Slovakia*, pp. 198ff.; and Joseph A. Mikus, *La Slovaquie dans le Drame de l'Europe*, pp. 185ff. Additional sources are cited in *Dokumentation der Vertreibung*, IV/1, 159.

[99] U.S. House of Representatives, 83d Congress, Select Committee on Communist Aggression, *Special Report No. 8, Czechoslovakia*, Washington, 1954, pp. 13-14; *Dokumentation der Vertreibung*, Vol. IV/1, *loc. cit.*, and Vol. IV/2, Report No. 131. In evaluating the agreement of February 7 it should be remembered that a low rank in the Soviet army is frequently a cover for important espionage or infiltration functions. Major Viliam Zingor, who later turned against the Communist government of postwar Czecho-Slovakia, was executed on October 19, 1950.

[100] *Dokumentation der Vertreibung*, Vol. IV/1, pp. 160-64, and Vol. IV/2, Reports Nos. 129 and 131-35; "The 1944 Communist Revolt in Slovakia," *Slovakia*, September-December, 1957, pp. 28-34. For testimony of Rev. Joseph Poess, one of three survivors of the Glaserhau massacre, see Select Committee on Communist Aggression, 83d Congress, *Hearings*, pp. 1287-93.

For a few days the insurgents controlled much of central Slovakia, blocking the main east-west highways and railroads. Slovaks who opposed the revolt, especially priests and known anti-Communists, were hunted down and tortured or shot.[101] The real leaders of the revolt were Soviet commissars, the most prominent being Velichko, commander of the partisans from Kiev, and his deputies, Yegorov and Chernogorov. Slovaks who assisted them, including the Communists Dr. Gustav Husak and Laco Novomesky and the "liberals" Dr. Jozef Lettrich, General Mikulas Ferjencik, Dr. Martin Kvetko, and Dr. Samuel Bellus, were later rewarded with prominent roles in postwar politics.[102]

Except for a minority of leftists and anti-clerical "Czechoslovaks," the Slovak people remained loyal to their republic and to their president, Dr. Jozef Tiso. They did not want the revolt which the Communists and "liberals" had thrust upon them. An entire brigade of Slovak prisoners of war, which had been "reoriented" in the Soviet Union and then dropped by parachute to help the revolt, deserted en masse. Unlike many of their officers, the enlisted men of the Slovak army had little sympathy for the revolt, and executed the orders of insurgent commanders unwillingly or not at all. Loyal elements in the garrisons of Nitra and Trnava frustrated a plan to march on Bratislava. After German forces, whose help had been requested by President Tiso, opened a counteroffensive from that city on September 5, the revolt collapsed with but scattered resistance.

The Communist leaders knew that the revolt would fail—in fact, it was intended to.[103] But their plans to flee were upset when anti-Communist Slovaks burned the airplanes in which the commissars and their principal Slovak accomplices intended to escape to the Soviet Union. While most of the insurgent military units— whose rank and file had been shanghaied into the revolt

---

[101] For accounts of atrocities against Slovaks, see *Slovakia, loc. cit.*

[102] Philip A. Hrobak, "The Slovak Uprising of 1944," *Slovakia*, September-December, 1954, pp. 4-22.

[103] This is evident from the fact that a Russian advance which the insurgents had been led to expect was not forthcoming, while the Kremlin objected to assistance by the Western powers since Slovakia lay within the Soviet zone of operations. See Benes, *Memoirs*, p. 253, and Lettrich, *op. cit.*, pp. 210 and 212ff.

—surrendered without firing a shot, the hard core of the insurgents retreated into the forests, from which they emerged from time to time to plunder and to ravage. The Communist Karel Schmidke and the "liberal" General Mikulas Ferjencik went to Moscow to work out strategy for the future.[104] The "Slovak Revolt" of 1944 did, however, accomplish what Benes and the Communists intended: it destroyed the independence of the Slovak Republic. Until 1944, the Germans had interfered relatively little in Slovakia. But when President Tiso was forced to call for help they entered in full force, occupying the country until the Red Army drove them out in 1945. As Reitlinger comments: "The repression of the rebellion was from the beginning an SS affair."[105] This gave the Communists and their "liberal" collaborators an excuse to claim that the Slovak Republic had depended on Nazi support, and to smear as "Quislings" those Slovaks who had been politically active under the Tiso government.

---

[104] Hrobak, *loc. cit.*, pp. 17-22; statement of Dr. Joseph A. Mikus, Select Committee on Communist Aggression, *Tenth Interim Report*, Washington, 1954, pp. 163-65; Stephan Blasko, *Slovakia in Blood and Shackles*, New York, 1954, *passim; Slovak Newsletter*, August and September, 1949.

[105] Reitlinger, *op. cit.*, p. 392.

IV

TOTALITARIAN DEMOCRACY
1945-1948

THE "NATIONAL FRONT" IS ORGANIZED
IN MOSCOW

AFTER completing its investment of Subcarpathian Ruthenia, the advancing Red Army crossed the Eastern border of Slovakia on October 18, 1944. A German counteroffensive in the Budapest area delayed progress during November and December, but the Russian invasion of Slovakia was resumed in full force in January, 1945, and substantially completed by April 4, on which day forces of the "Second Ukrainian Front" under General Malinovsky captured Bratislava.

Under a Czechoslovak-Soviet agreement signed in London of May 8, 1944, Minister Antonin Nemec had followed Russian forces into Ruthenia as Czecho-Slovak "Commissioner." The agreement provided that: "As soon as any part of the liberated territory ceases to be a zone of direct military operations, the Czechoslovak Government takes over completely the power of administration of public affairs. . . ."[1] The Russians, however, never permitted Nemec to assume authority, and he was eventually forced to leave the area.

Undaunted by Russian failure to honor the agreement in Ruthenia—which the Kremlin was preparing to annex without waiting for formal Czecho-Slovak consent[2]

---

[1] For full text of agreement, see Margaret Carlyle, ed., *Documents on International Affairs, 1939-1946*, Vol. II, *Hitler's Europe*, London, 1954, pp. 321-22. A contemporary Russian comment appears in *Izvestia*, May 9, 1944, and is translated in *Soviet War News*, Soviet Embassy, London, May 10. Regarding Russian "violation" of this agreement, see Ivo Duchacek, *The Strategy of Communist Infiltration—The Case of Czechoslovakia*, New Haven, 1949, pp. 6-9.

[2] Benes' secretary, Edward Taborsky ("The Triumph and Disaster of Eduard Benes," *Foreign Affairs*, July, 1958, p. 680), speaks of the "Soviet rape of Ruthenia." The weight of evidence, however, indicates that Benes was prepared to cede Ruthenia without a struggle. As early as 1939 he told Soviet Ambassador Maisky (*Memoirs*, p. 139): "The question of Subcarpathian Ruthenia will be

—Dr. Benes and the majority of his ministers traveled from London to Moscow in March, 1945. Minister of Information and Deputy Foreign Minister Dr. Hubert Ripka remained in London to manage liaison with the Western Powers. He was joined in April by former mayor Dr. Petr Zenkl, of Prague, who had just emerged from a Nazi concentration camp and who assumed the presidency of the National Socialist party.[3] Dr. Benes arrived in Moscow with the intention of reorganizing the "government" to include Communist ministers, a plan which he and Gottwald had discussed during his Moscow visit of 1943, but which had been postponed until the cabinet should leave London for fear of alarming the British.[4] Benes is reported to have told his friends in London that if a Communist were appointed Minister of the Interior (controlling the police), it would mean that the Bolshevists were running the government.[5] In the Soviet capital, it was agreed that each party in the new "National Front" cabinet would have three ministers or ranking state secretaries. The Communists, however, obtained a double quota by dividing into "separate" Czech and Slovak Communist parties.[6] Of six "non-partisan technicians" appointed to the cabinet, two were Communists and two others were evidently considered "politically reliable," an assumption justified by their subsequent conduct.[7] The Communist

---

solved between us later and we will surely agree!" Dr. Michal Zibrin relates in his pamphlet, *Benes' Trip to Moscow and Czechoslovak Propaganda,* Chicago, 1954: ". . . When [Czecho-Slovak Ambassador] Fierlinger on behalf of his government submitted objections to what was going on in Ruthenia, Stalin wrote a letter to Benes on January 23, 1945. I was in the office of Ambassador Fierlinger in Moscow. In his letter, Stalin upbraided Benes, saying 'You yourself told me in Moscow of your willingness to give Ruthenia to the Soviet Union.' This quotation is according to the official Czech embassy record. Dr. Fierlinger himself assured me there that Stalin was right, and that Benes and his government in London were playing a comedy, because they were afraid of the consequences." The treaty ceding Ruthenia to the Soviet Union was signed in Moscow on June 29, 1945, by Fierlinger and Soviet Foreign Commissar Molotov.

[3] Ripka, *Czechoslovakia Enslaved,* p. 36 ; Jaksch, *Europas Weg nach Potsdam,* pp. 417-18. As Jaksch indicates, Zenkl had belonged to a preferred category of political hostages, who were exempt from forced labor and who enjoyed superior accommodations and food. Ripka states that "he was in excellent form ; he had lost none of his vitality and energy."

[4] *Memoirs,* p. 273.

[5] Louis Clair in *New York Call,* as quoted by *Slovenska Obrana,* Scranton, Pa., August 5, 1945.

[6] Ripka, *op. cit.,* pp. 29-30.

[7] The Communists in this category were Professor Zdenek Nejedly, Minister of Education, and Vlado Clementis, state secretary in the Foreign Ministry. The "nonpartisan" General Svoboda, who had proved a pliant instrument as commander of Czecho-Slovak troops in the U.S.S.R., supported the Communists in

party thus obtained control not only of the Ministry of Interior, but of those of Information (controlling the press and radio), Agriculture (in charge of redistribution of land), Social Welfare, and Education. With the aid of their "nonpartisan" supporters and left-wing Social Democrats such as Fierlinger and Lausman, they attained a working majority in the cabinet.[8]

The reorganized "government" then adopted a program which Dr. Ripka, writing in 1950 for a Western audience, attributes to the Politburo and describes as "a plot destined to permit the Communists to seize power immediately after liberation." The principal elements of this plan were the following:

1. As the principal instruments of Communist power, "National Committees" of "representatives of the people"—in fact local Soviets under Communist control—were to replace the traditional provincial, district, and local administrations. (The effect of this seeming decentralization was to subordinate ministerial control over local administration to that exercised by the Communist party.)

2. Autonomy for Slovakia, with a "parliament" (Slovak National Council) and a "cabinet" (Board of Commissioners), the objective being a Sovietized Slovak province. (Since the Slovaks rejected Communism decisively in the 1946 elections, the Communists shifted back to "Czechoslovak" centralism.)

3. Suppression of "several parties of the right, particularly the Czech Agrarians and the Slovak Catholic Populists, accused of having fascist tendencies and of having collaborated with the Germans." (The Agrarians were the largest Czech party and the Slovak Populists or Hlinka party, as we have seen, represented a majority of the Slovak nation.)

4. Uniting of all permitted political parties in a "National Front" coalition, with opposition parties prohibited. (General Eisenhower rejected a Soviet proposal for such an arrangement in the United States Zone of Germany as "not in accord with American concepts of democracy.")

5. "Punishments striking at traitors, collaborationists and Fascists," whereby the Communists "would be enabled to intimidate or suppress their political adversaries."

6. "The collectivization of the entire national economy . . . prefaced by the nationalization of industry and the banks and

the 1948 crisis, and remained in his post as Defense Minister until 1950. See Ripka, *op. cit.*, pp. 30, 278-80; Jaksch, *op. cit.*, pp. 389, 442. General Ferjencik's record is discussed in a subsequent section of this chapter.

[8] Ripka, *op. cit.*, pp. 29-32; Jaksch, *op. cit.*, p. 416; Jan Stransky, *East Wind Over Prague*, London, 1951, pp. 51-53; Philip A. Hrobak, ed., *Czecho-Slovakia, Victim of Communist Aggression* (collection of contemporary news articles), Middletown, Pa., 1945.

by a new agrarian reform. The unions, the co-operatives, the Sokols, the Boy Scouts, the gymnastic societies and various cultural institutions were to be unified—in other words, subjected to Communist control."
7. "Finally, alliance with the U.S.S.R. and the other Slav countries was to constitute, if not the only aim, at least the principal aim of our foreign policy."[9]

Explaining that this was a program for the bolshevization of Czecho-Slovakia, Ripka sums up: "In short, in the political, economic, military, and cultural domain, Czechoslovakia must follow in the wake of the U.S.S.R."

Since the leaders of the non-Communist parties in the National Front are now for the most part in the United States and other Western countries, where they hold most of the better positions available to "professional anti-Communists,"[10] one might suppose that they would have objected to this program or, if that were too risky, have kept silent about it. That such was not the case is indicated by the following quotations, selected from literally hundreds of similar news clippings:

. . . we deliberately intend to do all that we can to support these national committees and to establish them as the bearers of the national political will of the broad masses of the people. They shall become the firm constitutional foundation of our Republic. (*Pravo lidu*, official organ of Social Democratic party, Prague, June 13, 1945.)

. . . Our alliance with the Soviet Union is the main pillar of our security and our foreign policies, however, we will not fail to promote and strengthen our friendly ties with the Western Powers. . . Today I would like to call your attention mainly to the fact that we are living in a revolutionary age and thus we shall have to draw its extensive consequences in our policies. . . We pay homage to the Marxist doctrine and are aware of what constructive and useful work a policy based on Marxism has done, particularly for the working class. I stand side by side with those who sincerely and deeply desire closest cooperation with both the Communist and Social Democratic Parties. . . (Speech by Dr. Ripka, "Czecho-

---

[9] Outline based on Ripka, *op. cit.*, pp. 27-28. Material between quotation marks quoted verbatim; comments in parentheses supplied by author.

[10] See Slovak Liberation Committee, *Documents*, and Philip A. Hrobak, *"Czechoslovakism" Versus Americanism*, Middletown, Pa., 1953, both of which deal at length with the background and public statements of exiles in prominent "anti-Communist" positions. See also files of *Tschechischer Exilpressedienst* ["Czech Exile Press Service"] and *Informationsdienst Bohemia* ["Bohemia Information Service"—Czech], Munich and Cologne; and Czech periodicals *Narod* ["The Nation"] and *Narodni Demokrat* ["National Democrat"], Chicago, and *Krestanska Demokracie* ["Christian Democracy"], New York.

slovakia's Structural Changes," reported in *Svobodne Slovo*, June 20, 1945.)

. . . Those who are responsible for the wrongs, injustices and crimes against the people of Czechoslovakia must be punished for them. . . Naturally, when the law which deals with these crimes and criminals is passed, it will have to apply retroactively. (Jan Papanek, *Czechoslovakia*, New York, 1945.)

. . . The Democratic Party unreservedly accepts its share of responsibility in establishing complete state control of all productive work. (Dr. Fedor Hodza in Provisional National Assembly, November 14, 1945.)

Deviating forces shall be jailed. . . Deviating forces are today eradicated and liquidated. Today only the Democrats and Communists, and members of other political parties [of the National Front], bear the responsibility of determining which forces shall control Slovokia and in which direction Slovakia shall go. (Dr. Jozef Lettrich, *Cas*, Bratislava, No. 130, 1946.)

It is probably true that some of the non-Communist ministers had mental reservations about the program which Ripka correctly describes as a Communist plot. The fact is, however, that the entire cabinet, including the ministers carried over from London and those added in Moscow, put their signatures to the laws and decrees which carried it into effect—to the extent that they did not actually prepare them.[11] As we have seen, Benes had, as early as December, 1943, agreed to Points 1 ("National Committees") and 4 (the "National Front"), and had failed to object to Point 3 (suppression of conservative parties).[12]

THE KOSICE PROGRAM

The reorganized "government," with Benes as president and the leftwing Socialist Zdenek Fierlinger as premier,[13] followed the Red Army into Czecho-Slovakia

---

[11] The most important of these decrees are reprinted in English translation in W. K. Turnwald, ed., *Documents on the Expulsion of the Sudeten Germans*, Munich, 1953, Appendices VIIa to XIII; decrees affecting Slovakia alone are cited in Slovak Liberation Committee, *Documents*, pp. 29-30. A much fuller collection, in German, appears in *Dokumentation der Vertreibung der Deutschen aus Ost-Mitteleuropa*, Vol. IV/1, Appendices 2-21. According to Ripka, *loc. cit.*, "M. Jaroslav Stransky, Minister of Justice, had submitted to us an act on the punishment of traitors and collaborationists, striking first of all at the Sudeten Germans."

[12] Benes, *Memoirs*, pp. 270-71.

[13] Fierlinger was the Kremlin's choice. Ripka (*op. cit.*, p. 31) states: "We would have preferred to have Gottwald in the Premiership in order to avoid

—already truncated by the *de facto* detachment of Ruthenia. Benes and his ministers established temporary headquarters at Kosice in eastern Slovakia, where they began to exercise governmental functions. The question of whether, when, and in what areas this *de facto* government installed by the Russians became a legal government involves complex issues of international and constitutional law and political theory which cannot be discussed here. Diplomatic recognition is only one of many criteria.[14]

While in Kosice, the Benes government adopted the notorious Kosice Program of April 5, 1945. This was a detailed blueprint for the Sovietization of Czecho-Slovakia, some of its outstanding features being:

1. *A new "democratic antifascist" Czecho-Slovak Army patterned after the Red Army,* with "iron but democratic" military discipline. To facilitate joint operations, the organization, equipment, and training are to follow Soviet standards. To assure the necessary ideological link between the army and the people [Communist jargon for assuring control by the party], the concept of a "non-political" army, a "cloak for reactionary and anti-democratic tendencies," is to be abandoned. "Education officers" [politcommissars] are to be attached to each unit. The officer corps, purged of "anti-democratic" elements, is to be schooled in Soviet military experience; the Red Army will be requested to detail instructors, and as many Czecho-Slovak officers as possible will be sent to Soviet military academies.

2. *Alliance with the "victorious Slavic great power in the East" as the irrevocable guide line of Czecho-Slovak foreign policy.* Following a "Slavic line," Czecho-Slovakia will seek closer relations with other Slav states, but will also promote closer ties of "a new and really democratic Hungary" and "an independent and democratic Austria" with their Slav neighbors. Friendly relations with democratic Western Powers "in the anti-Nazi front of the United Nations" will be continued.

3. *Replacement of the traditional district and local administrations with popularly elected "National Committees,"* vested with police powers and supervising their own staffs of local officials. The National Committees are to administer all state laws and policies on the local level. [Organization and state-local relation-

any misunderstanding and to put the responsibility for their policy upon the Communists themselves."

[14] Raschhofer, *Die Sudetenfrage,* pp. 262-302; Korkisch, "Die verfassungsrechtliche Entwicklung in der Tschechoslowakei bis zur Verfassung vom 9. Mai 1948" ["Constitutional Law in Czechoslovakia to the Constitution of May 9, 1948"], *Zeitschrift für ausländisches Recht und Völkerrecht,* XIII, 670ff.; F. Durcansky, *The International Aspects of the Slovak Question,* pp. 23-35; Taborsky, *The Czechoslovak Cause in International Law, passim.*

ships are substantially the same as in the Soviet Union. The distinction between "self-government functions" and "delegated functions," normal in continental Europe, is replaced by the principle of "dual subordination," under which local officials are answerable both to the local deliberative body and to the corresponding officials on the higher administrative level. To operate without conflict, this system requires the mediating and disciplinary force of the Communist party. So long as the Communists have not completed their take-over, they can use the "autonomy" of local authorities to frustrate non-Communist administrators in the central government. The National Committees are in fact local *Soviets*—they have, since their first appearance, served as what Stalin calls "transmission belts" for the will of the Communist party.][15]

4. *The expulsion of Sudeten and Carpatho-Germans and Magyars.* Czecho-Slovak citizenship may be retained only by those Germans and Magyars who fought for Czecho-Slovakia *and* were either imprisoned in jails or concentration camps or, if they fled abroad "participated in the struggle for the restoration of Czechoslovakia." [This definition excluded the anti-Nazi Sudeten German Social Democrats, who were ready to support the Republic, but insisted on political rights for their national group.]

"The Czechoslovak citizenship of the other Czechoslovak German and Hungarian citizens will be cancelled. Although they may again express a choice for Czechoslovakia, public authorities will retain the right of individual decision. Those German and Hungarian transgressors who are under indictment for crimes against the Republic and the Czech and Slovak nations and who are condemned, will lose their citizenship and will be expelled from the Republic for ever—if not under sentence of death.

"Germans and Hungarians who immigrated into Czechoslovak territories after the Munich Pact in 1938 will, if not sentenced to capital punishment, be expelled from the Republic at once, except those persons who worked on behalf of Czechoslovakia."

5. *Prosecution and punishment* of "all war criminals, traitors, and active helpers of the German and Hungarian oppressors. The government will carry out its task without delay and will spare no one." German and Hungarian "war criminals" and lesser Czech and Slovak "traitors, collaborators and fascist elements" are to be tried before "Special People's Courts" [modelled after the People's Courts of the Soviet Union], attached to the National Committees [local Soviets]; major Czech and Slovak offenders are to be tried before National Courts. "The German and Hungarian culprits convicted will be handed over to Soviet organs."

---

[15] On February 3, 1944, shortly after his return from Moscow, Benes urged the formation of underground National Committees in Czecho-Slovakia. Their legal status was established in a constitutional decree of December 4, 1944, which was confirmed by the postwar cabinet on August 3, 1945. On local government in the U.S.S.R., see W. W. Kulski, *The Soviet Regime*, Syracuse, 1956, pp. 206-11; on "transmission belts," see Joseph Stalin, *Problems of Leninism*, 1926, Chapter V.

"Persons guilty of high treason, like Hacha, all members of the Beran Government who confirmed Hacha's so-called Berlin Pact of March 15, 1939, and those who welcomed Hitler when he arrived in Prague, will be brought before the National Court. The Government will take care that all members of the 'Protectorate' Government of March 16, 1939, Tiso and the members of the so-called Slovak Governments since March 14, 1939, as well as members of the so-called Slovak Parliament shall be brought before the court." [This provision would be unconstitutional in the United States, both as a "bill of attainder" and as an ex post facto law.] Those tried are to include the functionaries of all organizations active in the Protectorate or the Slovak Republic.

"Bankers, industrialists, and big land owners who helped the Germans to plunder the land and wage war will also be punished without mercy." [Since Czech industry and agriculture, and to a lesser extent those of Slovakia, had supported the German war economy, this provision served as a "death sentence" to private enterprise. Advance liquidation of the "class enemy" shortened the time necessary to complete the Bolshevist revolution.][16]

6. *Suppression of the Czech Agrarian, Tradesmen's and National Union Parties, the Hlinka Slovak People's Party, and those parties which joined the latter in 1938.* [By maintaining the fiction that all political activity after Munich was "treasonable," the Communists, with "liberal" assistance, were able to paralyze the organs most representative of the Czech and Slovak peoples.]

7. *Confiscation of the industrial and agricultural property of those who supported the German and Hungarian occupiers* [a definition which, as we have seen, included practically all businessmen and large land owners] *and of citizens of enemy countries.* [By declaring that German and Magyar inhabitants of the areas ceded in 1938 acquired Reich or Hungarian citizenship at the time, the Benes government established a "legal" basis for treating these people as "foreigners" when their homelands were reoccupied by Czecho-Slovakia.][17]

8. *A welfare state,* with social security "from the cradle to the grave," and state-operated workers' rest homes in the palaces and summer homes of the "foreign nobility and other parasitical gentry."

9. *An educational and cultural purge.* All German universities and schools are to be closed, and there is to be "a revision of our relation to German and Magyar culture through the exposure of

---

[16] As Jaksch points out (*op. cit.*, p. 425), the protectorate was a productive workshop for Hitler's war machine. Acceptance of Nazi war orders was, of course, compulsory, but there was little sabotage. Czech employers and workers took advantage of the boom: both industrial and farm productivity were higher than in the Reich itself. As in World War I, the Czechs as a whole did much more for the Central Powers than for the Allies. Benes, the Czech "liberals," and many Western "friends of Czechoslovakia" were taken in by the ideological master stroke of the Communists—shifting the burden of this "collective guilt" to the bourgeoisie.

[17] Annexation of a territory coupled with refusal to accept its inhabitants is unauthorized in international law and is a violation of elementary human rights. Raschhofer, *loc. cit.*

the reactionary elements contained therein. . ." Cultural policy will have a "Slavic orientation," with major emphasis on the U.S.S.R.: textbooks are to be purged of anti-Soviet content. New professorial chairs will be established: for Soviet history, economics, and law.[18]

The following ministers who came to the West as "anti-Communists" after February, 1948, signed the Kosice Program: General Mikulas Ferjencik, Antonin Hasal, Bohumil Lausman, Vaclav Majer, Dr. Adolf Prochazka, Dr. Hubert Ripka, and Dr. Jaroslav Stransky. They also signed a number of decrees carrying the Kosice Program into effect, such as that of May 19, 1945, confiscating the property of Germans, Magyars, and other "unreliable" elements, and the totalitarian "Retribution Decree" of June 19, 1945, which defined "crimes against the Republic" and established the detailed organization of the People's Courts.[19]

THE NATIONAL FRONT IN COMMUNIST STRATEGY

Apologists for the National Front often invoke the doctrine of the "lesser evil," according to which Benes, Ripka, Stransky, and the other non-Communist "liberals" had no practical alternative to co-operation with the Communists. Had they resisted Communist demands, it is contended, they would have been cast aside as ruthlessly as the London Polish government, which the Allies abandoned at Yalta.[20] It is further argued that the United States and Great Britain were remiss in consenting to Russian occupation of so much of Central Europe: since it was apparent that only Russian-approved governments could return to their homelands, the Czech politicians could hardly be blamed for making their peace with the

---

[18] The foregoing summary is based on the text of the Kosice Program (20 pages) given in *Dokumentation der Vertreibung der Deutschen aus Ost-Mitteleuropa*, IV/1, 184-203. Wording within quotation marks is directly translated; the comments in brackets are those of the author. Quotations in paragraphs 4 and 5 are based on the English translation given in Turnwald, *Documents on the Expulsion of the Sudeten Germans*, pp. 264-65 (Articles VIII and IX of Kosice Program).

[19] See note 11, *supra*.

[20] Jan Stransky (son of Minister Jaroslav Stransky), *East Wind Over Prague*, New York, 1950, pp. 51-53; see also Ripka, *op. cit.*, pp. 10-11.

Kremlin.[21] Benes' wartime secretary, Dr. Edward Taborsky, mentions "Benes' incessant endeavors to persuade the Anglo-Saxon Powers that they could cut themselves off from the fate of Central Europe only at their own gravest peril."[22]

This author is not prepared to defend the Roosevelt administration against the charge of having catered excessively to Russian demands during World War II. It must be added, however, that the influence of Benes and his associates was hardly such as to curb American pro-Sovietism. Although Benes did, during the period of the Hitler-Stalin Pact, utter some mild cautions against "exaggerated Sovietophile feelings and Communist propaganda" which Taborsky carefully cites,[23] they were but a trickle against the flood of pro-Soviet panegyrics which poured from his pen and those of his associates throughout the war.[24] If Benes had desired to warn Roosevelt against the dangers of Russian expansion in Central Europe, he had an excellent opportunity during his visit to Washington in May and June, 1943. What he actually said is apparent from his confidential summary of a five-hour conference held in the White House on May 13, 1943, which reads in pertinent part:

1. In regard to Russia the President's attitude is that it is necessary to trust Russia and also to continue to co-operate loyally and fully after the war. He wants to give practical expression to this by meeting Stalin soon and by discussing all questions with him quite frankly and realistically. For the time being please do not speak of this possibility.

2. Roosevelt also takes a realistic view of Polish-Soviet relations. At least he has succeeded in stopping any further polemics. But he is taking the right view of the difficulties on the Polish side and on the form of a solution of the Polish-Soviet frontier dispute. . . .

5. I informed the President about my negotiations with the Soviets and of their and our point of view for the regulation of our mutual relations in the form of a treaty—also of their assurance that they do not intend to interfere in our internal affairs

---

[21] Stransky, *loc. cit.*, relates that in March, 1945, the Czech Communists threatened that failure to reach agreement with them would result in establishment of a Soviet-sponsored "progressive" government, which "would not even negotiate with the London reactionaries."

[22] Taborsky, *op. cit.*, p. 679.

[23] *Ibid.*, p. 675.

[24] See, in particular, Hubert Ripka, *East and West*, London, 1944, and statements quoted therein.

and of their readiness in principle to come to an agreement with democratic Poland also. The President took note of this with visible satisfaction and *recognized that in our attitude to Russia we were proceeding on the right lines*.[25]

While Benes, who published his *Memoirs* in Prague in 1947, would hardly have included any reservations about Russian intentions which he might have expressed to the President, it seems certain that, had he disagreed with Roosevelt, he would have reported this interview somewhat differently. He also appears to have been willing to tell Stalin, on behalf of Roosevelt, that while the United States could not officially support Russian annexation of the Baltic republics, actually it would not interfere.

Although official Washington had for some time been adjusting itself to the prospect of Russian hegemony in east-central Europe,[26] it was at the Teheran Conference of November-December, 1943, that the switches were finally set for Red penetration in depth. This is true on two scores. Confirmation of the Casablanca policy of "unconditional surrender" promised to create a power vacuum in Central Europe which, for geographical reasons, the Russians were most likely to fill.[27] Secondly, rejection of Churchill's proposal for an Anglo-American expedition through Trieste into the Balkans in favor of the militarily unproductive invasion of southern France opened the road to the Red Army as far as Prague and Vienna.[28] Dr. Benes, who passed through Teheran on his way to Moscow, and who had "discussions with most of the participants in this conference," must have learned much more than is contained in the vacuous communiqué

[25] Benes, *Memoirs*, p. 193. (Emphasis supplied.)

[26] Robert Sherwood, *Roosevelt and Hopkins*, New York, 1948, pp. 748ff.; R. C. Snyder and E. S. Furniss, Jr., *American Foreign Policy*, New York, 1954, pp. 666-68.

[27] See F. O. Miksche, *Unconditional Surrender*, London, 1952, particularly chap. VIII (pp. 251-80); George F. Kennan, *American Diplomacy, 1900-1950*, Chicago, 1951, chap. V. The alternative to "unconditional surrender" was a peace which would have left Germany defeated and minus Hitler, but militarily intact. Such a peace would have kept Russia out of Central Europe, permitting orderly evacuation by the Germans and establishment of free governments.

[28] For an account of the Teheran Conference and its political consequences, see Georg Rauch, *A History of Soviet Russia*, New York, 1957, pp. 352-57. Stalin was particularly insistent that the Balkan project be abandoned. Roosevelt's military advisers, who often failed to appreciate the political aspects of the war, did not relish a campaign in difficult and remote terrain, and helped to swing the President to Stalin's view. General Mark Clark comments on this episode: "[Stalin] knew exactly what he wanted in a political and military way; and the thing he wanted most was to keep us out of the Balkans, which he had staked out for the Red Army." (*Calculated Risk*, New York, 1950, p. 370.)

released to the public. He sums up his reaction to Teheran as follows:

. . . So far as our country was concerned, the decisions on the whole coincided with our long pursued policy of securing first victory in the war and then a victorious peace—victorious for us as well as the others. *I therefore regarded the Teheran Conference as a great success,* and I moulded all my further discussions in Moscow as well as my later ones in London and our negotiations with the Americans to fit the results of Teheran. *This also covered the advance of the Soviet Army into Central Europe and on to our territory, which I regarded as a certainty*—especially after Teheran—though I did not exclude the possibility that the Western Allies would also try to reach it.[29]

Although veterans of the London "government" and the National Front would have us believe that they favored Anglo-American occupation of as much of Czecho-Slovakia as possible, the total behavior of Benes and his associates from 1943 to April, 1945, was such as to convey the impression that they welcomed "liberation" by the Red Army. This impression was, furthermore, entirely correct, since the exile cabinet was determined to carry out policies which required (a) the utter prostration of Germany, and (b) direct Russian military support.

Suppose, for a moment, that the London "government" had broken with the Kremlin after the Bolshevist treachery in connection with the August, 1944, Warsaw revolt —a break which would have strengthened Churchill's hand against the "soft" policy of Roosevelt, Hopkins, and Harriman.[30] Moscow would doubtlessly have responded by setting up a "people's democratic" regime analogous to its Polish "Lublin Government." This showdown, however, would probably have compelled a revision of Western military and political strategy, perhaps even including a compromise with Germany permitting Anglo-American occupation of the Danube Valley. Failure to obliterate Germany, however, would have precluded mass expulsion of the Sudeten Germans, and the presence of Western troops would have forced Benes

---

[29] *Memoirs,* p. 253, italics supplied. For Teheran summary agreement, see Baltzly and Salomone, *Readings in Twentieth-Century European History,* New York, 1950, pp. 504-5.

[30] See Winston Churchill, *Triumph and Tragedy,* Boston, 1953, pp. 287ff.

to seek agreement with the conservative resistance in Bohemia.[31] Without the Red Army, Benes could not have liquidated the Slovak Republic: an American commander would have insisted on political freedom for the Slovak people, most of whom supported the Tiso government.

It is true, therefore, that the politicians of the London "government" were forced to co-operate with the Communists, but for a reason which their apologists do not mention: *the policies of the London "government" itself made such co-operation inevitable.*

So far as the Kremlin is concerned, the non-Communist ministers of the National Front played an essential though temporary role. To allay Western suspicions and to assure undisturbed entry into Central Europe, Moscow kept its intention to create a chain of Communist satellites very much in the background. As a propaganda cover, used initially in all the European satellites, the Communists adopted the tactic of the "United Front," expounded by Georgi Dimitroff at the 1935 Congress of the Comintern, and successfully used to establish Communist control of the Republican government during the Spanish Civil War.[32]

A "United Front" government is defined as "a government of struggle against fascism and reaction," formed "on the eve of and before the victory of the Soviet revolution." Dimitroff describes the conditions necessary for the formation of such a government as follows:

First, the state apparatus of the bourgeoisie must already be sufficiently *disorganized* and *paralyzed*, so that the bourgeoisie cannot prevent the formation of a government of struggle against reaction and fascism;

Second, the broadest masses of toilers, particularly the mass trade unions, must be in a violent state of revolt *against fascism and reaction, though not ready* to rise in insurrection, to *fight*

---

[31] Pilsen, which was occupied by American troops from late April to October, 1945, was for that time the center of anti-Communist resistance in Czecho-Slovakia. See Jaksch, *op. cit.*, pp. 424ff.

[32] Proceedings of the Seventh World Congress of the Communist International, Moscow, July 25–August 20, 1935. Reprinted in U.S. House of Representatives, Committee on Un-American Activities, *The Communist Conspiracy, Strategy and Tactics of World Communism*, Part I, Section C (House Report No. 2242, 84th Congress, 2d Session), Washington, 1956, pp. 294-372. By liquidating large numbers of Trotskyites, Anarchists, and other dissidents, the Communists seriously weakened Republican manpower, thus facilitating the ultimate victory of the Nationalist army under General Franco.

under Communist Party leadership for the achievement of Soviet power;

Third, the differentiation and Leftward movement in the ranks of Social-Democracy and other parties participating in the united front must have already reached the point where a considerable proportion of them demand *ruthless measures against the fascists and the other reactionaries,* struggle together with the Communists against fascism, and openly come out against that reactionary section of their own party which is hostile to Communism.[33]

The "United Front" government is neither permanent nor an end in itself. It represents a transitional stage, during which "reactionaries" are liquidated and mass organizations brought under Communist control.[34] As Dimitroff explains:

Final salvation this government *cannot bring.* It is not in a position to overthrow the class rule of the exploiters, and for this reason cannot finally eliminate the danger of fascist counter-revolution. Consequently it is necessary *to prepare for the socialist revolution!* Soviet power and *only* Soviet power can bring such salvation![35]

Confirming the transitional nature of the "United Front," the Congress declared that: "The establishment of the united front of the working class is the decisive link in the preparation of the toilers for the forthcoming great battles of the second round of proletarian revolution."[36]

The situation which promised to obtain in Czecho-Slovakia upon "liberation" by the Soviets, with thousands whipped to frenzy by propaganda from both London and Moscow, seemed made to order for a "United Front," of which the Czecho-Slovak National Front was a prime example. Certainly Benes, Ripka, and their colleagues must have been familiar with the speeches of Comrade Dimitroff and therefore have known what was to follow. The one excuse which has *not* been made on behalf of the National Fronters is that they walked into the situation with their eyes shut!

---

[33] Report of Georgi Dimitroff, August 2, 1935, *ibid.,* pp. 321-22. (Italics in original.)

[34] Resolution on the Report of Georgi Dimitroff, August 20, 1935, Part II, *ibid.,* pp. 351-55.

[35] Dimitroff Report, *ibid.,* p. 325.

[36] Resolution on Dimitroff Report, Part VII, *ibid.,* p. 360.

WHY THE RUSSIANS "LIBERATED" PRAGUE

The foregoing ideological digression gives us the background to understand the situation which arose in the spring of 1945, when Russian and American forces approached Bohemia from opposite directions. Both the Russians and their Czech friends in London wanted to avoid the establishment of a postwar government in Prague under Western auspices, since they feared that the free decision of the Czech people might go against them. Benes, Jan Masaryk, and, after their departure, Ripka, took pains to assure the Western Allies that Czecho-Slovakia would not "go Soviet," while the Russian envoys, Bogomolov and Gusev, importuned United States Ambassador Winant to assure that the Red Army would be allowed to capture Prague.[37]

Churchill, already suspicious of Russian intentions, cabled on April 1, 1945, to President Roosevelt, urging that Western troops move as far eastward as possible. But the President felt that raising a political issue on the eve of victory was an "unfortunate reaction." A few days later, the British Chiefs of Staff urged that General Eisenhower be directed to take Berlin. But their American counterparts replied that strategy would have to be determined by "imperative military considerations," namely the destruction and dismemberment of the German armed forces.[38] President Roosevelt's death on April 12, 1945, and Mr. Truman's need to learn what Roosevelt had failed to tell him about European politics and America's secret commitments, paralyzed temporarily Washington's ability to make fundamental political decisions.

[37] See statements of Benes and Ripka in the *New York Times*, February 20, and April 15, 1945, respectively; also *News Flashes from Czechoslovakia, passim.* Bogomolov was Soviet ambassador to the occupied powers, while Gusev had replaced Maisky as Soviet ambassador to the United Kingdom; information on their activities developed in interview with a former member of the London "government." The emotionally unstable Winant, our member of the tripartite European Advisory Commission charged with postwar planning, was no match for his hard-boiled Russian counterpart. After the American public had been lulled into the belief that Western forces would occupy Germany as far as the Oder (see map in *Newsweek,* April 10, 1944), Winant consented to a demarcation line which gave Russia not only East Germany (now under U.S.S.R./Polish administration) but Central Germany as well (the present Soviet Zone).

[38] Forrest C. Pogue (of Office of Chief of Military History, United States Army), "Why the Russians Got Berlin and Prague," *Journal of Modern History,* Vol. XXIII, No. 4, December, 1951. Dr. Pogue incorporated the information contained in this article in his book, *The Supreme Command* (Vol. IV of *The United States Army in World War II*), Washington, 1954, pp. 500ff.

On April 24, the Russian command accepted General Eisenhower's proposal that Western forces advance as far as the Elbe and Mulde rivers in Germany. General Antonov, Acting Chief of Staff of the Red Army, added that the Soviets proposed to take Berlin and the Moldau River Valley in Bohemia, including Prague. Since the American Third Army was approaching the Bohemian border, the British Chiefs of Staff urged the political advantage of liberating Prague and as much of Czecho-Slovakia as possible. General Marshall, however, cabled to General Eisenhower: "Personally and aside from all logistic, tactical, or strategic implications I would be loath to hazard American lives for purely political purposes." Eisenhower replied: "I shall *not* attempt any move I deem militarily unwise merely to gain a political advantage unless I receive specific orders from the Combined Chiefs of Staff."[39]

Although President Hacha's government of the Bohemia-Moravia Protectorate, which had functioned under Nazi supervision since March, 1939, was a puppet regime powerless to prevent the Gestapo's brutalities, it does not follow that it was a Quisling or traitor government. Like all Czechs, Hacha and his ministers were prisoners. Hacha refused to declare war against the Allies, telling the Germans: "You deprived me of all power and I have nothing to declare."[40]

As the Red Army advanced through Slovakia and the Western armies swept across Germany, Hacha considered how to get the Reich Germans out of Bohemia and Moravia without major battles which would have devastated the country. The problem was complicated by the fact that Karl H. Frank, the Nazi Protector, could not make up his mind to evacuate the thousands of Reich citizens who were crowding Prague.[41] Members of his staff, how-

---

[39] Pogue, *loc. cit.* For a psychological explanation of the "delusion . . . of total victory" which blinded American statesmen and soldiers to political realities, see Kennan, *op. cit.*, chaps. V and VI.

[40] V. L. Borin, *Against the Hangman*, London, 1951, p. 11.

[41] Neither Hacha nor conservative members of the resistance wished to deport the Bohemian Germans, of whom 41,700 lived in Prague in 1930. Officials of the Reich Protectorate authorities and of Nazi military and economic agencies and their families, however, together with 50,000 patients in eighteen military hospitals and a recent stream of refugees from the East had swelled the German population to 200,000 by April, 1945. Plans to evacuate these people were not put in effect until it was too late. See *Dokumentation der Vertreibung*, IV/1, 51-53.

ever, had for some time been holding secret talks with Hacha's associates and with underground leaders who opposed both Nazism and Communism. Their plan was to turn over power to a conservative and pro-Western Czech government, whereupon German forces would leave the protectorate. Although such a step would have provoked a clash of Western and Russian war aims, it met with no favor when Frank proposed it in Berlin early in 1945.[42] In mid-April, the Hacha cabinet suggested directly to Frank that he relinquish his powers to the protectorate government. The *Reichsprotektor*, with Hitler's last vain boast of a new "wonder weapon" ringing in his ears, was at first inclined to clap them in jail. During the next several days, however, he reconsidered.[43] Although General Schörner's large army remained intact, it would be impossible to beat off the Russians and Americans at once. At Frank's suggestion, the Czech General Klecanda made an unsuccessful effort to contact the Allied high command, with the objective of negotiating an agreement whereby the German army and administration could leave without bloodshed.[44]

At the end of April, the Czech National Committee, organized secretly by officers and civilians not compromised by service under the Nazis, appeared in the open. The *Wehrmacht* began to withdraw westward and the committee prepared to assume power as a Czech government, instructing the people not to attack the Germans, who were leaving in any case. Prague was vacated, except for a rear guard and a number of hospital patients. On April 30, Mr. Bienert, premier under Hacha, and Manager Vambersky of the Skoda Works arrived at

---

[42] Jaksch, *op. cit.*, p. 419.

[43] Jaksch, *loc. cit.*, describes Frank's visit to Hitler on April 16, 1945. The Führer, unwilling to lose "the arsenal of the Reich," rejected anew Frank's plan for an agreement with the Czechs, adding that he proposed to "bring about the decision of the war" within three weeks. Frank was so impressed with Hitler's talk of a new weapon that he suspended the evacuation of German civilians. A few days later, Speer notified Frank that Hitler was leaving matters in Bohemia to the latter's judgment. Frank then realized that the choice was between leaving Prague peacefully or being thrown out.

[44] *Czech Press Service*, London, May 1, 1945; *Denni Hlasatel*, Chicago, May 3, 1945; Defense speech of General Vladimir V. Klecanda before the National Court at Prague, August 2, 1946 (Czech manuscript). Klecanda reached the Swiss border, but the Swiss authorities would not permit him to proceed further. He was accused of treason because of this trip, but convinced the court that he had acted in the interest of the Czech people and was acquitted. Threatened after his acquittal with a court-martial, he committed suicide.

United States forward headquarters and asked for American protection of the Czech nation.[45] The same day, Churchill cabled to President Truman:

"There can be little doubt that the liberation of Prague and as much as possible of the territory of Western Czechoslovakia by your forces might make the whole difference to the post-war situation in Czechoslovakia, and might well influence that in nearby countries. On the other hand, if the Western Allies play no significant part in Czechoslovakian liberation that country will go the way of Yugoslavia.

"Of course, such a move by Eisenhower must not interfere with his main operations against the Germans, but I think the highly important political consideration mentioned above should be brought to his attention."[46]

American protection of the Czech nation was exactly what the Communists and "liberals" of the Kosice government did not want. Should a home-grown regime assume power peacefully in Prague, the best that could be achieved would be a compromise, whereby conservative elements would retain substantial power. Something had to be done to wreck the Czech National Committee. In the Prague area, a Communist-dominated "Revolutionary Council" made preparations for an armed revolt, *which was totally unnecessary for ridding Bohemia of the German army.* By forcing the Germans to turn and fight, the Communists could prevent a peaceful transfer of power, make investment of Prague militarily unattractive to the Americans, and at the same time provide a "justification" for Russian "liberation" of the city.

On May 1, Dr. Ripka, who was still in London, commandeered the Czecho-Slovak service of the BBC. Alternating in shifts with the Communist deputy Hodinova-Spurna for ten hours, he harangued the people of Prague to mount the barricades and help the glorious Red Army which was coming to liberate them. But the attempt to make a revolution by radio did not work. The city remained quiet and, on May 5, the Czech National Committee went on the air in Ceske Budejovice, announcing

[45] *Czech Press Service*, May 1, 1945; Stransky, *op. cit.*, pp. 112-15; Ripka, *Czechoslovakia Enslaved*, pp. 35-38. Last sentence based on consensus of information from Czech sources. Reports of this episode conflict (see Jaksch, *loc. cit.*), but it seems clear that while Klecanda failed to make contact with the Americans, Bienert and Vambersky did reach them but obtained no satisfaction.

[46] Churchill, *Triumph and Tragedy*, p. 506.

an agreement for peaceful withdrawal of the Germans.[47] In the meantime, United States forces had entered western Bohemia and had penetrated to the Plzen-Karlsbad line, if not farther.[48] When, on May 4, General Eisenhower offered to advance to the Elbe and the Moldau, thus bringing the Americans into Prague, General Antonov made strong objections. As the Russians claimed that they had held back in northern Germany at American request, Eisenhower agreed not to proceed beyond Plzen.[49]

Since a non-Communist Czech government, which did not even call itself "Czechoslovak," was coming into being without American assistance, the Russians intervened directly. Communist agents, strengthened by reinforcements dropped by parachute, seized Radio Prague and proclaimed an uprising, shouting their slogan *Smrt nemeckym occupantum!* ("Kill the German occupiers!") over the loud-speakers on the street corners. This time the people, who were in a high state of nervous tension, turned out *en masse* and attacked German installations. The departing Germans returned to rescue their rear guard, and an SS armored division, which was bypassing Prague, moved in to clear the city. Although Reich Protector Frank had been willing to turn over his powers to a conservative Czech government, he refused to surrender to the "Revolutionary Council." The Czech National Committee was not able to cope with

---

[47] *Czech Press Service*, May 7, 1945, plus information developed by investigation.

[48] Jaksch (*op. cit.*, p. 418) reports that American troops had reached the Pisek-Beraun-Rakonitz line, within twenty to forty miles of Prague, from which they later *retreated* to agreed positions. Dr. Otakar Machotka, vice-chairman of the leftist "Revolutionary Council," later stated that reports to this effect were falsified and were circulated to facilitate "an overturn for the benefit of a certain group by the grace of the German Minister of State, who desired to resign in favor of a new Czech government." (Interview, *Svobodne Slovo*, May 3-11, 1946, cited in *Dokumentation der Vertreibung*, IV/1, 54-55.) Official publications are remarkably silent on how far United States troops really did advance. As late as March, 1956, Major General John A. Klein, the Adjutant General, informed the author that access to the pertinent Army files could not be permitted since they "are predominantly security classified and no downgrading action is practicable at this time." It seems clear, however, that between April 30 and May 5, if not later, United States forces could have entered Prague without interference. The author has interviewed a member of Patton's army who, with several others (but without permission), drove to Prague in a jeep and returned safely to the American lines.

[49] Pogue, *loc. cit.* As Pogue observes, Eisenhower was anxious to occupy Lübeck on the Baltic in time to keep the Russians out of Denmark. Actually, the Russians advanced so slowly along the coast that they could hardly have reached Lübeck before Western forces, even if they had so desired. See map of situation at end of April, 1945, in Chester Wilmot, *The Struggle for Europe*, New York, 1952, p. 701.

the German *Wehrmacht,* nor with the Communists and their allies, who were operating under exact instructions.[50] A renewed Czech appeal for American entry into Prague brought only negative results.[51]

The nature of the Prague uprising was later made clear by Dr. Otakar Machotka, vice-chairman of the "Revolutionary Council," who explained that the revolt had been launched two days ahead of schedule to frustrate the establishment of a Czech government with German consent.[52] A similar picture is given by a participant in the uprising, who told the author:

"Complete plans had been made for establishing an independent provisional government, which would take over on the departure of the Germans. Its leaders were not active in public office during the Protectorate and therefore not to be classed as 'collaborators' of the Nazis. This group had sent Klecanda and Vambersky to contact the Americans and ask for United States occupation of Prague. They were not negotiating with the Germans, but they did not advocate attacking the Germans, since Prague would be rid of them in any case without bloodshed in a few days. The military adviser of this group was General Kutlvasr, who took command in Prague after the uprising started and tried to make the best of a bad situation.

"The uprising, instigated by the Communists, completely upset the plans for the provisional Czech government. Since the Communists were the only ones who had clear instructions, this tactic permitted them to infiltrate themselves into the National Committees—not to be confused with the Czech National Committee—which the Communists themselves took the initiative in forming. The Communists kept this tactic so secret that neither I nor any of my non-Communist friends knew about it."

[Author's question:] "What started the fighting?"

[Answer:] "The fighting started simultaneously in a number of places after the broadcast which I mentioned."

[Question:] "Was the fighting necessary?"

[Answer:] "It was absolutely unnecessary, because the Germans had only one interest: to get to the west to surrender to the Americans. The only reason they intervened in Prague was

[50] Pogue, *loc. cit.*; *Czech Press Service,* May 7, 1945; Edward L. Delaney, *False Freedom,* Los Angeles, 1954, pp. 83-100.

[51] The *Third Army Intelligence Report,* one of the few documents which has been "downgraded" (unpublished: AG Records Center, Alexandria, Virginia), contains the following entry: "5 May 1945: Five representatives of Czech underground stated they had driven from Prague through Pilsen; that Czech partisans controlled Pilsen, where German garrison confined in barracks. Partisans also reported that German commander of Prague stated he would not fire on US troops but refuses to surrender to partisans."

[52] Interview cited in note 48.

to rescue their own forces and to protect the line of retreat for units still to the east of Prague."
[Question:] "Did you see any Russian officers?"
[Answer:] ". . . On the 7th I saw a crowd of armed civilians gathered around a major of the Soviet Army in Soviet uniform who was making a speech in Russian about the eternal brotherhood of the Czech and Soviet peoples. He stated that he had been parachuted several days before, that 'his unit' had gotten everything under control, and that the Red Army group of Marshal Koniev would arrive in a matter of hours."[53]

During the course of May 6, the SS cleared the barricades in most of Prague at a cost of at least two thousand killed and some forty thousand wounded. While this was going on, the Communist-controlled radio broadcast appeals in Russian for reinforcement from NKVD headquarters in Kiev, and appeals in English for American help, which the Communists were reasonably sure would not be forthcoming.[54] Dr. Ripka in London—who according to contemporary observers had up to that point taken a dim view of American intervention in Bohemia —now joined the chorus, asking for American entry into Prague on May 6 and again two days later.[55] On May 7, the Russian Vlassov Army, which the Germans had organized from Soviet prisoners of war, turned against the *Wehrmacht:* the Germans resorted to aerial bombardment of partisan strongholds, with heavy civilian casualties. By this time the Czech National Committee was thoroughly disorganized, and the Communist-dominated "Czechoslovak Revolutionary Council" had control of the situation.

Despite renewed Czech appeals and a telegram from Churchill to General Eisenhower, United States headquarters honored its commitment to the Russians to stay west of the Plzen-Karlsbad line.[56] On the evening of

---

[53] Confidential interview. For similar accounts, see Emil Franzel, "Prag im Mai 1945," *Die Welt* (Hamburg), May 4, 5, and 6, 1950; also Olga von Barenyi, "It Started With Red Paint, a Czech Eyewitness Report of the Prague Revolution," *Sudeten Bulletin*, Munich, May, 1955.

[54] These broadcasts were reported in detail by the *Czech Press Service*, May 7, 1945, and were also heard by the informant cited in note 53. See also Jaksch, *op. cit.*, p. 420.

[55] Pogue, *loc. cit.*; Ripka, *op. cit.*, pp. 36-37. It should be noted that Ripka did not appeal for Western assistance until *after* Radio Prague had done so.

[56] Churchill, *op. cit.*, p. 442. The fact that American inaction was at Russian insistence did not prevent the Communists from exploiting it in anti-American propaganda. Bartosek-Pichlik, *Hanebna role amerikych okupantu v zapadnich Cechach v roce 1945* ["The Disgraceful Role of the American Occupants in West-

May 8, German evacuation began under an agreement with the "Revolutionary Council" calling for safe conduct in exchange for the surrender of weapons.[57] The following morning, the first forces of Marshal Koniev arrived in Prague after a forced march from eastern Saxony, and all promises to permit peaceful German withdrawal were quickly forgotten. By May 10, the Red Army had "liberated" the city: the Communist leader Gottwald and the fellow-traveling Premier Fierlinger appeared on the scene immediately thereafter. Their first step was to make sure that the Czech National Committee would have no part in the Czecho-Slovak government.[58]

Dr. Benes and certain of his apologists later contended that they had always hoped for Western rather than Russian occupation of Czecho-Slovakia. Taborsky criticizes "the reluctance of the Anglo-Saxon powers to assume adequate responsibility and to assert their proper influence in Central and Eastern Europe," and gives a dramatic account of Benes' elation over the news that General Patton's forces had entered Bohemia.[59] Confirming what Taborsky describes as his "bitterest disappointment" at the order that Patton halt at Plzen, Benes later told Bruce Lockhart that the decision not to advance was a "great and perhaps decisive misfortune. . . Neither then nor now was this decision comprehensible to him."[60]

While there is no reason to doubt that Benes exclaimed "Thank God!" when Taborsky informed him of the American advance, or that his feelings expressed to Lockhart were sincere at the time, attempts to project this attitude backward constitute an *ex post facto* revision of history. The essential point is not what Benes said privately after having tasted Russian methods of political control, but what the Czecho-Slovak "exile gov-

---

ern Bohemia in 1945"], Prague, 1951, asserts that the United States deliberately halted its advance to give the Nazi General Schoerner time "to suppress the wave of revolution which arose throughout the land upon the entry of the Soviet Army."

[57] A German text of this agreement, translated from *Mlada Fronta* of June 2, 1945, appears in *Dokumentation der Vertreibung*, Vol. IV/1, p. 59.

[58] Ripka and Stransky, *loc. cit.*

[59] Taborsky, *op. cit.*, p. 680.

[60] Cited by Jaksch, *op. cit.*, pp. 443-44.

ernment" stated to the Allies at a time when revisions of political and military strategy were still possible. Considering the entire record, including that recounted by Benes in his *Memoirs*, the Western Powers had no reason to believe that the Czechs were in any way dissatisfied with the prospect of Russian "liberation." And indeed, as we have seen, such "liberation" was a *sine qua non* for the fulfillment of their chauvinist aspirations.

GENOCIDE AGAINST THE SUDETEN GERMANS

In seeking Allied support for his plan to expel the Sudeten Germans and Magyars from a Czecho-Slovakia restored to its pre-1938 boundaries, Dr. Benes emphasized repeatedly that the "transfers of population" would be "carried out, so far as possible, universally, decently and humanely." He summarizes his argument to both the Western Powers and the Russians as follows:

> Though this would mean a grave and long drawn-out crisis for the persons actually involved, it would nevertheless provide *a better and more humane solution than fresh inhuman massacres in the post-war period through outbreaks of civil war and brutal vengeance causing the continuation of nationality struggles for centuries* thus frustrating again and again the social and economic progress of mankind. Moreover, the transfer could be closely controlled and co-ordinated and could be carried out under decent and humane conditions.[61]

The statements of Benes and his associates to the Czech people, however, were such as to make a "humane" expulsion—if such a thing can be imagined—virtually impossible. Summarizing a radio speech broadcast on October 27, 1943, Benes wrote:

> In our country the end of this war will be written in blood. The Germans will be given back mercilessly and manifold everything that they have committed in our lands since 1938. The whole nation will be caught up in this struggle, there will be no Czechoslovak who does not take part in this task and there will be no patriot who does not take just retribution for the suffering the nation has experienced.[62]

---

[61] Benes, *Memoirs*, p. 222 (italics in original). Benes has the temerity to claim in a footnote that the expulsion actually was carried out humanely with the exception of "some, very few excesses which were unworthy of the country of Masaryk," which he condemned "publicly and categorically."

[62] *The Central European Observer*, London, XX, No. 22, November 12, 1943, 353.

On returning from Moscow in February, 1944, Benes declared to the exile "Council of State": "The revolution [in Czecho-Slovakia] must be violent. It must be a violent people's reckoning with the Germans and the fascist thugs, a bloody, merciless struggle."[63] General Ingr, commander of the Czecho-Slovak forces abroad, adjured his compatriots:

When our day comes, the whole nation will apply the old Hussite battle cry: "Beat them, kill them, leave none alive." Everyone should look around now for the appropriate weapon to harm the Germans most. If there is no firearm at hand, any other kind of weapon that cuts or stabe or hits should be prepared and hidden.[64]

Although President Roosevelt and the British War Cabinet had tentatively approved a transfer of *some* Sudeten Germans, Benes had reason to doubt that the Western Allies—once relieved of the pressure of war and to the extent that they had a choice in the matter —would permit the indiscriminate total expulsion which he had in mind.[65] He was probably aware that the American State Department, although it did not consider it "expedient" to oppose general population transfers, preferred a minimal and "selective" movement of Germans.[66] Foreign Minister Eden had rejected flatly Benes' "Ten-Point Plan" of November, 1944, stating that a decision on the Sudeten Germans would have to be part of a general postwar settlement.[67] Benes and Ripka therefore adopted the tactic of the *fait accompli,* playing heavily on the propaganda theme of German collective guilt and inciting to individual acts of violence. Their attempts to generate a "spontaneous" popular uprising against the Germans were abetted by the Communists, who were determined to reap the benefits of intensified hatred between Czechs and Germans. Lon-

---

[63] Quoted in *Einheit* (published by Sudeten German Communists), London, No. 4, February 12, 1944.

[64] *News Chronicle,* London, November 4, 1944.

[65] Jaksch, *op. cit.,* pp. 400-406, 414, cites extensive British criticism of the proposed expulsion. See also "Two Versions of Non-Predetermination," in Chapter IX, *infra.*

[66] *Foreign Relations of the United States, The Conferences at Malta and Yalta, 1945,* Washington, 1955, briefing papers on Germany (January 12, 1945) and Poland (undated), pp. 189-90 and 232-34.

[67] See "Planning the Expulsion of the Sudeten Germans," in chap. III, *supra.*

don and Moscow broadcast simultaneously the National Front's proclamation of February 26, 1945: "Attack the accursed Germans and kill the occupants! Punish the traitors, and force cowards and saboteurs of the national struggle to be silent!"[68]

1. MASSACRES IN PRAGUE AND CENTRAL BOHEMIA

The broadcasts over Radio Prague which began on May 5, 1945, were not merely a call to armed revolution against the *Wehrmacht* and the *Reichsprotektor* but an incitement to mob violence against the defenseless German civilian population. Those who survived shudder when they recall a certain *agent provocateur*, whose frequent harangues during the several days of the revolt caused the rabble to shed every civilized inhibition. "Kill the Germans wherever you find them!" this agitator would urge in macabre tones. "Every German is our mortal enemy. Have no mercy on women, children, or the aged! Kill every German—wipe them out!"[69]

Almost as soon as the revolt broke out, the Revolutionary Guard—consisting of every Czech who cared to join —began rounding up the Germans and herding them into schools, cinemas, and barracks. Few were permitted to take any food with them, and almost none was provided in the internment centers. Conditions were worst in the cinemas, which in Prague are mostly underground and which were packed far beyond their normal capacity—men, women, and children were forced to sit in artificial light for several days, almost suffocating from the lack of air. From time to time, prisoners were ordered out to remove the barricades—while working on the streets they were beaten, whipped, tarred, and in many cases murdered. Many committed suicide in desperation. After the entry of the Red Army, the

[68] *Einheit*, No. 5, March 10, 1945. See also Jaksch, *op. cit.*, p. 426.

[69] Günter Karweina, "Prag, die blutige Stadt" ["Prague, City of Blood"], *Neue Illustrierte*, Köln, November 1, 1958, pp. 49-59. There are numerous similar published accounts. See, for instance, Franzel, *loc. cit.*; Jürgen Thorwald, *Das Ende an der Elbe* ["Finale on the Elbe"] Stuttgart, 1950, pp. 300ff; and "Hinter den Kulissen von 'Free Europe'" ["Behind the Scenes in Radio Free Europe"], *Sudetendeutsche Zeitung*, February 19, 1955.

Germans were transferred to large collection camps such as the Strahov Stadium where over ten thousand were housed, the Riding Academy, and the Slavia Stadium. Here they were kept on a starvation diet—with Russian soldiers admitted every night to rape the women and girls—until their further transfer to forced farm labor or concentration camps.[70]

It must be emphasized that the mistreatment of the Germans was *not* an act of the entire Czech people. Like the Nazi extermination of the Jews, it was the crime of a small minority. Czech patriots who had resisted Nazism at the risk of their lives were the strongest objectors to Nazi methods employed by their own countrymen. Some paid for their convictions in prison, since any attempt to help a German was branded "collaboration." Other Czechs, while they refrained from active atrocities, were cowed by the master propagandist's dictum: "Death to anyone who protects the Germans!"[71]

Every nation, including our own, has its rabble element: the human nullities who stage lynchings and pogroms or become storm troopers, venting their spleen in the anonymity of the mob. The most vicious among the Prague rabble were precisely those who had licked the boots of the Nazis, and who sought to clear themselves by last-minute "partisan" activity. They were lions against the German civilians in the absence of an effective *Wehrmacht,* but their courage sagged when General Schörner's troops began to reoccupy the city. The master agitator of Radio Prague therefore invented some atrocities. "The SS is nailing children to the wall!" he cried. "The SS is burning the Hradcany Castle. They have filled a merry-go-round in Pankrac with murdered Czech children!"[72]

The atrocity stories told over the Prague radio were pure fiction. Although the SS had been one of Hitler's primary instruments of liquidation, its concern during the Prague revolt was to extricate the Germans with as

---

[70] *Dokumentation der Vertreibung,* IV/1, 60-65.

[71] *Ibid., loc. cit.* and Vol. IV/2, pp. 133ff, 150; Jaksch, *op. cit.,* pp. 425-26; Karweina, *loc. cit.*

[72] *Dokumentation der Vertreibung,* Vol. IV/1, p. 55, Vol. IV/2, p. 110; Karweina, *loc. cit.*

few casualties as possible, an aim which would not have been served by indiscriminate murder or arson. The reputation of the SS, however, lent plausibility to the stories, and in the atmosphere of excitement the masses believed them without question. Enraged at the supposed wanton brutality of the SS, the mob—now joined by those spurred by vengeance rather than pure sadism —began to *do* to the Germans what they had been *told* the SS was doing to the Czechs. It is reported that the perpetrator of this psychological coup, the anonymous agitator who has been justly called "the real butcher of Prague," was not a Communist but a "liberal" National Fronter.[73]

The results of this unconscionable hatemongering, which represent the climax if not the catastrophe of Dr. Benes' politics, are best described by the victims, whose sworn affidavits have been collected in the "Sudeten German White Book."[74] The following condensed excerpts represent typical rather than extreme cases. The author has, in fact, censored out certain gory details, to avoid turning the stomachs of his readers.

Report of the physicist K. F.—Prague: "Partisans crowded in from the street and drove some 30 men to Weinberg Avenue to clear away the barricades. . . . After the first hour we were all covered with blood, as a result of kicks and blows upon the head and the neck. Everything from shovels, iron bars and lead pipes up to poles was used on us.

"Our shoes were taken away from us and we had to walk barefoot over the glass splinters on the ground . . . and afterward were driven to work again, where everything started once more.

"[That evening] we were loaded in a lorry and driven to a former German college at Stefansgasse 22. All our belongings were left behind and we never saw any of them again. In the college we were forced to stand against the wall with our hands raised until one after another collapsed. We were then taken to another room where what they called the 'Gestapaci' were kept. There were about 50 of us. We were ordered to hit each other in the face and when that was not carried out to the full satisfaction

[73] Karweina, *loc. cit.*; *Sudetendeutsche Zeitung,* February 19, 1955. Students of mass psychology are familiar with the phenomenon of "transference," whereby members of a crowd believe that they have seen what has only been told to them. See Gustave LeBon, *Psychology of the Masses* (originally published Paris, 1895), chap. II, Section 2.

[74] Wilhelm K. Turnwald, ed., *Documents on the Expulsion of the Sudeten Germans,* Munich, German edition 1951, English (abridged) edition 1953. A number of statements in this volume also appear in Vol. IV/2 of *Dokumentation der Vertreibung.* The authenticity of this documentation is of the highest order.

of our jailers, we were shown how to do it properly. When I collapsed again, a burning match was held to my toes until I came to. Then I had to get up again. The second time I was permitted to lie a little longer. Then they trampled on my face, but since there was still no reaction on my part, I was left lying there. Anyone who put up the slightest resistance was shot dead.

"The afternoon of May 10th, a group of armed men came in and selected the six youngest and strongest men, I being one of them. . . . We reached the corner of Wassergasse and there we were confronted with our task: Three naked bodies, burned with petrol, were hanging by their feet from a large hoarding. The faces were multilated beyond recognition with all the teeth knocked out. . . . The roasted skin stuck to our hands as we half carried and half dragged the bodies to the Stefansgasse.

"I had hardly washed the blood off when our guards entered, looking for the six of us; I suddenly realized what was bound to happen now. We had seen far too much to be allowed to live. . . . While being knocked about, we were asked our names and professions and then given the order: 'To the death cellar!'

"The first of us was done with and lying on the floor in his own blood. Then the second had his turn. I should have been fourth. But as the second victim was lying on the floor, the door opened and a Czech, who looked somewhat more intelligent and who, judging by the guards' manner, had a certain amount of authority, entered the cellar. Later I learned that he was a nephew of Minister Stransky. He asked who we were and after a good deal of hesitation, he had me and a boy of 17, a former member of the Hitler Youth, brought out of the room, because we were the only ones who could speak Czech. . . .

"When we passed the guard, he grinned and remarked that we were the first ones to leave the cellar alive."

Report of Helene Bugner—Prague: "My labor group consisted of 20 women, among them some 60 to 70 years old. We were in charge of Professor Zelenka. When we stepped out of the house, Professor Zelenka handed us over to the mob with the following words: 'Here are the German bitches for you.' Calling us German whores, the mob forced us to kneel down and then our hair was cut off with bayonets. Our shoes and stockings were taken off, so that we had to walk barefoot. With each step we were inhumanly beaten with sticks, rubber truncheons, etc. Whenever a woman sank to the ground, she was kicked, rolled in the mud, and stoned. I myself fainted several times; water was poured over me and I was forced to continue working. When I was quite unable to do any more work, I received a kick in the left side, by which two of my ribs were broken. During one of my fainting fits they cut a piece of about 0.6 square inches out of the sole of my foot. These tortures lasted the whole afternoon. Among us were women far advanced in pregnancy and nursing mothers, who were ill-treated in the same way . . . one of the women had a miscarriage.

PRAGUE

Hradcany Castle and St. Vitus Church in the background. The Charles Bridge over the Vltava (Moldau) River is in the foreground.

PLATE II

SLOVAKIA
Lomnicky Stit Peak in the High Tatra Mountains
PLATE III

SLOVAKIA
Presov. City Park and Catholic Church
PLATE IV

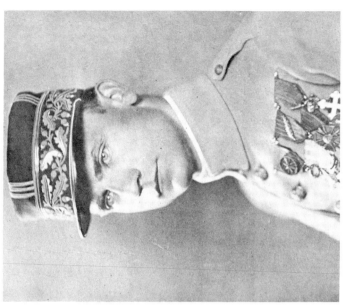

FOUNDERS OF THE CZECHO-SLOVAK REPUBLIC

Professor Thomas G. Masaryk, first President of Czecho-Slovakia.

General Milan R. Stefanik, champion of Slovak freedom within Czecho-Slovakia. Killed May 4, 1919.

PLATE V

THE CZECH COMMUNISTS SHOW THEIR POWER

Communist demonstration in Prague, May 1, 1947. Note the pictures of Benes, Stalin, and Tito.

PLATE VI

THE CZECH PEOPLE SHOW THEIR TRUE FEELINGS

The people of Plzen cover a Third Army memorial with flowers and American flags on May 5, 1948, when the Communists were already in power. The Communists removed the decorations during the night.

PLATE VII

THE COMMUNISTS FORCE BENES' HAND

A huge turnout of trade-unionists and other citizens fills St. Wenceslaus Square, Prague, on the final day of the "February Revolution," February 25, 1948.

PLATE VIII

THE END OF THE ROAD

President Benes swearing in Klement Gottwald as head of the new government two days after the Communist coup d'etat of February 25, 1948.

PLATE IX

ANTI-COMMUNIST LEADER OF CZECHO-SLOVAKIA
General Lev Prchala, chairman of the Czech National Committee

PLATE X

ANTI-COMMUNIST LEADER OF CZECHO-SLOVAKIA
Dr. Rudolf Lodgman von Auen, first speaker of the Sudeten-German
Landsmannschaft.

PLATE XI

ANTI-COMMUNIST LEADER OF CZECHO-SLOVAKIA

Minister Matus Cernak, leader of the Slovak National Council Abroad. He was assassinated July 5, 1955.

PLATE XII

"In the evening we went home. I was so disfigured from the maltreatment and tortures that my children no longer recognized me. My face was crusted with blood and my dress reduced to blood-stained rags. Two women living in our house committed suicide in despair; another woman became insane. . . . "Three weeks later we were sent to the camp at Hagibor. There 1200 persons were lodged in four barracks. All fell sick with hunger dysentery, for the diet consisted of a cup of thin water-gruel twice a day for the children and for the grown-ups a cup of black coffee with a thin slice of bread morning and evening and watery soup at noontime. . . . Each evening the forced labor groups returned to the camp badly beaten up. Medical care was completely lacking. . . . Epidemics of measles, scarlet fever, whooping-cough, and diphtheria broke out, which could not be dealt with.

"One day we were ordered to parade. We had to stand in the open air for seven hours, while a terrific thunderstorm with hail and a high wind, which unroofed two barracks, burst right over our heads. The very same day we were transported from the station in open coalwagons . . . the space between us was so small that there was hardly room for us to stand. At three o'clock in the morning we arrived at Kolin while it was pouring with rain. Two women died of exhaustion while marching from the station. . . . The Czech Red Cross nurse admitted groups of Russian soldiers to the camps each night and called their attention to several attractive women and girls, who were raped, sometimes up to 45 times a night in the most inhuman and barbarous way. . . .

"After several days I was sent, together with 45 other women, among them a woman with six small children, to a Czech estate, in order to work there. . . . Receiving the same kind and amount of food as at Hagibor, we had to do the hardest agricultural work, even on Sundays. The children received the same food as the adults without one drop of milk, so that three out of four died. All the children under a year old had already died in the camp at Prague. . . . When my child like the others got scarlet fever and I implored the foreman to get the doctor, he simply told me: 'The Narodni vybor [National Committee] has ordered that Germans should not get medical attendance.' Every night the villagers sent groups of Russian soldiers to our lodgings, who raped the women.

"As a consequence of my rib-fracture I contracted pleurisy and was sent to Prague, in order to be transferred to Germany. When I arrived in Prague, the transfers had already been suspended and I stayed in camp there until Christmas. The camp was so crowded that none of the inmates had enough room to lie down. We and our children had to sleep in a squatting position on the bare floor. . . . Often there was no water for three days. Children and adults contracted scurvy of the mouth and festering abscesses. Moist exanthemas, tuberculosis, spotted typhus, smallpox, and children's diseases broke out. Every child had rickets. Women gave birth to children, wearing the same dresses and underwear they had worn for months. Most of the infants died. Only a few mothers were able to feed their babies."

Report of Hans Freund—Prague: "I myself witnessed the following scene at the Sparta Square in Prague: we were marched to the well-known sports ground and after being commanded to 'halt' we were asked for our German military papers. About 50 men handed over the pay-books while some 500—and I was among these—did not deliver them. The 50 men were rounded up and had to stand facing the wall. Afterwards the gates were shut and the 50 men were mowed down from two sides with old German machine guns, which were served by two women.

"While marching to the Sparta sports ground I saw a group of Czech women take a German woman of 20 or 21 years of age, who was just getting into a truck, tie her up together with her child and throw both into the river Moldau.

"Our daily food ration consisted of 1.4 ounces of bread, a cup of soup, sauerkraut, and coffee. Four weeks later we were taken over by the Russian army and sent to Dresden. When the Russians took over the prisoners, a Czech lieutenant named Jaro Prochazka was shot by an adjutant because he attempted to torture us, which the Russian colonel would not allow. On our march to Dresden elderly people, who were unable to walk any further, were simply shot by the escorting partisans."[75]

Upon his arrival in Prague, Klement Gottwald, chairman of the Communist Party and deputy premier in the National Front government, announced the deportation of the Sudeten Germans. The proclamation which he issued on May 11, 1945, in the name of the government declared that the Germans and Magyars had forfeited Czecho-Slovak citizenship, and ordered the local National Committees to "punish them severely" and to confiscate the property of "the foreign nobility, Germans, traitors, and collaborators."[76] Two days later President Benes arrived in Prague, and "rows of Germans were set on fire as human torches in his honor."[77] Benes re-

---

[75] Turnwald, *op. cit.*, Reports 1, 4, and 10 in German edition; 1, 2, and 3 in English edition. Reports have been quoted from the English edition. While not changing the language, the author has condensed the material and has rearranged Freund's statement in chronological order.

[76] *Cechoslovak*, London, May 18, 1945; cited in *Dokumentation der Vertreibung*, IV/1, 70-71.

[77] Report of Dr. Hans Wagner, Turnwald, *op. cit.*, p. 21. Dr. Wagner, a representative of the International Red Cross (which the Benes government refused to recognize), was not arrested until May 17 and was therefore able to observe events up to that date.

sponded to the situation by declaring on May 16: "Our slogan will be that we must purge our country of everything which is German—culturally, economically, and politically."[78]

Following Radio Prague's summons to revolution and revenge, Czech units at various places in central Bohemia and Moravia began attacking German troops, resident German civilians, and the numerous columns of refugees which were passing through the "Protectorate." Some German military units managed to defend themselves and to inflict considerable losses on the partisans. The latter reacted by taking all the more violent revenge on German civilians, particularly after the German forces had disbanded or surrendered to the partisans.

Gottwald's proclamation of May 11 was followed by the mass arrest of Germans in various "ethnic islands" such as Iglau-Stecken and areas near Vyskov (Wischau) and Olomouc (Olmütz), as well as the scattered German residents of Czech communities. The entire German population of Iglau was interned in the concentration camps of Altenberg, Obergoss, and Helenenthal, which were as overcrowded as the Prague camps. Inmates were roused at 0415 hours for a day of heavy labor without lunch and were beaten and tortured on their return to camp, women and girls were raped each night by Russian and Czech soldateska, and children and adults died of starvation and disease.[79] Some of the Iglau Germans were driven on foot to Austria in late June, 1945—during which trek many infants and aged died of exhaustion or exposure—while the remainder were held in the camps until their transfer to Germany in 1946.

One of the most gruesome episodes was the notorious Brno "Death March" of May 30-31, 1945, in which

---

[78] Quoted by Jaksch, op. cit., p. 427. Although Benes claims in his *Memoirs* (p. 237) that he "always opposed" excesses against the Sudeten Germans "very strenuously," his first recorded public statement to that effect was in a speech made on June 15, 1945, at Plzen, *after* the British government had sent a sharp note of protest. See *Dokumentation der Vertreibung*, IV/1, 113-14.

[79] *Ibid.*, Vol. IV/2, Reports 31-33 and 95, pp. 177-97 and 433-35. The diet during the first week consisted of ¼ liter thin soup and ¼ liter "coffee," after which two to four ounces of bread or two potatoes were added. Margaret Zimmermann, an inmate of the Obergoss camp, reported that among 800-1500 inmates there were 10 to 15 deaths each day. At this rate the average length of survival was little more than three months.

25,000 Germans of that city were driven thirty miles on foot to the Austrian frontier. The Austrian government—which perhaps hoped to induce the Czechs to return the Germans to Brno—refused to admit the refugees, who were lodged for weeks in a grain elevator in the border town of Pohrlitz, where hundreds died in an epidemic. Details of this operation are described by a Red Cross nurse as follows:

Report of M. von W.—*Brno:* "At nine o'clock in the evening of May 30, 1945, the Germans were evicted from their apartments. The whole night long men, women, and children had stood in crowds in the monastery garden in Alt-Brünn (suburb of Brno). In the early dawn we were driven out to the garden and lined up in the yard of the monastery. A staff captain then arrived with a throng of partisans and gendarmes and shouted: 'Deliver up all gold, money, and savings-bank deposit books!' Following this order the partisans, gendarmes, and he himself rushed up to the defenseless women and elderly people and tore all their jewelry, money, and valuables out of their luggage and from the bodies of the assembled. Each of the partisans had boxes full of money, silverware, and jewelry. . . .

"The march began. Since the assembled Germans had had to stand in the open air all night long on the streets and in the monastery garden, many collapsed after a few kilometers. After marching for close to 10 miles, near the village of Raigern, those among us who, tired and exhausted, were unable to walk any further, were driven into the camp at Raigern. Upon their arrival there they were assembled by female partisans, stripped naked, and both men and women searched for jewelry and money. Their garments were literally cut to tatters during the search for hidden valuables. Countless persons were beaten to death and, according to the statements of many who reached Pohrlitz, finally shot. Scenes beyond all description took place on the road to Pohrlitz; especially when, in the afternoon, a terrible thunderstorm burst and flooded the ditches. The tired and exhausted marchers slipped on the soaked ground and although whipped and beaten, were unable to get up again. The ditches were filled with articles of clothing, bags, and food which the exhausted men and women had dropped, and amidst these all those who had collapsed and who finally died of exhaustion.

"The majority dragged themselves to Pohrlitz where, however, thousands died.

"I myself reached Pohrlitz, together with thousands of men, women, and children, on the evening of Corpus Christi Day. In the darkness I came to a car repair shop, where I crouched exhausted and spent the night. All night long I heard the cries for help of women being raped; early in the morning those able to continue the march were driven back on the road with whips and blows and forced to walk in the direction of Austria. Those unable to go any further—about 6,000 persons—were lodged in the nearby grain elevators, where they camped on the bare concrete floor.

"I was appointed as nurse to hut IV, although there was scarcely anything I could do, as neither medicaments nor any other means were available. I still remember the first killing—a soldier was chasing a woman. He jumped over the exhausted women on the ground and landed with both feet on the head of an eight-year-old girl, killing her immediately.

"In the early morning we heard a three-year-old girl crying for her mother; the woman had committed suicide by taking poison. The baby was dead too, since the woman had pressed it against her breast until it had died. A Czech gendarme in passing asked me why the woman's face was so blue. I replied that she had probably poisoned herself. He then cursed her, calling her a Nazi whore and a filthy sow for committing suicide after two days in camp; and he ordered me to 'throw the sow into the latrine together with her bastard.' I protested, saying that I was a Red Cross nurse and, being bound by my oath, could not execute such an order even if he were to shoot me. He then called for three other women, whom he intimidated more easily. . . .

"The mothers of small children and babies attempted to feed their children by cooking half-rotten potatoes, turnips, and dry bread to an eatable pap. They built themselves a very primitive outdoor stove from tiles and sheet iron. A gendarme arrived on the spot and was brutal enough to ruin the painfully prepared meal for the almost famished children by demolishing the stove with a kick.

"Night after night all the women, including the sick and even the very old ones of 70 years of age or more, were raped. The partisans let the soldiers into the camp and the women were misused twice or more times each night. . . . I became witness of the suicide of an old married couple. Both hanged themselves. . . . I saw how Czech gendarmes deprived the dead couple of their documents and then tied a slip of cardboard around their wrists, on which they wrote: 'Unknown, without documents.' This was the custom with all those thousands who died there. 60 or 70 persons died daily in the camp, the bodies being robbed of their shoes and frequently also of their garments; the corpses were piled in a heap and lay in the sun for hours covered with blowflies. . . . The cause of death in most cases was hunger typhus.

"Mass graves had, of course, to be established around Pohrlitz. The corpses were buried only a few inches below the surface, so that very soon a smell of corpses could be noticed everywhere. The newly arrived Czechs now began to protest; they said: 'We don't want to have these German swine around here. They infect the entire territory and spread epidemics.' It was therefore decided that on June 18 the sick persons and the mothers with children (most of them almost famished) were to be taken away in carts, while the others who were still capable of work were kept in the camp for another day. This transport of patients was led up to the Austrian border, into the so-called no man's land. Arriving there the unfortunate people were left in the woods, in the flood region of the Thaya River, and abandoned to swarms of mosquitoes. Nobody knew of these people's presence there; and almost all of them starved to death and were only found when their corpses were already bloated or eaten up by mosquitoes."[80]

Those Germans of Brno who escaped this ordeal were assigned to slave labor on southern Moravian estates, which the Czechs had confiscated from their German owners.[81] Some escaped to Austria, while others were eventually deported to Germany.

2. TERROR IN THE SUDETENLAND

At times during World War II, Dr. Benes had for tactical reasons indicated a willingness to leave part of the Sudetenland to Germany. In view of the total collapse of the Third Reich and the "non-political" attitude of the United States, such a compromise no longer seemed necessary in May, 1945, and the National Front government now asserted its sovereignty over the entire area ceded to Germany in 1938. While the British would have preferred to postpone a boundary settlement, the Benes government's claim was recognized by the Soviet Union and the United States, whose forces were occupying Bohemia and Moravia.[82] Once the Na-

---

[80] Turnwald, op. cit., condensed from Report 7 in English edition (No. 19 in German edition). See also Dokumentation der Vertreibung, Vol. IV/2, Report 97, pp. 438-54.

[81] The district surrounding Pohrlitz was, until the expulsion, inhabited almost entirely by ethnic Germans.

[82] It will be recalled that Eden had stated on August 5, 1942: "At the final settlement of the Czechoslovak frontiers to be reached at the end of the war, [His Majesty's Government] will not be influenced by any changes effected in and since 1938." This language, while a repudiation of Munich, did not commit the British to any particular boundary. Molotov, on the other hand, had stated in his note to Benes on June 9, 1942, that the Soviet Union "takes its stand on the pre-Munich Czechoslovak frontiers." For sources, see chap. III, note 86, supra. On May 19, 1943, Benes reported that Secretary Hull, discussing the Munich Agreement, had said that ". . . so far as the United States was concerned, all its effects on Czechoslovakia were null and void." (Memoirs, p. 194.) The Department of State's briefing paper of January 12, 1945, also indicates acceptance of the pre-Munich boundary, as well as American belief that only "more than 1,500,000" Sudeten Germans would be expelled. (Malta and Yalta, pp. 189-90.)

tional Front had established itself in Prague, its assumption of political control in the border districts met with no Allied opposition.

In areas of mixed population, the local Czechs established National Committees—which in some cases were removed for dealing too mildly with the Germans.[83] Administrators for purely German communities were appointed by Vaclav Nosek, the Communist Minister of the Interior. Political police forces moved into all areas as rapidly as they could be organized.

The tactic of the *fait accompli* included, as we have noted, the stage-managing of the expulsion as a "spontaneous" revolutionary act of the Czech people. To accomplish this, units of the Revolutionary Guard were dispatched to the Sudetenland, where their members were promised preference in the public services, the police, and in the redistribution of confiscated German farm and industrial property.[84] In some cases entire units of the Revolutionary Guard were incorporated into the SNB, which at that time combined general and secret police functions.[85] In other cases, groups of partisans were permitted to undertake punitive expeditions on their own initiative; they would move into a Sudeten town, beat and shoot victims denounced to them or selected at random, and plunder the houses and apartments. In many cases, the partisans held public executions, with the entire German population, including the families of the victims, as unwilling witnesses.[86] It was often hard to tell which measures of retribution were officially ordered and which were merely sadistic acts of individuals—a situation highly satisfactory to Benes, Ripka, and the other germanophobe ministers, who could dis-

[83] *Dokumentation der Vertreibung*, Vol. IV/1, pp. 68-69, and Vol. IV/2, Reports 11, 42, 44, and 126-28.

[84] See Article XI of Kosice Program ; Decree of June 21, 1945, No. 12, § 7, sec. 6 ; Decree of October 25, 1945, No. 108, § 7, sec. 3 ; also *Dokumentation der Vertreibung*, Vol. IV/1, p. 69, note 3. Numbers of Czecho-Slovak laws and decrees, including those hereafter cited, refer to their promulgation in the *Sbirka zakonu a narizeni republiky Ceskoslovenské* ["Collection of Laws and Decrees of the Czecho-Slovak Republic"].

[85] SNB=*Straz Narodni Bezpecnosti* ["National Security Guard"]. It is now restricted to general police duties, its political functions having been transferred to the StB and the PVS. See "The Police State" in chap. VI, *infra*.

[86] *Dokumentation der Vertreibung*, Vol. IV/1, pp. 69-70, and Vol. IV/2, Reports 2, 37, 39, and 128. See also Turnwald, *op. cit.*, English edition, Reports 34, 40, 51, 53, 75, and 102.

claim responsibility for those atrocities which gave rise to protests.[87]

The deployment of partisans produced spectacular though limited results. One of their first operations, at Landskron in the eastern Sudetenland, is described by an eyewitness as follows:

Report of Julius Friedel—Landskron: "About 11 o'clock on May 17, hundreds of armed Czechs, so-called partisans, arrived in trucks. The German men and with them many women and children were driven to the market place; the houses were thoroughly searched to insure that all men were present, old and young, also invalids and those seriously ill. The individual groups of Germans were escorted by yelling Czechs, heavily armed, who shot blindly in all directions and knocked down anyone who came in their way. . . . More than a thousand German men were rounded up in the market place in the early hours of the afternoon. They were ordered to fall in and they stood there with their hands above their heads, waiting for what would happen next.

"The men were forced to lie down on the pavement, to stand up quickly, and then to get in line again. The Czechs passed down the lines, kicked the men, preferably on the shins or in the genitals. They hit them with whatever lay convenient to their hands; they spat at them and fired wildly with their rifles.

"Many men were too badly wounded to get up again and lay in great pain. But this was not enough. There was a large water tank for air raids in front of the town hall. Into this the victims of this terrible madness were finally thrown one after the other. As they came to the surface, they were struck at with sticks and poles and kept under water. The Czechs even shot into the mass and the water slowly reddened. Whenever anyone tried to scramble out of the tank, they stamped on his fingers; some of the men were fished out of the water, but they were already dead. Others, who lay prostrate on the ground, were squirted with the fire hose, or were tortured in indescribable ways. While all these atrocities

---

[87] *Dokumentation der Vertreibung*, Vol. IV/1, pp. 87-88. Among those who contributed to inflaming Czech opinion against the Sudeten Germans, mention should be made of the Communist Vaclav Kopecky and the "liberals" Prokop Drtina and Ivan Herben. On May 29, 1945, Minister of Information Kopecky called for a "mighty national offensive to purge our border districts of the Germans" (*Einheit*, No. 12, June 16, 1945). Drtina, one of Benes' secretaries in exile and later Minister of Justice, and Herben, after 1948 on the staff of the *New Yorkske Listy* and a script writer for Radio Free Europe, were the authors of the pamphlet *My a Nemci* ["We and the Germans"], published by the National Socialist party (Prague, 1945), which contains the following sentences: "The devil speaks German" (p. 3); "There are no good Germans: there are only bad and worse" (p. 5); "The Czech father who does not educate his children to hate the mendacious culture and inhumanity of the Germans is not only a bad patriot but a bad father. How can one bring up a Czech child to love such Germans?" (p. 7); "The entire German people is responsible for Hitler, Himmler, Henlein, and Frank, and the entire people must bear the punishment for the crimes committed. Each of us must consider it an inhuman thing if the Germans should escape their total punishment" (p. 13).

were taking place, the so-called People's Court established itself on the sidewalk in front of the district council building. . . . "One after the other, with their hands above the head, the Germans had to appear before the tribunal. . . . The last 20 or 30 paces up to the tribunal had to be made in a creeping position. Arriving there each one received his sentence, written on his back with a piece of chalk. About 170 to 200 feet distant from the tribunal, on the opposite side, was a gate; up to this the victims had literally to run the gauntlet. Many of them collapsed on their way, even before the sentence could be carried out. . . ." [The witness then describes various killings, giving a list of twenty-four victims and twenty-five suicides.][88]

A similar massacre befell the men of Saaz, a city of 20,000 in the western Sudetenland. On June 3, 1945, German males between thirteen and sixty-five years of age—some 5,000 in all—were marched ten miles to the barracks at Postelberg, which became a concentration and liquidation camp. Here they were starved, beaten, and tortured for days, several hundred being arbitrarily shot and heaped into mass graves. On June 7, 275 men were locked all night in a tightly closed room without windows; scores suffocated and others went insane in this "black hole of Calcutta." A few days later the survivors, together with their families, were transferred to slave-labor camps where conditions were only slightly better than in the concentration centers of Prague or Iglau.[89] Mass murders also took place at Joachimsthal, Ober-Lipka, Totzau, and other places too numerous to mention.[90]

In areas near the border, the Revolutionary Guard also undertook to drive the Germans out of the Sudetenland altogether. On June 9, the 8,000 German men of Komotau were ordered to assemble on the market place with extra clothing and food for three days. To start proceedings, fifteen were beaten to death and all food except bread was confiscated. Ironically enough, the Sudeten German Communists—who had not been exempted from the order to line up—were singled out for

[88] Turnwald, *op. cit.*, condensed from Report 6 in English edition (Report 18 in German edition). A similar account is given in *Dokumentation der Vertreibung*, Vol. IV/2, Report 48.

[89] Turnwald, *op. cit.*, Report 11, English edition (29 in German edition); *Dokumentation der Vertreibung*, Vol. IV/2, Reports 58-60.

[90] Turnwald, *op. cit.*, *passim*, especially Reports 51, 75, and 102, in English edition.

a special beating. The Czech Communist party had authorized them to wear red arm bands instead of the white bands mandatory for other Germans: these red bands aroused the ire of the local Czech commander, who ordered his men and some of the non-Communist Germans to beat the Communists. The men of Komotau were then marched some twelve miles to the border of Saxony (Soviet Zone of Germany), sixty or more who could not keep up the pace being shot on the way. The Russian commander in Neudorf, however, refused to admit the expellees, who were forced to spend the night sitting on the highway. A number slipped away in the darkness and managed to rejoin their families, but the majority were taken to concentration camps to serve as slave laborers.[91] A parallel episode took place on the Bavarian border on May 13, when the American frontier control refused to admit several hundred Sudeten Germans being expelled from the village of Vollmau.[92]

3. THE MASS EXPULSIONS AND POTSDAM

Adventures in mayhem and plunder in the Sudetenland attracted only a relatively small "carpetbagger" element among the Czechs. The majority took no part in the persecutions, and a considerable number risked life or freedom to stave off atrocities or alleviate the lot of the victims.[93] As Minister Ripka complained: "We were too slow and too considerate with the Germans. *The people failed to carry out the government's plan* during the first two months after liberation, and the entire operation of driving out the Germans was there-

---

[91] *Dokumentation der Vertreibung*, Vol. IV/1, p. 110, and Vol. IV/2, Reports 55 and 90.

[92] Turnwald, *op. cit.*, English edition, Report 112.

[93] Acts of kindness by Czechs and Slovaks are reported in K. O. Kurth, ed., *Documents of Humanity*, Kitzingen/Main, 1952 (English edition), pp. 155-84. See also *Dokumentation der Vertreibung*, Vol. IV/1, pp. 111-12, and Vol. IV/2, Reports 24, 26, 32, 36, 49, 51, 52, and 54. The Czech humanitarian Premysl Pitter, who had established homes for Jewish and Czech orphans during Nazi rule, overcame the resistance of the National Front authorities and was able to rescue hundreds of Sudeten German orphans from the camps, particularly those whose parents had perished from mistreatment.

by delayed."[94] The National Front regime therefore turned to more radical measures.

Beginning early in June, 1945, the Czecho-Slovak army —consisting largely of troops which General Svoboda had organized in Russia—swept across the northern Sudetenland, driving as many Germans as possible into the Reich.[95] The Soviet Military Administration had by now instructed its commanders in Saxony not to obstruct the entry of the Sudeten Germans, but had made no efforts to provide food or quarters for half a million uprooted people. The German official publication *Dokumentation der Vertreibung* describes the details of the "wild expulsion" as follows:

. . . Armed troops appeared in towns and settlements without warning, sealed them hermetically, and ordered the Germans to leave their houses within a short interval and assemble at designated points. Frequently the victims were not even allowed to pack the most necessary articles, but were dragged unceremoniously from their homes. In places near the border as well as elsewhere when no transportation was available, the assembled Germans were immediately set in motion toward the border. Goaded to a faster pace by the escorting soldiers or Revolutionary Guards, these processions of misery—in which women with small children and the aged and feeble were the dominant element— dragged their way to the frontier in marches which often lasted for days. Forced to endure the jeers of Czech civilians and the brutalities of their guards, who threatened to shoot laggards on the spot and often carried out this threat, the expellees were forbidden assistance by the Germans in the villages traversed. . . . In a few cases those who could walk no more, particularly the aged, were carried to the border in horse-drawn wagons or trucks.

Baggage was limited; most expulsion orders permitted only hand baggage and hand-wagons in which to carry it. In many cases the Czech escorts and local authorities provided teams or trucks to carry the baggage, but frequently the deportees were forced to carry it themselves throughout the trek—often abandoning pieces by the wayside in their exhaustion.

Once across the border, the expellees were left to their own devices. . . . Those who reached Silesia were caught up in the simultaneous Polish expulsions. Others, whom the Czechs were not able to expel to Silesia or whom the Polish militia returned

[94] Minister of Foreign Trade Dr. Hubert Ripka in interview with Reuters correspondent Jon Kimche, July 20, 1945, quoted by Jaksch, *op. cit.*, p. 427 (retranslated from German, italics supplied).

[95] According to Jaksch (*ibid.*, p. 428) the "wild expulsion" under the Svoboda army began on June 11, 1945. It did not extend to the western Sudetenland, which was occupied by American troops.

to Czecho-Slovakia, were interned in Czech camps and later deported to Saxony by rail.

In addition to the treks on foot, Germans from the eastern and northern Sudetenland were also moved by train, in open coal cars into which 30 to 60 people with their baggage were crammed. These transports frequently took several days to reach the Saxon border, sometimes continuing into Saxony and as far as Brandenburg.

Since hundreds of thousands of expellees from the Sudetenland and from nearby Silesia converged on Saxony, tremendous masses of human beings accumulated there. . . Fantastic rumors intensified the confusion of the multitudes which, ravaged by starvation and epidemic, were hunted from place to place without plan or purpose. Many lost the last remnants of their possessions to marauding Soviet soldiers.[96]

It has been estimated that between 550,000 and 650,000 Sudeten Germans were deported to Germany during the course of the "wild expulsion," in addition to some 150,000 expelled to Austria.[97] The Saxons, whose capital of Dresden had been destroyed shortly before and whose Russian occupants were "living off the land," could do little to help these people. Their plight was poignantly described by a Dutch citizen, who after traveling from the Sudetenland through the Soviet Zone of Germany reported to the British Military Government in Lübeck as follows:

I saw a great many of these people, who number almost half a million, literally starving on the highways. I saw children and infants lying dead in the ditches, victims of hunger or epidemic, their arms and legs no thicker than a man's thumb. These evacuees tried to collect the garbage from the Russian field kitchens, often already in a state of putrefaction, to assuage their infernal hunger. Transportation facilities are either non-existent or totally inadequate. These people are therefore obliged to remain outdoors for weeks in all sorts of weather.[98]

While the Sudeten Germans in towns near the border were being expelled, many thousands of others were herded into concentration camps. The inmates were assigned to factories and construction gangs as slave labor-

---

[96] *Dokumentation der Vertreibung*, IV/1, 106-8. (Author's translation.) For individual experiences, see *ibid.*, Vol. IV/2, Reports 71-76, 78, 81, 87-89, 94, and 126.

[97] *Ibid.*, IV/1, 112. Approximately 118,000 Sudeten Germans were later transferred from Austria to Germany.

[98] Quoted by Jaksch, *op. cit.*, p. 428.

ers. They were beaten and tortured at work and in the camps, and the women served the pleasure of the local Russian garrisons. Nazi concentration camps such as Theresienstadt were continued in operation by the National Front with only a *partial* change of inmates— since Jews of German nationality (as registered in the 1930 census or thereafter) were subjected to the same treatment as other Germans.[99] Richard Stokes, a British member of Parliament who visited Czecho-Slovakia in October, 1945, reported that there were fifty-one concentration camps and that the ration of those who did not receive extra food from their employers was "750 calories a day, which is below the Belsen level."[100]

Those Germans who were not immediately expelled or confined in concentration camps were subjected to a variety of discriminations. As Turnwald tells us:

. . . They were only allowed to be on the streets at certain times (curfew), they had to wear white badges as a distinguishing mark, they were not permitted to use any public means of communication (trains, buses, streetcars) or to leave or change their residences. They were forbidden to walk on the pavements. They were not allowed to write letters to one another or to visit restaurants, cinemas, or theatres. . . . Gold, silver, jewelry and other valuables, radios, cameras, and optical instruments had to be surrendered. Special ration cards for Germans were issued, without coupons for meat, eggs, milk, cheese, and fruit. All German schools and kindergartens were closed. . . .[101]

Although the National Front government attempted to suppress the truth about the genocide[102] being com-

[99] *Dokumentation der Vertreibung,* Vol. IV/1, pp. 80-83 and 97-104, also Second Supplementary Volume, p. 138. See further H. G. Adler, *Theresienstadt 1941-1945,* Tübingen, 1955, pp. 211-14 and 743. In Report No. 15 in Turnwald, *op. cit.* (English edition), Dr. E. Siegel describes the maltreatment of Jews at Theresienstadt and notes that Czech personnel "often remarked that Adolf Hitler had done a bad job, since there were still plenty of Jews alive."

[100] *Manchester Guardian,* October 10, 1945. According to Jaromir Luza, a supporter of the National Front's expulsion policy, the number of camps was increased to 107 (with an average of 1200 inmates) after the Potsdam Conference (*Odsun* ["The Expulsion"], Vienna, 1953, p. 23; cited in *Dokumentation der Vertreibung,* IV/1, 117). After the disclosures of Stokes and G. E. R. Gedye (*Daily Herald,* London, October 9, 1945) some of the most brutal camp officials were arrested for embezzlement of prisoners' assets and there was a slight improvement in camp conditions.

[101] Turnwald, *op. cit.,* pp. xxi-xxii.

[102] According to the United Nations Genocide Convention of December 9, 1948, the crime of genocide includes the following acts committed with intent to destroy, in whole or in part, a national, ethnic, racial, or religious group: (a) killing members of the group, (b) causing serious bodily or mental harm to members of the group, and (c) deliberately inflicting on the group conditions of life calculated to bring about its physical destruction in whole or in part.

mitted against the Sudeten Germans, a certain amount of information leaked out. Wenzel Jaksch and his Social Democratic colleagues in London reported the facts to British and American statesmen, and occasional articles appeared in the press. In June, 1945, the British Foreign Office notified Prague that His Majesty's Government: (a) did not consent to a mass deportation of the German minority, and (b) considered in any case that the question could not be decided by Czecho-Slovakia alone but also belonged to the competence of the Control Powers [over Germany].[103] The Prague cabinet therefore, after Premier Fierlinger had obtained renewed assurances of the Kremlin's support, requested the Allies to place the expulsion on the agenda of the forthcoming Potsdam Conference, submitting a detailed deportation plan on July 22.[104]

The Communist-controlled "Information" Ministry in Prague then mounted a massive propaganda offensive, a central feature of which was the myth of (nonexistent) "Werewolves" or Nazi partisans. The unexplained explosion of a munitions dump at Aussig was blamed on the "Werewolves," whereupon an enraged Czech mob, *encouraged by soldiers and police,* took "revenge" by murdering at least one thousand Germans on the bridge over the Elbe.[105] Left-wing journalists helped to deceive the Western public; the Communist reporter Ralph Parker, whose articles appeared in the London *Times,* the *Glasgow Herald,* and the *Manchester Guardian,* compounded the "Werewolf" stories and described the Aussig massacre as an "enforcement of Czech authority."[106]

It must be remembered that 1945 marked the high point of anti-German "collective guilt" propaganda, systematically guided by the Communists, who exploited

---

[103] *Keesing's Archive,* London, XV (1945), 275 E; see also the *Observer,* London, June 17, and the *Daily Express,* London, June 18, 1945.

[104] *Keesing's Archive,* XV, 232 E and 318 D.

[105] *Dokumentation der Vertreibung,* Vol. IV/1, pp. 71-72, and Vol. IV/2, Report 53 (by a Czech administrative official of Aussig); Turnwald, *op. cit.* (English edition), Reports 12 and 13. The Czech report (reprinted from *Londýnské Listy,* London, July 15, 1948) indicates that careless storage of munitions caused the explosion. Estimates of the number of Germans killed run from 1,000 to 2,700.

[106] Jaksch, *op. cit.,* pp. 429-430. A similar report by Stefan Litauer was printed in the London *News Chronicle.* Parker's articles were circulated in the United States through the leftist Overseas News Agency; he later wrote for the Moscow *New Times.*

the revulsion generated by Nazi atrocities.[107] The result was an ideological frenzy in which the Morgenthau Plan to make Germany a "cow country" could find highest-level acceptance, in which a United States Military Governor could be instructed to "take no steps . . . looking toward the economic rehabilitation of Germany,"[108] and in which the American Association for Orthopsychiatry could seriously discuss collective psychotherapy for the German people. The Western statesmen went to Potsdam without the backing of a unified or correctly informed public opinion; they lacked both the will and the political conception necessary to resist the *fait accompli* which Soviet Russia and its Polish and Czech satellites thrust upon them. To stop the Russian advance into Europe meant thinking in terms of the balance of power, and such thoughts were ruled out by the "unconditional surrender" psychology which had prevailed since the Casablanca Conference.

As Truman, Attlee,[109] and their advisers saw the situation, there was nothing they could do to prevent the expulsion of fifteen million Germans from the Reich east of the Oder-Neisse line, from Czecho-Slovakia, and from the German settlements of eastern Europe. They honestly believed that they had obtained the maximum possible concession from Stalin in Article XIII of the Potsdam Agreement, which sanctioned the transfers of Germans from Poland, Czecho-Slovakia, and Hungary, but provided that they would be "effected in an orderly and human way" and that further deportations would be suspended until the Allied Control Council for Germany had worked out a plan for receiving and distributing the expellees.[110] Publication of the Potsdam Agree-

---

[107] As Miksche observes (*Unconditional Surrender*, p. 257): "It was certainly not without deep design that an ideologically internationally-minded Communism launched the most fanatical anti-German propaganda after the war. The waves of blind hatred which overshadowed even the minds of statesmen in the West precluded any realistic consideration of a policy of European equilibrium, and their postwar attitude broke up Europe completely." On Communist infiltration of American propaganda agencies, see Julius Epstein's pamphlet *The O.W.I. and the Voice of America*, New York, 1951.

[108] JCS 1067, April, 1945, released in Department of State *Bulletin*, October 21, 1945.

[109] Clement Attlee, leader of the Labor party, succeeded Winston Churchill as Prime Minister on July 27, 1945, after the Potsdam Conference had already started.

[110] For a fuller citation, see "Two Versions of Non-Predetermination" in chap. IX, *infra*.

ment was, however, followed by a wave of protest in Great Britain and the United States, both against the expulsions as such and against the barbarous treatment of Germans—now fully reported in the press and denounced by political personages and churchmen in both countries.[111]

Actually, the helplessness of the Western Powers at Potsdam was largely self-imposed. While they had given away their best trumps at Teheran, at Yalta, and in the final weeks of the war, they still held some playable cards. They could deny the Russians reparations from their zones, they could block urgently needed UNRRA shipments to Poland and the Balkans, and their armies, not yet demobilized, were in much better fighting condition than the "exhausted and partly demoralized" Red Army.[112] American troops occupied part of Czecho-Slovakia, so that Truman was in a position to say: "Either you will discontinue the persecution of Sudeten Germans, or we shall annex Western Bohemia to the United States Zone of Germany!" To take a firm position against the expulsions, however, would have meant laying down the law to Russia. While a break at this time would have saved millions from Communist tyranny, it was psychologically not in the cards: we were still prisoners of our wartime delusions.

Annoyed by Western criticism and fearful that the Allies might revoke their Potsdam commitment, the Prague government continued expulsions to the Soviet Zone at a slower rate and made life as miserable as possible for the Sudeten Germans who remained. President Benes gave a policy speech on October 14, 1945, in which he said: "Our entire action in the matter of their expulsion to the Reich must be humane, decent, correct, morally justified, exactly planned, and firmly agreed with all Allies." But he also declared:

We have recently been criticized in the international press for resettling the Germans in an unworthy and inadmissible manner. . . . We are accused of simply imitating the Nazis in their cruel and uncivilized methods. Whether these charges may be

---

[111] Jaksch, *op. cit.*, pp. 434-38.
[112] Miksche, *Unconditional Surrender*, p. 252.

true in their details or not, I declare absolutely and categorically: Our Germans must go away to the Reich, and they will go away under all circumstances.[113]

Many who opposed mass deportations on principle came to feel that it was more humane to move the Sudeten Germans than to leave them to be starved and tortured in concentration camps. This consideration doubtlessly influenced Allied agreement to a resettlement plan which was approved by the Control Council on November 20, 1945, and placed in operation in January, 1946.

Beginning on January 25, 1946, four trains daily (six from February 25 to July 15) were admitted to the United States Zone, each carrying 1,200 expellees. Czech treatment of evacuees remained unsatisfactory, but improved somewhat following American intervention in April. Incoming expellees were distributed to towns and villages throughout the zone, where rooms were requisitioned for them: it became the normal thing to live "doubled up" in postwar Germany. Saturation of available housing made it necessary for the American Military Government to discontinue the program after November 30, 1946, at which time more than 80 per cent of the Sudeten Germans had been moved. Although a lack of firm statistics prevents an exact accounting, the following is a reasonably correct summary of the expulsion to that date.

EXPULSION OF SUDETEN GERMANS, 1945-1946[114]

German population of Czecho-Slovakia, May, 1945 (A) .. 3,391,000
Germans expelled from Czecho-Slovakia:
   In "wild expulsion," 1945 (B) 750,000
   To Soviet Zone after Potsdam, 1945 (C)   70,000
   To United States Zone, 1946 (D) 1,183,000
   To Soviet Zone, 1946 (E) 750,000

---

[113] *Pravo lidu*, October 16, 1945.

[114] Compiled by author from figures cited in *Dokumentation der Vertreibung*, IV/1, 112-35. A : German estimate based on Czecho-Slovak census of 1930, corrected for natural growth and war losses. B : Consensus of German and Czech estimates ; actual figure may vary up to 50,000 either way. C : Statement by Czech officials in negotiations with U.S. Military Government, January, 1946. D : Official statistics of Bavarian Refugee Commissioner. E : Estimates from Czech sources. Over 52,000 Germans are known to have left Czecho-Slovakia since 1946, and it seems probable that at least 100,000 fled "illegally." Estimates of the number of Germans now in Czecho-Slovakia vary from 180,000 to 200,000.

	2,753,000
Remainder:	638,000
Estimated present in Czecho-Slovakia, November 1946 (E)	400,000
Not accounted for (includes those who died in massacres and concentration camps, those who fled, and prisoners of war discharged in Germany)	238,000

The story of the tribulations of the Sudeten Germans and other expellees after their arrival in Germany, and of their contribution to economic reconstruction in the German Federal Republic, is beyond the scope of this book. Readers who are interested in this subject are referred to the publications of the German Federal Ministry for Expellees and of the numerous religious and philanthropic groups which have interested themselves in expellee and refugee problems.[115]

TOTALITARIAN LAWS AND THEIR ADMINISTRATION

To provide a "legal" basis for the expulsion of the Sudeten Germans and for the "building of socialism" under the Kosice Program, the National Front regime passed a spate of legislation, most of which would be unconstitutional by American standards. Among the most important of these enactments[116] are the following:

1. *Decree of the President of the Republic, May 19, 1945, No. 5* [see footnote 84]: This decree invalidated all property transfers made after October 29, 1938 "under the pressure of the occupation or national, racial, or political persecution." More importantly, it paved the way for confiscation through the following provisions:

---

[115] See particularly German Federal Ministry for Expellees, Refugees, and War Victims, *Expellees and Refugees in Germany*, Bonn (revised periodically), and *Die Betreuung der Vertriebenen*, Bonn (undated); *After Ten Years: a European Problem—Still No Solution*, Frankfurt, 1957; ECA Technical Assistance Commission on the Integration of the Refugees in the German Republic, *The Integration of Refugees into German Life*, with technical appendices, Bonn, 1951 (distributed by National Planning Association, Washington, D.C.); publications of Research Group for European Migration Problems, published in English by Martinus Nijhoff, The Hague; *The German Expellee Problem*, lectures delivered at the International Conference of Red Cross Societies, Bonn, 1951; American Friends Service Committee, *After Seven Years*, Philadelphia, 1952.

[116] *Dokumentation der Vertreibung*, Vol. IV/1, Appendices 3-23, gives the full text (in German) of twenty-one laws, decrees, and notices dating from May 19, 1945 to May 6, 1948. Turnwald, *op. cit.*, Appendices VIIa and IX-XIII, gives full English translations of six of these enactments.

Article 2

1. The property within the Czechoslovak Republic of politically unreliable persons shall be placed under national administration according to the further provisions of this decree. ...

Article 4

The following shall be considered politically unreliable persons:

(a) Persons of German or Magyar nationality.

(b) Persons who engaged in activity directed against the state sovereignty, independence, integrity, the democratic-republican form of government, the security, and the defense of the Czechoslovak Republic, who incited to such activity, or who solicited other persons to engage therein, and who intentionally supported the German and Magyar occupants in any manner. . . . . [There follows a "bill of attainder" against members and functionaries of various organizations.]

Article 5

Those juristic persons shall be deemed politically unreliable, the management of which deliberately and intentionally served the German or Magyar war effort or fascist or Nazi purposes.

Article 6

Persons who indicated their nationality as German or Magyar in any census since 1929 or who became members of national groups, organizations, or political parties consisting of persons of German or Magyar nationality shall be considered persons of such nationality.

2. *Decree of the President of the Republic, June 19, 1945, No. 16:* This so-called "Retribution Decree" punished *ex post facto* not only Nazi crimes against persons and property (already covered by the regular penal code) but also political activity hostile to "Czechoslovak" centralism. Severe penalties were imposed for "crimes against the state" committed during the "time of the increased threat to the Republic"—during most of which the Czecho-Slovak Republic did not legally exist. These crimes included attacks against the Republic (death), endangering the security of the Republic (twenty years to life imprisonment, in extreme cases death), and being an official or leader of the Nazi party, the Sudeten German party, or the Hlinka Guard (five to twenty years).[117] Those who approved or defended "the enemy rule on the territory of the Republic" through the press, radio, or theater or in public assembly—meaning those who supported the Slovak Republic, the Protectorate, or German rule in the Sudetenland—were liable to terms of five to twenty years. For

---

[117] Concerning non-Nazi and anti-Nazi elements in the Sudeten German party and the basically non-totalitarian character of the Hlinka Guard, see chaps. II and III, *supra.*

statements made "with the intention of destroying the moral, national, or state consciousness of the Czechoslovak people," the punishment could be increased to twenty years, life imprisonment, or even the death penalty. Czecho-Slovak citizens abroad who "hampered the movement directed at liberating the Czechoslovak Republic in its pre-Munich constitution and unity" were threatened with five to twenty years imprisonment. Most of Dr. Benes' opponents in Western countries took the hint and remained in exile.

Part Two of the "Retribution Decree" established Soviet-type "Special People's Courts" to try political offenders. The People's Courts, each consisting of one professional judge and four lay "People's Judges," followed court-martial procedures and rendered their verdicts by majority vote. A person acquitted could be tried again in an ordinary or state court for the same offense. The utter brutality of this system of totalitarian "justice" is suggested by the following excerpt:

Article 31

1. There shall be no appeal from a judgment of the Special People's Courts. An application for pardon, by whomever filed, shall be without dilatory effect.

2. As a rule the death penalty shall be executed within two hours after judgment has been announced. Upon express request of the person convicted such period may be extended one additional hour. If the accused was tried in absentia the death penalty shall be executed within 24 hours after his apprehension.

3. The Special People's Court may also decide that the death penalty shall be executed in public. . . . In this case the court may extend the period of two hours, but not beyond twenty-four hours, to assure public attendance at the penal execution.[118]

3. *Decree of the President of the Republic, June 21, 1945, No. 12:* This decree confiscated "immediately and without compensation, for the purposes of the land reform," all farm property belonging to:

(a) "all persons of German and Magyar nationality, without regard to their citizenship,"

(b) "traitors and enemies of the Republic," as determined *administratively* by the Provincial National Committee (with decision by the Ministries of Agriculture and Interior [both controlled by Communists] in doubtful cases).

(c) Stock and share corporations, "the management of which knowingly and intentionally supported the German war effort or Nazi or fascist purposes."

A further decree (No. 108 of October 25, 1945) ordered the

---

[118] An amendment of January 24, 1946, modified this article, eliminating the provision for public executions.

confiscation without compensation of all remaining property of Germans, Magyars, and political offenders (as defined in the decree of June 19), establishing so-called "Funds of National Regeneration" to administer and distribute such property.

4. *Constitutional Decree of the President of the Republic, August 2, 1945, No. 33:* This edict disposed of the citizenship of ethnic Germans and Magyars by providing:

Article 1
1. Czechoslovak citizens of German or Magyar nationality who acquired German or Magyar citizenship under the regulations of a foreign occupation power have, on the date such citizenship was acquired, lost their Czechoslovak citizenship.
2. Other Czechoslovak citizens of German or Magyar nationality shall lose Czechoslovak citizenship on the effective date of this decree.

Persons affected could retain Czecho-Slovak citizenship by *proving* "that they remained loyal to the Czechoslovak Republic, that they never offended against the Czech and Slovak people," *and* "that they either participated actively in the fight for liberation or suffered under the Nazi or fascist terror."[119]

By calling the German government in the Sudetenland and the Hungarian administration in southern Slovakia "foreign occupation powers," the Prague regime attempted to assert the *illegality* of the transfers of territory accomplished in 1938 together with the *legality* of citizenship changes incident thereto. This legal *tour de force* is defeated by the universally recognized principle that only *de jure* transfers of territory can alter the citizenship of inhabitants. Conversely, re-annexation of territory previously ceded implies the repatriation of the population concerned.

5. *Decree of the President of the Republic, September 19, 1945, No. 71,* establishing compulsory labor for persons denied Czecho-Slovak citizenship by the decree of August 2. Men from fourteen to sixty and women from fifteen to fifty years of age (with certain exceptions) were required to perform any work "in the public interest," at any location, as assigned by the local National Committee. An implementing regulation issued by the Minister of the Interior on December 2, 1945, provided for the billeting, feeding, and discipline of forced laborers when housed in camps or away from their homes.[120]

6. *Law of May 8, 1946, No. 115:* This retroactive measure, passed by the Provisional National Assembly under Communist pressure, provided that:

---

[119] Only a few Sudeten Germans, mostly Communists, were able to benefit from this provision. The majority of Sudeten German anti-fascists were expelled; promised preferential treatment did not always materialize. See *Dokumentation der Vertreibung,* IV/1, 103-4 and 127-34.

[120] No. 500 in *Uredni list Ceskoslovenské republiky*—Official Gazette of the Czecho-Slovak Republic, December 11, 1945.

Article 1

Any act committed between September 30, 1938, and October 28, 1945, the object of which was to aid the struggle of the Czechs and Slovaks for the recovery of their freedom, or which constituted a just reprisal for deeds of the occupation forces and their accomplices, is not illegal, even if it would otherwise be punishable by law.

Article 2

1. For persons already sentenced for such offenses, the procedure for the reopening of criminal cases will be followed.

The law of May 8, 1946, representing the climax of totalitarian "justice," constituted *carte blanche* legal approval of all murders, tortures, and other atrocities committed against Germans and Magyars during the Benes-Gottwald "national revolution."

Czechs and Slovaks also suffered under the totalitarian legislation of the National Front. Since most factories and large farms had, willingly or unwillingly, provided supplies for the German army and made shipments to the Reich, the effect of the retribution and confiscation decrees was to liquidate the major part of the business class, thus paving the way for rapid "building of socialism" and smashing the economic center of anti-Communism. Many left-wingers, however, were not above taking "capitalist" advantage of the situation, which is described by a Czech source as follows:

. . . The simple fact that an active Communist or member of the National Front wanted to have a house, a business, a farm, or a position held by an innocent citizen was sufficient to have the latter thrown into jail under a false accusation.

. . . The decree of June 19, 1945, which became the basis of the arbitrary acts of the police, was called the "Retribution Decree" because it was primarily directed against those citizens who professed true democracy and who opposed nationalization. In general, the confiscation of property and the intimidation of those who still held it became the avowed aims of this measure. Moreover, murderers and other criminals were promised pardon for the acts they had committed.[121]

When Minister of Justice Drtina made his final report on the work of the Special People's Courts, it turned out that 475 Germans and 234 Czechs had been con-

---

[121] *Declaration*, February, 1953, issued by Alliance for Liberation and Freedom in Czechoslovokia, New York, Professor Frank Kral, Chairman.

demned to death, while 443 Germans and 293 Czechs were sentenced to life imprisonment. Prison terms averaging more than ten years were meted out to 19,888 other persons.[122] Among these was Dr. Josef Cerny, leader of the Agrarian party, who spent two years in prison. His associates, George Stribrny and Rudolf Beran, were sentenced to life imprisonment and twenty years respectively. Dr. Emil Hacha, third president of Czecho-Slovakia and president of the Protectorate, was not even tried, but was beaten to death in a Prague jail.[123] Monsignor Dr. Joseph Tiso, the respected president of the Slovak Republic, was falsely accused of Nazism and sentenced to death by a judge of the National Court who declared, *before the trial*, "I will hang Tiso!"[124]

In Bohemia and Moravia, the political police and concentration camps were administered by the Communist Minister of the Interior, Vaclav Nosek, sometimes with the local help of non-Communists who appeared in Germany as "democratic exiles" after 1948.[125] In Slovakia, however, these activities were directed by the "nonparty technician," General Mikulas Ferjencik, who had aided the Soviet commissars in the 1944 "revolt." He was appointed Commissioner of the Interior in a deal between the Communists and the non-Communist Dr. Jozef Lettrich, president of the Slovak National Council. A competing candidate for the job, Dr. Fabian, was arrested to get him out of the way.

The Executive Decree on Labor Camps for Slovakia, issued by the Board of Commissioners on June 14, 1946,

---

[122] Prokop Drtina, *Na soudu naroda* ["The People's Court"], three speeches by Minister of Justice Dr. Prokop Drtina on the activities of the Special People's Courts and the National Court, Prague, 1947, pp. 11ff. See also Mikus, *La Slovaquie dans le Drame de l'Europe*, pp. 216-47; "People's Courts in Czecho-Slovakia," *Slovakia*, May, 1951, pp. 3-6; and Andrej Gemersky, "Nationalization of Private Property in Slovakia," *Slovakia*, September-December, 1954, pp. 44-49.

[123] Borin, *Against the Hangman*, pp. 11-12; Jaksch, *op. cit.*, p. 443.

[124] Delaney, *False Freedom*, pp. 101-7; Michal Zibrin, "The Case of Dr. Joseph Tiso," *Slovakia*, August, 1952, pp. 1-24; Mikus, *op. cit.*, pp. 229-40.

[125] Frantisek Kroupa, who conducted a reign of terror at Joachimsthal, and Vaclav Hrnecek, deputy commander of the Budejovice concentration camp from May, 1945, to November, 1946, are cases in point. On Kroupa, see Turnwald, *op. cit.* (English edition), Report 51; *Sudetendeutsche Zeitung*, Munich, February 21 and April 25, 1953. The most detailed English-language exposé of concentration camp conditions in the Czech lands is found in: United States Court of the Allied High Commission for Germany, Area Five, *Office of the U.S. High Commissioner for Germany, Plaintiff, v. Vaclav Hrnecek, Defendant* (Crim. 52-A5-486), *Opinion, Findings of Fact, Conclusions of Law and Sentence*, by Presiding Judge Leo M. Goodman, Munich, May 26, 1954. Hrnecek was sentenced to eight years imprisonment on fourteen counts of aggravated assault; his career as an exile is mentioned briefly in chap. IX, *infra*.

provided *confinement in a camp without trial* for persons who "by their actions—contrary to the people's democratic spirit—threaten the reconstruction of the state, national security, the peace, public order . . . as well as those persons who profess an ideology inimical to the state or an ideology inciting other persons to such hostility . . . or persons who failed without ground to appear at their work . . . within the framework of the law making labor universally obligatory."[126] Since the majority of the Carpatho-Germans had already been evacuated or interned pending deportation, this decree was directed largely against recalcitrant Slovaks, the adherents of Dr. Tiso in particular.

General Ferjencik supervised a number of concentration camps. According to his own official report, 3,224 persons were confined in these camps in 1946, 1,297 of them by *administrative decision of the police.* In numerous cases his inquisitors tortured prisoners and extorted false testimony to "frame" political opponents. He covered up political murders and refused to investigate the mass graves of victims of Red Army and Communist massacres. When General Ferjencik left office in 1948, the Communist press praised him for his efforts.[127]

THE JOACHIMSTHAL URANIUM MINES

There are major uranium mines at Joachimsthal (Jachymov) in the western Sudetenland, north of Karlsbad. These are a major source of atomic materials for the Soviet nuclear weapons program which is, of course, principally directed against the United States. In the last days of World War II, when the United States Army occupied western Bohemia, it stopped just short of Joachimsthal. Several days passed before the Red Army arrived to take the town, including the uranium mines.

It is hard to believe that American intelligence did

126 Slovak Liberation Committee, *Documents*, pp. 29-30.
127 Stefan Blasko, *Slovakia in Blood and Shackles* (a history of General Ferjencik's political career) ; Mikus, *op. cit.*, pp. 277-84; *Slovak Newsletter*, August and September, 1949.

not know that these mines existed. It would have been simple enough to occupy the area and stay there long enough to assure that they would not be exploited by the Russians. Since United States forces were then occupying German Saxony immediately north of Joachimsthal —where there are also uranium mines (which we also turned over to the U.S.S.R.)—and since the entire area is German rather than Czech, a minor border adjustment would have put all the uranium in the United States Zone of Germany. After all, even in 1945, we were not (officially) sharing our atomic technique with the Kremlin.

Be that as it may, the Czecho-Slovak government did not offer to make the uranium available to the West. During the war President Benes, Foreign Minister Masaryk, and Dr. Ripka signed a secret pact leasing the mines for ninety-nine years to the Soviet Union. This was supplemented by an agreement of October, 1945, granting the Soviet government the use of the mines free of charge, with all investments to be paid for by the Czecho-Slovak Republic.[128]

Dr. Bohdan Chudoba, a deputy of the People's party, tried to launch a parliamentary investigation of the free gift of uranium to the Kremlin. He was promptly attacked by his own party's newspapers, accused of uttering untruths, and threatened with reprisals. It later turned out that the attacks had been instigated by Dr. Ripka's protégé, Dr. Ivo Duchacek. In June, 1948, after Dr. Duchacek had left Czecho-Slovakia, he admitted in a *New York Herald Tribune* interview that he had covered up the truth about the uranium mines. His excuse was that he had been bound by an agreement with the Communist party.[129]

---

[128] Josef Josten, *Oh, My Country!*, London, 1949, pp. 186-87; Otto Friedman, *The Breakup of Czech Democracy*, London, 1950, p. 133. This section is, however, based largely on interviews with Czech and Slovak exiles having direct personal knowledge of the uranium transactions.

[129] *New York Herald Tribune*, June 8, 1948, interview with Dr. Ivo Duchacek on his arrival in Paris.

V

THE 1948 "FEBRUARY REVOLUTION"

THE COMMUNIST-LIBERAL HONEYMOON

MEMBERS of the "liberal" Czech and Slovak parties who sought asylum in the West after February, 1948, oftcn picture the so-called "February Revolution" or "Gottwald Putsch" as the sad end of a struggle between Communists and anti-Communists — a battle nobly lost. But how seriously did the non-Communist "National Fronters" really fight Communism?

Whatever secret motives the "liberals" of the National Front may have harbored, they played to perfection the role assigned them by Comrade Dimitroff's "United Front" strategy: to spread the impression of honest and harmonious co-operation between Communists and liberals, deceiving the free world, while turning over the levers of power to the Communist party. One of the first steps in this "silent revolution" was the creation of a "National Bloc" of socialist parties within the National Front. An agreement to this effect was signed in June, 1945, by Dr. Peter Zenkl and Ministers Fierlinger and Gottwald, representing the National Socialist, Social Democratic, and Communist parties respectively. The document explained that while the three parties would remain separate organizations, they would pursue a common policy and program.[1]

Dr. Ripka later stated his opinion that the "National Bloc" was conceived as a step toward the eventual merger

---

[1] *Dohoda o spolecnem postupu stran Narodniho bloku pracujiciho lidu mest i venkova* ["Agreement for Co-operation Among the National Bloc Parties of the Urban and Rural Workers"], *Knihovnicka Aktualit* ["Little Current Affairs Library"], Gustav Bares, editor, No. 2, Prague, June, 1945. The author is indebted to Dr. Joseph A. Mikus for translating this document and providing a valuable analysis of its significance.

of the three socialist parties into a single body. In the meantime, he indicated, the bloc was to exert pressure on the Social Democrats, and more particularly on the National Socialists, bending them to the will of the Communists and forcing the Czech Catholic People's party and the Slovak Democrats into a minority position within the government.[2] To accomplish this, the "National Bloc" agreement provided for co-ordinating committees in which the three parties would reach unanimity before the discussion of important matters in local or regional National Committees.[3] Communist power was further enhanced by the decision of the three parties to foster centralized and exclusive trade unions, professional and peasant associations, and an inter-party Czech Youth Federation.[4] The monopoly enjoyed by these organizations, which progressively assumed the character of "Communist Fronts," was later confirmed by the "Law on Organizations" of July 12, 1951.[5]

The non-Communist politicians competed with the Communists to take credit for the deportation of the Sudeten Germans. Dr. Ivo Duchacek, Ripka's former assistant and (in his own words) "close collaborator," made a long speech in parliament in March, 1946, claiming the expulsion as the accomplishment of the middle-class parties, the National Socialist party and Dr. Ripka in particular. Dr. Ripka was at least honest enough not to deny his role in the expulsion. In his book *Czechoslovakia Enslaved* he admitted authorship of the plan, and he even tried—though without appreciable success—to convince Americans that uprooting more than three million people was a masterpiece of statesmanship.[6]

---

[2] Hubert Ripka, *Le Coup de Prague*, Paris, 1949, p. 19.

[3] These committees were similar to the "Antifas" (Anti-Fascist Committees) used to enforce "bloc politics" in the Soviet Zone of Germany.

[4] National Bloc agreement, paragraphs 4-9. Paragraph 4 reads: "The parties of the National Bloc agree that in the liberated Republic the organizations of trade unions, cooperatives, professional groups, spiritual and physical culture, as well as the youth organization will, from the outset, have a nation-wide and exclusive character. Independent of political parties, they will be organized on the principle of free membership and their leadership shall be elected by democratic procedure. The parties of the National Bloc consider it their duty to promote the formation of such organizations and to oppose energetically any attempt to split them. These nation-wide organizations shall be granted the right to criticize the government and the public administration." Such centralized organizations, which serve as instruments of control, propaganda, and "Bolshevist criticism," play a major role in all Communist countries.

[5] See the section on "Totalitarian Indoctrination" in chap. VI, *infra*.

[6] Ripka, *Czechoslovakia Enslaved*, p. 26; Slovak Liberation Committee, *Docu-*

Other "liberal" politicians, including Jan Stransky, Fedor Hodza, Juraj Slavik, Martin Kvetko, and Jozef Lettrich made speeches for home consumption only favoring the expulsions or opposing the granting of minority rights. Lettrich went so far as to say that German- or Hungarian-speaking Jews should "share the fate of Hungarians and Germans."[7]

When politicians of the National Front visited Western countries or entertained foreign guests during the years 1945-47, they asserted categorically that their country was "once more" a model democracy, often adding an explanation of Czecho-Slovakia's unique function as a "bridge between East and West." Many American newsmen were taken in by such propaganda and a few became its active propagators, so that the public was subjected to a barrage of misleading dispatches such as the following:

Stanislav Dvorak, new Czechoslovak consul in Cleveland, today asserted that "Czechoslovakia is absolutely independent, both politically and economically, from Russia. . . ." Dvorak said that he was amazed at the number of American people who were asking him about "Communist Czechoslovakia. . . ." (*Cleveland Press*, August 19, 1946.)

"There is no iron curtain over Czechoslovakia," Jan Masaryk, chairman of the Czechoslovak delegation to the United Nations General Assembly, asserted yesterday. . . Declaring that his country had "voluntarily and gladly" signed a treaty with the Soviet Union, which it was resolved to fulfill, M. Masaryk . . . suggested that anyone who believed in the existence of an iron curtain over Czechoslovakia "should go over and see for himself." (*New York Times*, October 29, 1946.)

"Czechoslovakia is governed by a democratic government which is not influenced or controlled by any foreign government. Czechoslovakia has a representative government, which the people elected freely. President Benes is acclaimed in the whole world as one of the leading statesmen in Europe, and his experienced and firm hand is leading Czechoslovakia to complete reconstruction." (Fiorello H. LaGuardia, as quoted by *New Yorksky Dennik*, August 25, 1946.)

The two-year plan became law with a maximum of publicity

_____

ments, pp. 26-27; speech by Ripka quoted in *Sudetendeutsche Zeitung*, Munich, July 19, 1952; see also *News from Czechoslovakia*, Vol. 8, No. 142, New York, October 1, 1946, and section on the "Council of Free Czechoslovakia" in chap. IX, *infra*.

[7] *Cas*, Bratislava, June 2, 1945; Slovak Liberation Committee, *Documents*, pp. 25-28; "The Czechoslovaks and Anti-Semitism," *Slovak Newsletter*, November, 1950; Mikus, *op. cit.*, pp. 272-76.

and of insistence on the idea that it represented an open challenge to free enterprise to demonstrate in a peaceful contest
which system could assure the better standard of living. . . .
Political leaders here . . . are convinced that Czechoslovakia
alone is in a position to show the world how collectivist economy
and individual liberty can be combined and eastern and western
ideals can find a common meeting ground. (Albion Ross, *New
York Times*, October 29, 1946.)

Prague— . . . Most observers here are inclined to doubt United
States fears that Russia is going to try to develop in Czechoslovakia, Austria and Germany the kind of Communist police state
that prevails in Rumania, Bulgaria and Poland. . . . One popular
theory in Prague is that the Russians always withdraw from the
West sooner or later for fear of being contaminated. (James
Reston, *New York Times*, August 5, 1947.)

The two dark spots on Czechoslovakia's otherwise bright horizons
are the restiveness in Slovakia and the increasingly truculent
political warfare between the two leading Czech parties—Communist and national socialist. Neither Czech leaders nor foreign
observers expect a crisis which might endanger the coalition
government. . . . (Maurice Hindus, *St. Louis Post-Dispatch*, July
8, 1947.)

Czechoslovakia is a country where approximately four out of
ten people voted the Communist ticket . . . in an election as fair,
free and untainted as any in the most advanced Western country . . . on a basis of perfectly free and fair competition among
political ideas. . . . I have been told that there is no danger to
Czechoslovak independence from Russian greed and expansionism
but that there is a danger of too much "dictation" within Czecho-
slovakia by Czechoslovak Communists. (Owen Lattimore, ONA
dispatch, *New York Times*, September 19, 1947.)

The myth that a local Communist party is "just one
more domestic party" can be recognized as a familiar
feature of the Kremlin's "confuse and control" propaganda.

Many members of the "liberal" parties, the Czech
Catholic People's party and the Slovak Democrats in
particular, opposed the Communists from the beginning
or became disgusted by bolshevist tactics. This was especially true in the local and intermediate levels of government. But their ability to resist was limited by the
fact that, during the Soviet occupation, the Communists
had assumed the chairmanship of many National Com-

mittees and had ensconced themselves in the local and district police and agriculture departments.[8]

The "liberal leadership had, moreover, embraced the Kosice Program, the totalitarian features of which we have already noted. While they did at times oppose Communist measures within the cabinet, their public statements were not such as to inspire militant resistance. Among the utterances of prominent "liberals" during the later period of the National Front we find the following:

> The Democratic Party knows that the Slovak Nation can be assured of a happier, more secure, and a brighter future only by working together with the Communist Party. (Dr. Jozef Lettrich, *Cas*, February 1, 1946.)

> Never in history was Russia so mighty, never were the forces of socialism so colossally forged together. This is a new historical epoch. Nevertheless some people think in a stick-in-the-mud fashion. It has not yet been possible to convince everybody of the need for the overthrow of capitalism. (Ferdinand Peroutka, *Tak nebo Tak* ["So or So"], Prague, 1947, p. 8.)

> Question: "Why does no opposition party exist in Slovakia?" Answer: "The need for an opposition party in reality has not yet arisen in our country." (Pavel Viboch in press conference in England, reported in *Cas*, Bratislava, May 15, 1947.)

> . . . Our Soviet friends possess in the people of Czechoslovakia and most especially among the members of the National Socialist Party devoted allies, dependable and tested friends. From the bottom of our hearts: "Cheers for the people of the Soviet Union. Long live the mighty Soviet Union. . . Long live in health and strength the great statesman Stalin." The permanent alliance of the Soviet Union and Czechoslovakia should be the more developed, strengthened, and firmly established in the interests of its peoples and in the interest of a general European peace. (Resolution of the Central Executive Committee of the National Socialist party, signed by Peter Zenkl, chairman, and Krajina, secretary, *Svobodne Slovo*, November 7, 1947.)

Let us declare war against the fear of Bolshevism and forbid, at the same time, the formation of any anti-Communist front

---

[8] Ivo Duchacek, *The Strategy of Communist Aggression—The Case of Czechoslovakia*, New Haven, 1949, pp. 8, 15-16. Duchacek, a supporter of the National Front himself, indicates: "In the autumn of 1945, a month before the withdrawal of the Red Army, nearly all chairmanships of National Committees were in Communist or pro-Communist hands. So was the leadership of most police and agriculture departments in local or district National Committees. The police and agriculture departments were of the utmost importance in a country where it was the duty of the local police to arrest collaborators and fascists according to the judgment of the local government, and where the Ministry of Agriculture and its local agencies were authorized to confiscate and distribute property which had formerly belonged either to fascists or to Sudeten Germans" (p. 15).

whatsoever. (Vaclav Majer in *Pravo lidu*, organ of the Social Democratic party, November 25, 1947.)[9]

Dr. Ivo Duchacek, who surely cannot be suspected of bias against his political mentors of the National Front, has given the following apt characterization of the weakness of "liberal" opposition to Communism in postwar Czecho-Slovakia:

But tactics of weakening the Communist Party by close cooperation with them were very confusing to the democratic rank and file, which was supposed to fight the Communists bravely on the local level, while democratic leaders almost seemed to be "honeymooning" with them on the national level.[10]

LIBERALS ARE EXPENDABLE

Elections for the National Assembly, the single-house parliament of the revived Czecho-Slovak Republic,[11] took place on May 26, 1946. Competition among the parties of the National Front was relatively free even though, as Dr. Ripka points out, the Communists used their control of ministries such as Interior and Information (including the radio) to bring pressure on the voters. The disenfranchisement of between 250,000 and 300,000 Czechs and Slovaks, "suspected of having collaborated with the Germans," cost the non-Communist parties at least ten of the three hundred seats.[12] The Agrarian, Tradesmen's, National Democratic, Slovak People's and Slovak National parties remained forbidden, and their adherents had to choose the National Front parties which they least disliked.

The Communists won 38 per cent of the votes (42 per cent in the Czech lands, 30 per cent in Slovakia) and thus secured the largest single fraction in parliament. Led by the fellow traveler Zdenek Fierlinger, the Social Democrats, who had obtained 13 per cent of the seats, were ready to assist the Communist party in ex-

---

[9] For more such quotations see, among other sources, the files of *Slovak Newsletter*, and Hrobak, *"Czechoslovakism" Versus Americanism*, Middletown, Pa., 1953, *passim*.

[10] Duchacek, *op. cit.*, p. 33.

[11] The Senate or upper house of the first Czecho-Slovak Republic was not re-established after World War II.

[12] Ripka, *Czechoslovakia Enslaved*, pp. 46-47.

ercising legislative control.[13] The cabinet was reorganized to reflect the results of the election, with the Communist leader, Klement Gottwald, as premier. The non-Communist parties, including the Social Democrats, retained a numerical majority in both the parliament and the cabinet.[14]

Somewhat shaken by the leftist electoral landslide and concerned to demonstrate the practical value of Dr. Benes' "bridge between East and West" theory, the non-Communist ministers now endeavored to promote a United States loan of $200,000,000 to Czecho-Slovakia. Although the Communists did not gainsay a project which might pay off in hard currency, they were at that time gravitating toward the Zhdanovite line of "inevitable conflict and Soviet victory": the Communist and Communist-influenced press in Czecho-Slovakia echoed Russian charges of "dollar diplomacy" and "Wall Street imperialism."[15] While officials of the Export-Import Bank were willing to discuss a loan of $150,000,000, Secretary of State Byrnes was not a man to be gulled; on August 26, 1946, he ordered negotiations suspended and froze the unexpended $40,000,000 of a $50,000,000 credit previously granted for the purchase of surplus property. After noting how Czecho-Slovakia and other satellite states were employing the relief extended by UNRRA, Mr. Byrnes announced in December, 1946, that the United States would no longer support that organization. He was not inclined to use American taxpayers' money to finance Communism or Russian imperialism.[16] A final attempt to maintain a foothold in the Western camp was made on July 7, 1947, when the Czecho-Slovak

[13] Curt Beck, "Politics and Political Organizations," in Vratislav Busek and Nicolas Spulber, eds., *Czechoslovakia*, New York, 1957 (hereinafter cited as "Busek-Spulber"), p. 66.

[14] The Gottwald cabinet, formed on July 3, 1946, consisted of nine Communists, three Social Democrats, four National Socialists, three People's party members, and four Slovak Democrats. None of the parties were anti-Communist, though individual anti-Communists were elected on several tickets. The difference between the Social Democrats and the other non-Communist parties was not basic but rather a matter of the *degree* to which they were willing to collaborate with the Communist party. See Slovak Liberation Committee, *Documents*, pp. 6-7; Mikus, *op. cit.*, pp. 216-22; House Committee on Communist Aggression, *Special Report No. 8*, pp. 19-20.

[15] See Josef Kalvoda, *Titoism and Masters of Imposture*, New York, 1958, pp. 56-61; Georg von Rauch, *A History of Soviet Russia*, New York, 1957, pp. 391-93.

[16] See John C. Campbell, ed., *The United States in World Affairs, 1945-47*, New York, 1947, pp. 156-57, 329-38; Raymond Dennett and Robert K. Turner, eds., *Documents on American Foreign Relations, 1945-46*, Boston, 1948, pp. 371-72, 875.

cabinet—with the approval of Communist ministers who had misjudged the Kremlin's wishes—voted to send a delegation to the Marshall Plan conference in Paris. Upon telephoned instructions from Moscow, however, the cabinet promptly reversed itself and voted unanimously *not* to take part in the conference, thus avoiding "an act directed against the Soviet Union and our other allies."[17]

Propaganda for the National Front had been based on the theory that the Communists and "liberals" would work together under a common program. But as time went on, the Communists became increasingly dictatorial, often shutting off discussion of measures which they "railroaded" through the parliament or the cabinet. To undermine the other parties they invented intrigues and plots, which the "liberals" sometimes disingenuously promoted. Ripka devotes considerable space to a description of the Communist attack on the Slovak Democratic party, directed at eliminating certain conservative and Catholic elements whom the Reds had accused of "plotting against the Republic."[18] A little later in his narrative, however, Ripka tells of a meeting at Karlsbad with Zenkl, the Stranskys, father and son, Drtina, Krajina, and Julius Firt, where Ripka suggested "that we should ask the Slovak Democrats to take the initiative in getting rid of certain undesirable elements which had insinuated themselves into their ranks. . ."[19] These "undesirable elements" were precisely the victims of the Communist intrigue. The attitude of Dr. Lettrich, the "liberal" chairman of the Slovak Democrats, is indicated by his speech of November 16, 1947, in which he said: "It is with joy and satisfaction that we Democrats take cognizance of the fact that our security organs have saved us . . . from . . . an anti-State plot."[20] Similar intrigues were directed against conservative

[17] Busek-Spulber, chronology, p. 438; *New York Times*, July 11, 1947; Ripka, *op. cit.*, pp. 69ff.

[18] *Ibid.*, pp. 96ff.

[19] *Ibid.*, p. 110.

[20] Dr. Jozef Lettrich, at a meeting sponsored by the Democratic party in Bratislava, November 16, 1947, quoted by Jiri Brada, *History of the Council of Free Czechoslovakia and of the Personnel of Radio Free Europe*, Munich, 1953, p. 21.

Czechs, particularly those who belonged to the Catholic People's party.[21]

Serious disagreements within the National Front arose during the latter half of 1947. These were to some extent arguments as to *how far* socialism should be carried, a matter which was rather academic since 60 per cent of Czecho-Slovak industry (in terms of employees) had already been nationalized by June, 1947.[22] There were also, increasingly, conflicts over power and jobs.

Although the Kremlin could have installed an out-and-out Communist government in Prague in 1945 without too much difficulty, its policy was—as we have observed—to make haste slowly. Not wishing to alarm the United States, which might have delayed demobilizing its forces in Germany, Stalin had waited until after the 1946 election before allowing an overt Communist to head a "United Front" cabinet. The "silent revolution" did not, however, proceed quite so smoothly as expected. Although the "liberals" managed to keep the West assured that Czecho-Slovakia was nothing more than a "progressive" democracy, it was not so easy to fool the Czech and Slovak peoples, who were daily witnesses and victims of what was happening.

The general atmosphere in Czecho-Slovakia in late 1947 and early 1948 was that of growing disillusionment with Communism. The Czechs and the Slovaks were becoming sick of the police state and of economic regimentation. However unsatisfactory the "liberal" parties might be, they were at least the lesser of two evils: a popular current swept them toward unwilling opposition to Communism. The Communists began to fear that they would lose control in the elections then scheduled for the summer of 1948. They therefore began to plan a *coup d'état* to prevent the holding of free elections.[23]

[21] Annex, "Czechoslovakia," *Monthly Bulletin of the International Peasant Union*, Vol. I, Nos. 8-9, Washington, September-October, 1950, pp. 30-35; statement of Dr. Joseph A. Mikus, House Committee on Communist Aggression, *Tenth Interim Report*, Washington, 1954, pp. 165-67; Joseph Bystricky, "The Slovaks and Dr. Joseph Lettrich," *Slovakia*, December, 1951, pp. 48-52. For General Ferjencik's role in the fabrication of "plots," see Blasko, *Slovakia in Blood and Shackles*, pp. 18-22, 30-39.

[22] *Statistical Digest of the Czechoslovak Republic*, Prague, 1948, p. 55, cited in U.S. Bureau of the Census, *The Population of Czechoslovakia*, by Waller Wynne, Jr., Washington, 1953, p. 4. On the scope of nationalization, see *ibid.*, pp. 3-6.

[23] Duchacek, *op. cit.*, pp. 30-35; House Committee on Communist Aggression, *Special Report No. 8*, p. 21; Borin, *Against the Hangman*, p. 14.

Although the "liberals" had served Communist tactics admirably during the first two years of the National Front, they now became a political liability. It grew increasingly clear that the Communists regarded the "liberals" as expendable: to be dumped overboard when their utility had ended. Needless to say, the "liberals" did not appreciate this view.

It might even be said that the "liberal" parties competed with the Communist party to become the chosen instrument of Russian policy. This is suggested by Dr. Ripka's appearance with Soviet Ambassador Zorin under the motto "Faithfully with the Soviet Union Forever" in November, 1947, as well as by a speech of January, 1948, in which he said:

. . . Let us rely on the U.S.S.R. a great power which is menaced by Germany as much as we are. Should anyone claim that he who will not side with the Communists is against the U.S.S.R. —he sins against this very alliance. Such a pretension would also constitute an insult to the Soviet Government, which formulated its relation to us quite clearly. . . Socialism means to us the supreme form of democracy.[24]

Whether President Benes could have stayed the impending disaster is not a major question. His former secretary, Dr. Taborsky, feels that Benes missed two opportunities to head off a Communist takeover. The first was after the election of 1946 when the president, in view of abuse of power by the Communist Minister of the Interior, could have insisted on appointing a non-Communist to that position—Taborsky's candidate being Jan Masaryk(!). The second was in July, 1947, when Benes might have thwarted the Kremlin's demand for withdrawal from the Marshall Plan, thereby (as Taborsky saw it) forcing the Communist ministers to resign. When the crisis finally came in February, 1948, Benes was unwilling to risk civil war and possible Russian intervention.[25] The possibility that genuine opportunities

[24] *Svobodne Slovo*, Prague, November 7, 1947, and January 22, 1948.

[25] Edward Taborsky, "The Triumph and Disaster of Eduard Benes," *Foreign Affairs*, July, 1958, pp. 682-84. Taborsky admits that Masaryk was "not well qualified," but points out that in view of his devotion to Benes, the president would have been his own Minister of the Interior. That the Communists would have resigned on being outvoted over the Marshall Plan seems to this author a rather doubtful thesis.

to "rescue" Czecho-Slovakia were missed at these late dates is highly problematical. What is not problematical is the fact that Benes' policy in the first place created a situation calling for rescue.

THE COMMUNISTS TAKE OVER

As there are a number of detailed accounts of the events of February and March, 1948, in Prague, only the bare essentials will be recited here. Those who wish to read more will find a good objective account in Otto Friedman's *The Collapse of Czech Democracy* (London, 1952), written by a Czech who supported the National Front without being blind to its weaknesses. The eye-witness reports by Ripka (*Czechoslovakia Enslaved*) and Jan Stransky (*East Wind Over Prague*) are also valuable if read with discrimination.

The specific bone of contention in February, 1948, was the refusal of Vaclav Nosek, Communist Minister of the Interior, to carry out the cabinet's resolution ordering him to dismiss certain party comrades he had appointed as police commissioners. Premier Gottwald, of course, supported Nosek in his insubordination against the command of the non-Communist majority. This majority, incidentally, included the Social Democrats, whose pro-Communist leader, Fierlinger, had been replaced in November, 1947, by the "moderate" socialist Bohumil Lausman, who *appeared* to be leading his party toward greater independence.[26]

There were several possible ways of dealing with the issue. Which, if any, might have succeeded is of course a speculative question—it may well be that Communist infiltration of the government had already made the situation hopeless. In any case, effective measures against the Communists would have required prompt and firm action by the non-Communist ministers and by President Benes. The ability to act, however, seemed precisely the missing ingredient.

One method would have been to call out the army

and have it remove the Communist police commissioners by force. Although Defense Minister Svoboda tended to side with the Communists, President Benes was commander of the armed forces, in which non-Communist elements still dominated. Another alternative would have been for President Benes to dismiss the Communist ministers and appoint others, a step which Article 70 of the Czecho-Slovak Constitution empowered him to take. In view of the fact that the Czech Communist party had over 1,200,000 members,[27] this action too would probably have required military support and, in all probability, the proclamation of martial law.

The idea of forming a government without the Communists, however, seemed incredible to the National Fronters. On February 9, 1948, when the cabinet crisis was already brewing, Ferdinand Peroutka, reflecting the thinking of the National Socialist party, wrote in the magazine *Dnesek:*

> In Czech politics, in Czech national life, it is urgent that we come to an understanding with the Communist party. . . . If there is any thought of forming a coalition against the Communists with the aim of excluding them from the government . . . it is possible to answer with certainty that no reasonable man would dream of it, for to do so would amount to inviting catastrophe. The Communist Party shall remain the greatest force in our political scheme even after the elections are over; and socialism shall remain the foundation of our national life. . . . Coming to terms with the Communists is the golden theme of our political philosophy.[28]

The step actually taken by twelve ministers of the National Socialist, Catholic People's, and Slovak Democratic parties—including Zenkl, Ripka, Jaroslav Stransky, Prochazka, Sramek, Hala, and Kocvara—was to hand their resignations to President Benes. They believed, as they have claimed, that by threatening dissolution of the cabinet they could force the Communists to

---

[27] The Czech Communist party (not including Slovakia) had 1,281,138 members as of November 28, 1947, and 1,602,223 members on March 21, 1948. For statistics on the Czech and Slovak Communist parties, see Slovak Liberation Committee, *Documents*, pp. 6-7.

[28] Cited, *ibid.*, p. 22. In answer to criticism, Mr. Peroutka later explained (in the article quoted in Chapter IX, "The Council of Free Czechoslovakia") that he wrote this passage to *counteract* Communist propaganda. For an analysis of his position, see the author's article, "Psychological Warfare's Policy Feedback," *Ukrainian Quarterly*, Spring, 1953, pp. 113-15.

negotiate. Their position was weakened, however, by the fact that Bohumil Lausman, disappointing the hopes of the "liberals," refused to align the Social Democratic party with the anti-Gottwald faction.[29] The attempt to resolve the crisis by negotiation gave the Communists exactly what they needed—time to organize mass demonstrations and to mobilize "action committees" in public agencies and industrial enterprises.[30] Lack of a functioning cabinet made it difficult to proceed against these clearly subversive moves. The sudden return of the Soviet diplomat Zorin to Prague and his open support of Gottwald raised an implied threat of Russian intervention. Although Benes had once declared that he would "fight to the bitter end" should the Communists attempt to seize power by violence,[31] he capitulated when faced with the show of force. As Taborsky relates, he refused offers of support from generals of the army, explaining that "the Russians would not tolerate" Gottwald's arrest.[32] Instead of disciplining Gottwald and Nosek, he *accepted* the resignations of the twelve ministers, appointing successors chosen by Gottwald. The new cabinet, consisting of twelve Communists and twelve fellow travelers, took office on February 25 and obtained a vote of confidence of 230 of the 300 members of parliament on March 11, 1948. The other seventy members, in hiding or fearing reprisals, did not attend.[33]

The repressive measures which the National Front had from the beginning aimed against its political opponents were now felt by its erstwhile ministers and their political supporters. The "action committees" provided the impetus for a wave of dismissals which swept public agencies, business enterprises, and editorial offices. The spring of 1948 saw a mass flight from Czecho-Slovakia, not only of those who had made and justified the policies

[29] Close observers of Mr. Lausman's conduct during World War II could have expected as much. Lausman, who left Czecho-Slovakia in 1949 and returned in 1953, has never been an anti-Communist, but has proved adept at fooling Czech and American "liberals." See Kalvoda, *op. cit.*, pp. 134-49; chap. IX, *infra*, "Radio Free Europe."

[30] Sidor, *op. cit.*, p. 54; Mikus, *op. cit.*, pp. 287-88.

[31] Taborsky, *loc. cit.*, p. 683.

[32] *Ibid.*, p. 684.

[33] Several deputies who voted *for* Gottwald later turned up in the West as "anti-Communist" exiles.

of the National Front, but also of those who, within the Front or outside it, had led a shadowy conservative opposition.[34]

Yet not all the "National Fronters" really had to flee for their lives. The comment of the Communist newspaper *Tvorba* (Prague, December 29, 1948) was: "It is true that nine-tenths of them were fleeing without reason as they were not exposed to any danger." While this Communist story was perhaps exaggerated, it was not cut out of whole cloth.

Many who had really fought Communism had difficulty in escaping. Others left without police interference, some received passports, and a few were able to drive to Germany in their own cars. Occasionally, Communist agents escorted "escapees" over the border.[35] The story of Dr. Hubert Ripka's escape seems significant. In March, 1948, Ripka left Prague in the company of two priests, Monsignor Sramek and Monsignor Hala, who had been ministers in the National Front government. The three proceeded to a small air field near Rakovnik, some thirty-five miles due west of the capital. Here they waited in a shack on the edge of the field for a French airplane which was to pick them up. The Czech secret police got wind of the affair and covered the air field with their men. The French pilot arrived and, seeing the men on the field, flew away without landing. Ripka then left the shack and walked *right past the secret police* into the woods. Monsignori Hala and Sramek were arrested and sent to prison. A few days later the plane returned and picked up *Ripka alone* without any difficulty.

An examination of the political implications of the flight of the Czecho-Slovak "liberals" is undertaken in Chapter IX. Suffice it to note here that, as Mr. Peroutka has made abundantly clear, the "National Fronters" would have continued collaborating with the Communists had not the latter decided that it was time to get rid of them.

---

[34] House Committee on Communist Aggression, *Special Report No. 8*, pp. 22-25.

[35] Based on the author's interviews with refugees, police officials, and members of intelligence agencies.

VI

THE "PEOPLE'S DEMOCRACY"

THE COMMUNISTS DICTATE A CONSTITUTION

SINCE March, 1948, Czecho-Slovakia has proceeded further along the path chosen by the exile "government" during World War II and pursued by the National Front throughout the first postwar years. It is currently a "people's democracy," which, in Communist parlance, represents a transitional stage on the road to socialism, more advanced than that of the United Front.[1] Formally independent, the Prague government receives its orders from Moscow through the ultra-orthodox Communist party and a large staff of resident Soviet officials who function as a Russian colonial administration. Dr. Benes has passed from the scene, having been succeeded by three Communist presidents: Gottwald, Zapotocky, and Novotny.

During the months preceding the "February Revolution," a committee of parliament had been drafting a revised constitution. The Communists now edited this document to suit their own purposes: it was adopted by the parliament on May 9, 1948, by a vote of 246-0 with 54 members absent. President Benes was given thirty days to sign the new constitution. With the document still awaiting his signature, he resigned on June 7, and the constitution was signed by Premier Gottwald, who was elevated to the presidency on June 14. Trade-union boss Antonin Zapotocky, who had made organized labor a pliable instrument of Communist political warfare, assumed

---

[1] See C. E. Black, "The People's Democracies of Eastern Europe," in Taylor Cole, ed., *European Political Systems*, New York, 1954, especially pp. 221-36; see also "Volksdemokratie" in *SBZ von A bis Z*, Bonn, 1956, 3d edition, Deutscher Bundes-Verlag, p. 281.

the premiership. Dr. Benes retired to his country home, where he died on September 3, 1948. Although his health had failed markedly since the end of World War II, it is not unreasonable to speculate that his death was hastened by the manifest bankruptcy of his own policies. The political orientation of the 1948 Constitution is apparent in the Preamble, which states, among other things:

We have now resolved that our liberated state shall be a national state, rid of all hostile elements, living in harmony in the family of Slav states and in friendship with all the peace-loving peoples of the world. We want it to be a people's democratic state in which the people, through their representatives, not only make the laws but, through their representatives, also put them into operation. We want it to be a state in which the entire economy serves the people and is so directed that the general welfare increases without economic crises and with a just distribution of the national income. By this road we want to reach a social order in which the exploitation of man by man will be completely abolished—socialism.[2]

Although the new constitution abandons the concept of a "Czechoslovak nation," it repeats the half-truth that: "The Czechs and Slovaks, two brother nations, members of the great Slav family, lived together in one state a thousand years ago . . ."[3] The Czechoslovak Republic, Article II asserts, "is a unitary State of two Slav nations possessing equal rights, the Czech and the Slovak. The territory of the State forms a single and indivisible whole."

The structure of government established by the 1948 Constitution is a hybrid between Soviet forms and those of the first Czecho-Slovak Republic, the concessions to tradition not being such as to preclude monolithic party control.[4] Supreme legislative power is vested in a single-

[2] *The Constitution of the Czechoslovak Republic,* English translation with amendments to date, Orbis, Prague, 1958, 108 pp. The purged "hostile elements" are of course the Sudeten Germans. According to Andrei A. Zhdanov, formulator of the "two camps" theory, only socialist states are "peace-loving," capitalist states being imperialist warmongers. The definition of "people's democracy" reflects the Leninist rejection of separation of powers, which is considered a bourgeois doctrine obstructing the will of the people.

[3] *Ibid.,* Preamble. Admission that there are two nations does not imply any genuine concession to self-determination, but merely reflects Soviet nationality policy of "nationalism in form, socialism in substance."

[4] The formal constitutions of the U.S.S.R., Yugoslavia, and most other Communist states are typified by concentration of power in the parliament, with a weak cabinet dependent on parliamentary confidence and lacking power to

chamber National Assembly of 368 deputies elected for six years.[5] With one third of its members constituting a quorum, the Assembly passes ordinary laws by simple majority and constitutional amendments by vote of three fifths of all the deputies.

Soviet precept is apparent in the Presidium of the National Assembly, which in its personnel and powers duplicates the Presidium of the Supreme Soviet of the U.S.S.R. Consisting of twenty-four deputies elected by the assembly for one year, the Presidium is vested with the right of judicial review, being empowered to give binding interpretations of laws and to judge the constitutionality of acts of the assembly or the Slovak National Council. When the assembly is not in session, the Presidium exercises full powers on "urgent" matters: the only things it cannot do are amend the constitution or elect a president or vice-president of the republic. As in the Soviet Union, most legislation is accomplished by decree of the Presidium, the assembly meeting twice a year to ratify laws placed in effect in the meantime. Urgent matters "which would otherwise require an Act" may be proposed only by the Government (cabinet); they must be signed by the president, the premier, and not less than half the members of the government.

The office of president of the republic, which has no counterpart in the Soviet Union or Poland, and which was not introduced in Yugoslavia until 1953, represents a concession to the Masaryk-Benes tradition of presidential leadership. Elected by the National assembly for seven years, the president summons and prorogues the assembly, and may dissolve it, except during the last six months of his term. He may veto any act of the assembly, but the latter may override the veto with an absolute majority of the deputies. The president appoints cabinet ministers and recalls them *if they resign;* he *may* assume the chair at cabinet meetings. While

dissolve. Such a constitution works well only when a single party controls *both* parliament and cabinet. In the French Fourth Republic, with its multitude of splinter parties, combination of a strong assembly with a weak cabinet led to political chaos.

[5] Constitutional Law No. 26 of May 26, 1954, which increased the number of deputies from 300 to 368, also introduced single-member districts in place of the former party-list system and provided that each deputy could be recalled by his constituents.

the government is held responsible for the president's official acts, he may nevertheless be impeached by the Presidium and convicted by a three-fifths vote of the National Assembly.

Although the formal powers granted the president of Czecho-Slovakia by the 1948 Constitution are no greater than those of the President of the French Fourth Republic, it is significant that the Communist leaders Gottwold, Zapotocky, and Novotny, each Moscow's proconsul in his time, have preferred the presidency to the premiership as a base of operations. As of this writing (December 1959), President Novotny is the most powerful figure in Czecho-Slovakia, but his power stems largely from his position as First Secretary of the Czech Communist party.

The "Government," as the cabinet is called, depends upon the confidence of the assembly, which may be withdrawn by majority vote, an absolute majority of the deputies being present. In contrast to French practice under the Third and Fourth Republics, a vote of nonconfidence against an individual minister does not require the resignation of the entire government.

The Constitution of 1948 abolished the traditional provinces of Bohemia, Moravia, and Silesia, grouping the municipalities and counties in nineteen artificial administrative regions (*kraje*). At each level there is a popularly-elected National Committee, which in theory selects the heads of the local administrative departments —who are actually chosen by the Communist party.[6] The Czech Communists have introduced the Soviet principle of "dual supervision," according to which an official is responsible not only to his National Committee but also, and primarily, to the corresponding official on the next higher level. National Committees at all echelons are considered organs of state power and are both "under the constant control of the working people" and "subordinate to the Government."

The Communist Constitution also provides what can

---

[6] The central secretariat of the party supervises the placement of party members in government posts at all levels. Such control over personnel, manipulated with dexterity by Stalin and Khrushchev in the U.S.S.R., is a key source of power within the party. See Merle Fainsod, *How Russia Is Ruled*, Cambridge, 1953, Harvard, pp. 152-79.

best be described as bogus self-government for Slovakia. There is a Slovak National Council or "Slovak Legislature" of 104 members elected for six years, with a Presidium analogous to that of the National Assembly. The powers of the Slovak National Council were originally limited to the enumerated fields of culture, education, public health, endowments, local boundaries, city planning, agriculture, and care of orphans; even in these areas it could legislate only in conformity with the Uniform National Economic Plan and with national laws. The council was summoned and adjourned by the premier of the *central* government in Prague, without whose signature acts of the council could not take effect. The central government could annul acts of the Slovak National Council which it considered unconstitutional, beyond the council's powers, or in conflict with the Economic Plan or the Budget Act. Finally, the premier, with the concurrence of the Government, could dissolve the Slovak National Council altogether.[7]

There are regional administrative departments for Slovakia, headed by commissioners who form a board or "Slovak cabinet." Until 1956, the commissioners were appointed and recalled by the government in Prague. While they were also theoretically accountable to the Slovak National Council on matters within the jurisdiction of that body, the council lacked the disciplinary powers with which to enforce this responsibility.

Constitutional Law No. 33 of July 31, 1956, expanded the legislative powers of the Slovak National Council to include regional planning and budgeting and "matters of a national or regional character, if these require special provisions to secure the full economic and cultural development of Slovakia." The administrative functions of the Bratislava Commissioners were at the same time extended to all fields except foreign affairs, foreign trade, national defense (including heavy industry), and road and air transport. On paper, Slovakia was granted constitutional autonomy comparable to that of a Union Republic in the U.S.S.R. The Slovak National Council is

---

[7] Chapter Five of the 1948 Constitution, containing these provisions, has been superseded by Constitutional Law No. 33 of July 31, 1956, which is included in the 1958 Orbis edition of the Constitution.

now summoned and adjourned by its own Presidium; Slovak laws become effective when signed by the chairmen of the Council and Board of Commissioners and the commissioner charged with enforcement. The commissioners, who collectively exercise police power and supervise National Committees in Slovakia, are now appointed and removed by the Slovak National Council without the intervention of the central government.

These seeming concessions are, however, "Indian gifts," since the machinery of central control remains. Power to declare a Slovak law unconstitutional or *ultra vires* is vested in the Presidium of the National Assembly.[8] The rule of "dual supervision" is implicit in the juxtaposition of Article 23 of the 1956 law, which makes the commissioners responsible to the Slovak National Council, and Article 24, which requires them to "be guided by the principles embodied in government directives. Individual commissioners shall also conform in principle with the directives of the appropriate ministers." The government has power to void a decision of the board or a single commissioner which it believes to violate the law or its own "fundamental directives."

Actually, however, the powers of the Czech cabinet to annul decisions of the Slovak authorities are held in reserve for the unlikely occasion of a revolt within the Communist party. Under the principle of "democratic centralism," continuous control is exercised through party channels; the ostensibly independent acts of the Slovak National Council and the commissioners are "pre-decided" in accordance with party directives. As will be shown in Chapter VIII, the "Slovak Communist Party," managed by the Czech Karel Bacilek, is in reality a subordinate branch of the Czech Communist party and completely subservient to Prague. In view of the large number of Czechs assigned to "Slovak" agencies, and the systematic purging of all Slovaks—even Slovak Communists—suspected of "bourgeois nationalism," the Bratislava regime today can best be described as a Czech-Communist administration for Slovakia.

---

[8] The Presidium of the Supreme Soviet of the U.S.S.R. exercises the same power to review legislation of Union Republics. See articles 20 and 49 of the Soviet Constitution and comment in Kulski, *The Soviet Regime*, pp. 193-94.

THE POLICE STATE

Despite their success in frightening President Benes with mass demonstrations, the Czech Communists never succumbed to the delusion that the "February Revolution" was a popular uprising. They knew, as their Muscovite mentors have always known, that the continuance of a Communist regime in power depends on the ruthless suppression of political opposition. It was therefore necessary to abolish even the limited degree of freedom which had existed during the National Front period.

With the parliamentary elections of May 30, 1948, the Communists introduced the "unity list" nominations common to all "people's democracies." Theoretically the various parties agree how many seats shall be held by each party: in practice, the Communists decide the distribution and exercise a veto over nominations by other parties. The voter, therefore, can only approve the preselected candidates or cast a blank ballot. To discourage negative voting, the Communists intimidated many into balloting openly in the 1948 election, in spite of which there were 10 per cent of "no" votes, most of which were cast in Slovakia. By passing the word around that use of the voting booth was a matter of interest to the secret police, the Communists have achieved majorities in the high nineties in more recent elections. Shortly after the 1948 election, the Communists "invited" the Social Democrats to join the Communist Party en masse, a measure which assured a 75 per cent majority in the National Assembly and most National Committees.

In October, 1948, the Communist-controlled assembly passed a new "Defense of the Republic Act," which imposed criminal penalties not only on acts of overt resistance but also on "the spreading of rumors detrimental to state policy." There followed the "Law on the Democratization of the Courts" of December 22, 1948, which assured that the judiciary, as in the Soviet Union, would henceforth be an instrument of "socialist justice." Armed with these "legal" weapons, the Gottwald regime intensified persecution to the point at which all known anti-Communists were either in exile or in concentration camps.

The magnitude of the Red Terror is suggested by the fact that there are currently some 250 known concentration and forced-labor camps in Czecho-Slovakia, with an estimated total of 380,000 inmates. The largest camp, at Joachimsthal (Jachymov), is administered by the Soviet KGB, which employs the 30,000 prisoners as uranium miners. There are three other large camps with 9,000 or more inmates and many smaller camps, including several for priests and nuns.[9] The inmates are forced to perform heavy labor on a starvation diet, of which the following "menu" is typical:

Breakfast:	Bitter black coffee Bread A small portion of jam *or* sugar for coffee, but not both
Lunch:	Weak soup Potatoes One piece of bread
Supper:	Black coffee Bread Jam or margarine two days per week[10]

From 1948 to 1954, penal boards attached to district National Committees could, without trial or hearing, commit persons who "endangered public safety" to forced-labor camps for periods up to two years. As President Zapotocky cynically observed: "When such people vacate an apartment, this is their one and only contribution to socialist construction." Since 1954, confinement at forced labor following a prison sentence may be imposed by regional parole boards, while the district penal boards may order correctional labor without confinement.[11]

The former political role of the National Security Police (SNB) is now divided between the secret police (StB) and a special militarized police, the PVS (*Pohranicni a vnitrni straze*), organization of which com-

---

[9] *Sudetendeutsche Zeitung*, January 24 and February 7, 1953, and January 8, 1955.

[10] *Der Sudetendeutsche*, March 3, 1952.

[11] *Sudetendeutsche Zeitung*, January 8, 1955; Stephen Kocvara, "The Constitutional System," in Busek-Spulber, p. 58.

menced in 1953. Both are supervised by the Ministry of the Interior. The PVS, which corresponds to the military detachments of the KGB (Committee for State Security) in the Soviet Union, served as a vehicle for the ambitions of Interior Minister Rudolf Barak, at that time engaged in a feud with the Minister of Defense, Dr. Alexei Cepicka. In 1954 Minister Barak convinced his colleagues that the army, though recently purged, was not sufficiently reliable for frontier duty. Accordingly, as the PVS expanded, it took over the guarding of the border, the regular army being withdrawn to the interior. The PVS also manages all concentration camps which are not directly Soviet-operated.

Only fanatical Communists are selected as officers of the PVS, and all ranks are subjected to thorough indoctrination. Pay scales are much higher than in the army; enlisted men of the PVS earn more than many industrial workers.[12]

Like any police agency vested with unlimited powers, the PVS has at times proved difficult to control. Although American forces and the West German border police kept the PVS from raiding Bavaria, there were numerous incidents along the Bohemian frontier with the Soviet Zone of Germany. PVS men are granted bounties up to one thousand crowns and passes for each arrest, and since there were few victims left in the Sudeten German border villages, groups from the PVS formed the habit of raiding nearby Saxony, kidnapping inhabitants, and then charging them with illegal entry into Czecho-Slovakia. Since "friendship within the socialist camp" was the order of the day in Sovzone Germany, the press there was instructed not to mention such incidents.[13]

TOTALITARIAN INDOCTRINATION

A Communist state cannot limit itself to stamping out political opposition: it must, to maintain power, invest all phases of human activity with political con-

---

[12] *Slowakische Korrespondenz*, Munich, August, 1958, p. 3.

[13] *Sudetendeutsche Zeitung*, November 7, 1954.

tent. Since "nonpolitical" voluntary groups, if left to themselves, are likely to become hotbeds of opposition to a regime exercising a political monopoly, all organizations in Czecho-Slovakia have been *gleichgeschaltet* ("co-ordinated") in Nazi fashion.

The "Law on Organizations" of July 12, 1951, provides:

> To guarantee the democratic rights of the people, to strengthen the people's democratic system, and to support socialist construction, organizations are established. The state guides the development of all organizations and sets the conditions for their activity.

Under this law, a limited number of organizations are permitted and all others prohibited. Of the recognized organizations, all of which serve as "fronts" for the Communist party, the largest is the URO (Unified Trade Union) with 3,500,000 members. Next in importance is the CSM or Youth Federation, which enjoys a monopoly, since parties and churches are forbidden youth groups of their own. Although originally founded as an "interparty" organization under the 1945 National Bloc agreement, the CSM was affiliated with the Communist party by a decision of the latter's Eleventh Congress in June, 1958, and is now the equivalent of the Russian Komsomol. Its branches for younger children are the Pioneers (boys and girls from six to twelve) and the Svazaci (adolescents from twelve to seventeen). There are also the CSZ or Women's League, the Association for Czecho-slovak-Soviet Friendship, the Czecho-Slovak Red Cross, and SVAZARM, which specializes in the para-military training of glider pilots, radio amateurs, pigeon and dog breeders, and the like. All these organizations are required to combine "political education" with their other activities, and to turn out for demonstrations when wanted.[14]

The 1948 Constitution deals with education as follows:

> All schools shall be state schools. . . .
> All education and instruction provided shall be consistent with the results of scientific research, and shall be in consonance with the people's democratic order.

[14] Information supplied by Munich office of Slovak National Council Abroad. See Rudolf Sturm, "Propaganda," in Busek-Spulber, particularly pp. 116-20.

The supreme direction of all education and all instruction, as well as the supervision thereof, shall be the responsibility of the State.[15]

The Communist regime has interpreted these provisions as a mandate to begin political education in the kindergarten, attendance at which becomes compulsory at the age of three. Here, children are regaled with "progressive stories," play "peace games," and memorize edifying ditties such as the following:

> Grandfather and Grandmother
> Eat the bread from our mouths.
> When Grandfather and Grandmother exist no more
> There will be more bread for the rest of us.[16]

The effect of this curriculum on family life is poignantly described by a Czech mother, who wrote to an American friend, in part, as follows:

Milenka is healthy and rather tall for her age. You wouldn't recognize her. She's changed—changed in so many ways. . . . It all started two years ago. I'd heard so many disturbing rumors about the kindergarten and didn't want Milenka to go there. For a while she stayed with grandfather. But then I was called before the trade-union council in my factory. They told me that my child must be educated as "a patriotic member of the working class." I had to send her there.

Pretty soon Milenka came home with strange stories and new versions of old fairy tales. Little Red Riding Hood was a poor working girl and the bad wolf only looked like a wolf, but was really a capitalist. Cinderella was being "exploited" by her stepmother, and the good fairy had become a lady shock worker or stakhanovite. Once I sat by her bedside and told her the story of Schlaraffenland, where milk flows in the rivers and roast pigeons fly through the air. I'd always loved that fairy tale when I was a kid. But Milenka gave me a funny look and said, "That's a silly story, mother. There is no such country." I had to go out. I felt the tears coming up and was afraid she might see me cry, and report me to her teacher. Yes, I've become afraid of my own child. . . .

The other day she came home and said, "Mother, President Gottwald was the greatest son of our country, wasn't he?" and she gave me a quizzical glance. I quickly said, "Yes, he was." I knew she was watching me. Later I talked to the mothers of

---

[15] *Constitution*, Orbis edition, Sections 13 and 14.

[16] Taught to children in the Prague public schools. *Sudetendeutsche Zeitung*, July 23, 1955, and July 14, 1956.

other kids. They, too, had been asked that question by their children. The kids had orders to report to the teacher what we mothers had said!

Milenka is already a member of a children's collective. They perform certain tasks together and build things out of cubes—factories, never castles. . . .

My child doesn't know the beautiful songs of our country. Instead she sings Czech translations of Red Army marching songs, Three Tankers and The Grenade. Worst of all, Milenka learns no prayers in kindergarten. Prayers have been abolished because "they distract the minds of the children and lead them to faulty admiration of the imaginary [God]."[17]

In the primary school, according to Deputy Education Minister Anna Karlovska, children are to be "stripped of all bourgeois habits and prejudices. Every aspect of the children's education must be unconditionally on the basis of Marxism-Leninism. The pupil must be taught to love peace so passionately that he will be ready to defend it to the last drop of blood."[18] Between the ages of six and nine, children receive their red scarves as members of the Pioneers, after which their spare time is absorbed by activities such as military drill, political discussions, scrap collecting, and espionage—mainly against their own parents.[19] Vacations are spent in "shock brigades" in the factories or on the collective farms.

Recently, however, the Communist regime has been obliged to admit deficiencies in its youth program. In spite of the handsome uniforms, titles, and medals, two thirds of the young people from six to twenty-six have managed to stay out of the CSM and its affiliates, indicating a general distaste for organized "recreation."

[17] Joseph Wechsberg, "They're Afraid of Their Own Children," *Saturday Evening Post*, April 18, 1953, pp. 38-39. Wechsberg also cites the official monthly, its name translated "Pre-School Education," to the effect that: "We shall teach the children to love the Communist Party . . . we must create and stimulate the children's eagerness to become valuable party members when they grow up. There must be more political education in kindergartens. . . . With the children, their parents must also be educated. . . . The kindergarten teachers must inform the parents of the principles of socialist education." Permission to reprint granted by Paul A. Reynolds and Sons, 599 Fifth Avenue, New York, N.Y.

[18] Cited by Wechsberg, *loc. cit.*, p. 139.

[19] The *Sudetendeutsche Zeitung*, July 23, 1955, reports the case of a construction worker of Prague who was denounced by his own son for criticizing the works council of his plant and cursing the "friends from Moscow." The father was sent to a concentration camp, while his son received a special commendation from the district organization of the Pioneers. Wechsberg, *loc. cit.*, also cites some cases of denunciation, a practice typical of both Nazi and Communist youth groups.

Furthermore, the deliberate effort to undermine the influence of parents has backfired, producing not dedicated young Communists but undisciplined and destructive *Paskovstvi* and *Somrastvi*, the Czech equivalent of "zoot suiters" and "teddy boys." The Communist party was finally forced to urge parents to take their obligations more seriously—to assert precisely that authority which the state itself had sought to destroy.[20]

A major reorganization of the school system was launched by the party at its CC Plenum of April, 1959. Following changes sponsored by Khrushchev in the U.S.S.R., increased emphasis is now placed on vocational training and on combining work with study. Attendance to the age of fifteen will be compulsory in a nine-grade "polytechnic work school," designed to prepare the child for production as well as further education. Students at apprentice schools, workers' middle schools, and general (college preparatory) middle schools will all hold jobs; as rapporteur Jiri Hendrych explained to the CC, child labor under capitalism is exploitive—under socialism it is an essential part of a "rounded education." College students will be required to perform manual work and to devote three times as many hours as formerly to the study of Marxism-Leninism. As in the U.S.S.R., academic accomplishment is bound to suffer if the reform is carried out thoroughly. Special commissions of the Communist party have been appointed to check faculty and students for loyalty and to decide the eligibility of the latter for further education.[21]

The Czecho-Slovak Communist party also mounts a mass adult "education" program for, as the Minister of Planning has declared, "the transition from capitalism to socialism requires not only reconstruction of the material base but also a re-thinking of men's thoughts."[22] Workers are generally expected to attend regular indoctri-

[20] "The Crisis of Czech Youth," *Sudetendeutsche Zeitung*, October 27, 1956. Concerning similar youth problems in the Soviet Union, see *Problems of Communism*, Washington, U.S. Information Agency, VI, No. 3 (May-June, 1957), pp. 15-29.

[21] Johann Gottfried Herder-Institut, Marburg/Lahn, *Wissenschaftlicher Dienst fuer Ost-Mitteleuropa* ["Scientific Service for East-Central Europe"] (hereafter cited as *Wissensch. Dienst*), IX (1959), 181-84; also *Sudeten Bulletin*, Munich, VII, No. 9 (September, 1959), 186-87.

[22] Quoted by Rudolf Wenzel, "The Party Is Everything, Comrades!," *Sudetendeutsche Zeitung*, September 24, 1955.

nation sessions, while the 1,422,200 members of the party (as of the Ninth Congress) progress through a curriculum ranging from a basic "candidates' course" to a three-year "evening university of Marxism-Leninism." The effectiveness of this program is, however, hampered both by a lack of competent instructors and by the evidently lukewarm enthusiasm of many comrades.

PERSECUTION OF THE CHURCH

Once Slovak independence had been crushed and the Sudeten Germans expelled, the greatest remaining obstacle to the "re-thinking" demanded by a Communist regime was the Catholic church. It is significant that persecution of the Church began long before the "February Revolution." The National Front government, despite the presence of Msgr. Sramek and Msgr. Hala of the "Catholic" People's party in its cabinet, was basically antireligious in its orientation.

Religious persecution has always been most severe in Slovakia, where the majority of the clergy supported Father Tiso and the Slovak Republic. Shortly after its entry into Prague in 1945, the National Front government ordered the arrest of the Slovak bishops Jan Vojtassak and Michael Buzalka, some 170 priests, and several thousand Catholic laymen. The bishops and most of the other prisoners were released after several months, however, since the time was considered premature for a direct attack on the Church.[23]

The government then issued a decree nationalizing all property of the Church in Slovakia, transferred the parochial schools to the state, and expelled teachers known for their religious convictions. It also dissolved the Catholic Youth, Men's, and Women's societies and the Catholic Charity, and confiscated their property. When Archbishop Karol Kmetko of Nitra, in July, 1945, collected 260,000 signatures for a petition favoring private schools,

---

[23] Slovak Catholic Federation of America, *Memorandum On the Present Status of Slovakia and the Situation of the Catholic Church and Its Bishops Under Communist Rule in Slovakia*, Chicago, May 16, 1956, pp. 8-10.

his action was declared illegal and a number of priests and laymen who had helped him were imprisoned.[24] The "trial" of President Tiso aroused massive resentment among Slovak Catholics. The National Front decreed that any demonstrations favoring Tiso's release would be "illegal," and Commissioner of the Interior Ferjencik was granted special powers to suppress them. There were a number of arrests, including that of Father Zenican, accused of inspiring a demonstration at Kralovany.[25] Tiso's trial could, indeed, be interpreted as a symbolic trial of the entire Catholic church in Slovakia. As the Protestant *Baseler Nachrichten* observed: "The trial of Monsignor Tiso, like that of Archbishop Stepinac in Yugoslavia, is solely for the purpose of liquidating anyone who maintains an opposing political outlook."[26]

The Czech lands were also the scene of religious persecution while the National Front coalition was still in office. According to a report made during the spring of 1947:

Agents of the Czech police, headed by Communist Minister of Interior Vaclav Nosek, have adopted the practice for which several Nazi agents were recently placed on trial—spying on the sermons of priests. . . . Recently the Rev. Stephen Trochta . . . was held and cross-examined by the Czech police (SNB) for sermons given during a retreat in the church of St. Maurice at Olomouc, Moravia. . . . There are other instances of priests having been seized by the police and cross-examined for references to totalitarianism and communism in their sermons. It was recently brought to light that the SNB sent a spy in clerical garments to the seminary of a religious order to listen to theology professors' lectures.[27]

After the "February Revolution," Archbishop Josef Beran of Prague, the Primate of the Roman Catholic Church in Czecho-Slovakia, made every effort to avoid a conflict with the Gottwald-Zapotocky regime. The archbishop even sang a festive *Te Deum* on June 14, 1948, on the occasion of President Gottwald's inauguration. The Communist party was, however, determined to liquidate the Church as an independent center of

[24] *Ibid.*, p. 9.
[25] *National Catholic Welfare Conference News Service*, April 9, 1947.
[26] Quoted in *Slovak Newsletter*, April, 1957, p. 2.
[27] *NCWC News Service*, May 7, 1947.

moral authority—if it could not stamp it out altogether, it could at least take over its administration. This was done in successive stages, beginning in June, 1949, when the government issued decrees to the effect that: (a) Church officials are forbidden to hold meetings without government sanction; (b) all pastoral letters, circulars, instructions, orders, and proclamations must be submitted to the Ministry of Education before issue; and (c) disciplinary measures of the Church "for political reasons" are invalid and punishable by law.[28] During the same month the regime sponsored the organization of a so-called "Catholic Action" movement looking toward a Czech "National Catholicism."

The Church refused to accept these attacks passively. The hierarchy indicated that the Catholic church would continue to uphold its ideas of a Christian society in public life and in education, and that it would strive for the repeal of enactments which endanger the religious freedom of Catholics.[29] On June 20, 1949, the Vatican declared the regime's "Catholic Action" movement schismatic and excommunicated its leaders and followers.[30] Archbishop Beran continued to issue uncensored pastoral letters, although many priests were arrested for reading them and the archbishop himself was threatened with charges of treason.

In October, 1949, the Communist regime had the rubber-stamp National Assembly pass a law confiscating the remaining property of the Church and converting priests into public officials, paid by the state and controlled by a newly organized Office for Church Affairs. This agency was given power to appoint priests to their offices, as well as to transfer and dismiss them. The government took over the operation of religious seminaries, and all priests, bishops, and other Church officials were required to take an oath of loyalty to the regime. Although the Vatican objected strongly to this encroachment on the independence of the Church, it permitted Czech and Slovak priests to take the oath (without which

[28] J. Hutchison Cockburn, *Religious Freedom in Eastern Europe*, Richmond, Va., 1953, John Knox Press, p. 73.

[29] "Bulletin of Catholic Priests," June 15, 1949, cited by Cockburn, *loc. cit.*

[30] Slovak Catholic Federation of America, *Memorandum*, May 16, 1956, p. 10.

they would have received no salaries), provided they did not violate their obligations to the Church itself.[31] The majority of bishops reserved their own attitude to the taking of the oath, and refused salaries for themselves.[32] Suffragan Bishop Josef Eltschkner, of Prague, however, took the oath with other clergymen on February 17, 1950, and began to ordain priests who had graduated from new Communist-sponsored religious seminaries.[33]

The first head-on collision between the Catholic church and the Communist regime occurred in February, 1950, when the Office for Church Affairs nominated the fellow-traveler Father Buchta as Vicar-General of Ceske Budejovice (Budweis). Bishop Hlouch refused to appoint him, since Buchta had been excommunicated by the Vatican. Buchta, nevertheless, having the backing of the Prague government, assumed the duties of Vicar-General and appointed a number of "progressive" priests to parishes within the diocese. The affair dragged on until April, 1952, when the government removed and interned Bishop Hlouch and appointed Buchta in his stead.[34]

By 1951, the Communist government was ready for a frontal assault on the Church, which began in Slovakia. Bishops Jan Vojtassak (of Spis) and Michael Buzalka (Auxiliary Bishop of Trnava), who had been jailed for several months in 1945, were again arrested, together with Bishop Paul Gojdic of the Greek-Catholic diocese of Presov. On January 15, 1951, after a trial in which they were denied defense counsel and the right to summon witnesses, the three bishops were convicted of treason, subversive conspiracy, and espionage. Bishops Buzalka and Gojdic were condemned to life imprisonment, while the seventy-three-year-old Bishop Vojtassak was sentenced to twenty-four years in prison.[35]

---

[31] There is a historical precedent for this position in the Vatican's acceptance of the French Civil Constitution of the Clergy, under which French priests, since the Revolution of 1789, have been paid by the state. Except in revolutionary times, French governments have not interfered with the teaching of the Church.

[32] Cockburn, op. cit., pp. 78-79. Cockburn gives a useful summary of the main provisions of the law in question, Act No. 218 of October 14, 1949.

[33] Vratislav Busek, "Church and State," Busek-Spulber, p. 148.

[34] See ibid., p. 151, for a list of prelates imprisoned or interned.

[35] For a detailed account, see Joseph A. Mikus, The Three Slovak Bishops,

It was obvious that the three bishops were guilty of nothing more than loyalty to their Church and to Slovakia, combined with outspoken opposition to Communism, and that the purpose of their trial was to intimidate bishops who so far had defied the government. During the next three months, three Slovak bishops took the loyalty oath, reserving their canonical obedience to the Pope. Three other bishops, Monsignori Stefan Barnas, Vasil Hopko, and Stanislav Zela, were later sentenced to long prison terms.[36]

On March 10, 1951, Czech secret police occupied the chancery of Archbishop Beran in Prague. The archbishop himself was banished from Prague and placed under house arrest in a remote village. The Office for Church Affairs then installed Canon Antonin Stehlik as Vicar Capitular of the Archdiocese. A few days later, Stehlik and five other churchmen, including four bishops, took the oath of allegiance to the regime. In Rome, the Sacred Consistorial Congregation, of which the Pope is the head, excommunicated all persons connected with the removal of Archbishop Beran.[37]

As things stand today, the Czech Communists have largely succeeded in organizing a schismatic church, which the regime can manipulate to suit its propaganda needs. Among its leaders are Father Josef Plojhar, cabinet minister and chairman of the purged "People's Party"; Canon Benes, chairman of the "All-State Peace Committee of the Catholic Clergy"; and Prelate Jan Stehlik of Prague. Father Plojhar regularly praises the Soviet Union and the October Revolution, while Canon Benes recently returned from a trip to Moscow to praise that city as "the head and heart . . . of all the people throughout the world who long for peace. . . ." Nearly all high ecclesiastical offices are filled by prelates who have been excommunicated, "brainwashed," or intimidated. As of 1956, almost 18 per cent of the Catholic

---

Middletown, Pa., 1956. (Slovak National Council Abroad, Box 285, Middletown, Pa.)

[36] On the inhuman treatment meted out to these bishops, including beatings and exhausting physical exercises in the nude, see Bulletin of the *Slovak National Council Abroad* (Box 285, Middletown, Pa.), August, 1957, and *German News* (München 22, Germany, Triftstrasse 1/I), March, 1958.

[37] *Collier's Year Book*, New York, 1952, p. 189.

parishes were administered by schismatic priests, and there is little doubt that this proportion has increased in the meantime. Hundreds of loyal secular priests, and the majority of the members of religious orders, suffer in prison or in forced labor camps; of over one thousand who have been released, not one has been permitted to resume his spiritual office.[38]

The devout Catholic layman is in a quandary: shall he accept communion from an excommunicated priest, shall he stay away from church altogether, or shall he risk arrest by attending "underground" religious services? If he confesses, he has no assurance that the secrecy of the confessional will be observed, since priests are required to report all "subversive" matters to the police.[39]

As a further divisive tactic, the Communist government has vigorously promoted an artificial growth of the Orthodox church. In Slovakia, the entire Greek-Catholic diocese of Presov[40] was maneuvered into the Orthodox church. At a "peace rally" held on April 18, 1950, 820 delegates of Communist-sponsored "Committees for a Return to Orthodoxy" together with one hundred priests adopted a resolution breaking off from Rome. It was Bishop Gojdic's resistance to this coup which precipitated his arrest and imprisonment.[41]

Under the supervision of the Metropolitan of Moscow since 1945, the Orthodox church in Czecho-Slovakia was raised to the status of an "autocephalic" church in 1951, the new metropolitan being the former Russian Exarch Yelevferiy. Appearing at Yelevferiy's coronation, Zdenek Fierlinger, at that time Minister of Church Affairs, declared that the autocephalic Czecho-Slovak Orthodox church would contribute to the maintenance of world

---

[38] Slovak Catholic Federation of America, *Memorandum*, May 16, 1956, p. 13; Heinrich Kern, "The Clergy in Czechoslovakia," *Sudeten Bulletin*, VII, No. 7/8 (July-August, 1959), 148-50.

[39] On April 18, 1958, for instance, Father Albert Hedera of Bratislava was sentenced to twenty-four years' imprisonment. His "crime" was failure to report to the authorities matters confessed to him by "traitors." *Bulletin of the Slovak National Council Abroad*, June, 1958, p. 1.

[40] The Greek Catholics or Uniates are a branch of the Roman Catholic Church which uses the Slav liturgy and has married clergy, but conforms to Roman teachings in doctrinal matters.

[41] Slovak Catholic Federation of America, *Memorandum*, p. 10.

peace and would demonstrate the existence of "religious freedom" in Czecho-Slovakia.[42] As in the Soviet Union, there is a government-supported atheist movement, which bears the disarming name of "Society for the Dissemination of Scientific and Political Knowledge." With state printing plants, the radio and television at its disposal, it subjects the public to a barrage of propaganda ridiculing belief in God and reviling the clergy. This campaign is suspended locally when convenient to the regime, as was the case when the so-called "Christian World Peace Conference" met in Prague in April, 1959. Yet the outpouring of money and effort to stamp out religion seems to be having little effect. As late as July, 1959, the Communist organ *Rude Pravo* found it necessary to warn parents that attendance at religious classes would cause "serious psychological damage" to their children. Shortly afterward, Comrade Vasil Bilak, the party's expert on schools, deplored the fact that "in the areas with the most industry—in Zilina and Bratislava (both in Slovakia)— the largest percentage of children attend religious instruction. The systematic religious instruction of the children from early youth has caused most of the students to enter college with an idealist world outlook."[43]

The schismatic prelates of Prague hoped that the newly elected Pope John XXIII's announcement that he intended to seek contact with Eastern churches would open a gambit whereby they could be restored to grace while continuing to serve their Communist masters. They were quickly disillusioned, however, by the Pope's message congratulating the still-imprisoned Archbishop Beran on his seventieth birthday. Since then the battle has continued. During the spring of 1959 a number of Slovaks were sentenced for operating a secret theological seminary, but this is doubtless not the last of such endeavors. Churches have survived persecutions before and experience suggests that they survive best

---

[42] *Der Sudetendeutsche,* April 12, 1952. On governmental control over the Orthodox church in the Soviet Union, see Kulski, *op. cit.,* pp. 259-62.

[43] *Rude Pravo,* July 3, 1959; *Sudeten Bulletin,* VII, No. 9 (September, 1959), 187. For further complaints against the persistence of religion among students, see *Pravda* (Bratislava), February 24, 1959; *Vysoka skola,* No. 6-7 (June, 1959), pp. 171-74; *Wissensch. Dienst,* IX (1959), 103, 339-40.

when they refuse to compromise with forces contradicting their basic principles.

"MORE ORTHODOX THAN THE KREMLIN"

The political history of Czecho-Slovakia since 1948 has been relatively free of the feuds between major Communist leaders which have characterized politics in Poland, Hungary, and the Soviet Union. Intrigues, denunciations, and liquidations have been as frequent as in other Communist states, but the majority of victims have been second-string comrades. Mighty heads have rolled, but never in such number as to shatter the integrity of the central leadership. Throughout the decade, political control has remained in the hands of the same small group of doctrinaire Marxists, aptly described as "more orthodox than the Kremlin."[44] This clique has enhanced its monopoly of power by maintaining a high turnover in the intermediate ranks of the party.

Although the 1949 congress of the Czecho-Slovak Communist party was held in an atmosphere of relative optimism, it was not many months before the leaders were looking for scapegoats on whom to blame deficient fulfilment of the Five-Year Plan. In a message on New Year's Day, 1951, President Gottwald inveighed against traitors, wreckers, spies, and saboteurs: agents of the United States, the Vatican, and Tito's Yugoslavia. Within the next few weeks, some two hundred upper and middle-echelon Communists were arrested, and the first major purge was under way.

Among the more prominent victims were Foreign Minister Vlado Clementis,[45] Party Secretary Otto Sling of Brno, former Deputy Secretary-General Maria Svermova, and Dr. Ripka's former associates, Otto Katz and Evzen Loebl. The lesser purgees included most of the Communist members of the British Broadcasting Company's Czecho-Slovak staff during World War II. The charge

---

[44] J. F. Appleby in *Ost-Probleme* (published by U.S. Embassy, Bad Godesberg, Germany), October 25, 1957, p. 957.

[45] Clementis, a Slovak, was removed on March 14, 1951, and replaced with Vilem Siroky, another Slovak, who later became premier. On Clementis' role in England during World War II, see chap. III.

was that of a massive conspiracy to overthrow the regime and realign Czecho-Slovakia with the West. The purge was accompanied by the dismissal of all Foreign Office personnel suspected of Western ties, including the Czecho-Slovak ambassadors to the United States, Britain, and France. Defense Minister Svoboda had already been "kicked upstairs" to the position of "Vice-Premier in Charge of Physical Culture," and replaced with Gottwald's son-in-law, Dr. Alexei Cepicka. Secretary-General Rudolf Slansky of the Communist party was removed from that post on September 7, 1951, and arrested on charges of espionage on November 27. On January 23, 1952, the Communist party's chief purger, Minister of National Security Ladislav Kopriva, was himself purged and replaced with Karel Bacilek— today First Secretary of the Communist party in Slovakia.

After thorough preparation and rehearsal of "confessions," the show trial of Clementis, Slansky, and their associates was held in Prague in November, 1952. All the defendants admitted plotting the overthrow of the Czecho-Slovak government on behalf of the United States, Great Britain, and Yugoslavia.[46] A number also confessed economic sabotage designed to discredit Soviet industrial methods and equipment. Coinciding with the later abandoned trial of the Kremlin doctors, the process had anti-Semitic overtones: Truman and Ben Gurion were accused of plotting together against the Czecho-Slovak state. Another villain in the piece was Dr. Ripka, with whom most of the defendants had been associated. The stage managers had them confess that they assisted the "imperialist agent" Ripka in infiltrating the Communist Party![47] Clementis, Slansky, and nine others were hanged in Prague on December 30, 1952.

---

[46] The conviction of Associated Press correspondent William N. Oatis of "espionage" on July 4, 1951, was clearly intended to lend credence to these charges. On May 15, 1953, after Oatis had served his propaganda purpose, he was "pardoned" and released. What is considered normal reporting in the West is "espionage" under Communist law.

[47] This charge is obviously absurd: even Benes (*Memoirs*, p. 113) called Ripka "clearly leftist," and his pro-Bolshevist and pro-Soviet utterances, some of which are quoted in this volume, are a matter of public record. Detailed reports of the trial are contained in *Rude Pravo* (organ of the Czecho-Slovak Communist party), Prague, November 21-26, 1952. An analysis of the trial with particular reference to its anti-Semitic aspect is contained in the *American Jewish Year Book for 1954*, New York, 1954, pp. 287-95.

President Gottwald contracted pneumonia while attending Stalin's funeral, and died on March 14, 1953. The National Assembly elected Zapotocky to the presidency, while Vilem Siroky became premier. The Prague government saw no immediate reason to change its policies, but after Malenkov had promised Soviet citizens a greater supply of consumer goods, unrest spread in Czecho-Slovakia. The currency reform of May 30, 1953, which wiped out individual savings, went beyond the threshold of endurance, and the country was swept by riots and strikes. On June 1, 1953, a crowd of some five thousand workers from the Lenin (Skoda) Works stormed the city hall of Plzen, where insurgents exercised control for a few hours until security troops arrived from Prague.[48]

The regime's first reaction was to crack down on all forms of disobedience. In early July, however, the government reversed itself and decided to make some concessions to the public. These included permission for farmers to leave collective farms,[49] a revision of production schedules to provide more consumer goods, and a series of price cuts.[50]

The Czecho-Slovak cabinet was reorganized on September 11, 1953. The number of ministers was reduced from forty-six to thirty-three and the Presidium or "inner cabinet" was cut from eleven to five: Premier Siroky, First Deputy Premiers Jaromir Dolansky and Alexei Cepicka, and Deputy Premiers Vaclav Kopecky and Jindrich Uher.[51] The Ministry of State Security was merged into the Ministry of the Interior under Rudolf Barak, a specialist in political police operations. Former Interior Minister Nosek was "demoted" to the Manpower portfolio, while former security chief Bacilek was detailed to Bratislava to manage the Communist party in

---

[48] Free Europe Committee, *Eyewitness Account of the Pilsen Rebellion,* New York, August 12, 1954.

[49] This was only a temporary expedient. Zapotocky warned the farmers: "In the future you will have to re-establish the cooperative from which you escape today." *Rude Pravo,* August 2, 1953, cited by Ivo Duchacek, "Czechoslovakia: New Course or No Course?," *Problems of Communism,* Washington, U.S. Information Agency, IV, No. 1 (January-February, 1955), 12-19.

[50] Duchacek, *loc. cit.,* gives a description of governmental measures during 1953 and 1954.

[51] Cepicka, Kopecky, and Uher also headed the Ministries of Defense, Culture, and Agriculture, respectively.

Slovakia. Antonin Novotny, who had assumed charge of the central secretariat of the party in March, was officially designated First Secretary, a position which enabled him to achieve personal power analogous to that of his Soviet colleague, Khrushchev.

Although some one thousand collective farms were dissolved during the latter half of 1953, things quieted down so that the drive for collectivization could be resumed in 1954. In June of that year, the Czecho-Slovak Communist Party held its Tenth Congress, with Khrushchev as the guest of honor. The congress committed itself to the principle of "collective leadership" and elected a new Central Committee of eighty-four members, of whom only thirty-three had served in the CC elected in 1949. Although the party continued its policy of moderate concessions to industrial workers, it is significant that no Czech Communist has ever referred to this policy as the "new course" (the term current in the U.S.S.R. and Sovzone Germany), and that no gesture has ever been made suggesting the possible rehabilitation of Clementis, Slansky, and other victims of liquidation.[52]

When Khrushchev sounded his famous blast against Stalin at the Twentieth Congress of the CPSU in February, 1956, Communist leaders in Prague refrained from expressing more than mild agreement. Novotny stated explicitly that he saw no reason to change the Czecho-Slovak party line,[53] and intellectuals were warned not to carry criticism of Stalin to the point where it undermined the principles of Communism. It may well be that Novotny and his friends anticipated the explosions to which "anti-Stalinism" would lead in Hungary, Poland, and the U.S.S.R. itself. Khrushchev's recent return to orthodoxy has required no accommodation on the part of the Prague Communists, who have never countenanced any degree of "revisionism."[54]

The Hungarian Revolution of October, 1956, had no

[52] Trials of persons alleged to have been associated with Slansky, as well as of "Slovak nationalists" and "Zionists," continued during 1954.

[53] E. Mühlberger, "Novotny's Triumph," *Sudetendeutscher Artikeldienst*, Munich, June 21, 1958, p. 7.

[54] For a detailed account of recent ideological developments in the Czecho-Slovak Communist party, see J. F. Appleby, "Der Tschechoslowakische Mustersatellit" ["The Czechoslovak Model Satellite"], *Ost-Probleme*, Bad Godesberg, Germany, October 25, 1957.

immediate repercussions in Bohemia or Moravia.[55] The Czech secret police, however, vented its nervousness by constructing an imaginary plot which, as usual, was laid at the door of United States intelligence agencies. A number of culprits were arrested and, after being held incommunicado for several weeks, made the desired "confessions." At the same time, the Czech Communist party purged a number of members and functionaries for "following the arguments of the Hungarian fascists and counter-revolutionaries." When Khrushchev visited Prague in July, 1957, he emphasized his "unreserved confidence in the Czecho-Slovak Communist party."[56]

President Zapotocky died of a heart attack on November 13, 1957. He was succeeded by Antonin Novotny, who has retained his position as First Secretary of the Communist party, the key source of power. The second most powerful man in Czecho-Slovakia today is probably Interior Minister Rudolf Barak, who controls the secret police.[57] For the Czech Communists, the shots which felled Imre Nagy on the eve of their Eleventh Congress in 1958 were the confirmation of their "hard" policy. Since then, the resurgence of the "Stalinists" in Poland and the relative absence of ideological disturbances in the Soviet Union—a by-product of Khrushchev's successful scientific and diplomatic circus which has distracted attention from theoretical questions—has tended to make "revisionism" a dormant issue in Czecho-Slovakia.

---

[55] Two contributing reasons may be given: The standard of living in the Czech lands, although low by Western standards, is higher than in other satellites, with the exception of Sovzone Germany. Secondly, there were no serious differences among the leaders which insurgents or "deviationists" could exploit.

[56] *German News*, Munich, I, No. 10, October, 1957, 9-10; Mühlberger, *loc. cit.*

[57] Early in 1956, Barak succeeded in forcing the resignation of his enemy, Defense Minister Cepicka, who was replaced by Bohumir Lomsky, a graduate of the Moscow Military Academy and a man enjoying Barak's confidence.

VII

CZECHO-SLOVAKIA'S ROLE IN SOVIET STRATEGY

WORKSHOP OF THE "SOCIALIST CAMP"

AS A Soviet satellite, Czecho-Slovakia plays a role prescribed in broad outlines by the Kremlin. The Prague leadership, however, having demonstrated its reliability in times of crisis, enjoys considerable flexibility in working out the details.[1] Czecho-Slovakia's functions as a member of the "socialist camp" are determined partly by geography and economic resources, and partly by the tensions which continue to beset Czecho-Slovakia as an artificial state. On the latter score, there is significance in Karel Bacilek's remarks to the Central Committee Plenum of the Communist party in Slovakia on December 12, and 13, 1956:

> One of the weakest aspects of our ideological battle is the struggle against bourgeois nationalism. We must never forget that there is in our past a relatively long period of the so-called Slovak state. . . . And it must not be forgotten that the leadership of the Hlinka Populist Party before its withdrawal beyond national borders designedly left in Slovakia a number of its adherents, especially from among the younger generation of Populists. . . .
> It will be the bounden duty of all Party members to educate our entire nation to a fast federation with the Soviet Union, without which there would have been no Czechoslovak Republic nor any establishment of socialism in our land.[2]

The substance of Bacilek's statement is his admission that Czecho-Slovakia can exist only as a Soviet satellite.

---

[1] In October, 1956, when the Hungarian revolt was approaching its climax, an eleven-man Soviet delegation headed by Central Committee Secretary Aristov arrived in Prague "to study the work of the Czecho-Slovak Communist Party and to exchange experiences in the field of Party work." As Khrushchev implied in later statements, this precaution turned out to be unnecessary.

[2] *Pravda*, Bratislava, December 16, 1956, p. 3.

Czecho-Slovakia's economic role, shared to a certain extent with Sovzone Germany, is that of a supplier of machinery and capital goods to the Soviet orbit.[3] As in all other satellites, economic planning has taken the form of a Two-Year Plan followed by a series of Five-Year Plans. The purpose of the Two-Year Plan, launched in October, 1946, was to reorganize the economy so that it could be co-ordinated with the Soviet economic system.[4] The Five-Year Plans are, in fact if not in theory, subdivisions of the Soviet Five-Year Plan elaborated in Moscow.[5]

During the first Five-Year Plan, launched in 1948 after the "February Revolution," industries remaining in private hands were socialized and Czecho-Slovakia girded for its role as an arsenal of the Soviet bloc, second only to the Soviet Union itself. Heavy industry was expanded at forced draft, the costs—apart from a modest loan granted by the Soviet Union to start the program—being borne by Czech and Slovak workers in the form of lowered real wages. Approximately 20 per cent of the national income was channeled into industrial expansion, with over half of this investment allocated to mines, smelters, rolling mills, heavy machinery and chemical plants, and power stations.[6]

While exact capacity and production figures are hard to obtain, it is evident that the Communist government of Czecho-Slovakia has built an imposing industrial plant, with a *per capita* steel capacity equaling that of West Germany. The State Statistical Office claims that industrial production doubled between 1948 and 1953. Not only have the Lenin (Skoda) Works and other machine factories been greatly expanded, but twenty-four new

[3] Ivo Duchacek in *Problems of Communism*, IV, No. 1, 17.

[4] Albion Ross wrote from Prague on October 27, 1946: "The Left-Wing press is celebrating this weekend with the proclamation of the two-year plan as something on the order of the formal funeral of capitalism. The Social Democratic press said: 'Capitalism will never come back into our economy.' At the same time certain 'foreign countries' were accused of trying to tell the Czechoslovaks how to run their economic affairs." (*New York Times*, October 28, 1946.)

[5] The first Five-Year Plan ran from 1948 to 1953. Initiation of the second plan was delayed until 1956 so as to coincide with the Soviet Five-Year Plan.

[6] Vilem Brzorad, "Fuel, Power, and Producer Goods Industries," in Busek-Spulber, pp. 306-9. Comparable percentages of gross national income invested in manufacture, mining, and public utilities in 1955 were: United States 5.8% Great Britain 6.1%, U.S.S.R. 14.3% (derived from statistics quoted by Edward S. Mason in *International Stability and Progress*, The American Assembly, Columbia University, New York, 1957, pp. 74-75).

industrial complexes and hundreds of minor factories have been built and equipped, and the new hydroelectric plants of Slovakia turn out more power than all generating stations in Slovakia in 1937. Industrial planning in Prague is watched over by Soviet experts, who co-ordinate investment and production with the militarized economy of the Soviet bloc.[7]

The Czech and Slovak peoples have reaped little benefit from the new industrialization. Products not channeled into new investment or into armaments are, for the most part, exported to the Soviet Union or other satellites, while investment in consumer-goods industries has been deliberately neglected. Production of leather goods, ceramics, glassware, and textiles in 1954 was less than before World War II. Furthermore, industrialization has been pushed far beyond what the domestic raw material base can supply. Although industrial production doubled during the first Five-Year Plan, hard-coal mining expanded by only 13.8 per cent and soft coal by 45 per cent.[8]

The first Five-Year Plan had left the workers and farmers with considerable cash, but nothing on which they could spend it. To drain off this excess purchasing power, a new currency was introduced on May 30, 1953. Cash was converted at fifty old crowns for one new crown, pensions at five to one, and bank deposits at an intermediate rate. State securities issued since 1945 were repudiated altogether. After the resulting riots and strikes, the regime found it advisable to continue industrial growth at a much slower rate. Since then, real wages have improved somewhat, and a limited number of autos been made available, though consumer goods shortages have continued.[9]

Czecho-Slovak industrialization has also had its lo-

---

[7] Soviet and satellite plans and trade arrangements are co-ordinated through the COMECON (Council of Mutual Economic Assistance), established in 1949 as an eastern equivalent of the OEEC (Organization for European Economic Co-operation). It is Soviet policy to have each satellite specialize in certain industrial branches, so as to make the satellites dependent on each other and on the Soviet Union. See George B. deHuszar, "The Soviet Union and Her Satellites," in Thorsten V. Kalijarvi and Associates, *Modern World Politics*, New York, 1954, pp. 485-87.

[8] Duchacek, *loc. cit.*, p. 14.

[9] *Collier's Year Book*, New York, 1954, p. 164; J. F. Appleby in *Ost-Probleme*, October 25, 1957, p. 960.

gistic troubles. Activation of the hydroelectric plants in Slovakia was delayed when the Russians suddenly confiscated the turbines for use in the Soviet Union. Lack of spare parts led to a general breakdown of transportation in the fall of 1954. Delays of commuter trains disorganized factory production, and the workers rioted when wages for lost time were not paid.[10] Coal was for a long time a thorny problem. Soviet mining equipment, designed for the smooth seams of the Donbas, works badly in the irregular Slovak deposits. Since the Russians seldom provide enough spare parts, machines are deadlined more often than not, and miners find their earnings less than before "mechanization."[11] In the Moravske Ostrava district, in spite of rigid labor controls, over 37,000 miners managed to quit during 1955, and the Labor Offices were able to fill less than 20 per cent of the requisitions for new workers. Since home gardening and black marketing are frequently more profitable than mining, absenteeism runs as high as 30 per cent in a number of mines. Faced with increases of 45 and 25 per cent, respectively, in the production costs of hard and brown coal, the government introduced *khozrashot*, the Soviet system of business accounting, under which each plant must show a balanced budget.[12]

In spite of frantic efforts to boost coal production, including the moving of surface workers underground and the drafting of young workers from other industries, Czech and Slovak mines have seldom met more than 70 or 80 per cent of their plan quotas. Since new machinery to increase productivity is not available, the Communist party has attempted to force a speed-up.[13] This puts the foremen in a difficult position, between the party bosses and the police who demand that output be raised and wages held down, and the rank-and-file miners who are often mutinous, particularly in the Ostrava district, where Polish workers have become infected with the rebelliousness of their compatriots across

[10] *Sudetendeutsche Zeitung*, September 4 and December 11, 1954.
[11] *Slowakische Korrespondenz*, Munich, III, No. 3/4, March/April, 1955, 11.
[12] *Sudetendeutsche Zeitung*, December 17, 1955.
[13] See Vilem Brzorad, "Mining," in Busek-Spulber, p. 274.

the border. The foremen, who to the ordinary miners represent the disciplinary apparatus of the state, know that they are the first who would be lynched in the event of a political overturn. For this reason, coal production is a sensitive barometer of the political atmosphere, dropping sharply whenever unrest becomes acute, as it did during the Hungarian Revolution of 1956.

The current goal is to increase the production of all types of coal from seventy-seven million tons in 1956 to ninety-eight million by 1960. While Vice-Premier Dolansky indicated in September, 1957, that greater efforts would be needed to achieve this goal, there have been no serious crises in the coal industry since then. More recently, motor fuel has become a serious problem. During the summer of 1959, a breakdown of machines and a lack of spare parts at the main Western refinery near Brüx, combined with failure by the Soviet Union to deliver crude oil promised to its counterpart at Bratislava, produced such an acute shortage that vacationists were forced to abandon their cars while the state bus lines were forced to cancel all excursions. This experience led the economic administrators of Prague, despite their unshattered faith in Soviet planning, to look for alternate sources of supply in the Middle East.[14]

Czecho-Slovakia's role as a workshop of the "socialist camp" requires that women be workers rather than housewives. Today, they constitute 40 per cent of the labor force, and two thirds of the workers in light industry.

During the first Five-Year Plan, pressure was exerted by reducing the rations of nonemployed women, except those with small children in localities without day nurseries. The 1953 currency reform, which reduced the purchasing power of wages, was calculated to force 400,000 additional women into the labor market. A law passed in 1954 makes work compulsory for every woman under forty-five, unless she has a child under four years of age. The immediate effect of this law was a boom in births. The state has continued, however, to encourage female employment by establishing community kitchens

---

[14] *Sudetendeutsche Zeitung,* July 25, 1959.

and laundries, providing beauty parlors and fashion shows in the factories, and requiring children of three or more to attend kindergarten. At present, over 700,000 children are cared for and fed collectively, a practice which not only frees their mothers for factory or farm work, but also makes the children available for indoctrination during their formative years.[15]

By pushing workers to the margin of endurance, Czecho-Slovakia has become the Soviet bloc's largest exporter of turbines, generators, marine engines, textile machinery, locomotives, automobiles, trucks, and buses, as well as general-purpose and specialized farm machinery. Since 1954, the Soviet bloc has yielded its place as principal market to the underdeveloped areas of the Near East and Southeast Asia,[16] where Czecho-Slovakia spearheads the Communist trade offensive among "neutralist" states.[17]

COLLECTIVE FARMS AND EMPTY LARDERS

Although Czecho-Slovakia was a net exporter of foodstuffs before World War II, it is today a land of chronic food shortages.[18] Aside from the loss of Sudeten German manpower, to which we shall return in a later section, the principal reason is the collective farm system.

During the National Front period, the Communists said little about socializing agriculture, since they wanted the farmers' votes. After the "unity" elections of May 30, 1948, however, the regime embarked on a campaign to force farmers into collective farms, or "agricultural unit co-operatives" as they are called in Czecho-Slovakia.

---

[15] Kocvara, *op. cit.*, and Ivo Duchacek, "Education," in Busek-Spulber, pp. 55 and 167, respectively; *Sudetendeutsche Zeitung*, July 23, 1955, and December 1, 1956.

[16] United Nations, Economic Commission for Europe, *Economic Survey of Europe in 1956*, Geneva, 1957.

[17] The Prague regime also dispatches specialists who combine technical assistance with propaganda. Further expansion of exports is, however, hampered by renewed inflation, which has caused the Czecho-Slovak crown to drop from its official value of 13.9 cents to less than three cents on the free market. An effective attack on inflation requires a further reduction of the investment rate, to which the cabinet reluctantly consented in 1957, and more goods for the domestic market. To reduce administrative overhead, the regime recently adopted a decentralization analogous to Khrushchev's reforms in the U.S.S.R. Appleby, *loc. cit.*, p. 961; *Prace* (Prague), November 24, 1957.

[18] See Wanklyn, *Czechoslovakia*, chap. VI; Ernest Koenig, "Agriculture," in Busek-Spulber, *passim*.

Individual land ownership was limited by law to fifty hectares, and delivery quotas discriminating against the individual farmer were imposed. Collectives were given priority in the distribution of seeds, tools, and fertilizer, and in the services of the state-owned machine-and-tractor stations. For Czech and Slovak farmers, who look back to many decades of prosperous individual operation, the collective farm system was totally lacking in incentives. Since the state had a bare minimum of consumer goods to offer, self-interest dictated working as little as possible for the collective and concentrating on private gardening for home consumption. Deliveries lagged: farmers, inside or outside the collectives, became experts at cheating the government, often cultivating "secret" plots unknown to the authorities.[19]

Persuasion, however forceful, did not expand the collectives as fast as the Communists desired. In 1952, therefore, the party mounted a hate campaign against the remaining individual farmers, now labelled "kulaks" or class enemies. When the collective farms failed to meet their quotas—which was normally the case—ways were found to blame the "kulaks," who were accused of secret sabotage, aid and comfort to American agents, and even complicity in the "germ warfare" in Korea. A Ministry of Bulk Purchases was created, with squads of snoopers trained to seek out hidden stocks of food, possession of which was a sufficient ground for expropriation. This reign of terror resulted in rapid growth of the collectives—and an alarming decline in food production.

As noted in the previous chapter, the government, to avoid a total breakdown in food supply after the disorders of June, 1953, permitted farmers to leave the collectives, the number of which dropped from 8,284 to 7,201.[20] This temporary measure was "suspended" on April 1, 1954, and the drive for collectivization quietly resumed. Collective farm workers, however, tended to

[19] Duchacek, *loc. cit.*, pp. 13-14; Koenig, *loc. cit.*, pp. 245ff.; *Collier's Year Book*, 1953, pp. 216-17.
[20] Czecho-Slovak official sources as cited by Duchacek, *loc. cit.*, p. 17.

migrate to industrial jobs, and crops rotted in the fields for lack of manpower. Party efforts to recruit 105,000 new agricultural workers yielded a total of 22,636, most of whom had no farm experience whatever.[21] To make matters worse, the Russians ordered substantial shipments of potatoes, fruits, and dairy products to the Soviet Union and Sovzone Germany, where the political situation was considered more critical than in Czecho-Slovakia. During the summer of 1954, meat was practically nonexistent, and milk, butter, and even bread were in short supply. Emergency squads of factory workers and students, sent to help in the potato harvest, took to burying potatoes in the fields and then returning at night to fill their own sacks.

After the heavy floods of 1954, the United States offered a relief shipment of canned meat. Rejection of this offer by the Prague government led to local rioting and attacks on Communist functionaries.[22] Meanwhile, a major portion of the potato and sugar-beet crops rotted in the fields, while an abnormal number of fires destroyed part of the grain crop.[23] To prevent a repetition of this catastrophe in 1955, the regime established a special office to mobilize seasonal workers for the collective farms.

Tourists in Czecho-Slovakia are often impressed by the apparently ample quantities of food available in cities such as Prague, Brno, and Bratislava. This propaganda effect is accomplished by reducing deliveries to smaller towns and villages, where numerous retail stores have been arbitrarily closed, and those which remain offer little and that of poor quality. Throughout rural Czecho-Slovakia there are frequent complaints of fail-

---

[21] *Sudetendeutsche Zeitung,* October 9, November 13, and December 18, 1954. It is obvious that once a farmer is reduced to the status of a hired worker, he will go where he can earn the highest wage. Communist factory managers, pressed to meet their quotas, tend to hire without questions all the "bodies" they can get, thus defeating manpower controls.

[22] *Sudetendeutsche Zeitung,* July 31 and August 14, 1954. Refusal to accept the American meat was a factor contributing to a typhoid epidemic, since the hungry population took to butchering livestock drowned in the floods.

[23] The fires were attributable to two factors: (a) improper storage of grain, which had been harvested wet and artificially dried, and (b) arson by collective farm managers to hide below-quota harvests. In the Brno district alone, there were thirty fires on collective farms during the fall of 1954, not reported in the Communist press. *Sudetendeutsche Zeitung,* November 13, and December 18, 1954.

ing milk deliveries, moldy bread, and rotten potatoes. Priority has been given to increasing the food supply in industrial centers, since it is there that riots and strikes are most feared. The favorable harvest of 1956 produced little improvement, since the Kremlin pressured its puppets in Prague into exporting much of the surplus to the Soviet Zone of Germany, where the Communists evidently fear unrest more than they do in Czecho-Slovakia.[24] The admittedly improved food situation in the so-called German Democratic Republic, where food rationing was finally abolished in May, 1958, has thus been achieved partially at the expense of Czechs and Slovaks. The sight of over two thousand cars loaded with fresh vegetables and fruits, potatoes, and meats being shipped out before the eyes of a population hovering on the edge of famine caused a breakdown of morale among Czech farmers. As a result, at least one third of the Moravian sugar-beet crop remained unharvested in the fields, with a loss of some fourteen thousand tons of refined sugar.[25]

The collective farms dissolved in 1953 were re-established by the end of 1956; by October, 1957, there were 10,736 "agricultural unit co-operatives" which, together with the state farms, occupied 60 per cent of the cultivated land. President Novotny announced on March 25, 1959, that 80 per cent of Czecho-Slovak agriculture was now collective; the party has resolved to achieve 100-per-cent collectivization by 1960.[26] Although farm production was simultaneously increased (by one third of the amount planned) it is still below the prewar level of 1936. A large number of elaborate and expensive combines were purchased from the Soviet Union in 1958, but since the Russians as usual failed to supply spare parts, the majority of these machines could not be used. Plans to thresh the wheat electrically in 1959 were frus-

[24] West Berlin constitutes a serious breach in the Iron Curtain, and the Sovzone authorities have been able to reduce but not eliminate contacts with West Germany, where the standard of living is among the highest in Europe.

[25] *Sudetendeutsche Zeitung*, November 17 and December 8, 1956. *Rude Pravo*, February 28, 1957, reports continued shortages, particularly in dairy products.

[26] *Rude Pravo*, September 11, 1957, and report of CC Plenum of September 30-October 2, 1957, both cited in *Ost-Probleme*, October 25, 1957; *Rude Pravo*, June 23, 1958, and March 20-22, 1959; *Wissensch. Dienst*, IX (1959), 140-42.

trated by a general breakdown of the power supply. The only recourse available to the party was a wholesale roundup of vacationists, who suddenly found themselves engaged in "volunteer" farm work. Since the Communists must by now be aware that collective farms will never yield as much as those of private farmers afforded proper incentives, it is clear that collectivization is a political rather than an economic policy.[27] Left to themselves, farmers constitute a conservative and religious class, which is bound to conflict with a radical materialist dictatorship. To eliminate the seedbeds of possible counterrevoultion, the Kremlin has decreed the liquidation of the independent peasantry in all its satellites.

ARMED FORCES DESIGNED FOR AGGRESSION

From 1948 to 1950 the army, the Western-trained officers of which tended to be non-Communist or anti-Communist, was neglected in favor of the SNB or militarized police. In April, 1950, however, the "nonpartisan" Defense Minister, Svoboda, was replaced by the Communist, Dr. Alexei Cepicka, who lost no time in purging officers of Western leanings, even at the cost of a temporary decline in military efficiency. A reorganization of the Czecho-Slovak army on Russian lines was then initiated under the supervision of a special Soviet military mission of one hundred officers. "Deputy commanders for political affairs" were appointed at all levels; Soviet insignia, training programs, and service regulations were adopted; and plans were made to convert to Soviet weapons as rapidly as they could be obtained.[28]

Under the guidance of Soviet officers, the reorgan-

---

[27] As a device for increasing the food supply, collective farming has proved of doubtful value even in the Soviet Union where, in the past, individual peasants cultivated mainly for their own subsistence. In countries with a tradition of commercial farming, collectivization, with its inferior incentives, reduces the food supply. This has been the experience in all European satellites. Yugoslavia has improved its food situation by permitting the dissolution of collectives, a step which orthodox Communists decry as "economism."

[28] *Süddeutsche Zeitung*, 28/29 October 1950. See also Curt Beck, "The Government," in Busek-Spulber, pp. 99-100. This, and all other information on military affairs, espionage, etc. in this and the following chapters, has been checked with independent Czech, Slovak, and German sources in Europe.

ized army widened the military zone along the Bohemian-German frontier, demolishing entire villages and building a complex network of barbed wire, mine fields, and watchtowers.[29] A major expansion of the Czecho-Slovak armed forces began in 1952: the official defense budget, reflecting only a fraction of military expenditures, rose from 22.4 billion crowns in 1952 to 41.8 billion in 1953. As the army grew, specialized units were trained to use new equipment, such as an improved version of the Telefunken radar-flak system, the "Stalin organ" multiple rocket launcher, and Russian-made atomic artillery. It was reported in 1954 that all divisions were fully motorized, largely with vehicles of Czech manufacture.

The Czecho-Slovak general staff is quartered in the Hradcany Castle in Prague, along with a Soviet military mission having liaison officers attached to Czecho-Slovak divisional and subordinate headquarters, plus a large intelligence division.[30] Other satellites also have their military missions in the Hradcany, which seems to be emerging as a common "Pentagon" for the Warsaw Pact states. Soviet officers serve on the faculty of the Czecho-Slovak Military Academy and as field instructors, while candidates for the Czecho-Slovak general staff attend the Frunze Military Academy in Moscow. In 1953, when the Soviet Union was not yet ready to admit the rearming of the "German Democratic Republic," members of its *kasernierte Volkspolizei* were sent to Czecho-Slovakia for training in ground combat and military aviation.[31]

Soviet influence is particularly apparent in the training of special army units for partisan fighting behind the enemy's lines. First organized by General Zdenek Hruska, a Czech with Soviet citizenship, the partisan units acquire skill in Soviet tactics which were tested in Korea, some of the instructors being North Korean veterans. The smallest partisan groups consist of only

---

[29] This "no man's land," the major purpose of which is to prevent escapes, was later taken over by the PVS.

[30] As of 1955, the Soviet mission was headed by Colonel General Gussev and contained the Russian atomic warfare expert Malertcheff. Its total personnel has been estimated at over four thousand, of whom the majority are in military intelligence. *Sudetendeutsche Zeitung*, November 6, 1954, and February 12, 1955.

[31] *Sudetendeutsche Zeitung*, May 16, 1953. German pilots were not permitted to solo, lest they escape to the West.

seven or eight men, including a polit-officer, two interpreters, and a radio operator. They are equipped with special light machine guns and bomb catapults.[32] Another Russian-inspired innovation is a special academy for political officers, in which emphasis is laid on Communist ideology and techniques of mass suggestion. Estimates of the size of the Czecho-Slovak armed forces vary, and it is evident that the number of men in uniform varies from time to time.[33] Of greater significance than the number of troops is the fact that the army and the air force are merely the spearheads of a military organization encompassing a large part of the population. A decree of January 1, 1956, makes military training compulsory in secondary schools, for girls as well as boys. The curriculum includes target practice with carbines and machine guns, grenade throwing, care of weapons, trench digging, camouflage, air-raid protection, and first aid: field exercises must be held once a month. Additional military training outside school hours is provided by the CSM (Youth Federation) which conducts armed maneuvers and grants medals for military valor.

Secondary-school graduates are mobilized in the SVA-ZARM, headed by the partisan-trainer General Hruska, with 279,000 members between sixteen and twenty-six years of age. Under the direction of army reservists, SVAZARM members enjoy weekly field exercises and orientation marches. Those who sign up for "motorized tourism" learn shooting from moving vehicles, grenade throwing, and radio operation. Others practice parachute jumping and hand-to-hand combat. Women members are trained as grenade throwers and sharpshooters.[34] Since all this takes place in the name of "peace," even

---

[32] *Sudetendeutsche Zeitung*, July 18, 1953, and November 6, 1954. For a technical discussion of partisan tactics, see F. O. Miksche, *Secret Forces*, London, Faber & Faber, 1950.

[33] The *Statesman's Year Book* for 1955 (London, Macmillan) gives the strength of the army as 200,000, organized in twenty divisions, including mechanized and armored, plus an additional 190,000 men in the air force and security forces. These figures are confirmed by the *World Almanac* for 1958, while *Information Please* cites a somewhat smaller figure. According to an official statement of the Prague government, cited in the *Sudetendeutsche Zeitung* of August 4, 1956, the army was reduced by 10,000 men that year.

[34] Rudolf Wenzel, "Volksdemokratische Wehrertüchtigung" ["People's Democratic Military Training"], *Sudetendeutscher Artikeldienst*, Munich, April 26, 1958, pp. 1-3.

the (schismatic) Catholic church has given its blessing:

As a matter of principle the Czech Catholic has no objection to military service and military training for women. It is true for women, too, that war cannot be combatted with ideological manifestoes, but only with peacetime military training.[35]

Czecho-Slovak military maneuvers are often aggressive in nature. The 1953 fall and 1954 spring maneuvers in western Bohemia were simulated attacks on West Germany, the PVS having sealed off the border to prevent escapes. SVAZARM detachments played an active role in both exercises: the 1954 maneuver was the "baptism of fire" for several all-women combat detachments as well as a number of women tank drivers and aviators. The 1954 fall maneuvers were planned around a simulated Czecho-Slovak attack on Bavaria, supposedly coordinated with Russian and Polish thrusts through North Germany toward Holland. A group of forty Soviet officers served as evaluators.[36]

Since the advent of the "Geneva Spirit" in 1955, the Czecho-Slovak general staff has refrained from stating its maneuver problems in such provocative terms. The offensive nature of the Czecho-Slovak army and air force, however, as well as the presence of missile bases, is suggested by the size of military districts closed to the general public. These areas are many times larger than the maneuver grounds available to the United States Army in western Germany.

The 1955 *Administrative Index of Czecho-Slovak Communes*, published in Prague "for official use only," lists no less than 348 settlements, including four cities, as having become "defunct" (*zanikla*) since 1945.[37] Aside from the Sudeten German border villages which disappeared because there was no one to live in them, the vanished communes fall into four major areas:

---

[35] Mrs. Ruzena Vackova in *Katolik*, Prague, October 20, 1957. Since for the Communists "war is peace," it follows that those duped by Moscow-inspired "peace" propaganda, including certain Protestant church groups in the United States and Europe, are in fact supporting the most flagrant militarism.

[36] *Sudetendeutsche Zeitung*, November 7, 1953, May 29, 1954, and September 18, 1954.

[37] *Administrativni Lexikon obci Republiky Ceskoslovenske*, Prague, 1955, cited in *Sudetendeutsche Zeitung*, December 8, 1956, with maps of the areas involved.

(a) An oval area 20 kilometers long and 15 kilometers wide between Ceske Budejovice (Budweis) and the Austrian border (54 villages and towns);

(b) An area of at least 350 square kilometers east of Karlsbad, containing 68 vanished communities including the city of Duppau;

(c) A somewhat smaller area southwest of Reichenberg (28 villages and towns);

(d) An area in northern Moravia east of Olomoue, containing the former city of Liebau and 23 other vanished communities.

Strategically, the four military zones form a trapezium, with Prague approximately in the middle. It is probable that, in addition to serving as maneuver grounds, they figure in the operations of the Czecho-Soviet joint missile command, which has its headquarters in Troppau (Opava) and its advance base in Reichenberg.[38]

The Czecho-Slovak armaments economy has become an important adjunct to Soviet foreign policy. In addition to the artillery, tanks, and military vehicles produced by the Lenin (Skoda) Works and other large machine factories,[39] a large part of the production of the twenty-four industrial combines and many smaller plants has direct or indirect military uses. Czecho-Slovakia is today a major supplier of both small arms and heavy weapons to areas where the Soviet Union desires to stir up trouble; a number of Egyptian, Syrian, and Yemenite officers have been detailed to Czech military centers for training in their use.[40] The regime also has its aircraft factories, which produce modern military planes from Soviet designs.[41]

Two of the largest chemical plants are devoted to military production. One of these, constructed since 1952 and now employing over eight thousand workers, is at

[38] See INFORM, Baltimore, October 15, 1957. Control of atomic warheads will doubtless remain in Soviet hands.

[39] These include the Gotwaldove zavody or Brno Weapon Works, the Kliment (Mannesmann) Works at Komotau, and the V. M. Molotov Mining and Foundry Company at Bohumin.

[40] Czech Struggle, London, March, 1958, p. 2.

[41] Under the Soviet budgeting system introduced in 1952, military expenditures are largely "buried" in the civilian budget, and account for at least 50 per cent of government expenditures. Czech propagandists boast that Prague spends only 10 per cent of the budget for "defense" and 30 per cent for "cultural and social objects," but neglect to mention that the latter include uniforms, weapons, ammunition, vehicles and airplanes for the SVAZARM. Armament orders are lumped together with civilian contracts in the industrial category, and the rubric "nutrition" includes rations for the armed forces. Sudetendeutsche Zeitung, May 9, 1953, and December 18, 1954. See also Nicolas Spulber, "National Income and Product," Busek-Spulber, pp. 237-39.

Vlasim, Bohemia. Here, phosphorus grenades and napalm bombs are produced under the supervision of Soviet technicians. Samples of each lot of bombs are tested: the best are shipped to the Soviet Union, the remainder apportioned among the satellites.[42] The other of these plants is the "Synthesia" poison gas factory at Semtin, near Pardubice. The "Synthesia" laboratory, guarded by Russian as well as Czech security police, is devoted to the development of new and more lethal gases—including "nerve gas," which cannot be detected without special instruments and which kills in four minutes. In a special "Experimental Sanatorium" at Bohdanec, guarded by PVS troops, the new gases are tried out on human beings. Victims are selected from the mental hospitals at Bohnic near Prague, Kosmanos, and Dobrzan, and the prisons of Pankrac (Prague), Bory (Plzen), and Leopoldov in Slovakia. These Nazi-style experiments consumed seventy-two human lives during a six-month period in 1953-54: the bodies were cremated, secretly and without religious ceremonies, under the supervision of the PVS. In a few cases, the ashes were returned to respective families, along with the routine notice that the victim had "died while being transferred to another institution."[43]

ESPIONAGE CAPITAL OF EUROPE

Since the "February Revolution," Czecho-Slovakia has become the "chosen instrument" for Communist infiltration in Western Europe. Aside from Czecho-Slovakia's proximity to Germany and Austria, and the reliability of its government from a Communist point of view, the existence of large emigré colonies—including the thousands of refugees still in Germany and Austria—opens unusual opportunities to the Czech agent. These opportunities are enhanced by the equivocal orientation of

---

[42] A description of this plant is given in the *Sudetendeutsche Zeitung*, April 16, 1955.

[43] *Sudetendeutsche Zeitung*, June 26, 1954. Other mental patients have been used as human guinea pigs for experimental medicines produced in a chemical plant at Rostock (12 km. north of Prague), often with fatal results. In the spring of 1954, when it was desired to test a new anti-typhus medicine, infected lice were introduced among the inmates of a forced labor camp near Jachymov so as to produce the desired epidemic.

many exile politicians and organizations of "Czecho-slovak" persuasion.[44]

Among the various espionage schools in Czecho-Slovakia, the most noteworthy is the Foreign Institute in Prague,[45] which recruits its students among Communists with linguistic ability. Courses are small and intensive, and the students receive large stipends. The minority who pass with honors become full-fledged agents, while others are "demoted" to a school for sabotage. Needless to say, any student whose Communist orthodoxy becomes doubtful is transferred immediately to a concentration camp.

The curriculum includes sociology, individual and mass psychology, public speaking, and the organization of strikes, demonstrations, and riots. Agents are prepared for the following specific tasks:

(a) Infiltration in trade unions, incitement of discontent, and provocation of disturbances;

(b) Observation, guidance, and enlistment of people with potential Communist sympathies;

(c) Contact with prominent politicians, scientists, and industrialists—observation of their personal weaknesses, such as alcoholism or homosexuality, which lend themselves to blackmail or other exploitation;

(d) Infiltration into prominent positions in government, business, or industry, which can be used as bases for influence or sabotage;

(e) Infiltration of Czech and Slovak exile organizations and German expellee groups, and the establishment of spy networks within them.[46]

When not masquerading under a false nationality, the Czech spy usually pretends to be a legitimate emigré. If assigned to Germany, he may try to obtain refugee credentials[47]—and is quite likely to offer his services to American agencies as an *anti*-Communist. Prague agents have been able to infiltrate with relative ease into

---

[44] More is said on this subject in the following chapters. For obvious reasons, Slovaks are used as agents much less frequently than Czechs.

[45] Not to be confused with the Foreign Institute in Exile of Leiden, Holland, discussed in chap. IX.

[46] *Sudetendeutsche Zeitung*, October 4, 1952, and May 2, 1953.

[47] This was not too difficult from 1948 to 1953, when refugees were certified by the International Refugee Organization, which inherited many left-wing employees from its predecessor UNRRA. It is much harder now that German and American agencies have assumed full control over the refugee camps and the screening process.

socialist-oriented organizations such as the Council of Free Czecho-Slovakia and its affiliate in Germany, the Czechoslovak National Alliance.[48] Since in earlier years many refugees and expellees were unemployed for long periods after arriving in Germany, while others had close relatives in Czecho-Slovakia or feared denunciation for collaboration with the Nazis, there were ample opportunities for Communist agents to exert pressure. The German press is replete with stories of refugees and expellees who were blackmailed into furnishing intelligence for Prague—including employees of the United States Army.[49] Now that the refugee population has stabilized and jobs are plentiful, operations of this sort are somewhat less frequent.

Austria has been another major field of operations. Aided by the fact that the Soviets occupied part of Vienna until 1955, Prague agents achieved considerable influence within the large Czech community in that city, including control over the Comenius School, the Sokol (which became a recruiting ground for the SVAZARM), and even the two Czech football clubs. In January, 1953, Czech agents kidnapped from the U.S. Sector of Vienna an Austrian wanted for questioning in connection with the Slansky affair. Through their headquarters in Urfahr, the Soviet-occupied town across the Danube from Linz, they were, until 1955, able to kidnap a number of Czech and Slovak refugees from the United States Zone of Austria. Collaborating with Communists among the Italian railroad workers, Czech agents in Austria delivered money, propaganda materials, and even weapons to the Italian Communist party.[50]

In recent years, Prague has intensified political infiltration abroad, including the financing of Communist parties and "peace" movements.[51] Early in 1957, a conference of Czech and French Communist leaders dis-

---

[48] *Bohemia Information Service* (German), Munich, June 8, 1951; *Bohemia* (Czech), Munich, April-May, 1953; *Slovak Newsletter,* July, 1957, and *passim.*

[49] For case histories of spies convicted by U.S. and German courts, see *Sudetendeutsche Zeitung,* August 8, 15, 22, 29, and September 12, 1953, February 13, 1954, and December 10, 1955.

[50] *Neues Österreich,* Vienna, March, 1953; *Sudetendeutsche Zeitung,* May 2 and August 29, 1953.

[51] Foreign currencies for this purpose are, in part, obtained through the sale of gift parcels for delivery in Czecho-Slovakia, such as the "DAREX" packages sold in New York. Those who buy these parcels are, in the long run, hurting their friends rather than helping them.

cussed methods of interparty co-operation and issued a communiqué designed to aggravate French distrust of German rearmament. Later that year, delegations of the Syrian and Algerian Communist parties, as well as a Syrian government group, visited Prague, where President Novotny and Premier Siroky promised that Czecho-Slovakia would support Arab nationalism to the limit. Through a special "Office for Friendly Relations with the Labour Party" in Prague, Ambassador Hajek in London, and certain members of parliament, left-wing Laborites are mobilized for the cause of coexistence and for the defeat of British policy in the Middle East. Meanwhile, the learned Professor Hromadka, head of the Church of the Czech Brethren, works the ecumenical circuit, explaining that there is no real conflict between Christianity and Communism.

Since Russians are politically suspect in Latin-America, Czecho-Slovak embassies in that part of the world have become increasingly active in guiding and financing Communist parties and "anti-imperialist" movements. Promising young agitators are brought to Czecho-Slovakia for guidance and training. A principal speaker at the International Trade-Union Conference of Working Youth held in Prague on July 14, 1958, was the Cuban Negro Lazaro Peña, vice-president of the World Federation of Trade Unions and a principal instigator of anti-United States hostility among our southern neighbors. There is little doubt that Czech as well as Soviet agents had their hand in the attacks against Vice-President Nixon in Peru and Venezuela.

To sum up: In Czecho-Slovakia, as in other totalitarian states, the dynamics of dictatorship create a climate of "permanent aggression." Peaceful coexistence with such a state is a logical and political impossibility.[52]

---

[52] House Committee on Communist Aggression (83d Congress), *Summary Report* and *Special Report No. 8*, Washington, December, 1954; Mikus, *La Slovaquie dans le Drame de l'Europe*, pp. 293-316 (government and politics) and 317-55 (totalitarian controls). For news stories and articles on current conditions in Czecho-Slovakia, see files of *Problems of Communism* (Washington), *Slovak Newsletter* and *Slovakia* (Middletown, Pa.), *East Europe* (New York, Free Europe Committee), *German News* (Munich), *Czech Struggle* (London), and *Bulletin of the National Council of Slovaks Abroad*. In German: *Ost-Probleme* (U.S. High Commission/U.S. Embassy, Bad Godesberg), *Sudetendeutsche Zeitung* (Munich), and *Pressedienst der Heimatvertriebenen* (Göttingen). In Czech: *Narod* and *Narodni Demokrat* (Chicago), *Bohemia* (Munich), *Krestanska Demokracia* (New York), and *Rozpravy* (Brussels). In Slovak: *Jednota* (Middletown, Pa.), and *Slobodné Slovensko* (Munich).

VIII

THE CHALLENGE TO AMERICAN POLICY

THE ACHILLES' HEEL

THE FACTS recited in the foregoing chapters should make it evident that the Communist regime is not only a scourge to the Czech and Slovak peoples but also a direct menace to the United States and the rest of the free world. Hardly a week goes by without threatening manifestoes or violations of international law. Kidnappings by Prague agents continue, and raids and shootings across the German and Austrian borders are common occurrences.[1] Liberation of the Czechs and Slovaks from Communism is not, therefore, a matter of pure idealism, but a long-range goal which the United States and its allies must pursue for their own safety.

In political warfare as well as military, it is essential to attack the enemy at his most vulnerable point. The *greatest* weakness of the Prague regime is not the fact that, like all Communist dictatorships, it is based on terror rather than loyalty. It is, rather, the congenital weakness of *all* Czecho-Slovak governments—the weakness which impelled Dr. Benes to entrust his fortunes to the Kremlin. Czecho-Slovakia is a defective political entity, unable to exist without external sustenance. Just as the establishment of the Czecho-Slovak Republic and its existence during the 1920's depended on French support and German weakness, so is its survival today conditional on Soviet hegemony in east-central Europe.

---

[1] For an account of the kidnapping of the Slovak exiles Jozef Vicen and Dr. Jozef Bobek on Austrian soil in 1957, see the *Neuer Kurier*, Vienna, January 7, 1958, the *New York Times*, January 19, 1958, and the *Bulletin of the Slovak National Council Abroad*, February, 1958. For accounts of border violations, see the German and Austrian daily press, particularly for the week of August 4, 1958.

The experience of Czecho-Slovakia proves that there is only one way to impose a unitary national state on a multinational area: through sheer force. Even so, Czecho-Communist imperialism has proved incapable of digesting its conquered territories.

1. THE SUDETEN AREAS

In spite of the efforts of Prague politicians and Western "friends of Czechoslovakia" such as Harriet Wanklyn and Elizabeth Wiskemann to minimize the dislocation caused by the expulsion of the Sudeten Germans,[2] the fact remains that Czech efforts to settle the Sudeten territories have been a dismal failure. And much of the settlement which has been achieved is hardly of a permanent nature.

During the expulsion in 1945 and 1946, there was a rush of Communist and opportunist "carpetbaggers" from the interior of Bohemia-Moravia to the Sudeten districts. Some were interested only in acquiring movable property, some came to take personal revenge on the Germans, while others hoped to become homeowners or business proprietors at low cost. Most Czechs, however, felt a natural revulsion against taking what did not belong to them. It soon became apparent that resettlement would require state support: the government offered to pay moving costs, and to provide estates of one hundred hectares to farmers. Even so, much of the farmland remained vacant, and in many cases resettlement caused abandonment of productive farms in the interior. What happened in the towns is suggested by the following statistics:

	Population	
Town	Before Expulsion	After Expulsion[3]
Eger	40,000	19,000
Lobositz	17,000	2,000

---

[2] Miss Wanklyn, *Czechoslovakia*, pp. 238-41 and 291-92, admits serious shortages of agricultural and industrial manpower. But, she writes: "The German tradition in the Historic Provinces had to be uprooted, and it was worth any aggravation of existing difficulties to do so."

[3] Compiled from various Czech sources. The government, for obvious reasons, has never released any comprehensive population statistics.

Rumburg	12,000	1,800
Böhmisch-Eisenstein	5,000	0
Oberplan	1,500	300
Niederlichtenwalde	1,864	26 families

In 1947 the government began to shift Slovaks and Magyars to the Sudeten districts, and imported a few thousand Italian miners and Bulgarian and Rumanian farm workers. These, however, made up only a fraction of the 2.9 million Sudeten Germans who had been expelled.

In the military zone along the border, later widened to a depth between three and six miles, the vacancy problem was solved by the total demolition of all houses not needed for military use, including entire villages. But even in occupied areas, rapid deterioration of homes and business properties ensued since the state—concentrating its resources on heavy industry—was unwilling to supply paint, window glass, and building materials for repairs. Sudeten German workshops, mainly concerned with consumer needs, were left neglected,[4] and the entire contents of most bookshops and libraries was sold for pulp.[5] In 1952 the Resettlement Office scheduled 30,000 houses for destruction as being "beyond repair" or in "undersettled" areas, and two years later the Ministry of Agriculture discovered that of 127,000 Sudeten German farmhouses, only 3,200 were still habitable—if repaired. After usable building materials had been removed, the condemned houses were blown up with dynamite.[6]

From 1948 to 1952, establishment of settlers in the Sudeten German areas was largely a task of the *kraj* (administrative region) National Committees. But the program lagged, and during the winter of 1951-52 the population of the Sudetenland actually decreased.[7] In

---

[4] Attempts were made to continue certain export industries, such as Gablonz costume jewelry and Graslitz band instruments, but with indifferent results, since quality could not be maintained without skilled workers. These industries are now reestablished in West Germany.

[5] *Sudetendeutsche Zeitung,* March 7, 1954. In 1950 it was belatedly realized that the remaining books and archives of the Sudetenland might contain something of value, and an archival salvage operation was started.

[6] *Der Sudetendeutsche,* April 12, 1952, and *Sudetendeutsche Zeitung,* February 13, 1954.

[7] *Volksbote,* Munich, April 6, 1952, cites 70,000 as the approximate amount of the decline.

1952 administration of resettlement was centralized in Prague, and the entire country was divided into three zones for settlement purposes. Within Zone I, the interior zone, all politically unreliable elements and persons with relatives in Western countries or in concentration camps were to be moved from the larger cities to small towns and villages, where their surveillance would be easier. Zone II, containing most of the Sudeten German territory, was to be settled with those Sudeten Germans remaining in Czecho-Slovakia, with Slovaks, and with Ruthenians furnished by the Soviet Union. The strategy was to mix the nationalities in such a way as to provoke friction, so that members of each ethnic group would denounce "unreliable" elements in the others.[8] Zone III, the frontier zone, extending twenty to forty kilometers inland from the border, cannot be entered without a special permit, granted only after thorough investigation by the political police.[9]

The central Resettlement Office obtained no better results, and the population of the Sudetenland rose little, if any. During 1953, Czech peasants who had been settled close to the border were forced to move again to permit widening of the "no man's land." Observers in Bavaria could watch the systematic wrecking of villages, including the burning of churches formerly protected as historic monuments. Further inland, numerous settlers, upon finding themselves required to join collective farms, abandoned their homesteads and disappeared. In the wine district of Znaim and Nikolsburg, the vineyards were ruined by new settlers, who understood nothing of grape cultivation. Visitors to Aussig, Eger, and other Sudeten German cities in 1953 noted a tendency of local Czech administrations to order the wrecking of houses which were only slightly damaged or merely in run-down condition caused by nonuse. According to Erwin Wazula, a Sudeten German who visited his former home near Troppau several times in 1953 and 1954, not more than 80 per cent of the houses in that area were occupied, and these held about half the

---

[8] This strategy has backfired: Germans, Slovaks, Ruthenians and non-Communist Czechs tend to unite in passive resistance against their oppressors.

[9] *Sudetendeutsche Zeitung*, October 24, 1952.

former number of inhabitants. The remaining houses were rapidly falling to ruins, the doors, windows, and other woodwork having been removed for use elsewhere or as firewood.[10]

A new resettlement campaign launched in 1953 was equally fruitless, even though the government offered not only transportation but also loans for furniture and livestock. In the Zlin region, only six families and five single persons out of a population of 800,000 volunteered for resettlement. For lack of applicants, the government took to forcible recruiting in Slovakia, but many of the shanghaied Slovaks managed to sneak home. In the border counties of Nikolsburg and Znaim, which made preparations to receive 1,100 new farmers, only 78 actually arrived.[11]

As the factories built during the first Five-Year Plan swung into operation, the manpower shortage became increasingly critical. At the Tenth Congress of the Czecho-Slovak Communist Party in June, 1954, Premier Siroky was forced to admit that the total farmland under cultivation had shrunk by 500,000 hectares (1,235,000 acres) since the end of the war. It was the government's intention, he added, to recover 200,000 hectares by 1957, and to increase the number of farm workers by 320,000. Just where these people would be found, he did not say. The delegates then passed a resolution demanding that the population of the Sudeten districts be increased by at least 70,000.[12]

Of the 70,000 settlers demanded by the party, the Resettlement Office hoped to move 12,000 by the end of 1954. When a count was made, however, it was found that exactly 4,785 persons had been resettled during the year.[13] As a last resort, the government turned

[10] *Sudetendeutsche Zeitung,* April 25, September 12, and November 1, 1953, and December 1, 1956. See also chap. VII, note 21.

[11] *Sudetendeutsche Zeitung,* February 13, 1954; report of Secretary of Communist party, Kraj Brno, cited in *Sudetendeutsche Zeitung,* May 8, 1954.

[12] *Sudetendeutsche Zeitung:* June 19 and July 3, 1954, on Tenth Party Congress; August 21, 1954, on resettlement problems; and August 14, October 30, and December 18, 1954, on manpower problems in industry. See also *Ost-Probleme,* February 19, 1953 (Food Policy in Czecho-Slovakia), and March 18, 1954 (Colonization of the Sudetenland: articles from Western and Communist sources), as well as *Sudeten Bulletin,* Munich, November, 1954.

[13] *Sudetendeutsche Zeitung,* February 12, 1955. For accounts of attempts to settle gypsies in the Sudeten districts, see *ibid.,* October 9, 1954, and January 22 and March 19, 1955.

to wholesale compulsory resettlement.[14] No exact statistics are available, but a computation derived from the *Administrative Index of Czecho-Slovak Communes,* published in 1955, indicates that approximately 500,000 Slovaks have been moved out of Slovakia. While some of them joined the forces of Czech industrial combines, it is apparent that the majority were resettled in the Sudeten districts.

The limited success of both voluntary and forced efforts to replace the Sudeten Germans and to return their homeland to productivity is shown by the following statistics:

POPULATION OF BOHEMIAN BORDER REGIONS
(KRAJE)[15]

Administrative Region (Kraj)	Population	
	1930	1955
Hradec Kralove (Königgratz)	655,649	571,400
Reichenberg	730,291	497,400
Aussig	829,845	646,300
Karlsbad	645,994	311,800
Plzen (Pilsen)	667,234	567,500
Ceske Budejovice (Budweis)	613,850	510,500

In interpreting these figures, it should be noted that three of the regions as now defined, Hradec Kralove, Plzen, and Ceske Budejovice, are more Czech than German in their composition, while all contain some Czech elements. It should also be remembered that the present population includes forced laborers, such as the uranium miners of St. Joachimsthal, as well as Slovaks and Magyars who are likely to leave at the first opportunity.

Since 1955 the government has been more modest in its resettlement plans. The goal for 1956 was defined as "more than 5,000" and for the first time the Communist party was able to announce "almost 100%" fulfilment of the plan.[16] It is apparent that the regime has

---

[14] The Prague regime has never admitted that it engages in forced resettlement. It is obvious, however, that people will "volunteer" if threatened with worse alternatives, and reports of recent escapees indicate that such is often the case.

[15] *Administrativni Lexikon obci Republiky Ceskoslovenske,* Prague, 1955.

[16] *Pravda,* Bratislava, February 10, 1957, p. 1. An additional obstacle to resettlement is the fact that by now the majority of vacant houses are quite uninhabitable, or require repairs for which no materials are available. There are frequent reports of newly arrived settlers leaving in disgust. The government

given up the full resettlement of the Sudeten German territories as a bad job, and prefers that the subject be discussed as little as possible.[17]

2. SLOVAKIA

Prague's problem in Slovakia is not that of empty land, but of unruly people. Not only is underground opposition to the regime considerably more active than in the Czech lands, but there is no Slovak Communist leadership which Prague really trusts. To achieve acceptance as a leader among his own people, a Slovak Communist must show at least a superficial understanding of Slovak national aspirations. By doing so, he becomes guilty of "bourgeois nationalism" and, hence, a candidate for liquidation.

During World War II and for a short time afterward, Moscow experimented with the idea of supporting a Slovak national Communist movement distinct from the Czech Communist party. Since Slovak nationalism proved to be too deeply committed to the tradition of Stefanik, Hlinka, and Tiso, and to the Catholic church, the Kremlin shifted to the "Czechoslovakist" approach, and the leading Slovak Communists were liquidated. Clementis was the first to fall. His colleagues, Gustav Husak, Laco Novomesky, Ivan Horvath, Laco Holdos, and Daniel Okaly—leaders of the 1944 partisan revolt and executives in the post-1948 regional government— were convicted of "Titoism" and "Slovak separatism" on April 24, 1954, and sent to prison for terms ranging from eight to thirty years.[18]

In the eyes of Czech Communists, irrevocably com-

---

has therefore started a reconditioning program and is actually building new houses at industrial centers such as Brüx, Böhmisch-Leipa, St. Joachimsthal, and Troppau.

[17] For additional background on the population problem, see Waller Wynne, Jr., *The Population of Czechoslovakia*, Washington, 1953, U.S. Bureau of the Census; Alfred Bohmann, *Die Entvölkerung der Sudetenländer* ["The Depopulation of the Sudeten Regions"], Troisdorf, Germany, 1951; and Rudolf Schreiber, "Wirtschaftsgeschichte der Sudetenländer," in *Die Deutschen in Böhmen und Mähren*, pp. 268-90.

[18] Slovak League of America and Slovak National Council Abroad, *Memorandum Concerning the Czech-Communist Military Intervention in Slovakia*, Middletown, Pa., December 22, 1956, p. 4. The non-Communist partisan leader, Viliam Zingor, had already been executed on October 19, 1950, for "attacking the historical conception of a unified Czechoslovakia." See *Slowakische Korrespondenz*, May-June, 1954.

mitted to "Czechoslovakism," Slovaks are inherently unreliable. Beginning in late 1953, therefore, members of the "more mature" Czech Communist party were placed in the majority of key positions in Slovak administration and industry.[19] Prague's fears of unrest in Slovakia were not unfounded. In March, 1954, a wave of strikes broke out against the government's policy of requiring Slovak workers to fulfill higher norms for less pay than their Czech colleagues. The Slovak Communists Knotek and Neovesky supported the rank and file. When they were arrested, the strikes became so widespread that the government was forced to retreat, freeing the captive functionaries and partially equalizing working conditions. The transfer of Slovaks to the Sudetenland was therefore in part a political measure, directed at separating unruly elements from the mass of the Slovak people.[20]

As mentioned in Chapter VI, the Hungarian Revolution of 1956 provoked relatively little disturbance in the Czech lands. This statement definitely does not apply to Slovakia, which came close to having a revolution of its own.

As events in Hungary approached a climax, demonstrations took place in Bratislava, Levice, Lucenic, and Kosice. On October 27, 1956, Slovaks marched in the streets of Bratislava, carrying placards which read: "We Stand with New Hungary," "Out with the Czechs!" and "Freedom and Independence for Slovakia." The Prague government, meanwhile, dispatched six army divisions to Slovakia, suspended Slovak garrison officers above the rank of major, and mobilized a Czech workers' militia to replace Slovak factory guards. All Slovak political prisoners of any consequence, including Communists, were hastily removed to prisons in Bohemia and Moravia.

As the Kremlin prepared to crush Hungarian free-

---

[19] *Slowakische Korrespondenz*, Munich, III, No. 3/4, March/April, 1955, 10. This journal comments that since the liquidation of Husak, Novomesky, and almost every Slovak Communist of any consequence, it is almost absurd to speak of a Slovak Communist party. The apparatus presided over by the Czech, Karel Bacilek, could more accurately be described as the Czech Communist party for Slovakia.

[20] *Ibid.*, and *Pravda* (Bratislava), March 17, 1954.

dom with military force, Soviet troops moved into Slovakia. Slovak partisans blew up a large section of railroad track between Salgotarjan, Hungary, and Lucenec, Slovakia, as well as engaging Soviet forces in a battle near Presov. After the Red Army had installed the puppet premier Kadar in Budapest, there was heavy fighting in northern Hungary. Czech divisions moved to aid the Red Army, while Slovak partisans fought on the side of the Hungarian rebels.[21]

The Hungarian Revolution was crushed, but the Prague Communists remained worried about the prospect of a Slovak revolt. On December 9 and 10, 1956, Sovzone German and Czech party leaders met in Prague to discuss the possibilities of a revolutionary outbreak in Slovakia, similar to the revolt in Hungary, and also what measures should be taken to crush such a Slovak uprising in its earliest stages.[22]

There have been no major disturbances between the Hungarian uprising and the time of this writing. It is evident, however, that Slovak opposition to Prague and Moscow is smoldering, and will break out whenever the Czechs or Russians have serious troubles elsewhere. Significantly, there have been no announcements of trials of Slovaks who aided the Hungarian freedom fighters. This suggests either that the Slovak underground has been able to preserve security, or that the government fears that such trials, if public, would provoke further outbreaks.[23] Instead, the government has contented itself with trying and convicting a number of persons accused of "crimes" in the suppression of the 1944 Communist-inspired revolt.[24]

---

[21] See SLA-SNCA *Memorandum*, pp. 6-7; *Bulletin of the Slovak National Council Abroad*, February, 1957; *New York Times*, November 7 and 8 (Prague dispatches) and November 20 and December 15, 1956 (John MacCormac) ; *Salzburger Nachrichten*, December 17, 1956; *U.S. News and World Report*, December 21, 1956.

[22] *Dziennik dla Wszystkich* (Polish), January 10, 1957, cited in *Bulletin of the Slovak National Council Abroad*, February, 1957.

[23] In view of the number of Slovaks who participated in the Hungarian uprising, the latter hypothesis seems more likely.

[24] *German News*, Munich, April, 1958, pp. 7-8; *Bulletin of the Slovak National Council Abroad*, June, 1958, p. 1. As a matter of fact, nearly all the atrocities of the 1944 revolt were committed by Soviet agents, Slovak Communists, and other partisans, and not by the forces of the Slovak Republic. A considerable number of Slovaks (many to their later regret) took part in the uprising, and have these crimes on their consciences. The government, therefore, could take psychological advantage of mixed feelings among the people.

On the ideological front, Bacilek continues to beat the drums against "bourgeois nationalism" at party conferences and congresses.[25] But Slovak national feeling cannot be repealed by party decree. At the Central Committee Plenum of January 9 and 10, 1958, Bacilek—perhaps to justify the continued presence of Soviet troops in Slovakia—bore renewed witness to the tenacity of "bourgeois nationalism":

> Numerous former capitalists, kulaks, and former officials of the Slovak fascist state who are supported by foreign reactionaries have succeeded in obtaining posts in the Administration and even in our Party. These tendencies are all the more harmful since they show themselves at a time when the Communist Party is busy with economic decentralization.
>
> Bourgeois nationalism has also evinced itself in the economic apparatus, in the films, the press, the radio and television. It can be noticed in the central administration offices of the Slovak Commissioners. . . . The imperialists want to overthrow our people's democracy by using Slovakia as a channel. Bourgeois democracy is allied with Ludakism (Slovak separatism) and finds expression in an outcry against Czechs working in Slovakia.[26]

As the *New York Times* commented:

> Mr. Bacilek's speech is interpreted as an indication that the Slovak nationalists have been no more permanently reconciled by Communism to their domination by the Czechs in Bohemia and Moravia than by the democratic systems of the late Thomas G. Masaryk and the late Eduard Benes that preceded it.

The few Slovak "national Communists" who seek separation from Prague have been encouraged by recent preference shown to Slovak metallurgy, chemistry, and atomic energy in the Russian-dictated Czecho-Slovak investment plans. While Moscow justifies this emphasis on the ground of Slovakia's better accessibility to other East-block states, rumors circulate that a Slovak Soviet Republic may be in the offing. The Slovak people, however, so thoroughly identify Communism with "Czechoslovakism" that a change of this sort might open the floodgates to a revolution against Communism altogether,

---

[25] Bacilek's speeches at the CC Plenum of December 12-13, 1956 and the resolutions of the Party Congress at Bratislava on April 26 and 27, 1957, are quoted in the *Bulletin of the Slovak National Council Abroad*, February and June, 1957, respectively.

[26] The *New York Times*, January 13, 1958.

as did "national Communism" in Hungary. Subordination to Prague remains, at least for the immediate future, an essential instrument of Communist rule in Slovakia.[27]

EXILE POLITICS AND "CZECHOSLOVAKISM"

Political exiles from Czecho-Slovakia fall into three general categories:

(1) "Czechoslovak" politicians and their followers who uphold the Masaryk-Benes conception of a unitary state dominated by the Czechs. Members of this group, which includes most of the "liberal" officeholders, journalists, and academicians of the National Front, are adamant opponents of what they call "Slovak separatism" and are, with few exceptions, strongly anti-German. They are either totally opposed to the return of the Sudeten Germans or they make that return conditional on Sudeten acceptance of the privileged political role of "Czechoslovaks." The political center of this group is the Council of Free Czechoslovakia, about which more will be said later.

(2) Exiles who recognize the existence of separate nations within Czecho-Slovakia and therefore reject a unitary state. These exiles include oppositional members of National Front parties, those excluded from politics or imprisoned between 1945 and 1948, and some who never returned to Czecho-Slovakia after World War II. Their ranks are sometimes augmented by exiles who break away from the Council of Free Czechoslovakia. They are organized in separate Czech, Slovak, and Hungarian national groups, which cooperate on the common platform of equal self-determination. While these groups differ in their specific objectives, they agree that liberation must mean the end of the Czecho-Slovak state as it now exists. All these groups recognize the right of the Sudeten Germans to return to their homeland and to exercise self-determination equal to that of other nations.

(3) The Sudeten German expellees from Bohemia and Moravia, and the Carpatho-Germans from Slovakia, most of whom are now in the German Federal Republic.[28]

Relative influence among the first two groups is to some extent, though by no means entirely, a result of

---

[27] Heinrich Kuhn, "Moscow's Smoke Screen in Slovakia," *Sudeten Bulletin,* VII (1959), 11-12.

[28] According to the 1950 census, there were 1,918,000 expellees from Czecho-Slovakia in the Federal Republic (including the Saar and West Berlin), 916,000 in the Soviet Zone (including East Berlin), and 140,000 in Austria. It is probable that about 100,000 have since moved from the Soviet Zone to the Federal Republic.

United States policy. Some exile organizations are—directly or indirectly—subsidized by the United States government, while others are not.

The situation of the Sudeten Germans is different, since the entire ethnic group was expelled at a time when it lacked coherent political leadership. The Sudeten Germans in the German Federal Republic have, during the past decade, acquired both leadership and organization. Like other expellees, they enjoy full political rights and are proportionately represented in the Bundestag and the Land diets—both by older politicians formerly active in Czecho-Slovakia, and by a younger generation which is cutting its teeth in West German politics.

Although not committed to any one political party, the Sudeten Germans have retained a political cohesiveness which has surprised many Western observers and dismayed the Prague government. Their mass organization is the *Sudetendeutsche Landsmannschaft,* with 350,000 dues-paying members organized in districts and local chapters. The Landsmannschaft's annual rallies draw an average attendance of 250,000 and there are numerous regional meetings with 10,000 or more participants.[29] The Sudeten German Youth passes on the tradition of the homeland to the younger generation through study groups, dramatics, musical performances, and social activities. The SGY also conducts athletic programs and summer camps, and co-operates with other expellee youth groups in the *Deutsche Jugend des Ostens* ("German Youth of the East"). In matters of foreign policy, relations with Czechs, Slovaks, and other nationalities, and political questions involving the Sudetenland, the Sudeten Germans are represented by their council (*Sudetendeutscher Rat*), half of whose members are designated by the Landsmannschaft, the other half by the Sudeten German members of the Bundestag and the state diets. The Speaker (president) of the Landsmannschaft is an ex-officio member of the Presidium of the Sudeten-German Council.[30]

---

[29] Based on estimates by German police authorities.

[30] Minister of Transport Dr.-Ing. Hans Christoph Seebohm was elected speaker in October, 1959, upon the retirement of the first speaker, Dr. Rudolf Lodgman von Auen. The Carpatho-Germans are represented by the *Karpathendeutsche Landsmannschaft,* which co-operates with the Sudeten Germans on matters of common interest.

Through their organizations and their deputies in the Bundestag, the Sudeten Germans have consistently asserted their right to return to their homeland, a right supported by the German Federal government.[31] They insist at the same time on full self-determination, refusing to resume the role of a minority in a foreign national state. The status of the Sudeten districts and their inhabitants must, they maintain, be settled by free negotiation between the legitimate representatives of the Czechs and the Sudeten Germans, the historical "joint tenants" of Bohemia and Moravia. In 1950 the predecessor of the Sudeten German Council and the Czech National Committee of London entered into the so-called "Wiesbaden Agreement," a statement of principle supporting the return of the Sudeten Germans and the reorganization of the Bohemian Crown Lands as a federation, with both nations enjoying equal rights.[32]

Although both the Sudeten German leaders and the Bonn government reject the use of military force to recover the Sudetenland, it is clear that the *status quo* can last only so long as Czecho-Slovakia and its neighbors remain Soviet satellites. If genuine "disengagement" should occur and the Russians should retreat behind their own borders, a reunited Germany—supported by Austria and free Hungary—could exert political and economic pressure which no regime in Prague could resist. The dependence of the "Czechoslovakist" concept on prevailing Russian power was recognized by the ideologists of the National Front, whose views were reflected in Ferdinand Peroutka's magazine *Dnesek,* as follows:

---

[31] For text of Bundestag resolution of July 14, 1950, asserting "man's inalienable right to his home," see *Mitteleuropäische Quellen und Dokumente,* I, 104. More recently, in a discussion of problems which would be faced by a reunited Germany, Foreign Minister von Brentano stated: "The Federal Government expects that an agreement will also be reached with Czecho-Slovakia doing justice to the Sudeten Germans' claim to their homeland." *Sudetendeutscher Artikeldienst,* April 6, 1957, p. 2.

[32] Since no exile organization can make final commitments on behalf of the people at home, the provisional character of the "Wiesbaden Agreement" is recognized by both parties. It is significant, however, that a number of other exile groups, such as the Czech Christian Democratic Movement and the Czechoslovak Legion in Exile, have since endorsed the return of the Sudeten Germans. See Czech Christian Democratic Movement, *Memorandum,* New York, October 28, 1954; *Sudetendeutsche Zeitung,* November 13, 1954, and March 12, 1955.

If it came to a conflict between the East and the West and if the Soviet Union should lose, we as its allies would lose enormously and would be destroyed through the fact that the Germans would return to our country. But even if in that conflict we were on the side of the West, *which is practically unthinkable,* we could not avoid the same fate, namely the return of the Germans. For this reason the idea of being united with the Soviet Union for life and death is the most important principle of our foreign policy whether we like it or not. For this reason no government can afford to pursue anti-Soviet policies. . . .[33]

Once Soviet Russian power is withdrawn from Central Europe and Communist terror comes to an end, whatever government exists in Prague will also have to come to terms with the Slovaks. The former leaders of the Hlinka People's party and the younger Slovak politicians will return from the concentration camps and from exile: it is they and not the minority of "Czechoslovaks" who will lead Slovak opinion. Any arrangements for political association between Czechs and Slovaks will have to be voluntary on both sides, and it is safe to say that they will *not* be based on the concept of a "Czechoslovak nation."

THE IMPORTANCE OF SLAV-GERMAN RECONCILIATION

Although estimates of public opinion in enslaved countries are to be received with caution, it is significant that most observers rate Czech support for the Communist regime as considerably higher than that of the Slovaks. While exiles with very different viewpoints agree that between 80 and 90 per cent of the Slovaks want an independent Slovak state, and that even more oppose the present regime,[34] recent emigrés have expressed the belief that from 20 to 40 per cent of the Czechs support the Communist government, while many others take a "neutral" attitude. Czech opposition to

---

[33] "We are United with the Soviet Union for Life and Death," *Dnesek,* Prague, December 31, 1947. (Italics supplied.) In the New York *Staatszeitung* of March 17, 1953, Mr. Peroutka stated that he was out of town when the article appeared and that it "must have been written by someone else."

[34] The 80 per cent estimate is attributed to Dr. Martin Kvetko, a "Czechoslovak" holding a leading position in Radio Free Europe; the 90 per cent figure was published in the *Bulletin of the Slovak National Council Abroad,* April, 1957, p. 3.

Communism is also widespread, but often takes the form of "Schwejkism" rather than active resistance.[35] It cannot be denied that the Prague government still enjoys considerable mass support among the Czechs, as does the Warsaw Communist government among the Poles. Outside the relatively small caste of doctrinaire Marxists and opportunist Apparatchiks, loyalty to the regime and to the Soviet Union is based squarely on the fear of Germany. Through the expulsion of the Germans of Bohemia-Moravia and the eastern part of the Reich (now under Polish administration), the Kremlin acquired a political mortgage on Czecho-Slovakia and Poland which is exploited in propaganda of this sort:

Through the historical victory of the Soviet Union it was possible to reorganize our country so as to banish once and for all the dangers stemming from unsolved nationality problems and from the seditious propaganda which threatened our first republic. It is impossible to overestimate the historic importance of the fact that after a history of a thousand years the expulsion of the Germans has guaranteed the safety of our Fatherland as never before. Our peoples owe undying thanks to Comrade Stalin, who advocated this solution in Potsdam and fought it through against the resistance of the Western Powers.[36]

The main theme of Czech and Polish internal propaganda is the "aggressive" policy of Western Germany, pictured as being groomed for a new war of revenge by its imperialist masters in Washington. Prague and Warsaw politicians harp on the fear that the Germans, when they return to settle the Sudetenland and the Oder-Neisse territories, will repeat the atrocities committed by the Communist-led partisans in 1945 and 1946.

From the end of World War II until the "February Revolution," the Czecho-Slovak Communist line on the nationality question was based on the theory of collective guilt—*Nemec jako Nemec:* all Germans were alike,

---

[35] *Die Tschechoslowakei im Urteil der Spätheimkehrer* ["Czecho-Slovakia as Seen by Late Returnees"], Sudeten German Council, Munich, August, 1956; Rudolf Wenzel in *Sudetendeutsche Zeitung*, February 11, 1956; C. L. Sulzberger in the *New York Times*, March 10, 1956. The legendary soldier Schwejk, the literary creation of Jaroslav Hasek, provoked chaos in the Austrian army by carrying out orders to the point of absurdity. The pasting of propaganda placards reading "DODALO RUSSKO" ("A Gift from Russia") on empty freight cars is a typical example of "Schwejkism."

[36] *Rude Pravo*, No. 63, 1951.

and there was no room for them in Czecho-Slovakia.[37] Supporting Minister Kopecky's call for a "mighty national offensive" against the Sudeten Germans, the Communist Karl Kreibich wrote:

> Don't worry how many Germans will finally remain; the fewer the better. One thing is positive: There may never again be an organized political group of the German minority in the Czechoslovak Republic; there may never be a special German economic, political, or cultural tendency, nor any German national life of any sort. There can be no German statute, and the children must receive a Czech education, so that the number of Germans in the Republic is as small as possible and . . . so that not a district remains with a German majority.[38]

Although non-Communist "National Fronters" produced much of the most inflammatory anti-German propaganda,[39] it was the Communist party which reaped the political profit from the expulsion. The "liberals" therefore courted public favor with even more extreme chauvinism. In July, 1945, the National Socialist publishing house, "Melantrich," exhibited a map of "a just and great Czecho-Slovakia," including the partly Slavic Lausitz in Sovzone Germany, parts of Silesia and Austria, and a strip of eastern Bavaria. On September 18, Foreign Minister Masaryk claimed several Silesian districts, and on March 27, 1946, the *Svobodne Noviny* editorialized: "The Lausitz must become an autonomous territory . . . under Czecho-Slovak protection."[40] These demands remained academic, since the Kremlin was not prepared to support Czecho-Slovak expansion at the expense of its German or Polish satellites.

A change in nationality policy after the "February Revolution" was necessary for two reasons: the need to mobilize the Germans remaining in Czecho-Slovakia for the Five-Year-Plan and the fact that the Kremlin

---

[37] See Heinrich Kuhn, "Die kulturelle Situation der Deutschen in der Tschechoslowakei" ["The Cultural Situation of the Germans in Czecho-Slovakia"], *Mitteleuropäische Quellen und Dokumente*, II, Munich, 1957, 26-47.

[38] *Tvorba*, No. 5, 1945, cited in *Dokumentation der Vertreibung der Deutschen aus Ost-Mitteleuropa*, Vol. IV/1, p. 103n. Kreibich, later Czecho-Slovak ambassador in Moscow, was one of a few Sudeten Germans who ingratiated themselves with the Kremlin and the party by turning against their own countrymen.

[39] See "Genocide Against the Sudeten Germans" in chap. IV, *supra*, especially note 87.

[40] Jaksch, *Europas Weg nach Potsdam*, pp. 438-39.

was now forcing the development of a German Communist state. Under a new motto, *Neni Nemec jako Nemec*—"not all Germans are alike"—a distinction was made between the "peace-loving" Germans of the "German Democratic Republic" and the "warmongers" of West Germany, the expellee organizations in particular. Deportations of Sudeten Germans were brought to a halt in August, 1951, and those still in Czecho-Slovakia were provided with their own newspaper, *Aufbau und Frieden*, which proceeded to blame the excesses of the expulsion on the "bourgeois nationalists" who had fled in 1948.

Since propaganda plays upon the emotions, short-circuiting the intellect, a contradictory policy—whatever the logical hiatus—is seldom very effective, because it violates the rule of simplicity. It was hard to tell the Czechs why they should hate the West Germans and not the Sovzone Germans, particularly after Karlshorst[41] had begun to experiment with a nationalist political line for Germany and had authorized the recruitment of former Nazi officials for the "People's Police." A marked decline in anti-German feeling among the Czechs ensued, for which the Prague government attempted to compensate by stepping up the frequency and viciousness of its attacks on the Bonn government and the Western Powers. In 1955, however, anti-Western propaganda had to be softened in tone (though by no means eliminated) to conform with Khrushchev's "Geneva Policy" and the establishment of Soviet-West German diplomatic relations.

These events and the healing of wartime wounds have opened the way toward Slav-German reconciliation, a development which threatens to undermine the psychological basis of Russian control in east-central Europe. Such reconciliation has long been sought by the Sudeten Germans and other expellees, who in August, 1950, joined in sponsoring the "Charter of the German Expellees," a manifesto which asserts *Heimatrecht* ("the right to one's home") as a basic human right, but renounces any thought of revenge or retaliation.[42]

---

[41] Headquarters of the Soviet Control Commission for Germany in East Berlin.

[42] *Charter of the German Expellees* of August 5, 1950, multilanguage edition, Bonn, 1950.

In addition to their activities within the Czech-Sudeten German Federative Committee, an outgrowth of the Wiesbaden Agreement, Sudeten German leaders lose no opportunity for friendly contact with political exiles who are willing to accept the principles of *Heimatrecht* and of equality for all nationalities.[43] Czechs and Slovaks are frequent speakers at Sudeten German gatherings, and Dr. Lodgman always addresses a message to the Czech people on the occasion of the Sudeten German rally. Similar efforts to establish contacts and working relationships with Slav exiles are made by other expellee groups, unfortunately not always with the success attained by the Sudeten Germans.

The nationalist doctrine which emerged from the French Revolution is that each nation should have its own national state, and that this state should include all members of the nation. In east-central Europe, where centuries of dynastic politics had left a patchwork of nationalities intermixed with little regard for ethnic differences, nationalism was bound to provoke a series of disastrous wars. Today, Europe has drained the cup of nationalism to its bitter dregs, and is finally embracing a new European patriotism typified by the surrender of sovereign powers to the Coal and Steel Community and the Common Market.[44] Having suffered the consequences of nationalism more intensely than any other people except the Jews, the German expellees have taken the lead in the search for new political concepts which can put an end to the miseries of the past.

The ideological task of the Sudeten Germans and other expellees today is to demonstrate to their East European neighbors, behind the Iron Curtain and in exile, that the exercise of *Heimatrecht* does not mean a repetition of the atrocities and hardships inflicted by the Nazis during World War II and by the Communists and their

---

[43] The Committee's effectiveness is somewhat hampered by the fact that the Czech partner represents only part of the anti-Communist emigration. It is not and was never intended to be an exclusive channel of Czech-Sudeten German contact.

[44] Unlike conventional international organizations, which are associations of sovereign governments, the new European bodies are *true governments* in their respective fields, having an assembly elected by the national parliaments, an executive with power and personnel to enforce agency regulations, and an international court empowered to make final decisions. The success of these organizations disproves the theory that sovereignty cannot be divided.

helpers at the war's end. Quite to the contrary: the concept of *Heimatrecht* is inseparably linked to the sanctity of human rights and the political equality of all nationalities. As German and East European jurists agreed at a recent meeting, the traditional concept of "minority rights" is no longer adequate: there must be no privileged *Staatsvölker* ("ruling peoples") and no minorities who are "foreigners" in their native lands in the political structure of liberated Europe.[45] Since the national-state system affords self-determination to some and denies it to others, new forms of political organization must be found. As the expellee organizations view the return to their homelands, it will definitely *not* be accompanied by the expulsion or deportation of interim settlers, and the civil liberties and legitimate property rights of all concerned will be scrupulously observed.

As of this writing it cannot truthfully be said that "liberation is around the corner," but the political constellation has shifted abruptly in the past and will presumably do so in the future. For the time being, Slav-German reconciliation remains a major political imperative, since only such reconciliation can remove the fear of Germany which keeps large sectors of the Czech, Polish, and other populations psychologically tied to Moscow. The more concrete the forms of Slav-German collaboration, in the sense of working out methods of political partnership and mutual guarantee of human rights, the greater its propaganda effect. The Sudeten Germans, other expellees, and their East European friends are getting on with the job as best they can, but are hampered by the lack of funds, radio facilities, and great-power political and diplomatic support.

Prague and Warsaw have recently begun their own attempts to promote a "reconciliation" based on the *status quo*. After Gomulka's unsuccessful feelers in the direction of Bonn during 1957, Premier Siroky of Czecho-Slovakia—in the presence of a Polish delegation which visited Prague in July, 1958—made a parliamentary

---

[45] Augsburg round-table discussion of October 2, 1955 (with German, Czech, Slovak, Rumanian, Ukrainian, and other participation), *Unser Recht auf Heimkehr* ["Our Right to Return"], Frankfurt, 1956, pp. 66-96.

speech advocating West German–Czecho-Slovak diplomatic relations. He then wrote a letter to Chancellor Adenauer, delivered through the Soviet Embassy in Bonn, proposing a nonaggression pact between the NATO states and the members of the Warsaw Pact and asserting:

> There is no doubt that the normalization of relations between our two states on the basis of mutual respect for territorial integrity and sovereignty, of nonaggression, of mutual noninterference in domestic affairs, and of equality of rights would contribute to a relaxation of international tension.[46]

An agreement to coexist on the basis of the *status quo* of Yalta and Potsdam, riding roughshod over the rights of twelve million expellees, is not the way to achieve permanent peace. Since basic problems of human rights cannot be solved by ignoring them, such a "deal" with the Communist governments would only confirm the psychological bondage of the enslaved nations to Moscow. A "peace" made at the expense of the expellees would always remain shaky: wrongful possessors always live in fear that if the legitimate proprietors fail to regain their heritage by peaceful means, they will someday claim it by force. It is not only moral obligation to the expellees but the deepest interest of the satellite nations themselves, not to mention the need for a European settlement free of the seeds of future wars, which forbid the German Federal government and its NATO allies to sacrifice the *Heimatrecht* of the Sudeten Germans and other expellees on the altar of expediency.

Analogously, any exile movement which attempts to promote the liberation of its homeland without recognizing the equal rights of all inhabitants, including those who have been expelled, is trying to square the circle. Liberation without justice is a logical and political impossibility. Since Slavic chauvinism depends on Russian hegemony, exile politicians who build their programs around the former are forced, whether they like it or not, into the camp of "coexistence" and appease-

---

[46] *Sudetendeutsche Zeitung*, July 26, 1958. See also same newspaper, January 4, February 1, June 14, and July 12, 1958.

ment. As we shall see in our final chapter, this is exactly what happens.

The only way to liberate east-central Europe without war is to bring about a political climate in which the Kremlin finds (as it did in Austria) that the disadvantages and costs of Russian colonialism outweigh the advantages. This strategy requires the building of a solid anti-Communist front of European peoples based on partnership rather than mere coexistence.[47] Attitudes toward *Heimatrecht* and Slav-German co-operation are thus essential criteria for Americans faced with the tasks of developing a coherent and realistic East European policy and deciding which of the varied exiles from Czecho-Slovakia and other satellites should be given encouragement, financial support, and radiobroadcasting facilities.

---

[47] The distinction is indicated in the contributions of Dr. A. (Rumanian) and Dr. Becher (Sudeten German) to the Augsburg round table, *loc. cit.*

IX

THE AMERICAN RESPONSE

THE BANKRUPTCY OF "CZECHOSLOVAKISM"

C ZECHOSLOVAKISM," or Czech imperialism, as we have seen, was a major cause of the catastrophe which befell the Czech and Slovak peoples, as well as the Sudeten and Carpatho-Germans, at the end of World War II. The Roosevelt administration must bear its partial share of the blame, since it accepted, uncritically, Dr. Benes' claim to speak with authority for the Slovaks as well as the Czechs and since it consented to policies of the exile "government" which were certain to force Czecho-Slovakia into Russian tutelage. This attitude was typical of our general failure to do any positive thinking about the shape of postwar Europe until it was too late.

It is salutary to reflect upon our mistakes if they teach us to avoid similar errors in the future. Acceptance of the "Czechoslovak legend" has misled American policy into a sequence of blunders, some of which have seriously hurt the welfare and safety of the United States. The following are a few of the ill-advised decisions made at the close of World War II and thereafter:

1. By halting our troops on the Budejovice-Plzen line in April/May 1945, we permitted a Communist-dominated rather than an anti-Communist or at least a compromise government to come to power in Prague.

2. We permitted the Russians to obtain a major source of uranium which we could easily have denied them.

3. We permitted the Czecho-Slovak government to expel the Sudeten Germans from areas which had been liberated by American troops. Aside from the moral and political objections to mass

expulsions, they cost American taxpayers, until recently, more than $300,000,000 a year in financial contributions required to balance the German economy.[1]

4. We allowed Czecho-Slovak officials to remove hundreds of refugees from the United States Zones of Austria and Germany for trial in kangaroo courts as "war criminals," without holding hearings to see whether these persons could be presumed guilty of crimes. Although an American general had vouchsafed asylum to Monsignor Tiso and the Slovak government, they were consigned to totalitarian justice.

5. We agreed to treat *political* activity directed at the dismemberment of Czecho-Slovakia as a crime in the Nuremberg trial.

6. Although Czecho-Slovakia emerged from the war in better economic condition than most European countries, we permitted UNRRA to give it $275,000,000 worth of food, supplies, and equipment in 1946, much of which was really not needed. The Prague government sold the food at high prices, using the proceeds to finance nationalized industries.[2]

The "February Revolution" of 1948 should have stimulated the Department of State to undertake a fundamental reappraisal of its Central European policies. Did not the *dénouement* of "Czechoslovakism" demonstrate the need for a new concept, freed of the "Czechoslovak legend" and rooted in the realities of European politics? Were the politicians who had led their nation into the abyss entitled to recognition as "the most respected and authoritative leaders of the democratic forces of Czechoslovakia"?[3] And how did the Truman and Eisenhower administrations respond to the lessons of experience?

THE "COUNCIL OF FREE CZECHOSLOVAKIA"

We have already noted that the "February Revolution" was followed by an exodus of the non-Communist supporters of the National Front. The position of these "liberals" on the eve of the coup has been defined by Ferdinand Peroutka who, to justify his February, 1948, article upholding collaboration with the Communists, gave the following explanation:

[1] See *Germany Reports*, Press and Information Office of the German Federal Government, Bonn, 1953, pp. 108-28 on mass expulsions and p. 237 on United States aid. From 1945 to 1952, the United States spent $3,613,733,000 on aid to Germany (more than our total national budget in 1931), not including occupation costs.

[2] John MacCormac in the *New York Times*, May 29, 1946.

[3] Letter from James B. Carey of the CIO to Vice-President Nixon, protesting against investigation of Dr. Hubert Ripka by the Senate Internal Security Subcommittee, February 12, 1954, CIO Press Release, Washington.

As usual the Communists seek an excuse for their attack and as usual they do not admit the attack, but assert that they are being attacked. At that time their excuse consisted of the assertion that they had discovered a conspiracy with the objective of eliminating them from the government. And under this pretence they began to mobilize the masses for the decisive coup. The democrats defended themselves by *revealing the truth*, which was that *no one intended to throw the Communists out of the government.* My declaration, in this sense, was intended to protect the last position against Communism. The purpose of the sentence was to deprive the Communists of their excuse and to expose their carefully prepared lie.[4]

Gottwald's and Zapotocky's decision to maneuver their "liberal" allies out of the government at a time when their own positions were not in serious jeopardy has evoked a number of explanations, of which three will be mentioned:

1. The simplest assumption is that Communist power had been consolidated to the point anticipated in Dimitroff's "United Front" strategy, when the party, devoid of political gratitude and ready to "go it alone," liquidates its bourgeois and Social Democratic allies. If this thesis is coupled with Mr. Peroutka's reasoning, cited above, it is evident that the "National Fronters" would have continued co-operation with the Communists had not the latter arbitrarily forced them out of office.

2. Another possibility is suggested by V. L. Borin, who indicates that the Communist objective was "to send westwards again the Czechoslovaks who had rendered Moscow such invaluable services in the Second World War," that is, to disrupt and confuse anti-Communist activities in the West.[5] This view, with which the Slovak Liberation Committee concurs, is buttressed by the report that at a Communist party conference at Karlsbad in 1950, Minister of Interior Nosek and the Soviet delegate explained that the party had deliberately permitted the escape of the National Front politicians.[6] It does not, of course, follow from this thesis that the escapees were conscious agents of Communism. The Communist party knew, however, that their commitment to "Czechoslovakism" would lead them into conflict with

---

[4] Translated from New York *Staatszeitung,* March 17, 1953. (Emphasis supplied.)

[5] V. L. Borin, *Against the Hangman,* London, 1951, pp. 15-20.

[6] While the author has no conclusive proof that Nosek made the statement attributed to him, the report is from a reliable Czech source and in view of other factors can be rated as probably true. John Vlkolinsky, "Political Refugees or Red Agents," *Slovakia,* December, 1951, pp. 45-47, cites Robert Ingrim's "reinsurance" theory, according to which Benes and Gottwald made a secret agreement whereby the politicians and generals of the National Front were permitted to depart unmolested, in return for which they agreed to treat the Communists gently in case they should later return to assume political power in Czecho-Slovakia.

uncompromising anti-Communists such as the Czech groups headed by General Prchala and Professor Ghelfand and the Slovak organizations of Sidor and Durcansky.

3. A final thesis, advanced by most of the escapees themselves, is that the Communists forced out their "liberal" associates because they had finally seen the light and had begun to fight Communism.

While charity and fairness admonish us to accept the last thesis, that the non-Communist leaders of the National Front had begun to resist Communism, it must be admitted that they resisted it in the weakest possible way. The record of February and March, 1948, shows only minor efforts by the "opposition" to obstruct the final consolidation of Communist power. Certainly the resignation of Zenkl, Ripka, and the other ministers was not an adequate countermeasure. The lack of effective resistance is fully documented in the account written by Otto Friedman, who did not allow his admiration of President Benes to interfere with honest reporting.[7]

The ministers, bureaucrats, and editors of the National Front, the ink on their signatures of totalitarian decrees hardly dry, were greeted as VIPs by the United States authorities in Germany. Since the Department of State recognized them as democrats who had fought the good fight, the Army provided comfortable billets near Frankfurt, but the more active members moved on to Paris, which became their first center of political operations.

Shortly thereafter, the administration in Washington[8] decided to permit the party leaders of the National Front to enter the United States and to support the foundation of an exile council—the "Council of Free Czechoslovakia." The person entrusted with selecting the first group to be brought from Paris to New York to form the Council's executive body or "cabinet" was none other than Dr. Hubert Ripka, who hardly needs to be introduced to the reader at this point. Statements of exiles present in Paris in January, 1949, indicated that those picked by Ripka (in some cases against the wishes of party chairmen) were granted visas with a minimum of procedure.

---

[7] Otto Friedman, *The Collapse of Czech Democracy*, London, 1952, especially the chapter entitled "No Resistance."

[8] Information on the locus of responsibility for this operation within the government has never been released.

Within a few days the group was on its way across the Atlantic by air at the expense of the United States government.[9]

It soon became apparent that the Council of Free Czechoslovakia would continue the "National Front" policies which had turned Czecho-Slovakia into a Russian satellite.[10] At the first meeting of the Council's Paris branch, Mr. Peroutka declared that he would "endeavor to remove from the Council all members who will fight against socialism."[11] The magazine *Tribuna*, reflecting the prevailing trend of opinion in the Council, had this to say:

> Whoever reads the Communist press, even if he is non-party, believes no more in certain things, such as private initiative. . . . Private initiative is a thing of the past. (August, 1950, p. 2.)

> . . . Private possession of the means of production, ground, and capital is immoral, antisocial, unjust, inefficient, and disadvantageous. (April, 1951, p. 9.)

It is evident that the leaders of the Council never learned that the liquidation of the independent businessman is the liquidation of political freedom, in spite of the very practical lesson which they had gone through.[12]

The Council has also held that the expulsion of Sudeten Germans was right and proper, though most members will admit that there were some excesses. While Mr. Peroutka and Dr. Jaroslav Stransky, among others, have recently admitted that the expulsion was unjustified,[13] the Council has never officially repealed its state-

---

[9] According to a reliable Czech source, the group included Messrs. Blaho, Dieska, Feierabend, Hodza, Klimek, Majer, Prochazka, Peroutka, and Sabo.

[10] See *Declaration of Alliance for Liberation and Freedom in Czechoslovakia; Protesting Memorandum of Alliance of Czechoslovak Exiles in Chicago*, 1952; Miksche, *Danubian Federation*, pp. 5-9; Karl Geyer, "Meinungskämpfe im tschechischen Exil" [Differences of Opinion Among Czech Exiles"], *Der Europäische Osten*, Munich, December, 1954, pp. 139-42; and Leonard Reinisch, "Die dritte tschechisch-slowakische Emigration und die Sudetendeutschen" ["The Third Czecho-Slovak Emigration and the Sudeten Germans"], *Der Neue Ackermann*, Munich, November, 1951, pp. 11-18.

[11] *Navrat*, Paris, July 15, 1949.

[12] The official *Program of the Council of Free Czechoslovakia*, Washington, 1952, intended for American readers, advocates only partial socialism, stating: "We hold that both private and public property, freedom of contract and sound competition between private and public enterprise will form the basis of our future economic system. . . ."

[13] *Sudetendeutsche Zeitung*, March 3 and May 5, 1956.

ment of July 4, 1952, declaring that the "transfer" is "irrevocable."[14] It is interesting to compare the language adopted by the Council with the pertinent parts of a joint declaration of the Prague and Pankow (Sovzone German) Communist governments issued on June 23, 1950.

Prague — Pankow

The Government of the Czechoslovak Republic and the Provisional Government of the German Democratic Republic are convinced that their common obligation to maintain and assure peace is facilitated and at the same time confirmed by the fact that there are no contentious and open questions between their two states. Our two states have no territorial or border claims, and their governments emphasize expressly that the completed resettlement of the Germans out of Czechoslovakia has been accomplished irrevocably, justly, and finally. . . . Guided by the conviction that mutual support of their peaceful reconstruction is in the interest of both peoples and of all states interested in maintaining and assuring peace, the Government of the Czechoslovak Republic and the Provisional Government of the German Democratic Republic are resolved to strengthen the bonds of friendship between their peoples and states. (*Mitteleuropäische Quellen und Dokumente,* I, 102-4.)

Council of Free Czechoslovakia

We consider the transfer of Germans from Czechoslovakia to be irrevocable. The transfer was carried out following approval by the American, British, and French governments, in accordance with decisions of the Potsdam Conference and regulations of the Allied Control Council. By this decision the Great Powers obviously intended to prevent in future certain elements of population in Czechoslovakia and other states again becoming the tool of a foreign policy aimed at the destruction of those states. In this way, the Great Powers undoubtedly wished to contribute to security in Eastern and Central Europe, thereby better ensuring world peace. We are confident that, based on these assumptions, nothing will prevent Czechoslovakia from coming to terms with a democratic Germany concerning such friendly cooperation as will profit both neighboring countries and greatly contribute to the peaceful evolution of Europe.

Committed to policies conceived in the "United Front" with the Communists, the Council could never become an effective anti-Communist organization. As Dr. Stefan Kocvara said at a meeting on January 25, 1951: "I have lost all faith that the present Council of Free

14 *Program*, Washington, 1952.

Czechoslovakia is able to achieve anything in the struggle against Communism."[15]

Important officials in Washington, however, had decided to make the leftish Council of Free Czechoslovakia a chosen instrument of American policy. The National Committee for a Free Europe (later renamed the Free Europe Committee) was provided with government funds to supplement those collected by the Crusade for Freedom.[16] At public expense, the Committee undertook to finance the operations of the Council (as one of a series of exile councils), paying individual salaries to Dr. Zenkl (the chairman), Dr. Ripka (in charge of foreign affairs), and a score of other members.[17] The Czecho-Slovak section of the Committee's Mid-European Studies Center was entrusted to the Council's Dr. Julius Firt, a former socialist deputy who first visited the United States with the Communist Deputy Valo in 1944, when they lectured before the International Workers' Order.[18]

Various Czecho-Slovak politicians who collaborated with the Communists until 1948, and who were not given free salaries as leaders of the Council of Free Czechoslovakia, were assisted in other ways. Dr. Ivo Duchacek, who backstopped Ripka on the expulsion of the Sudeten Germans and the uranium gift to the Soviets, has been employed in high positions by the Voice of America and Radio Free Europe. General Mikulas Ferjencik, the secret police chief of Slovakia, was admitted to the United States over the protest of Americans of Slovak descent and now makes a comfortable living near Chicago. A number of minor "National Fronters" in Germany have been employed in various "intelligence" agencies, the value of which is—to understate the case

---

[15] Quoted in Slovak Liberation Committee, *Documents*, p. 10.

[16] The Committee has never admitted publicly the receipt of government funds, but it is obvious that its operations are on a larger scale than the "Crusade" income would permit. The "Fact Sheet" issued by Radio Free Europe in May, 1951, gives the 1950 "Crusade" receipts as $1,317,000. But Mr. C. D. Jackson, then president of the National Committee for a Free Europe, estimated the annual budget as "several millions" in a press conference on April 30, 1951. (Transcript released by RFE press office, Munich, pp. 7-8.)

[17] Free Europe Committee, *Weapon in the Struggle for Freedom*, leaflet, January, 1954; see also Slovak Liberation Committee, *Documents*, p. 10; and Dr. Michael Zibrin in *Slovakia*, September-December, 1954, pp. 30-34.

[18] Information from Czech sources, also *Sudetendeutsche Zeitung*, September 10, 1955. The International Workers' Order was a fraternal organization controlled by the Communist party.

—extremely doubtful. Former members of these groups have complained to the author that the Americans in charge failed to purge Communist infiltrators positively identified to them, while anti-Communist contacts in Czecho-Slovakia were regularly liquidated. Protection by American "intelligence" enabled Frantisek Kroupa, the notorious "hangman of Joachimsthal," to escape prosecution by a German court in 1952. Vaclav Hrnecek, deputy commander of the Budejovice concentration camp, sentenced to eight years imprisonment for multiple aggravated assault by United States Judge Leo M. Goodman in 1954, was at the time of his arrest *security officer* of an American-supervised "intelligence" detachment. After serving about six months, he was secretly released "for services rendered."[19]

The history of the Council of Free Czechoslovakia is one of constant infighting between the left-wing "Benes" group headed by Zenkl, Ripka, Firt, Lettrich, Papanek, and Slavik, which controlled the Council at its inception, and a growing "moderate" faction led by Osusky, Majer, and Prochazka and joined in 1953 by Peroutka. The organization would have split altogether in 1951 had not the members feared that they would lose their salaries.

Late in 1953, the Free Europe Committee insisted that the Council take in additional exile groups, such as the Agrarian party which had been prohibited under the National Front. The Zenkl-Ripka-Lettrich leadership was temporarily replaced by a "steering committee" in which the Czech Agrarian, Dr. Josef Cerny, and the independent Slovak, Dr. Stefan Osusky, played the dominant roles.[20] This committee labored for months with out finding an organizational formula acceptable to the Zenkl-Ripka group—who insisted that they were still

---

[19] The Bavarian Ministry of Justice informed the author that Hrnecek was released by an order of the United States High Commission Clemency Board dated December 23, 1954. The *Sudeten Bulletin* of September, 1955, reported that he had arrived in Chicago, implying a waiver of the immigration rule prohibiting entry of persons with criminal records. On Kroupa's crimes, see Turnwald, *Documents on the Expulsion of the Sudeten Germans*, English edition, Report 51. See also Heinz Kreutzmann, "Criminals in American Secret Agencies Alarm German Public," *Volkszeitung-Tribüne*, Omaha, Nebraska, June 25, 1953.

[20] H. F. March, "'Putsch' in the Council of Free Czechoslovakia," *Sudeten-deutsche Zeitung*, May 8, 1954. Dr. Osusky, former Czecho-Slovak ambassador in Paris, opposed Benes' pro-Soviet policies during the war. Both he and Dr. Cerny have records of consistent opposition to Communism.

the legal executives of the Council. A superficial compromise was reached later in 1954 and a new executive committee elected, since when the feud has continued with only minor interruptions.[21] From mid-1955 to the present, the central organs of the Council of Free Czechoslovakia have been paralyzed altogether.[22]

While it would be rash to predict the results of further efforts to rebuild the Council of Free Czechoslovakia, the following can be said with certainty:

1. Continued participation of politicians who supported the Kosice Program and the expulsions, and who have not mended their ways, precludes a consistent anti-Communist program.

2. Refusal to take a positive stand for self-determination and *Heimatrecht* limits Czech support to the chauvinist element and rules out support by other nationalities.

3. An organization which insists on retaining a "Czechoslovak" national state in a multi-national area, yet seeks escape from the Russian hegemony which alone can uphold such a state, must be eternally frustrated by the contradiction of its own policies.

RADIO FREE EUROPE

The Free Europe Committee's largest operation is Radio Free Europe, with studios in New York, Munich, and elsewhere. RFE's Czecho-Slovak section consists largely of members and supporters of the Council of Free Czechoslovakia—so much so that Radio Free Europe is commonly held to be a mouthpiece for the Council. Although the Council and RFE depend on the same source for funds, they are technically independent, a fact which is always emphasized by RFE spokesmen in answering criticisms.[23]

---

[21] *Sudetendeutsche Zeitung*, August 21, September 4, and December 18, 1954; January 29 and February 5, 1955.

[22] Vaclav Majer, at meeting of executive committee of Social Democratic party, as reported in *Sudetendeutsche Zeitung*, January 18, 1958.

[23] In his press conference of April 30, 1951, Mr. Jackson stated that the Council of Free Czechoslovakia had referred Mr. Peroutka and also refers other personnel, but that Radio Free Europe makes its own decisions. The overlapping of Council membership and RFE employment is, however, almost universal in the higher Czech and Slovak positions. See Jiri Brada, *History of the Council of Free Czechoslovakia and of the Personnel of Radio Free Europe*, Munich, 1953, and articles by George Brada in *Facts Forum Magazine*, Dallas, Texas, January-March, 1955.

1. GENERAL ORIENTATION

The chief of the Czecho-Slovak section of Radio Free Europe is Ferdinand Peroutka who, despite his earlier commitments to socialism and Czech-Soviet collaboration, has emerged on the conservative side of the Council of Free Czechoslovakia and now recognizes the political rights of the Sudeten Germans.[24] His principal assistant in Munich, Dr. Julius Firt—who transferred from the Studies Center and for a while assisted Mr. Peroutka in New York—represents the left wing of the Council, as do most of the personnel in the Munich studios.

The personnel of the Munich studio, as well as Radio Free Europe's broadcast policies, have been attacked repeatedly in the German and anti-Communist exile press, as well as in various American publications.[25] It is perhaps for this reason that some of the more controversial characters of the past are missing from recent personnel rosters. The Czech and Slovak staff, however, remains solidly "Czechoslovakist" in its orientation. Its more important members were identified prominently with the National Front; if not active in the Council of Free Czechoslovakia or related organizations, they are at least known to sympathize with the general political objectives of the Council. This characterization is not limited to full-time officials of RFE, such as Peroutka, Firt, Dr. Jan Stransky, Dr. Martin Kvetko; the editors Miroslav Kohak, Ivo Duchacek, Joseph Pejskar, and Karol Belak-Berger; or the economist Milos Vanek.[26] It

---

[24] "Peroutka on the Sudeten German Question," interview with Hermann W. Gaertner, *Sudetendeutsche Zeitung*, March 3, 1956.

[25] See *Sudetendeutsche Zeitung* and *Volksbote, passim;* also *Parlamentarisch-Politischer Pressedienst*, Bonn, May 31, 1951; *Münchener Allgemeine*, July 9, 1951; *Christ und Welt*, Stuttgart, October 16, 1952; *Revue*, Munich, January 17, 1953; *Bohemia* (Czech) Munich, December 23, 1953, February 19, 1955, and *passim; Slowakische Korrespondenz*, Munich, *passim*. Beginning in February, 1955, the *Sudetendeutsche Zeitung* ran a series by a former Czech employee of RFE entitled "Behind the Scenes in Radio Free Europe." For English-language sources, see *Slovak Newsletter, passim;* Slovak Liberation Committee, *Documents;* Brada, *op. cit.; Congressional Record*, April 25, 1955, Extension of Remarks of Hon. Usher L. Burdick; Kurt Glaser, *The Iron Curtain and American Policy*, Washington, 1953, and "The 'Russia First' Boys in Radio Free Europe," *National Republic*, Washington, February, 1953.

[26] Vanek, a charter member of the Czecho-Slovak Communist party, attended the 1920 Comintern Congress and remained a warm advocate of Czech-Soviet friendship after switching to the Social Democratic party. His incorrect prediction of a currency reform over RFE in 1952 set off a run on the black market in which many lost their savings. In view of personnel turnover, it is pos-

is also generally true of Czech and Slovak guest speakers, the list of whom has included such "Czechoslovak" politicians as Dr. Jaroslav Stransky, the late Dr. Hubert Ripka, Vaclav Majer, Dr. Jozef Lettrich, and Ivan Herben, but never "self-determinist" leaders such as General Lev Prchala, Professors Simeon Ghelfand and Bohdan Chudoba, Dr. Vladimir Pekelsky, the late Karol Sidor, Dr. Jozef Kirschbaum, or Professor Ferdinand Durcansky, even though the latter are figures of international prominence, whose appeal to anti-Communists within Czecho-Slovakia is unquestioned.

Radio Free Europe bases its policies on the assumption of a permanent Czecho-Slovak state. Although supposedly a symbol of "free speech," it enforces a rigid taboo against "separatist" ideas. It seeks to avoid any discussion of the Sudeten German question, and studiously ignores the activities and statements of expellees, especially those directed at Slav-German reconciliation. A request for the broadcasting of Dr. Lodgman's message of friendship for the Czech people on the occasion of the 1954 Sudeten German Rally was met with the reply that this "would not promote the common struggle of the free world against Communism."[27] This episode was repeated in 1958, when RFE refused to broadcast the award to General Lev Prchala of the Sudeten German Charles Prize "for the reconciliation of Central European peoples" and the General's acceptance speech in Czech, an event of obvious news importance, even for those who disagree with the General's politics. While the Americans in charge seek to avoid the transmission of deliberately *anti*-German statements, it is evident that they sometimes fail to control what goes out over the air.

2. THE "CZECHOSLOVAK FOREIGN INSTITUTE"
—INFILTRATION AND "REDEFECTION"

The preponderance of left-wing "Benesists" on the pay-

sible that some of the individuals named in this section may no longer be employed by RFE by the time this book appears in print.

[27] Letter from RFE European Director Richard J. Condon to Dr. Walter Becher of Consortium for the Protection of Sudeten German Interests, reporting decision of New York office, May 27, 1954, retranslated from *Volksbote*, June 5, 1954.

roll of Radio Free Europe is no accident. It was deliberately planned by Dr. Hubert Ripka, who alone among Czech and Slovak exiles appears to have had substantial funds at his disposal, the sources of which would bear investigation.[28] As will be seen, Dr. Ripka's project was largely successful, despite the claim—and in most cases the sincere belief—of the American managers of RFE that they maintain an independent personnel policy.

While in Paris in 1949, Ripka founded the *Zahranicni 'ustav* or "Czechoslovak Foreign Institute in Exile" as a center of ideological and political control over as much of the Czecho-Slovak emigration as possible. Beneath the cover of a scholarly research institute, a wide-flung network was built up on conspiratorial principles, with organizational techniques borrowed from the Communist party.

For a while, Dr. Ripka managed the central office of the Czechoslovak Foreign Institute in Paris. After difficulties with the French police, it moved to Leiden, Holland, where it was taken over by Vladimir Bruza, the man whom Gottwald's Communist government, *after the "February Revolution,"* sent to Moscow to negotiate the final agreement for Russian exploitation of the uranium mines. Other noteworthy adherents of the Institute included Dr. Karel Maiwald, known as a member of the Communist party after 1948; Frantisek Listopad, Paris correspondent of the Prague *Mlada Fronta* ("Youth Front") until 1949; and the Soviet agent Professor Bohumil Cerny.[29]

An important objective of the Institute is to safeguard socialism in Czecho-Slovakia if the present Communist government should be overthrown. A secret ideological directive commits the Institute to the Marxist view of society. There is also a secret organizational directive which provides for the formation of "operat-

---

[28] See Helena Kozeluhova, "Die mysteriösen Geldquellen Dr. Ripkas" ["Dr. Ripka's Mysterious Sources of Money"], *Sudetendeutsche Zeitung*, April 30, 1955.

[29] Information on Czechoslovak Foreign Institute was provided by Czech sources, through which the author was able to obtain copies of the directives of the Institute. See, however, Jiri Halek, "Podarena organisace: cs. Zahranicni 'ustav'" ["Strange Organization: CS Foreign Institute"], *Narod*, Chicago, February 17, 1954; Kalvoda, *Titoism*, pp. 138-40.

ing groups" or cells wherever adherents of the Institute live. Each such group becomes the nucleus of a larger "club," which provides a source of recruitment and enables the Institute to dominate various organizations and activities.

To place its adherents in key positions, the Institute maintains an employment office, with a special branch for American activities in Germany. Each adherent is pledged to notify the employment office of vacancies and to help secure jobs for other adherents and sympathizers. A number of persons associated with the Institute or its key personnel have found their way into Radio Free Europe, including Milos Vanek, Otto Graf, Miroslav Tetiva, Joseph Pejskar, Karol Belak-Berger, Kostrba-Skalicky, Dr. Pechacek, and Jaroslav Kusy. The secret directive states:

> With this system we hope to create a group democracy of an elite as opposed to the false conception of a democracy of the masses, which is especially prominent in exile. Thus we would strive to penetrate and dominate the political life as broadly as possible.
>
> The Czechoslovak Foreign Institute is to create a group within groups. The anonymity of its members is to constitute its great strength, *because it is not possible to defeat an invisible power.* (Emphasis in original.) [30]

The financial part of the directive provides that the Institute shall obtain income by trading in "valuables, securities, stocks, or products" with Communist countries. Since these have government trade monopolies, such operations require the collusion of Communist officials—who are by no means immune from the temptation to line their own pockets. For a while, a group as-

---

[30] Reference to "adherents" and "sympathizers" rather than "members" of the Czechoslovak Foreign Institute in the text is deliberate. It appears that the Institute, for obvious reasons, prefers to keep its relations with many of its collaborators on an informal basis. This technique, also used by the Communist party, makes it possible to deny "membership" whenever the connection should prove embarrassing. It may well be that Mojmir Povolny, director of the Institute's Philadelphia office, is technically correct in denying (in *Facts Forum News,* September, 1956, p. 54) that "a larger number of Radio Free Europe employees" are "members" of the Institute. Mr. Povolny is, however, stretching a technicality too far when he states that "Dr. Hubert Ripka is neither a founder nor a member of the Czechoslovak Foreign Institute in Exile." Dr. Ripka's role in bringing the Institute into existence and in managing its Paris office under the code name "Maly" are too well known to be obliterated from history at this late date. Indefiniteness of membership is, of course, part of the "invisibility" mentioned in the directive.

sociated with the Institute lived in Switzerland, where they published the *avant-garde* magazine *Skutecnost*. To provide funds, members of the group sold ball bearings, cadmium, and other strategic materials to Communist states. When this traffic attracted the attention of the Swiss police, the group moved to Munich, where most of the editors of *Skutecnost* obtained jobs with Radio Free Europe.

Two former associates of the Institute are of particular interest. One of them, Frantisek Kubal, who managed intelligence reports for the Institute in Paris and helped to edit its journal *Tribuna,* was arrested by French police and charged with illegally photographing American military installations for the Prague government.[31] He was sentenced to five years in prison.[32] The other was former Minister of Industry Bohumil Lausman, who had sided with the Communists in 1948 but left Czecho-Slovakia in 1949, spending some time in Belgrade as an adviser to Marshal Tito, who—let us note in passing—had never sought a quarrel with Soviet Russia and had asked an opportunity to prove his loyalty to Marxism-Leninism. As Kalvoda observes in his perspicacious study of Titoism, Lausman evidently came west with a double mission: (1) to acquaint Tito with the "stalking horse" role which the Kremlin had figured out for him, and (2) to sell the "Titoist" approach to Western psywar planners, thereby assuring Marxists a preferred position in "anti-Communist" propaganda and blunting its effectiveness. In late 1951 or early 1952, Lausman moved to Austria, where he became a regular commentator for Radio Free Europe. In December, 1953, he returned to Prague where, after "confessing," he re-emerged in the good graces of the Communist regime.[33]

---

[31] Kubal is mentioned by C. L. Sulzberger, "Reds Reshuffling European Spy Net," the *New York Times*, January 21, 1954.

[32] Kalvoda, *op. cit.*, p. 138.

[33] *Ibid.*, pp. 134-49. As Kalvoda mentions on p. 138, a third important figure in the Institute, Dr. Lev Sychrava, returned from London to Prague in January, 1956.
A letter by Lausman published in *Het Parool*, Amsterdam, June 2, 1954, establishes his connection with Bruza of the Institute. It also states that he would not return to Prague unless kidnapped, but the weight of evidence is that he returned voluntarily. The author has seen fiscal documents showing that Lausman was on the payroll of RFE, and such documents were also exhibited by Deputy Gaksch in the Bavarian Diet.

With personnel of the type indicated, Radio Free Europe is particularly vulnerable to infiltration and "redefection." Considerable embarrassment was caused by an article in the Czech paper *Bohemia* recounting the activities of the Soviet spy, Professor Bohumil Cerny, and his dealings with officials of the Council of Free Czechoslovakia and RFE.[34] Cerny, a former functionary of Zenkl's National Socialist party, was sent by Soviet intelligence in late 1948 to organize a network in Germany and Austria. As *Bohemia* points out, his success was largely attributable to his contacts with the Council of Free Czechoslovakia and its subsidiaries—and, of course, the Czechoslovak Foreign Institute, with which Cerny made connections soon after its establishment.

According to letters found in Cerny's effects, a certain Joseph Pejskar—later appointed an editor in Radio Free Europe—had authorized him to recruit members for the National Socialist party in exile. The names of persons so recruited were forwarded to the secret police in Brno. In some cases, the Communists sent "escapees" to join the National Socialist party under Cerny's guidance, one of these being Vera Faborska, later convicted of espionage by a United States occupation court.

During Cerny's career in Germany and Austria, he corresponded with Dr. Hubert Ripka, with Messrs. Busek, Kohak, and Vanek of Radio Free Europe, with editor Josten of the London *Czechoslovak,* and, of course, with Dr. Zenkl, then chairman of the executive committee of the Council of Free Czechoslovakia. About a month after receiving Zenkl's last letter of December 5, 1950, Cerny fled to Czecho-Slovakia after being warned that the CIC was hot on his trail.

After the exposure of Cerny and the Lausman affair, three employees of Radio Free Europe "redefected" to Prague at various times: Bruno Folta, Frantisek Zvolsky, and Rudolph Behal. The recent amnesty brought a further wave of "redefections," including Vladimir Kucera (radio name "Tonda Hornik"), Frantisek Hejna, Ales Molin, Marie Dvorak, Jiri Kalas, Stepan Kiripolsky,

---

[34] "Relations of Zenkl with a Soviet Spy," *Bohemia,* Munich, No. 22-23, April-May, 1953.

the actress Helena Busova-Kasal and her husband Karel Kasal, Antonin Vanha, and Bohumil Houser.[35] The return of the Kasals to Prague caused particular alarm, since Mr. Kasal had been an interviewer of escapees and therefore possessed confidential information on anti-Communist groups within Czecho-Slovakia.[36]

No statement is made or implied that the Free Europe Committee or any of the Americans in charge of Radio Free Europe are involved in the activities of the Czecho-slovak Foreign Institute or its members. They are doubtless very careful to have nothing to do with the Institute. But they cannot escape responsibility for the choice of personnel. And since, according to RFE's statement, prospective employees are thoroughly investigated, it cannot be presumed that this choice is made in complete ignorance.

3. BROADCASTS—THE "TITOIST" LINE

Since Radio Free Europe purports to offer a "complete" bill of fare, many programs are of the "entertainment" type. To criticize them would lead us out of the realm of politics and into that of aesthetics or perhaps sociology. We therefore leave the jazz concerts, radio plays, and chit-chat sessions with the passing remark that their necessity, and in some cases their good taste, is an open question,[37] and turn to those broadcasts with a directly political content.

A constantly recurring feature of the criticism which Radio Free Europe levels against the present Czecho-Slovak regime is the theory that the National Front was "democratic" (in the Western sense of the word) until February, 1948. This notion, which is basic to the propaganda of the Council of Free Czechoslovakia but which is hardly believable to Czechs and Slovaks

---

[35] *Slovak Newsletter*, July, 1957. Not all these people were in the Munich studios. Some were reporters in the refugee camps and elsewhere.

[36] *Sudetendeutsche Zeitung*, July 21, 1956.

[37] See Jiri Brada, *Programs of Radio Free Europe*, Munich, 1953 (mimeographed), and the series "Hinter den Kulissen des Senders Free Europe" ["Behind the Scenes in the Free Europe Station"] in the *Sudetendeutsche Zeitung*, beginning, February 5, 1955.

who lived through postwar history, is reflected in broadcasts such as the following:

> In the 1946 *democratic elections*, Siroky had failed to win the confidence of at least one-third of the Slovak people. . . .

> As far as prime ministers are concerned, Czecho-Slovakia has had no luck since 1945: Fierlinger, Gottwald, Zapotocky, Siroky —one worse than the other and all of them hand in hand responsible for the dark years of the criminal regime of Communist totality *installed in 1948*. . . . (Dr. Jozef Lettrich, "Night Commentary," April 7, 1953.)

> . . . the insidious putsch against Czechoslovak democracy in February, 1948. . . . (Vaclav Majer, labor program, August 6, 1953.)

> Toward the end of the last school year all . . . those who still had some knowledge of the *meaning of freedom* and who still remembered . . . *pre-February democracy* were graduating. (Antonin Kratochvil, students' program, October 27, 1953.)

> In February 1948, the freedom of the press in Czechoslovakia indeed was settled within one hour. (Ferdinand Peroutka, weekly talk, October 30, 1955.) [38]

A related theory, essential to the justification of Dr. Benes and to the "Czechoslovak" position as a whole, is that the Russian hegemony in east-central Europe which emerged from World War II is objectionable only because the Russians abuse it. Mr. Peroutka expounds this doctrine as follows:

> When the documents of the Yalta Conference were published, some people felt an urge to accuse this or that democratic leader, chiefly of lack of caution. Possibly there was not as much caution exercised as should have been, and the man who was attacked possibly should have armed himself with two pistols instead of one. But a discussion of the minor offenses of the democratic leaders would only conceal the major lesson and the major guilt: the Russian treason—and the major fact: the Russian system of deception. These facts must be presented clearly before the eyes of the world, without depressing discussions. The Yalta Conference did not turn into tragedy because of what had been agreed there, but because Russia has violated the agreements made there. (Sunday talk, April 2, 1955.) [39]

---

[38] Unpublished broadcast scripts furnished through the kindness of Mr. Jiri Brada. In these and other excerpts, the author has taken the liberty of editing Mr. Brada's English rendition, without, however, changing the meaning. (Emphasis supplied.)

[39] Unpublished broadcast scripts furnished by Mr. Brada.

Almost universally, the broadcasts reflect the view that socialism would be the ideal form of society if only the Russians did not distort it for their own nefarious purposes. The aim of liberation, as preached by Radio Free Europe, is not the abolition of socialism but the restoration of "true" socialism, a point illustrated by these excerpts:

> If only non-socialists and anti-socialists spoke against the Communist system, this would still be no proof of the errors in the system. Workmen, who were to be the bearers of the system, therefore also speak. We now present a man who is no adherent of capitalism, no enemy of the people, no reactionary—on the contrary, this man was a member of the Communist Party of Czechoslovakia, a director of textile plants. But he could not agree with the exploitation . . . he was and remained a socialist.
> The refugee: Bad materials, old machinery, very high quotas . . . I would remove these senseless quotas as well as the supervision in the factories by the local party organizations. . . .
> The first requirement of all socialists in the world, that is to work as little as possible and to earn as much as possible, was completely lost by Communism. . . The workers would like very much to be socialists and live in a socialist state. They learned the difference between the real socialism which is desired by all our people and the type which was introduced in Czechoslovakia. . . . ("I Chose Freedom," April 18, 1953.)

> Jack London was interested in anarchism and socialism. He took the books of Marx along on his trip to Alaska. . . . One can understand why the dying Lenin enjoyed reading Jack London, just as hundreds of Americans do. . . . Years later a decline of his work can be recognized—he became a convinced capitalist and a precursor of fascism. He preached the need for Nordic supremacy in Mexico. ("The Book of the Week," review of W. W. Brook, *The Years of Confidence*, about Jack London, April 19, 1953.)

> The farmers do not like the kind of socialism offered by the present Communist regime. (Farm program, April 30, 1953.)

> Socialism is a western word, and it is also a western invention. And what is still more important: it is a western practice and it is today's western practice.
> The democratic socialists esteem Marx as a man who was for his time very intelligent and very wise.
> The former esteem for property has generally relaxed. The men of this century discovered that property is not a necessary key to prosperity. And the men of this century agree at the same

time that prosperity is more important than property. (Commentary by Dr. Kulhanek, December 30, 1955.)[40]

Radio Free Europe has committed itself to the "Titoist" strategy of *not fighting Communism as such* but limiting its attacks to the specifically Russian or "Stalinist" variety. This political line, the value of which has been sharply criticized,[41] is reflected in commentaries such as these:

We have never adopted the theory that the Soviet Union is ruled by the dictatorship of the proletariat. From the very beginning we knew that it is a dictatorship against the proletariat. (Zdenek Sedivy, labor program, May 1, 1954.)

The October Revolution was socialist in the aims and impulses of its organizers and leaders. It was socialist in the hopes of the men who made it or supported it. The October Revolution was *not* socialist when we judge it according to what has come out of it. Men's motives and aims often differ from the eventual results of their acts. Just as Goethe's Mephistopheles was a ghost who "intended evil and created good," the very opposite can be said about the Bolsheviks: they intended good and produced evil. . . . the Bolsheviks' strategy was caught in a vacuum. They remained encircled by the Russian barbarism. And in this encirclement, nothing remained to the Bolsheviks but to remain barbarians too. (Holesovsky, "Calling the Communist Party," December 13, 1955.)

. . . the government resorts again and again to the last argument: the exiles would be sure to reintroduce private capitalism in Czechoslovakia. . . . The enraged government chases after the pamphlets and tries to order us to leave off and admit our program for the reinstatement of capitalism. We cannot oblige for the very simple reason that no such program of ours exists. Not once did the political leadership of the exile meet to resolve the reinstatement of capitalism. . . . (Ferdinand Peroutka, weekly talk, January 29, 1955.)

. . . in Yugoslavia the government calls meetings at which the citizens, including non-members of the Communist Party are

---

[40] First three excerpts from Brada. *Programs of Radio Free Europe,* Munich, 1953. Last excerpt unpublished script furnished by Mr. Brada.

[41] An analysis of the implications of "Titoism" and American aid to Communist states is beyond the scope of this volume. For views favorable to American support of Tito see Hamilton Fish Armstrong, *Tito and Goliath,* New York, 1951, Macmillan; U.S. Department of State, background bulletin, *Yugoslavia: Titoism and U.S. Foreign Policy,* Washington, June, 1952; U.S. House of Representatives, Hearings on Mutual Security Appropriation, 1957. For contrary views, see Bogdan Raditsa, "What Price Tito?" *American Mercury,* May, 1952; A. N. Dragnich, *Tito's Promised Land,* New Brunswick, N.J., Rutgers University Press, 1954; Kalvoda. *Titoism.* To make his position clear, the author will simply state that he agrees with Mr. Kalvoda that "Titoism" is the greatest weakness in American "cold warfare" strategy.

given free opportunity to criticize the Communist bureaucracy and they use it. And again: nothing happens to them. . . . Flattery of leaders disappeared in Yugoslovia.

In the Yugoslav parliament one recent government bill was adopted by only 85 votes against 75. In Yugoslavia, which remains a dictatorship, the elections are free to such an extent that last time several candidates not approved by the Party almost won in certain places. . . .

Yugoslavia is a country which, following its secession from Russia, began rapidly to approach democracy. A country that eased the unbearable and dignity-killing pressure imposed on man in other Communist countries. . . . (Peroutka, weekly talk, September 8, 1955.)[42]

The Czech and Slovak commentators of Radio Free Europe devote much time to the exegesis of Marx and Lenin, the manifest purpose being to convict the Prague leadership and the Kremlin of "deviationism." "Why," a speaker complained, "is it impossible to buy in Czechoslovakia the writings of the founder of scientific socialism? . . . The Stalinist theoreticians grossly falsified Marx's ideas." While this technique of "narrowing the target," as psywarriors call it, may have a limited value in special cases, listeners in Czecho-Slovakia who wait in vain to hear Radio Free Europe attack socialism or defend free enterprise will find it hard to disagree with the pointed observation of the Communist newspaper *Rude Pravo:*

Radio Free Europe has recently been filling the ether with sounds which evoke astonishment. Much is said on that station about Marx and Lenin and the need for preserving the purity of their doctrine and applying that doctrine to reality. In a broadcast of October 31, we even heard that "all the riches of the earth belong to the people and the workers."

It is certainly a great satisfaction to hear such words after so many years of abuse against Marx and Lenin and against the socialist society which we are building. There is only one thing we do not understand. What were these gentlemen running away from in 1948? . . . .[43]

While non-totalitarian socialists may be conceded a right to their opinions,[44] intellectual honesty would re-

---

[42] From unpublished scripts furnished by Mr. Brada.

[43] *Rude Pravo,* Prague, November 4, 1956.

[44] We must leave open the questions whether the aims of non-totalitarian social-

quire that the Crusade for Freedom inform American contributors of the "Titoist-socialist" orientation of Radio Free Europe's broadcasts. Such a one-sided program, which affords little or no scope to the supporters of free private enterprise, is in the author's opinion not a proper object of expenditure for United States government funds.

A corollary of the "Titoist" strategy has been the encouragement of "national Communism" in Poland and Hungary. Czech and Slovak medium-wave broadcasts were ended during the fall of 1956 and the program continued via short wave only: the opinion is heard in Munich that the main reason was to make available additional facilities for broadcasts to Poland and Hungary.[45] While there seems to be some truth in the claim that Radio Free Europe stimulated "Nagyist" resistance in Hungary, the fact that the 1956 uprising took an anti-Communist turn was strictly an "accident" so far as RFE was concerned.

Not only has Radio Free Europe failed to accomplish anything significant in the vital question of Slav-German reconciliation, but its broadcasts have at times supported the territorial-ethnic *status quo*—which, as we have seen, is no less important than Communist terror in welding Czecho-Slovakia and Poland to the Soviet bloc. The following are typical statements from earlier broadcasts which have tended to defeat efforts to build a common front against Bolshevism:

As long as the Germans do not recognize their present boundaries as definite, it is impossible to accept them in an organization which controls the political and strategic situation on both sides of the Atlantic. (Czech broadcast, February 21, 1952.)

... The Russians would offer to a neutralized Germany a common colonial rule over Central and Southeast Europe, so that the specter of Soviet imperialism would be accompanied by the even more frightful specter of German imperialism. (Czech broadcast, March 24, 1952.)

---

ism are logically or practically possible, and whether the socialism represented in RFE deserves that qualification.

[45] Discontinuance of the medium-wave broadcasts has made it difficult to monitor the programs. Reception of the RFE short wave is seldom satisfactory in Germany, and official transcripts of programs are hard to obtain. Reduction of the scope of the Czech and Slovak programs was followed by only a minor reduction in personnel.

Into this desert (Silesia), after years of *German* and Soviet *occupation*, came the Poles. . . . The efforts of the Poles to reconstruct and make economically productive their *recovered* territories is well known. . . . (Polish broadcast, September 19, 1952.)[46]

In recent years, provocative statements of this sort have been largely eliminated as a result of German protests. From a German point of view, the main complaint today lies in what Radio Free Europe does *not* broadcast.

Radio Free Europe's treatment of the "Slovak Revolt" of 1944 has been a source of considerable annoyance. Despite the evidence compiled and verified by the Kersten Committee proving the dominant role of Soviet agents in the uprising[47] and the protests of Americans of Slovak descent and their friends in Congress, Radio Free Europe has persisted in commemorating that event as a glorious victory for democracy. When the Communist government, in April, 1958, convicted a number of anti-Communists of atrocities during the revolt which were in fact committed by Russian agents and their collaborators, Editor Jan Lehota of RFE piously announced that: "Certainly there is not a person in Slovakia nor among us who would be identified with these bestial deeds"—a broadcast which earned Radio Free Europe the praise of Radio Prague.[48]

Finally, RFE's broadcast interviews with new refugees have often revealed the details of secret paths of escape, enabling the PVS (militarized border police) to block their use in the future. In other cases, listeners could identify persons who helped the escapees in Czecho-Slovakia and in the former Soviet Zone of Austria.[49]

4. REACTION TO CRITICISM

Radio Free Europe's response to criticism has, out-

---

[46] Cited in "Störsender Europas?" ["European Center of Disturbance?"], *Christ und Welt*, Stuttgart, October 16, 1952. Although these excerpts are eight years old, there is no evidence of any substantial change in the policies reflected therein.

[47] Eighty-third Congress, House of Representatives, Select Committee on Communist Aggression (former Representative Charles J. Kersten, chairman), *Special Report No. 8, Czechoslovakia*, December, 1954, pp. 13ff.

[48] Jarmila Uhrova, broadcast over Radio Prague, March 23, 1958, quoted in *Bulletin of the Slovak National Council Abroad*, June, 1958, p. 1.

[49] Brada, *Programs of Radio Free Europe; Sudetendeutsche Zeitung*, April 3, 1954. See previous section on the "redefection" to Prague of escapee interviewer Karel Kasal.

wardly at least, been one of defense rather than correction. As Public Relations Director Alton Kastner assured an inquirer, "All of our people, exile and Americans, are necessarily anti-Communist. They could not otherwise work for us. . . . Our exile colleagues are hand-picked by American officials of Radio Free Europe, after careful scrutiny of their records by experts who know just how to scrutinize personnel records."[50] Yet the continued high rate of dismissals[51]—in addition to resignations and "redefections"—suggests that the American management of Radio Free Europe is not wholly satisfied with its Czech and Slovak personnel situation.

RFE's personnel problems, however exasperating, are mainly a by-product of its "Czechoslovak" political orientation. Adherents of "Czechoslovakism" suffer acute anxiety when they attempt to cut the cord which binds them to Russia and to their fellow "Czechoslovaks" in Prague. Although the American management asserts that "all exiles at RFE . . . are employed on the basis of their professional ability, not their party affiliation" and denies any "direct relation" with the Council of Free Czechoslovakia,[52] Czechs and Slovaks who openly oppose socialism and "Czechoslovakism" are seldom hired and even more seldom retained for any great length of time. Such exiles can hardly avoid conflict with the station's political line and with the adherents of the Council of Free Czechoslovakia and the Czechoslovak Foreign Institute who are the nucleus of its Czech and Slovak staff.

In its fund-raising propaganda, the Crusade for Freedom emphasizes that the "privately operated" Radio Free Europe can "hew a tough anti-Communist line" prohibited to the government's Voice of America by dip-

---

[50] Letter, Alton Kastner (Director of Public Relations, Radio Free Europe) to Clyde M. Vandeburg (Executive Director, American Heritage Foundation), June 4, 1954, answering an inquiry from John K. Crippen, Park Ridge, Illinois. Made available through the kindness of Mr. Crippen. More recently, in reply to criticism by Fulton Lewis, Jr., RFE referred to its chief of security as "one of the founders, with Mr. J. Edgar Hoover, of the modern FBI . . . ," a statement which Mr. Hoover characterized as "literary license." See "Mr. Lewis and Radio Free Europe," *National Review*, New York, March 29, 1958, pp. 297-300.

[51] See, for instance, *Slovak Newsletter*, November and December, 1957, and April, 1958.

[52] Letter, Kastner to Vandeburg, June 4, 1954.

lomatic and political considerations. Only those portions of broadcasts which seem to prove this contention are released to the American public. Criticisms of RFE's program and personnel are, however, invariably met with the reply that the organization does not make policy but simply follows that of the Department of State.[53]

TWO VERSIONS OF "NON-PREDETERMINATION"

Since Radio Free Europe enjoys its broadcasting facilities in Europe through the good offices of the United States government, it must be assumed that its broadcast policies are at least tolerated by the Department of State. Were its emissions actually nothing more than elaborations of departmental policy, this fact would relieve the American management of personal onus, though it would not explain the need for a costly network duplicating the Voice of America. There are, however, important differences between the Czecho-Slovakia policy of Radio Free Europe and that indicated by responsible officials of the Department of State. Both are variations on the theme of "non-predetermination": the idea that Americans should not become involved in plans for the future of the enslaved nations.

According to Public Relations Director Kastner of Radio Free Europe:

> It is a fact that United States foreign policy envisages the restoration of the democratic Republic of Czechoslovakia that was founded by Masaryk with the full support of our government. Because Radio Free Europe, which is not a foreign office and does not make policy, follows U.S. policy on this matter, we are attacked constantly by proponents of an autonomous Slovakian Republic. We are attacked, too, for not disputing U.S. policy which asserts that some two million [sic] Sudeten Germans were expelled legally from Czechoslovakia in 1945 by order of the Allied Powers.[54]

The network's policy on the Slovak question has been specified in more detail by President Sheppardson of

[53] *National Review, loc. cit.* Letter, Robert E. Lang, director of Radio Free Europe, to Norma Leigh, Centralia, Washington, April 30, 1954 (courtesy of Miss Leigh) ; letter, Kastner to Vandeburg, June 4, 1954; letter, President Whitney Sheppardson of Free Europe Committee to Representative Alvin M. Bentley (Michigan), April 19, 1955 (courtesy of Mr. Bentley).

[54] Letter, Kastner to Vandeburg, June 4, 1954.

the Free Europe Committee, who wrote to Congressman Bentley, in part:

United States policy, we are informed, favors the eventual restoration of a truly democratic republic of Czechoslovakia; it does not favor the establishment of a republic of Slovakia. Radio Free Europe is not obliged to reiterate this fact in its broadcasts to Czechs and Slovaks; it refrains from discussing it. This means also that it refrains and indeed it should refrain—in view of U.S. policy—from promoting Slovak separatism over its facilities. . . .

The function of the Free Europe Committee is not to concern itself with future political and territorial arrangements in Europe. Its function is to carry on the present fight against Communism, especially behind the Iron Curtain. . . . our Slovak staff must be chosen for its intimate knowledge of present-day Slovakia and for its professional competence, not its party allegiance. . . . Some are Czecho-Slovak federalists, some even separatists. We honor them all for their belief that they must get on with the fight against Communism and wait to cross the separatist bridge, or federalist bridge, until they come to it, which is to say, until the time when the Slovak people will be free to speak for themselves.[55]

Critics of Radio Free Europe's policies, including the present author, have been accused of trying "to overthrow American foreign policy in the interest of certain foreign ethnic groups."[56] The bill of particulars is laid down by Director Lang, who states that:

The objectives of such persons seem to be these:

(a) To persuade the U.S. Government to abandon its recognition of the continued moral existence of a democratic Republic of Czechoslovakia and to advocate the establishment of an autonomous Republic of Slovakia.

(b) To persuade the U.S. Government to reverse its position on the expulsion of the Sudeten Germans and to favor their return to the Sudetenland (in Czechoslovakia).

(c) To throw such discredit upon the Czech and Slovak personnel of RFE as will result in their dismissal and replacement by a team which will use the prestige of this American station to advocate the causes defined in (a) and (b) and otherwise to promote sentiment in Czechoslovakia against the re-establishment of a democratic Republic of Czechoslovakia.[57]

Attempts to obtain a hearing on RFE for the *Heimatrecht* of the Sudeten Germans and their desire to restore

---

[55] Letter, Sheppardson to Bentley, April 19, 1955.
[56] Letter, Kastner to Vandeburg, June 4, 1954.
[57] Letter, Lang to Miss Leigh, April 30, 1954.

friendly relations with the Czechs, or for the self-determination of Slovakia, are dismissed as attempts to promote "aggrandizement of political power" on the part of the Sudeten Germans and Slovak autonomists.[58] According to Mr. Kastner: "We run an anti-Communist propaganda station, not a debating society. Our goal is the liberation of Czechoslovakia from Communism and not the triumph of any particular party or group. Our concern is for freedom and political morality, not for political power...."[59]

A recent authoritative summary of United States policy on Czecho-Slovakia is contained in a letter from the Department of State read by Congressman Bentley at a congress of the Slovak League of America. The full text of this statement is as follows:

In dealing with Central and Eastern European states, their territorial organization, and their national composition, the policy of the department has been predicated on the belief that support for the principle of self-determination makes it incumbent on us to await a conclusive manifestation of the will of the people of those states under free conditions, and to consider fully the consequences of any action in favor of a new state from the standpoint of the stability, security, and economic viability of Central and Eastern Europe generally. The focus of this policy is the creation of conditions under which the peoples of Central and Eastern Europe will be able freely to determine their own governmental and economic institutions, as well as their relationships with each other and with the other peoples of Europe.

With respect to the question of the future territorial organization of Czechoslovakia, it is the view of the department that the Czech and Slovak peoples should themselves determine under free conditions whether they will continue to live together in a common Czechoslovak state.

The Czechs and Slovaks have been united in one state since 1918, except for the period of World War II when the Czechoslovak Republic was dismembered through Nazi aggression. Advocates of a separate Slovak state seek to have this government take action which may be construed as an indication that the United States Government has changed its attitude toward the territorial state of Czechoslovakia, apart from its attitude toward the present Communist regime, and has come to favor the break-up of that state and the creation of a separate Slovak state.

The department believes, however, that a departure along this

---

[58] *Ibid.*
[59] Letter, Kastner to Vandeburg, June 4, 1954. The invective which follows is not pertinent to this discussion and is therefore not quoted.

line from continuing to deal with the historical concept of a united Czechoslovakia until the Czechs and Slovaks themselves may otherwise determine of their own free choice would have fateful consequences in Eastern Europe, consequences which would exist long after that area wins independence of Soviet domination. These consequences would involve such matters as the eventual political organization of all of Eastern Europe, the status of each of the many ethnic groups in that area, the relations of each such group to the United States and to Germany, Russia, and other European powers, and safeguards against the territorial, political, and economic fragmentation of Eastern Europe and even of Slovakia itself, since it includes national minorities.[60]

As the foregoing statements indicate, the Czecho-Slovak policies of Radio Free Europe and the Department of State agree up to a point and then diverge sharply. Both find the Czecho-Slovak state, apart from its Communist government, an acceptable political entity: neither is ready to take the initiative in proposing alternate forms of organization. But Radio Free Europe regards the perpetuation of Czecho-Slovakia as a closed question, whereas for the Department of State it is an open question to be settled under the rule of self-determination.

Mr. Kastner's assertion that the United States joined in "ordering" the expulsion of the Sudeten Germans from Czecho-Slovakia and Mr. Lang's inference that the American government opposes their return to their homeland are totally devoid of any factual basis. President Roosevelt's approval of the transfer of "as many as possible" of the Germans in Czecho-Slovakia, given to Benes in May, 1943, was informal and verbal.[61] It is not evident that Roosevelt knew how many people would be involved, and there is no record of any written commitment by the United States. Efforts of the Czecho-Slovak exile "government" to obtain formal approval of the expulsion by the Western Allies were unavailing. As has been shown earlier, the highest inter-Allied political planning organ, the European Advisory Commission, never took action on Benes' deportation plan, submitted to it

---

[60] Department of State letter of May 2, 1955, quoted by Representative Alvin M. Bentley in remarks at Thirty-fourth Congress of the Slovak League of America, Washington, May 23, 1955. Mr. Bentley was kind enough to make available the manuscript of his speech.

[61] Benes, *Memoirs*, pp. 186, 193-95.

in November, 1944, while the British rejected the plan flatly in January, 1945.[62] Nor was the attitude of the American State Department much more encouraging.[63] Since the surrender terms imposed on Germany in May, 1945, contained no mention of the expulsion, the National Front government in Prague and the Communist-dominated National Committees, with Russian backing but with no authority from the Western Allies, began rounding up the Germans and driving them across the pre-1938 border in disorganized and utterly brutal fashion.

According to James F. Byrnes, who as Secretary of State accompanied President Truman to Potsdam in July, 1945, the expulsion of Sudeten Germans from Czecho-Slovakia and of Reich Germans from territories east of the Oder-Neisse line was a *fait accompli* which the Americans and British were powerless to prevent or reverse.[64] United States consent to Article XIII of the Potsdam Agreement did not constitute moral approval of the expulsions as such, but represented merely an attempt—based on the assumption that the United States could do nothing to prevent the expulsions—to assure that they would be carried out under conditions as humane as possible.[65] The same is true of the various agreements which the United States Military Government for Germany made with the Czecho-Slovak authorities on the details of personnel movements.

---

[62] See "Planning the Expulsion of the Sudeten Germans" in chap. III, *supra*.

[63] See "Genocide Against the Sudeten Germans" in chap. IV, *supra*.

[64] James F. Byrnes, *Speaking Frankly*, New York, 1947, pp. 79ff.

[65] Article XIII of the Potsdam Agreement reads in pertinent part: "The three Governments, having considered the question under all its aspects, recognize that the transfer to Germany of the German population or part thereof, remaining in Poland, Czechoslovakia and Hungary, will have to take place. They agree that any such transfer that will take place should be effected in an orderly and humane way. Since the influx of a large number of Germans into Germany would increase the burden already being carried by the occupation authorities, they consider it desirable that the Allied Control Council should first of all examine the problem with special regard to an equitable distribution of these Germans among the different occupation zones. . . . The Czechoslovakian Government, the Polish Provisional Government and the Allied Control Council in Hungary will be . . . requested to suspend any further transfer for the time being until the respective governments have examined the reports of their representatives to the Control Council." Organized transfers of Sudeten Germans to the United States Zone were suspended until January, 1946.

Although the author does not agree that as of 1945 the United States could do *nothing* to prevent or modify the expulsions (American forces conquered much of the present Soviet Zone of Germany and did not withdraw from western Bohemia until the fall of 1945), such is the conclusion reached by the Walter Committee in its report, *Expellees and Refugees in Germany* (Washington, 1947, Report No. 1841, 81st Congress, 2d Session), which has been cited by the Department of State to justify the thesis of American non-responsibility for the expulsions.

So far as the return of the Sudeten Germans to their homeland is concerned, the Department of State has, to the date of this writing, never issued a definite pronouncement one way or the other.[66] To characterize advocacy of their return as an attempt to overthrow American foreign policy is gratuitous, since there is no policy to overthrow.

As the Department of State infers, the peoples of Central Europe cannot vote freely on their political future or anything else until Russian overlordship is eliminated. In the meantime, however, there is nothing in American governmental policy to prohibit discussion of alternate proposals for political organization and action, provided that radio time is fairly allocated between various parties and groups and that the views of the speakers are presented as their own and not those of the United States government.

Serious critics of Radio Free Europe have never demanded that the Council of Free Czechoslovakia or its members, other than obvious pro-Communists, be ruled off the air. They demand only that the station become a representative forum of exile opinion, with fair shares of time for the Czech (not "Czechoslovak") conservative groups such as the Czech National Committee, the Czech Christian Democrats, and the National Democratic party, for the Slovak National Council Abroad and the Slovak Liberation Committee, and for the organizations of the Sudeten and Carpatho-Germans and the Hungarian minority, which represent the historical partners of the Czech and Slovak peoples. All speakers should be held to a code of ethics, forbidding personal recriminations and statements which inflame inter-ethnic disputes. If such a change should turn Radio Free Europe into a "debating society," would that be a catastrophe? After all, RFE is supposed to be a window to the free world, where full and fair discussion is the way in which problems are solved.

---

[66] A number of Congressmen and Senators have issued statements sympathetic to the aspirations of the Sudeten Germans. See *Jenseits von Jalta und Potsdam* ["Beyond Yalta and Potsdam"], a collection of messages from members of Congress on the occasion of the 1957 Sudeten German Rally, and the issues of *Sudetendeutsche Zeitung* and *Volksbote* reporting the rallies of earlier years.

THE INADEQUACY OF
"NON-PREDETERMINATION"

Non-predetermination, as represented in both Radio Free Europe and the Department of State, is predicated on the theory that discussion of the future structure of liberated Europe will only cause dissension among anti-Communist forces. Let American propaganda concentrate on the single issue of fighting Communism, the non-predeterminists urge, and let all "controversial" issues be shelved until after liberation.

While it is not contended that Americans should try to make decisions which other peoples must ultimately make for themselves, there are several reasons why the refusal to discuss issues or let exiles discuss them—which is what "non-predeterminism" amounts to—is not an effective political tactic.

1. Central Europe did not fall under Nazi and later Communist rule by accident. It did so because of the structural weakness imposed by the 1919 peace treaties—a weakness which makes it easy for the Russians to "divide and rule." New political conceptions which will unite the divided peoples of Central Europe are thus *immediate* weapons against the *present* Communist tyranny. It is the task of the free world—including exiles and expellees—to forge such weapons.

2. Even though American-sponsored propaganda refuses to discuss the future of the enslaved areas in specific terms, Communist propaganda engages in constant polemics on this subject. The Prague and Warsaw radios, for instance, devote much of their effort to stimulating Czech and Polish fears of German "revenge." Unless American propaganda answers and *refutes* the Communists, it becomes defensive and negative.

3. When we refuse to face an issue, our mental processes dictate an unconscious presumption in favor of the *status quo*. Unless we bring out in the open, for instance, the issue of the return of expelled peoples and that of political reorganization in Central Europe, our policy falls into the rut of tending to leave things as they are. Fears by one nation of another cannot be cured by pretending that the problems which cause these fears do not exist: it is an elemental rule of psychotherapy that fears, of whatever nature, must be faced and overcome.

4. Even those agencies which claim that they do not judge or predetermine do so nevertheless when they hire certain exiles for their radio stations and research projects and reject others. The exile with a well-paid professional job has money and time for politics and propaganda, whereas his confrère who drives a

taxi or washes dishes has neither. Every personnel decision involving an exile is in fact a choice affecting the shape of post-
liberation Europe. Either we choose deliberately and with thought
for the future, or we pick exiles with nice manners, who speak
good English and "know the right people," accepting uncritically
whatever policies they choose to serve up.

The application of non-predetermination in American
public and private radio stations has led to an exclusively
"Czechoslovak" orientation of Czech and Slovak broadcasts and to a "Great Russian" tendency in programs
beamed at the Soviet Union. Thus, the programs have
little appeal for the many who feel that the Masaryk-
Benes republic and the national chauvinism on which it
was based are no longer positive values. Nor do they
reach effectively the non-Russian peoples of the Soviet
Empire, who seek freedom both from Communism and
from Russian colonialism.

Granted that the Czechs, Slovaks, Hungarians, Poles,
Ukrainians, and other enslaved peoples must ultimately
make their own decisions, American and other free radio
stations have an important role in preparing them to
do so. It is essential that public opinion be molded to
overcome national fears and hatreds, so that the forces
of freedom will all pull in the same direction.

A start in the right direction has been made by
the Czech-Sudeten German Federative Committee, which
since January, 1956, has conducted a daily Czech-language broadcast over Radio Madrid. For the first time,
Czech advocates of Slav-German reconciliation are able
to speak to their countrymen at home, while the Sudeten Germans have a vehicle for their message that
Heimatrecht is to be realized through Czech-German co-
operation, with full safeguards for the civil, political,
and economic rights of both peoples. The Madrid broadcasts have opened a new perspective: that of inter-
ethnic brotherhood, which alone can overcome the fears
which have clouded relations among the peoples of east-
central Europe.

The new radio program, which includes reports from
America as well as commentaries on European and world
problems, has met with a wide and positive response.

Visitors to Czecho-Slovakia have reported that the transmissions are frequently discussed and that they have contributed to an improvement in Czech-German relations. Where Sudeten Germans remain, Czech anti-Communists, who usually have the best receivers, have taken to inviting their German friends to hear and discuss the broadcasts. In spite of vigorous efforts of the Prague authorities to jam the Madrid wave length and to embargo the sale of short-wave receivers and parts, it is apparent that the program is still reaching a wide audience.[67] With a budget which is hardly more than 1 per cent of that of the Free Europe Committee, the Czech-Sudeten German Federative Committee is getting ahead as best it can with the job which Radio Free Europe should be doing. Clearly, a modest American contribution to this project would pay greater dividends than the millions today being spent on propaganda nullified by its own ideological contradictions.

LESSONS FOR AMERICAN POLICY

The concern for fellow men which Christianity shares with other major religions, as well as the basic needs of the safety of the United States, forbid us to "write off" the nations of Czecho-Slovakia or other enslaved countries. The only policy which can promise more than temporary breathing spells is the policy of liberation, meaning the consistent and determined use of all methods short of launching a third world war to push back the Iron Curtain of Communist power. Only such a policy can mobilize our most important allies—the enslaved peoples themselves.[68]

As the House Committee on Communist Aggression, under the capable leadership of former Representative

---

[67] *Sudetendeutsche Zeitung,* February 4 and 11, March 17, and June 30, 1956, plus information developed through inquiry. The local sponsor of the broadcasts in Madrid is the *Centro Europeo de Documentacion.* Because Otto of Habsburg is one of many members of this organization, detractors have spread the rumor that the program serves royalist interests. This is definitely not the case. Program content is controlled not by the Centro but by the Federative Committee. Neither of the latter's constituents, the Czech National Committee and the Sudeten German Council, has any commitment to the Habsburgs.

[68] An effective policy of liberation would include at least diplomatic support for anti-Communist revolts. There are, for instance, numerous non-violent sanctions, such as an economic and financial boycott, which could have been employed against Russia at the time of the Hungarian Revolution.

Charles J. Kersten of Wisconsin, pointed out in its Second Interim Report, "coexistence," as the Kremlin visualizes it, is "an acceptance of the greatest system of human slavery known in history." Any relaxation by the West, the Committee stated, would afford Bolshevism the opportunity to marshal its forces for "the final war of extinction against the free world."[69]

Although five years have now passed since the Kersten Committee completed its labors, events since then have only confirmed the conclusions of its *Summary Report*, based on a comprehensive study of Communist seizure of power over twenty different nations. The report contains the following findings which Americans should take to heart:

That the objective of Communist aggression is to destroy civilization as we know it and to replace it with a planned existence from which will emerge the new Soviet man completely responsive to the masters of the universal superstate.

That no pretext is too insignificant, if the Soviet Union is convinced the proper time has arrived, to serve as an excuse for an action of armed aggression.

That every effort at forming a political coalition between Communist and non-Communist groups for the establishment of a government can end in only one result: liquidation of the non-Communist groups.

That [the Communist] conspiracy which in the course of 37 years has occupied almost one-third of the earth's surface and enslaved over 800 million people is now engaged in the process of consolidating its empire and preparing for the final showdown with the free nations.

That any trade by the nations of the free world with the Communist empire, whether it be in war materials or consumer commodities, will assist the Kremlin in consolidating its empire and will strike a demoralizing blow at the millions behind the Iron Curtain who resist and await the day when they can overthrow the Communist tyrants.

That the Kremlin is now engaged in an all-out propaganda offensive as the advocates of "peaceful coexistence" between the Communist empire and the free world in order to gain time, delude the free world as to its real intentions, divide and destroy the free world alliances and thus prepare the way for World War III.

---

[69] Select Committee on Communist Aggression, 83d Congress, *Second Interim Report*, Washington, August, 1954, pp. 22-23.

Rejecting the Communist thesis that "peaceful co-existence" is the only way to avoid war, the Kersten Committee outlines proposals for "a positive, bipartisan, political offensive against the international Communist conspiracy and in behalf of the enslaved nations." It then marshals the facts showing that a policy of liberation, rather than appeasement or containment, offers the best prospects of forestalling ultimate war launched by the Communists at their own convenience. In short, active political warfare is necessary if we do not wish atomic war—which the Kremlin will not hesitate to start *if and when* it believes it can win. False hopes, such as those engendered by Mr. Khrushchev's recent American odyssey, should not obscure the fact that international Communism is continuing and even intensifying its political warfare, in the Far East, in Cuba, in Panama, in Guatemala, and wherever it sees an opportunity to weaken the American position.[70]

The enslaved nations want liberation, not only from Communism, but also from colonialist domination by other nations. The attempt by certain Czech politicians to establish their nation as a "master race," ruling over Slovak and Sudeten German "minorities," led inevitably to enslavement of the Czechs. Conversely, the fruits of liberation cannot be enjoyed in peace without self-determination and equal rights for enslaved and expelled peoples. Americans should therefore encourage those exile and underground movements which seek liberation *for others as well as themselves.* There is no place on our team for chauvinists who wish to extend their *national* states over other peoples and their homelands. Experience in Czecho-Slovakia and elsewhere shows that immoderate nationalists have a weakness for unholy alliances, such as Benes' pact with the Kremlin. In the end, such alliances destroy their makers and endanger civilization as a whole.

An equally important point, emphasized in Hungary by the efforts of the more determined rebels to oust not only the Russians but Imre Nagy as well, is that serious

---

[70] Same committee. *Summary Report*, Washington, December, 1954, pp. 3-11. See also James Burnham, *Containment or Liberation?* New York, 1952, and John Scott, *Political Warfare: A Guide to Competitive Coexistence*, New York, 1955.

opponents of Communism are seldom interested in exchanging Kremlin-style socialism for some other variety, such as that preached by Radio Free Europe. There are many behind the Iron Curtain who want to get rid of socialism altogether, and to return to the full freedom which is possible only under a system of private property and free enterprise. While it is not suggested that genuinely non-totalitarian socialists should be ruled off the radio, ample time should be given to proponents of free enterprise and "classical" economics.

The idea of re-establishing a "free Czecho-Slovakia" would make sense only if that state were acceptable to all nationalities living within it. To afford political and cultural freedom while remaining strong in the face of danger, a state must express the self-determination of all its national groups. It is conceivable that the territory of Czecho-Slovakia, in its pre-World War II boundaries, could be reorganized as a federation in which the Czechs, the Sudeten and Carpatho-Germans, the Slovaks, and the Ruthenians (should they vote to join rather than remain with a liberated Ukraine) could enjoy equal rights of self-government and cultural development. Since the name "Czecho-Slovakia," with or without the hyphen, implies a distinction between "ruling peoples" and "minorities," many would prefer a new name which would better express the equality of all member nations.

But if the national state is to be replaced by a multination federation, as it must be if Central Europe is to enjoy permanent peace, why limit such a federation to the present Czecho-Slovakia, an area which is geographically awkward and economically unbalanced? Would not a Danube Federation, including *at least* Austria, Bohemia, Moravia-Silesia, Hungary, and Slovakia be a sounder economic, political, and military unit, as well as affording better balance among the different nationalities?[71]

---

[71] Turnwald, *Renascence or Decline*, pp. 72-77; Mikus, *La Slovaquie dans le Drame de l'Europe*, pp. 391-409; Miksche, *Danubian Federation*, pp. 30-37. See also the books by Hertz and Macartney listed in the bibliography. A useful source on Danube area affairs is the quarterly *Mitteilungsblatt des Forschungsinstitutes für Fragen des Donauraumes* ["Bulletin of the Institute of Danube Area Affairs"], Salzburg, Austria (German with English summary).

TOWARD A NEW ORDER

Many of the settlements of east-central Europe have their roots in the dynastic politics of early modern times. In those days the highest object of civil loyalty was the monarch, with whose person the rights of sovereignty were associated. Enterprising kings filled their realms with as many settlers as possible, without seeking or enforcing ethnic uniformity. Conversely, the subject was little concerned with the nationality of his monarch: what mattered was that the sovereign ruled wisely and well.

The ideological effect of the French Revolution was to replace the monarch with the *nation* as the highest object of loyalty. Nineteenth-century nationalism, which was historically intertwined with classic liberalism, found its expression in the doctrine that (a) each nation should have its national state, and (b) this state should include all members of the nation. This doctrine was manifest in the thinking of Woodrow Wilson, and still lingers like a ghost from the past in the corridors of the Department of State.

In east-central Europe, where the people are mixed in an ethnic patchwork, and where there are hundreds of bi- or tri-national towns and villages, no nation can be brought within a single state without including members of other nations. Nationalism thus became a political poison which has provoked two world wars and a number of minor conflicts. It is no accident that today the Kremlin has adopted nationalism as one of its most effective tactical weapons.

The principle of self-determination, or rule with the consent of the governed, is a basic element of American political philosophy. It is unfortunate that Wilson confused this principle with the national-state idea, seemingly committing the United States to supporting separate national states under all circumstances.[72] The national state is, however, by no means the only way in which self-determination can be expressed. Today, the

---

[72] Actually, Wilson applied the concept of national self-determination selectively, approving the dismemberment of the Austro-Hungarian Empire, but insisting on preserving the integrity of "Russia." See Strausz-Hupé and Possony, *International Relations*, pp. 687-90.

traditional national states of Western Europe are moving in the direction of federation: in fact, the governments are being pushed in that direction by a growing current of public opinion. National states may be practical for mature nations which inhabit natural geographical units, and in some cases even for those which are historically necessary, as in the case of the Ukraine, a large nation which has been unable to achieve self-determination in association with Russia. There are, however, areas and circumstances in which national states do violence to geography, economics, and political common sense. Where many nationalities are interlocked and intermixed within a natural geographic-economic unit, the only way in which *all* nations can enjoy self-determination is to exercise it *jointly*.

The political struggle for freedom can never be fully effective if built around a merely restorationist ideology. What is needed in the fight to liberate east-central Europe is the promise of a new order to replace the "Balkanization" of the past and present—a political structure which will express the unity of free men, regardless of linguistic and cultural differences.[73] The type of propaganda most conducive to political action is that which looks to the future—which tells men what to fight *for* as well as what to fight against.

---

[73] It is beyond our present scope to examine specific proposals. The author believes that the problem of cultural autonomy in the Danube area could be solved by a "two track" federation analogous to the Moravian Equalization of 1905. There would be regional states for police and economic functions and national "corporations" for education and the arts, and perhaps for social welfare. A citizen would belong to the corporation of his choice regardless of his domicile, and corporations would provide their services wherever their members live. Thus, the local branch of the Czech corporation would operate the Czech schools in Vienna, while the Slovak corporation would serve its members in the ethnic islands of central Hungary. The corporations, being public-law agencies, would levy their own taxes and would enjoy budgetary independence. They should be represented in the Senate of the Federation.

§

GLOSSARY

OF CZECH AND SLOVAK NAMES

Transliteration follows the most common English usage: "OOR" rhymes with "poor" (not door), "OW" with "cow" (not slow), etc. "KH" is used for German "ch," as in Bach, and "ZH" indicates "s" as in "measure." Stressed syllables are printed in boldface. Where no transliteration is given, pronounce as in English.

Abbreviations: WW = World War; RFE = Radio Free Europe; CFC = Council of Free Czechoslovakia.

Banská Bystrica (**BAHN-SKA BIS-TRIT-SA**): city in central Slovakia, 1948 pop. 12,500.

Barak, Rudolf: Minister of Interior in Communist regime since 1953.

Batt, Bension: Russian Communist, editor of "Rudé Právo" under Czech alias Stěpán Budin (**SHTYEH-PAN BOO-DIN**); editor of "New Yorkské Listy" during WW II.

Belak-Berger, Karol (**BAY-LACK BEAR-GER**): Slovak editor, employee of RFE.

Belluš, Dr. Samuel (**BEL-LOOSH**): Slovak journalist, supported Communists in 1944 uprising. Commissioner of Information, 1946-48; employee of RFE.

Benau, Dezider (**BAY-NOW, DEZ-ID-ER**): Hungarian Communist, editor of "New Yorksky Dennik" during WW II.

Beneš, Dr. Eduard (**BEN-ESH**): principal collaborator of T. G. Masaryk during WW I, Czecho-Slovak Foreign Minister, 1918-35. Second president of Czecho-Slovak Republic, 1935-38 and 1945-48. Died September 3, 1948.

Beran, Rudolf (**BER-AHN**): Czech Agrarian leader; cousin of Archbishop Beran; premier under President Hácha, 1938-39. Imprisoned in 1946; died in prison.

Biheler, Oto (**BEE-HELLER, OH-TOH**): Communist, in Czecho-Slovak section of BBC during WW II; later military attaché and espionage agent in the United States.

Borin, Vladimir Ležak- (**BOR-IN, VLA-DEE-MEER LAY-ZHAK**): Czech political author. Former Communist; left party in

1934 and has since made outstanding record as anti-Communist.

Bratislava (BRAH-TEE-SLAH-VA): capital of Slovakia, pop. 184,400 (1949 estimate). German name: Pressburg.

Bruža, Vladimír (BROO-ZHA, VLA-DEE-MEER): Czech official; conducted Czech-Soviet uranium talks in Moscow, 1948; manager of Czechoslovak Foreign Institute in Leiden, Holland.

Budějovice [full name Ceské B.] (CHESS-KAY BOOD-YAY-O-VEE-TSAY): city in western Bohemia, pop. 43,800 in 1930; 38,200 in 1947. German name Budweis, whence Budweiser beer.

Čas (CHAHSS): Slovak word meaning "time," name of Slovak Democratic party newspaper.

Čechy (CHEKHY): Czech name for Bohemia, or "land of the Czechs."

Čepička, Alexei (CHEH-PITCH-KA, AL-EX-AY-EE): son-in-law of Klement Gottwald. Defense minister, 1951-56.

Černák, Matúš (CHAIR-NAHK, MA-TOOSH): Slovak diplomat, minister to Germany, 1939-44; later leader of Slovak National Council Abroad in West Germany. Outstanding fighter against Communism; assassinated July, 1955, with "package bomb."

Černy, Dr. Josef (CHAIR-NEE, YO-ZEF): Czech minister before WW II, leader of Agrarian party, imprisoned, 1945-47. Now in the United States.

Český Svaz (CHESS-KY SVAHZ): "Czech Union," the caucus of Czech deputies in the old Austrian parliament before WW I.

Chudoba, Dr. Bohdan (KHOO-DOH-BA, BOH-DAN, gutteral "h" in BOH): deputy of Czech People's party after WW II; fought leftist tendencies in party. Now professor at Iona College, New Rochelle, N.Y., and member of Czech National Committee.

Clementis, Vlado (KLAY-MEN-TISS, VLA-DOH): Slovak Communist. In London during WW II; foreign minister, 1948-52; liquidated, 1952.

Dnešek (DNYAY-SHEK): Czech word for "today"; magazine edited by Ferdinand Peroutka until February, 1948.

Ducháček, Dr. Ivo (DOO-KHA-SHEK, EE-VO): Czech journalist, assistant to Dr. Ripka in London and later People's party deputy; after 1948 an employee of Voice of America and RFE.

Ďurčanský, Dr. Ferdinand (DOOR-CHAHN-SKI): Slovak professor of international law and deputy; foreign minister, 1939-40; now chairman, Slovak Liberation Committee.

Fabian, Dr. Štefan (FAH-BEEAHN, SHTYEF-AHN): Slovak administrator, anti-Communist, proposed for Commissioner of Interior in 1946; imprisoned on fabricated charge to intimidate opposition to appointment of Dr. Ferjenčík.

Ferjenčík, General Mikuláš (FERR-YEN-CHIK, MIK-U-LASH): captain in Slovak Army, supported 1944 "revolt" and accompanied Communist leader Smidke to Moscow; promoted in

1945 to general and Deputy Defense Minister. In 1946, appointed Slovak Commissioner of Interior with Communist support; praised by Communist newspaper *Pravda* (Bratislava) on resignation. Now lives near Chicago.

Fierlinger, Zdeněk (FEER-LINGER, ZDYAY-NYEK): Czech left-wing socialist, ambassador in Moscow during WW II; premier, 1945-46. Supported Communists in 1948; has survived purges and is now speaker of Czecho-Slovak parliament.

Firt, Dr. Julius (FEERT, YOOL-YUS): Czech National Socialist deputy; in London during WW II and later published newspaper, "Svobodné Slovo," which supported expulsion of Sudeten Germans and friendship with U.S.S.R. Active in CFC and high official of RFE.

Frejka, Ludvík (FRAY-KA, LOOD-VIK): Czech name assumed by German Communist Ludwig Freund; on British "Daily Worker" during WW II; returned to Prague; liquidated, 1952.

Ghelfand, Professor Simeon (GHELL-FAND): Czech Catholic historian, Secretary-general of Czech Christian Democratic Movement in exile.

Gojdič, Monsignor Paul (GOY-DITCH): Greek-Catholic bishop of Prešov (PRAY-ZHOFF), Slovakia. Imprisoned in 1951 for attempting to prevent a break from Rome

Gottwald, Klement (GAWTT-VALD, KLAY-MENT): leader of Czech Communists; premier, 1946-48; led 1948 "February Revolution." Elected president after death of Benes; died in 1953, shortly after attending Stalin's funeral in Moscow.

Hácha, Dr. Emil (HA-KHA, AY-MEEL): third president of Czecho-Slovak Republic (November, 1938 to March, 1939); forced by Hitler to agree to Protectorate, of which he served as president. Beaten to death without trial after "liberation" in 1945.

Hála, Monsignor František (HAH-LA, FRAN-TI-SHEK): Czech priest and minister (People's party) in National Front cabinet.

Hasal, Antonín (HAH-SAL, AHN-TOH-NYIN): Czech general, minister in National Front cabinet; admitted to United States.

Havlíček, Karel (HAV-LEE-CHEK, KAH-REL): Czech journalist of nineteenth century; sought Czech self-government within a federated Austria.

Hajdu, Vavro (HY-DOO, VAV-RO): Slovak Communist; head of BBC Czecho-Slovak section during WW II. Later undersecretary in Foreign Ministry; liquidated in 1952.

Hlas Domova (HLAHSS DOH-MOH-VA): "The Voice of Home," weekly published in Prague and mailed abroad to encourage exiles to redefect to Communist Czecho-Slovakia.

Hlinka, Monsignor Andrej (HLIN-KA, AHN-DRAY): leader of Slovak self-determination movement and founder of Slovak People's party. Died in August, 1938; Slovak national hero.

Hodinová-Spurná, Anežka, Mrs. (HO-DEE-NO-VA—SPOOR-NA, AN-YEZH-KA): Communist deputy; in London during WW II.

Hodža, Dr. Fedor (HAWDD-ZHA, FAY-DOR): son of Milan

Hodža. Member of London "government" and secretary of Slovak Democratic party, 1945-48; active in CFC.

Hodža, Dr. Milan (MEE-LAN): first Slovak premier of Czecho-Slovakia (1936-38); resigned during Munich crisis. Later disagreed with Benes; died in 1944.

Hollý, Ján (HAWL-LY, YAHN): 1785-1849, considered the greatest Slovak poet of the nineteenth century; noted for his epic, "Svätopluk."

Hrneček, Václav (HER-NE-CHECK, VAT-SLAV): Czech deputy commander of the Budějovice concentration camp; sentenced to eight years imprisonment for atrocities, but released because of services for a U.S. intelligence agency.

Hruška, Zdeněk (HROOSH-KA, ZDYAY-NYEK): Czech Communist general and specialist in partisan warfare; chief of SVAZARM, the para-military "sports" organization.

Hrušovský, Professor Francis (HROO-SHOFF-SKI): Slovak historian, president of Slovak National Council Abroad, 1955-56; died, Cleveland, Ohio, September 9, 1956.

Hus, Jan (HOOSE, YAHN): 1369-1415, Czech religious reformer and nationalist; burned for heresy.

Husák, Dr. Gustav (HOO-SAK): Slovak Communist, leader in 1944 "revolt." President of Slovak Board of Commissioners, 1946-51; arrested in 1951 and sentenced to life imprisonment for "treason" in 1954.

Jáchymov (YA-KHEE-MOFF): Czech name for St. Joachimsthal, city in Sudetenland (1930 pop. 17,190, of whom 16,380 were German); noted for its uranium mines.

Jaksch, Wenzel (YOCKSH, VENT-SEL): leader of Sudeten German Social Democrats; in London during WW II, tried to forestall Sudeten expulsion. Now deputy in West German *Bundestag*.

Kirschbaum, Dr. Jozef (KEERSCH-BOWM, YO-ZEF): Slovak jurist and historian; president of Slovak National Council Abroad since 1956.

Klecanda, Vladimír Vojtěch (KLET-SAN-DA, VLA-DEE-MEER VOY-TYEKH): Czech general, in Bohemia during WW II. Attempted to contact Allied Headquarters to secure U.S. occupation of Prague; indicted for treason, but acquitted in 1946. Committed suicide to escape further persecution.

Kočvara, Dr. Stefan (KAWCH-VA-RA, SHTYEF-AHN): Slovak Democratic deputy, deputy premier, 1947-48. Member of CFC.

Kopecký, Václav (KO-PET-SKI, VAT-SLAV): Communist propaganda minister, 1945-48; promoted Sudeten expulsion; later deputy premier.

Košice (KO-SHEET-SAY): city in eastern Slovakia (1947 pop. 60,700); temporary seat of Czecho-Slovak government in 1945.

Krajina, Vladimír KRA-YEE-NA, VLA-DEE-MEER): Czech National Socialist, minister in National Front cabinet. Now in Canada.

Kramář, Dr. Karel (KRA-MARSH, KAH-REL): founder of Czech National Democratic party; first premier of Czecho-Slovakia and political rival of Benes.

Krofta, Kamil (KA- MEEL): Czech professor; foreign minister of Czecho-Slovakia, 1936-38.

Kubal, František (KOO-BAL, FRAN-TI-SHEK): Czech "exile" student; active in Czechoslovak Foreign Institute: imprisoned for espionage against U.S. military installations.

Kučera, Vladimír (KOO-CHE-RA, VLA-DEE-MEER): RFE commentator; returned to Prague, 1955.

Kutlvašr, General Karel (KUT'L-VOSH'R, KAH-REL: "KUT" rhymes with "put"): Czech general, anti-Communist; assumed command in Prague uprising of May, 1945, but failed to control course of events; later imprisoned by Communists.

Kvetko, Dr. Martin: Slovak commissioner, 1945-48, signed forced labor decrees and voted confidence in Gottwald March 12, 1948; now official of RFE.

Laušman, Bohumil (LOWSH-MAN, BO-HOO-MEEL): Czech socialist; Minister of Industry; supported Communists in 1948. "Fled" in 1949, consultant to Tito, commentator for RFE and French radio; returned to Czecho-Slovakia, December, 1953.

Lettrich, Dr. Josef (LET-TRIKH, YO-ZEF): chairman of Slovak Democratic party and president of Slovak regional parliament, 1945-48; now in United States; active in CFC.

Ležak-Borin, Vladimir. See Borin, Vladimir Lezak-

Locher, Dr. Karel (LAW-KHER, KAH-REL): Secretary of Czech National Committee, London; died in August, 1959.

Mach, Alexander (MAKH): Politician of pro-Nazi wing in Slovak People's party; appointed Slovak Minister of Interior at Hitler's demand in 1940; supervised deportation of Jews. Executed, 1947.

Majer, Václav (MYER, VAT-SLAV): Czech socialist, in London "government"; Minister of Food, 1945-48; active in CFC.

Masaryk, Jan (MAZ-A-RIK, YAHN): son of Thomas G. Masaryk. Foreign Minister in London "government" and in National Front until March 10, 1948, when he was thrown or jumped from a window, being killed instantly.

Masaryk, Thomas G., 1850-1937: professor, deputy of Czech People's party in Austrian parliament. Went abroad during WW I to work for establishment of Czecho-Slovak Republic, of which he became first president; retired in 1935.

Matoušková, Hilda, Mrs. (MA-TOH-SHKO-VA): Czech Communist, secretary to Dr. Ripka in Paris office of Czechoslovak Liberation Movement early in WW II.

Mojmír I (MOY-MEER): Slovak ruler (830-850); introduced Christianity, founded Great Moravian Kingdom.

Mojmir II: son and successor (894-906) of King Svätopluk; during his reign the Great Moravian Kingdom began to disintegrate.

Moravec, General František (MOR-A-VETZ, FRAN-TI-SHEK): director of military intelligence and secret police for the London "government." Later, head of a U.S.-financed "intelligence" agency noted for leaking critical information to the Communists.

Němec, Antonín (NYEM-ETZ, AN-TOH-NYIN): Minister in London "government," Czecho-Slovak Commissioner for Ruthenia, 1944-45.

New Yorkské Listy (NEW YORK-SKAY LIS-TEE): Czech-language newspaper; supports policies of CFC.

New Yorkský Denník (NEW YORK-SKI DYEN-NYIK): Slovak-language newspaper, same management as "Listy"; opposes Slovak self-determination and supports CFC.

Nitra (NEET-RA): city in west-central Slovakia, 1946 pop. 19,700.

Nosek, Václav (NO-SEK, VAT-SLAV): Czech Communist, Minister of Interior, 1945-53; died, 1955.

Novomeský, Ladislav (NO-VO-MEH-SKI, LAHD-EE-SLAV): Slovak Communist, active in 1944 "revolt" and postwar government; sentenced to ten years in prison in 1954.

Novotný, Antonín (NO-VAWT-NY, AN-TOH-NYIN): First Secretary of Czecho-Slovak Communist party and president of Czecho-Slovakia since 1957.

Osuský, Dr. Štefan (OH-SOO-SKI, SHTYEF-AHN): Slovak; Czecho-Slovak ambassador to France before WW II. Disagreed with Benes and did not return to Czecho-Slovakia after the war; member of CFC, but definitely not "left-wing."

Palacký, František (PAH-LAT-SKI, FRAN-TI-SHEK), 1798-1876: Czech historian and leader of nineteenth-century "renaissance"; advocate of federated Austria.

Papanék, Dr. Ján (PA-PA-NYEK, YAHN): Slovak; Czecho-Slovak representative in United Nations until dismissed by Communists in 1948; active in CFC and chairman of "American Fund for Czechoslovak Relief."

Pekelský, Dr. Vladimír (PEH-KEL-SKI, VLA-DEE-MEER): chairman of Democratic Czech Federalists, Köln; anti-Communist, opposed to CFC, favors Slav-German reconciliation.

Feroutka, Ferdinand (PEH-ROHT-KA): Czech journalist, National Socialist; chief of Czecho-Slovak section of RFE.

Plzeň (PL-ZEN'Y): city in western Bohemia, pop. 117,800 in 1947; German name Pilsen, noted for its beer.

Poděbrad, George (PO-DYEH-BRAD): Czech King of Bohemia 1458-71); undertook to improve Czech-German relations after the Hussite wars.

Praha (PRAH-HA): Prague, traditional capital of Bohemia and capital of Czecho-Slovakia, 1947 pop. 922,300.

Právo lidu (PRAH-VO LEE-DOO): "People's Justice," organ of the Czech Social Democratic party.

Prchala, General Lev (PR-KHA-LA): Czech general; urged that Czecho-Slovakia fight rather than yield to Nazis in 1938; commanded detachments in Poland in 1939. In London during WW II, but disagreed with pro-Soviet policy of Benes; did not return to Czecho-Slovakia after the war. Chairman of Czech National Committee; supports self-determination and Czech-German reconciliation.

Přemysl (PRSHEM-EES'L): Legendary peasant husband of the Czech princess Libuše (LEE-BOO-ZHAY) and founder of the Premyslide dynasty. According to the legend, a soothsayer told the princess to travel west and marry the first man she met plowing with an iron plow. If this is true, then Přemysl was probably a German.

Procházka, Dr. Adolf (PRO-KHAZ-KA): leader in People's party; member of London cabinet and Minister of Health, 1945-48; active in CFC.

Rázus, Rev. Martin (RAH-ZOOS): Lutheran pastor, poet, and leader of Slovak National party which co-operated with Hlinka's Slovak People's party to secure Slovak self-government; died, 1937.

Ripka, Dr. Hubert: leader in Czech National Socialist party, Minister of Information in London cabinet; promoted expulsion of Sudeten Germans and treaty with U.S.S.R. Minister of Foreign Trade, 1945-48; founder of Czechoslovak Foreign Institute and active in CFC; opponent of Czech-German reconciliation; died January 7, 1958, in London.

Rostislav (ROSS-TEE-SLAV): Slovak ruler (850-70) of Great Moravian Kingdom.

Rudé Právo (ROO-DAY PRAH-VO): "Red Justice," organ of Czecho-Slovak Communist party, today the most important daily in Prague.

Schwejk or Švejk (SHVIKE): Hero of story "The Good Soldier Schwejk," by Jaroslav Hašek (HAH-SHEK), with a gift for producing chaos without ever violating orders. Has become a symbol of Czech resistance to oppression.

Sidor, Karol, (SEE-DOR): Slovak ambassador to Vatican during WW II; first president of Slovak National Council Abroad. Died, 1954.

Široký, Vilem: Slovak Communist; premier of Czecho-Slovakia since March, 1953.

Skutečnost (SKOO-TETCH-NOST): "Reality," magazine published by exiles associated with the Czechoslovak Foreign Institute.

Slánsky, Rudolf (SLAHN-SKI): Secretary of Czecho-Slovak Communist party; liquidated, 1952.

Slávik, Juraj (SLAH-VIK, YOO-RYE): Slovak, member of London "government"; after WW II Czecho-Slovak ambassador in Washington; obtained asylum, 1948, active in CFC.

Šmidke, Karol (SHMID-KEH): Slovak Communist, active in 1944 "revolt"; traveled to Moscow with General Ferjenčík. Fell from grace, 1951, and died of "pneumonia" in a state sanatorium in late 1952.

Šramek, Monsignor Jan (SHRA-MEK, YAHN): premier of London "government" and minister (People's party) in National Front; arrested while fleeing in company of Dr. Ripka (who escaped arrest); died in prison.

Štefánik, General Milan R. (SHTYEF-AH-NYIK, MEE-LAN): Slovak scientist and general, member of Czecho-Slovak National Committee during WW I; killed by "accident" on May 4, 1919.

Stranský, Dr. Jan (STRAHN-SKI, YAHN): son of Jaroslav Stranský; National Socialist deputy; editor in RFE.

Stransky, Dr. Jaroslav (YAH-RO-SLAV): National Socialist minister in London and postwar cabinets; active in CFC, but has moved in direction of reconciliation with Sudeten Germans; lives in England.

Stříbrny, George (STRZHEE-BR-NEE): leader in Czech Agrarian party; imprisoned since 1946.

Stúr, L'udovít (SHTOOR, LYOO-DCH-VIT), 1815-56: teacher, writer, and editor, leader of Slovak renaissance; major role in unifying Slovak political thought (though Slovaks today reject his Pan-Slavism) and developing modern literary Slovak.

Svätopluk (SVA-TOH-PLOOK, "a" as in cat, "oo" as in moon): Slovak king (870-94) who expanded Great Moravian Kingdom to its greatest extent.

Svoboda, General Ludvík (SVO-BOH-DA, LOOD-VEEK): Czech general, commanded Czecho-Slovak troops in Soviet Union during WW II; Minister of Defense, 1945-50.

Svobodné Slovo (SVO-BOHD-NAY SLO-VO): "The Free Word," Czech National Socialist daily, noted for Sovietophile and violently anti-Sudeten German editorial policies.

Syrový, General Jan: Czech general, chief of staff in first Republic, appointed to head "non-political" cabinet during Munich crisis and served as acting president from resignation of President Benes to election of President Hacha.

Tiso, Monsignor Jozef (TEE-SO, YO-ZEF): leader of Slovak People's party after Hlinka's death; premier of autonomous Slovak government, 1938-39; only president of Slovak Republic. Sought refuge in U.S. Zone of Germany, but turned over to Communists; tried in National Court before Judge Igor (EE-GOR) Daxner, who had sworn to "hang Tiso." Hanged April 18, 1947; revered by Slovaks as national hero and martyr.

Tuka, Professor Vojtech (TOO-KA, VOY-TEKH): Slovak nationalist; sentenced to fifteen years imprisonment in 1928 on flimsy charges. Released in 1938, he became premier of Slovak Republic; his pro-Nazi policies were resisted by President Tiso and other moderate politicians.

Turčiansky Svätý Martin (TOOR-CHEE-AHN-SKI SVAH-TI MARTIN): city in northwestern Slovakia, 1946 pop. 10,600.

Valo, Josef (VAH-LO, YO-ZEF): Czech Communist deputy; spent

WW II in England, lectured to Communist Front groups in United States. Still active in Communist government.

Vaněk, Miloš (VAH-NYEK, MEE-LAWSH): Charter member of Czech Communist party, later left-wing socialist; now chief economic editor of RFE, Munich.

Viboch, Pavel (VEE-BOKH, PAH-VEL): leader in Slovak Democratic Party, 1945-48; employee of RFE, Munich.

Vojtaššák, Monsignor Ján (VOY-TASH-SHAK, YAHN): Bishop of Spiš (SPEESH), Slovakia; imprisoned since January, 1951.

Zápotocký, Antonín (ZAP-O-TOT-SKI, AHN-TOH-NYIN): Communist head of Czecho-Slovak Trade Union Federation; became premier after 1948 "February Revolution" and succeeded Gottwald as president in 1953. Died November 13, 1957.

Zenkl, Dr. Petr (ZENK'L, PAY-TR): Mayor of Prague before WW II, in concentration camp during war; released, 1945, and became chairman of National Socialist party; deputy premier, 1946-48. First chairman of CFC; may be considered the most prominent among the political heirs of Dr. Beneš.

Zibrin, Dr. Michal (ZEE-BRIN, MEE-KHAL): Slovak exile; former supporter of National Front, but broke with CFC and now one of its outspoken critics.

Žilina (ZHEE-LEE-NA): city in northern Slovakia, 1946 pop. 16,400.

Žingor, Vilem (ZHIN-GOR, VILL-EM): leader in 1944 "Slovak Revolt"; joined Communist party in 1946, but left it in 1947 and went underground; sentenced to death in 1950 for "bourgeois nationalism."

BIBLIOGRAPHY

BOOKS, PAMPHLETS, AND ARTICLES

Not all items cited in footnotes are included, but only enough for a rounded course of reading on Czecho-Slovakia. The titles listed below express widely different viewpoints, including the admirers as well as the critics of Masaryk and Benes.

BENES, EDUARD. *Détruisez l'Autriche-Hongrie!* ("Destroy Austria-Hungary!") Paris: Delgrave, 1916. 72 pp.

———. *Memoirs of Eduard Benes—From Munich to New War and New Victory.* (Originally published as *Pameti*, Prague, 1947.) London: Allen and Unwin, 1954. 346 pp.

BLASKO, STEPHAN. *Slovakia in Blood and Shackles.* New York, 1954. 68 pp. (Order from Catholic Slovak Sokol, 205 Madison Street, Passaic, N.J.)

BORIN, V. L. *Against the Hangman—The Martyrdom of Zavis Kalandra.* London: The Forty-Five Press, 1951. 31 pp.

BRADA, JIRI. "A Closer Look at Radio Free Europe," series of three articles, with rejoinder by Radio Free Europe, *Facts Forum*, Dallas, January-March, 1956.

BROUCEK, MILOSLAV J. *Ceskoslovenska Tragedie* ("The Czechoslovak Tragedy"). New York, 1956. (Order from author, 513 East 81st Street, New York 28, N.Y.)

BUSEK, VRATISLAV, and SPULBER, NICOLAS (eds.). *East-Central Europe Under the Communists—Czechoslovakia*, published for the Mid-European Studies Center of the Free Europe Committee. New York. Frederick A. Praeger, Inc., 1957. 520 pp.

CULEN, KONSTANTIN. *Tschechen und Slowaken im Staatsdienst in der tschechoslowakischen Republik* ("Czechs and Slovaks in Public Service in the Czecho-Slovak Republic"). Bratislava: Slowakische Bücherei, 1945. 103 pp.

DELANEY, EDWARD L. *False Freedom.* Los Angeles: Standard Publications, 1954. 180 pp.

DUCHACEK, IVO. *The Strategy of Communist Infiltration—The Case of Czechoslovakia.* New Haven: Yale Institute of International Studies (duplicated), 1949.

DURCANSKY, FERDINAND. *The International Aspects of the Slovak Question.* New York: Slovak Liberation Committee (1379 York Avenue), 1954. 35 pp.

Foreign Office of Great Britain. *Correspondence Respecting Czechoslovakia* and *Further Correspondence Respecting Czechoslovakia.* London: H. M. Stationery Office, 1938. Cmd. 5847 and Cmd. 5848 respectively.

FRIEDMAN, OTTO. *The Break-Up of Czech Democracy.* London: Gollancz, 1950. 178 pp.

GAUSE, FRITZ. *Deutsche-slawische Schicksalsgemeinschaft* ("Germans and Slavs as Partners in History"). Kitzingen/Main: Holzner Verlag, 1952. 312 pp.

German Federal Ministry for Expellees, Refugees, and War Victims. *Dokumentation der Vertreibung der Deutschen aus Ost-Mitteleuropa* ("Documentation on the Expulsion of the Germans from East-Central Europe"), edited by Theodor Schieder, Vols. IV/1 and IV/2. Bonn, 1957. 357 and 818 pp., respectively.

GLASER, KURT. *The Iron Curtain and American Policy.* Washington: Public Affairs Press, 1953. 36 pp.

Göttinger Arbeitskreis ("Goettingen Research Society"), *Sudetenland* (reference book on all areas of German settlement in Bohemia, Moravia, and Silesia). Kitzingen/Main: Holzner-Verlag, 1954. 207 pp.

HANTSCH, HUGO. *Die Nationalitätenfrage im alten Österreich* ("The Nationality Question in Old Austria"). Vol. I of "Vienna Historical Studies." Vienna: Verlag Herold, 1953. 125 pp.

HENDERSON, SIR NEVILE. *Failure of a Mission.* London, 1939; New York, 1940.

HERTZ, FREDERICK. *Nationality in History and Politics.* London: Kegan Paul, 1945.

———. *The Economic Problem of the Danubian States.* London: Gollancz, 1947. 223 pp.

HROBAK, PHILIP A. *Czecho-Slovakia—Victim of Communist Aggression* (collection of contemporary news articles and comments). Middletown, Pa.: Jednota Press, 1945. 64 pp.

———. *"Czechoslovakism" Versus Americanism.* Middletown, Pa.: Slovak League of America, 1953. 48 pp.

———. *Who Betrayed Slovakia to the Reds?* Middletown, Pa.: Slovak League of America, 1954. 31 pp.

———. *"Czechoslovakia"—History "Made to Order,"* a critical study of Kerner's *Czechoslovakia* (listed below). Middletown, Pa.: Slovak League of America, March, 1958. 80 pp.

HRUSOVSKY, FRANCIS. *This is Slovakia.* Scranton, Pa.: Obrana Press, 1953. 110 pp.

JAKSCH, WENZEL. *Sudeten Labour and the Sudeten Problem.* London: Sudeten German Social Democratic Party, 1945. 48 pp.

———. *Benesch war gewarnt!* ("Benes Was Warned!"). Munich: Verlag "Das Volk," 1949. 90 pp.

————. *Europas Weg nach Potsdam* ("Europe's Road to Potsdam"). Stuttgart: Deutsche Verlags-Anstalt, 1958. 522 pp.

————, and KOLARZ, WALTER. *Der Weg der letzten freien Deutschen* ("The Trail of the Last Free Germans"). London: Lincolns-Prager, 1940. 51 pp.

JOSTEN, JOSEF. *Oh, My Country!* London: Latimer House, 1949.

JUETTNER, ALFRED. *Aus den Akten—München 1938* ("From the Files—Munich, 1938"). Bonn: Sudetendeutsche Landsmannschaft, 1954. 24 pp.

KALVODA, JOSEF. *Titoism and Masters of Imposture.* New York: Vantage Press, 1958. 327 pp.

KERNER, ROBERT J. (ed.). *Czechoslovakia.* Berkeley and Los Angeles: University of California Press, 1945, 1949. 504 pp.

LAFFAN, R. G. D. *Survey of International Affairs, 1938*, Vol. II, "The Crisis in Czechoslovakia." London: Royal Institute of International Affairs, 1951.

LEMBERG, EUGEN. *Die Ausweisung als Schicksal und Aufgabe* ("Expulsion as Fate and Challenge"). Gräfelfing/Munich: Edmund Gans Verlag, 1949. 68 pp.

LETTRICH, JOZEF. *History of Modern Slovakia.* New York: Frederick A. Praeger, Inc., 1955. 330 pp.

LIPTAK, JOHANN. *800 Jahre Slowakei-Deutschtum* ("800 Years of German Settlements in Slovakia"). Stuttgart, undated (1948 or later). 128 pp.

MACARTNEY, C. A. *Problems of the Danubian Basin.* Cambridge, England: Cambridge University Press, 1932.

MACKENZIE, COMPTON. *Dr. Benes.* London, 1946.

MASARYK, THOMAS G. *Ceska Otazka* ("The Czech Question"). Prague: Pokrok Cooperative, 1908. 264 pp.

————. *The Making of a State.* London: Allen and Unwin, 1929.

MEYNEN, E. *Sudetendeutscher Atlas* ("Sudeten German Atlas"), with text and legends in German, English, and French). Munich: Arbeitsgemeinschaft zur Wahrung sudetendeutscher Interessen, 1954. (Order from Sudetendeutscher Rat, Trifftstr. 1, Munich.) Large folio, 28 plates and 56 pages.

MIKSCHE, LIEUT. COL. F. O. *Danubian Federation.* Camberley, England, 1953. 37 pp.

————. *Unconditional Surrender—The Roots of a World War III.* London: Faber & Faber, 1952. 468 pp.

MIKUS, JOSEPH A. *La Slovaquie dans le Drame de l'Europe* ("Slovakia in the Drama of Europe"). Paris: Les Iles d'Or, 1955. 475 pp.

MOLISCH, PAUL. *Vom Kampf der Tschechen um Ihren Staat* ("The Struggle of the Czechs for Their State"). Vienna and Leipzig: Wilhelm Braumüller, 1929. 164 pp.

————. *Die Sudetendeutsche Freiheitsbewegung in den Jahren 1918-1919* ("The Sudeten German Liberation Movement in 1918-1919"). Vienna and Leipzig: Wilhelm Braumüller, 1932. 190 pp.

PERGLER, CHARLES. *America in the Struggle for Czechoslovak Independence.* Philadelphia: Dorrance, 1926. 113 pp.

POGUE, FORREST C. (of office of Chief of Military History, U.S. Army). *The Supreme Command.* (Vol. IV of *The United States Army in World War II.*) Washington: Government Printing Office, 1954.

PREIDEL, HELMUT (ed.). *Die Deutschen in Böhmen und Mähren, ein historischer Rückblick* ("The Germans in Bohemia and Moravia, a Historical Survey"). Gräfelfing/Munich: Edmund Gans Verlag, 1950. 384 pp.

RASCHHOFER, HERMANN. *Die Sudetenfrage, ihre völkerrechtliche Entwicklung vom ersten Weltkreig zur Gegenwart* ("The Sudeten Question: Its Development in International Law from World War I to the Present"). Munich: Isar Verlag, 1953. 310 pp.

REITLINGER, GERALD. *The Final Solution.* London: Vallentine, Mitchell, 1953.

RIPKA, HUBERT. *Czechoslovakia Enslaved.* London: Gollancz, 1950.

————. *East and West.* London: Lincolns-Prager, 1944.

SKULTETY, JOSEPH. *Sketches from Slovak History.* Middletown, Pa.: First Catholic Slovak Union, 1930. 229 pp.

Slovak Liberation Committee. "Documents, giving True Backgrounds to the Negative Value and Inefficiency of the Broadcasting Organized by the National Committee for a Free Europe in Munich." London, 1951. 36 pp. Mimeographed. (Cited as "Documents" in the footnotes.)

TABORSKY, EDUARD. *The Czechoslovak Cause in International Law.* London, 1944.

————. "The Triumph and Disaster of Eduard Benes," *Foreign Affairs* (New York), XXXVI, No. 4 (July, 1958), 669-84.

THOMSON, S. HARRISON. *Czechoslovakia in European History.* Princeton, N.J.: Princeton University Press, 1943. 300 pp.

TURNWALD, W. K. *Renascence or Decline in Central Europe.* Munich: University Press, Dr. C. Wolf & Son, 1954. 89 pp.

————. *Sudeten German Picture Book* (consisting entirely of photographs with brief explanations). Munich: Christ Unterwegs, 1949. 104 pp.

———— (ed.). *Documents on the Expulsion of the Sudeten Germans* (English edition, condensed from a larger German edition). Munich: Arbeitsgemeinschaft zur Wahrung sudetendeutscher Interessen, 1953. 308 pp. (Order from Sudetendeutscher Rat, Trifftstr. 1, Munich.)

U.S. Bureau of the Census. *The Population of Czechoslovakia,* by Waller Wynne, Jr. "International Population Statistics Reports, Series P-90, No. 3." Washington: Government Printing Office, 1953. 72 pp.

U.S. House of Representatives, 83d Congress, 2d Session, Select Committee on Communist Aggression, *Second Interim Report.*

August, 1954. Washington: Government Printing Office, 1954. 25 pp.

———. *Fourth Interim Report—Hearings, 1954.* (Covering hearings held from May 3 to June 30, 1954, inclusive; pages 679 to 1448.) Washington: Government Printing Office, 1954.

———. *Tenth Interim Report—Hearings, 1954.* (Covering hearings on December 1-3, 1954.) Washington: Government Printing Office, 1954. 174 pp.

———. *Summary Report.* December, 1954. Washington: Government Printing Office, 1954. 43 pp.

———. *Special Report No. 8: Communist Takeover and Occupation of Czechoslovakia.* Washington: Government Printing Office, 1955. 30 pp.

WANKLYN, HARRIET. *Czechoslovakia.* New York: Frederick A. Praeger, Inc., 1954. 445 pp. (This book might better have been entitled "Economic Geography of Czecho-Slovakia"; history and politics are given only incidental treatment.)

WISKEMANN, ELIZABETH. *Czechs and Germans.* London: Oxford University Press, 1938. 299 pp.

———. *Germany's Eastern Neighbors.* London and New York: Oxford University Press, 1956. 309 pp.

PERIODICALS

These entries are limited to periodicals which are not widely known and which will be found in only the largest public libraries. All of the following are consistently anti-Communist and, in the author's opinion, generally reliable as to fact and interpretation.

English Language:

ABN Correspondence. English edition, monthly, $2.00 per year. Anti-Bolshevik Bloc of Nations, Postfach 70, München 33, Germany.

Bohemia: see under Czech Language.

Bulletin of the Slovak National Council Abroad. Monthly. Box 285, Middletown, Pa.

Czech Struggle: see under Czech Language.

Expellee Press Service: see under German Language, *Pressedienst der Heimatvertriebenen.*

German News. Published by Sudeten German members of German parliaments. Trifftstr. 1, München 22, Germany.

INFORM BULLETIN. Two or three times per month, and *INFORM* Quarterly. International Services of Information Foundation, Inc., 3 West 23d Street, Baltimore 18, Md. Concerned mainly with Soviet affairs, but often prints interesting items on Czecho-Slovakia and other satellites.

Slovakia. Quarterly, $1.00 per year. Slovakia, Box 150, Middletown, Pa.

Slovak Newsletter. Monthly, $2.00 per year. Slovak Newsletter, Box 150, Middletown, Pa.

Sudeten Bulletin. Monthly. Sudetendeutsche Landsmannschaft, 11 Karlsplatz, Muenchen 2, Germany.

Czech Language

Bohemia (Czech Democratic Federalists). Monthly, with occasional supplements in English and German. Bohemia, Horemannstrasse 54-58, Köhn-Ehrenfeld, Germany.

Brazda ("The Furrow"). Monthly of Republican (Agrarian) Party in Exile. c/o Vaclav Vostrez, Box 541, Hamilton, Ontario, Canada.

Czech Struggle/Cesky Boj. Czech and English, published by Czech National Committee. Monthly, $3.00 per year. 27 Rosedew Road, London W. 6, England.

Narodni Demokrat ("National Democrat"). Monthly. Narodni Demokrat, Box 185, Berwyn, Ill.

Rozpravy. Monthly. Mouvement Democratique Chretien Tcheque, Boite Postale No. 20, Bruxelles, Belgium.

German Language

Der europäische Osten ("The German East"). Monthly, subscription $6.00 per year. Joerg-Verlag, Schweigerstrasse 2, München 9, Germany.

Nord-Amerika. Catholic weekly, $4.00 per year. Nord-Amerika, 4543 North 5th Street, Philadelphia 40, Pa.

Pressedienst der Heimatvertriebenen. Weekly, with bi-weekly English-language *Expellee Press Service.* Goettinger Arbeits; kreis, Sternstrasse 2, Goettingen, Germany.

Slowakische Korrespondenz. Monthly. Slowakischer Nationalrat im Ausland, Postfach 27, München 22, Germany.

Sudetendeutsche Zeitung. Weekly. Sudetendeutsche Zeitung, 57 Bayerstrasse, Muenchen 15, Germany.

Sudtendeutscher Artikeldienst. Weekly. Der Sudetendeutsche Rat, 1 Trifftstrasse, Muenchen 22, Germany.

Slovak Language

Jednota. Weekly. Jednota, Box 150, Middletown, Pa.

Slovak v Amerike. Weekly. Slovak v Amerike, Whiting, Ind.

Slovenska Obrana. Bi-weekly. Obrana Press, Scranton, Pa.

Svobodne Slovensko. Bi-weekly. Slowakischer Nationalrat im Ausland, Postfach 27, München 22, Germany.

INDEX

Because of the large number of persons and places mentioned in this book, references to persons who figure only incidentally and to most geographical names have been omitted. Some subjects, on the other hand, such as nationalism and propaganda, are so pervasive that it was not feasible to index them.